THE RAINMAKER

THE RAINMAKER

A BIOGRAPHY OF

JOHN BALLANCE

JOURNALIST AND POLITICIAN

1839 – 1893

By Timothy McIvor

HEINEMANN REED

To Paula

Published by Heinemann Reed,
a division of Octopus Publishing Group (NZ) Ltd,
39 Rawene Road, Birkenhead, Auckland. Associated
companies, branches and representatives throughout the
world.

ISBN 0-7900-0024-5

©1989 Timothy McIvor
First published 1989

Design by Jane Connor/Godwit
Typeset by Typocrafters Ltd
Printed in Singapore

Contents

Foreword

THERE ARE TWO STATUES of former Prime Ministers at the front of New Zealand's Parliament Buildings. They mark the leadership contributions of John Ballance and Richard John Seddon. The Seddon statue is prominently displayed in front of the main steps. The Ballance figure is less flamboyant and less visible among the greenery in front of the General Assembly Library building. The placing and visibility of the two statues corresponds with the contemporary perception of the importance and contribution of the two men. Seddon's career has always considerably overshadowed that of his predecesor.

Yet Ballance had been a considerable politician, first as a minister in the Grey and Stout-Vogel ministries, but more significantly as the first Liberal Party leader and Prime Minister.

The far-reaching liberal reforms of the 1890s arguably owed more to him (and to William Pember Reeves) than to the larger public figures who came to dominate public awareness.

The documentation of Ballance's career and politics was always likely to redress some longstanding imbalances in perception and to show Ballance to be a substantial figure in New Zealand's political development.

The publication of Tim McIvor's biography fulfils that expectation very well. Dr McIvor makes a most welcome contribution towards giving John Ballance his rightful place as a major reforming politician during one of the most important stages in this country's history.

Russell Marshall
Minister of Foreign Affairs
MP for Wanganui

Ballance family tree

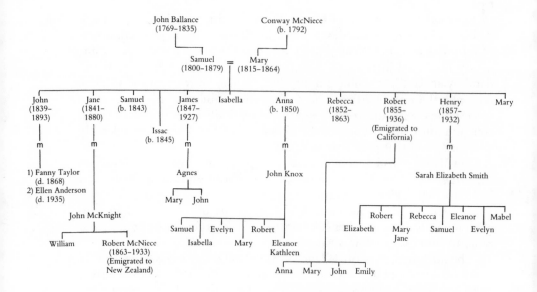

John Ballance
(1769–1835)

Conway McNiece
(b. 1792)

Samuel = Mary
(1800–1879) (1815–1864)

John
(1839–1893)

Jane
(1841–1880)

Samuel
(b. 1843)

Issac
(b. 1845)

James
(1847–1927)

Isabella

Anna
(b. 1850)

Rebecca
(1852–1863)

Robert
(1855–1936)
(Emigrated to
California)

Henry
(1857–1932)

Mary

m

1) Fanny Taylor
(d. 1868)
2) Ellen Anderson
(d. 1935)

m

Agnes

John Knox

Sarah Elizabeth Smith

m

John McKnight

William

Robert McNiece
(1863–1933)
(Emigrated to
New Zealand)

Mary   John

Samuel   Evelyn   Robert

Isabella   Mary   Eleanor
Kathleen

Robert   Rebecca   Eleanor   Mabel

Elizabeth   Mary
Jane

Samuel   Evelyn

Anna   Mary   John   Emily

Preface

JOHN BALLANCE DID NOT MAKE things easy for his biographer. He left no diaries, virtually no personal letters and only a limited amount of official correspondence. He had no children who might have kept his memory alive, nor did the niece he adopted. Ballance memorabilia are few and far between — scattered among relatives and museums. It is hardly surprising that he has been ignored by historians for so long.

Yet he is much too important a nineteenth-century political figure to be left alone; and a fairly comprehensive life of Ballance can be constructed from the source material that is available. Above all, there is the *Herald* newspaper which he founded. Ballance edited the paper until he first entered Parliament in 1875. Thereafter, he returned to the editorial chair during each recess (and when he was out of Parliament between 1881 and 1884), right up until the appointment of James Duigan as full-time editor in January 1891. Through the pages of the *Herald* the development of Ballance's career and views can be traced. There are also the Ballance Papers, which contain correspondence from his years as Premier and term as Colonial Treasurer in the Grey Government. Other material comes from a wide range of minor — including oral — sources.

Writing a biography, especially under these circumstances, is a bit like putting together a large and intricate jigsaw. Some pieces fall into place easily, others do not seem to fit anywhere. The amount of guesswork needed is considerable, particularly as some pieces are soon found to be missing. A picture that makes sense does eventually emerge. Yet the gaps remain. If only, for example, we knew more about his parents, his relationship with them and their influence on him. Why, when writing to an old friend in Belfast, did he make reference to 'my poor mother'?[1] Also, did his personal witness of death during the war against Titokowaru in 1868 move him so much as to have a major impact on his approach to race relations when he later became Minister of Native Affairs? Finally, what of Stout? Did Ballance have such high regard for him and his opinion simply because

[ix]

he had intellectual qualities Ballance aspired to but felt in his heart he could not match? Were there other personal characteristics of both men that bound them so closely together? If only Ballance's private correspondence or a diary existed. It would be fascinating to read how he felt about himself, other people and politics — particularly at critical points in his career.

This book is an attempt to resurrect Ballance, to give him a prominence that reflects his popularity at the time of his death and his significance as a major actor in a vital period in New Zealand's history. The work was written with few preconceptions about the man; perhaps this was inevitable given the slight attention historians had given him. At the start of the study, Ballance appeared as someone who tended to be swept along by events, without having any great influence upon them. A good man, but in many respects uninteresting and unexciting. By the finish, Ballance has become much more appealing.

Acknowledgements

M ANY PEOPLE CONTRIBUTED to this book and the thesis upon which it is based. I had a number of enjoyable interviews with descendants of the Ballance and Anderson families. In New Zealand, Shirley McKnight of Ohingaiti (whose grandfather was Robert McKnight, nephew of John Ballance) and her mother, Beeban McKnight, were particularly helpful and supportive in their genuine interest in what I was doing, as was Carol Anderson and the late John Hatherly of New Plymouth. Of the Irish Ballance descendants I would like to acknowledge especially the aid of Eleanor Crawford, granddaughter of Henry Ballance. My research in Wanganui benefited from the advice, information and practical assistance given to me by Arthur Bates, Wanganui historian and ex-Managing Director of Wanganui Newspapers, and Brian Henderson, Director of Wanganui Museum.

I would like to thank the following historians for their help: Keith Sinclair, Raewyn Dalziel, T. G. Wilson, James Belich, Helene Frey and Andrew Watkins. I am deeply grateful to David Hamer of Victoria University, who supervised the original Ph.D. thesis and whose assistance and advice was invaluable. As *The Rainmaker* was in its final stages of production, Professor Hamer's *The New Zealand Liberals: The Years of Power, 1891–1912* was published. This major study will be the standard work on what is a fascinating and critical phase in New Zealand's political development. Dr John Chrisp of Wellington took much trouble in reading and commenting upon material relating to Ballance's illness.

This book would not have been written had I not, in my early student days, developed a fascination for political history stimulated by Frank Wright of Queen's University, Belfast. To him I owe a considerable debt. Max Armstrong spent many hours going through the manuscript with a fine-tooth comb; for his time and intellectual rigour I am most grateful. Judith Wigglesworth kindly drew the maps. My parents provided much encouragement as well as practical assistance. Jill McIvor's enthusiasm extended to establishing the Ulster-New Zealand Trust, whose primary aim is to restore Ballance's birthplace near Glenavy, Ireland. My special thanks go to Carole Hoult, who typed the manuscript with great speed and efficiency, deciphering my hieroglyphics and making editorial corrections in the process.

Andrew Campbell of Heinemann Reed has been very helpful and encouraging in this project.

My greatest debt is to my wife, Paula, who read the drafts at various stages and checked proofs. Perhaps most important, she gave me vital support and kept me at the job in hand when energies flagged.

Tim McIvor
Wellington
January 1989

The people's premier

THE STATUE OF JOHN BALLANCE stands at one end of the grounds of New Zealand's Parliament Buildings. Around its base are inscribed the words: HE LOVED THE PEOPLE. It is not a tall or imposing statue and in fact has been increasingly hidden from view by the growth of trees and shrubs nearby. Nor is it at all a good likeness. Edward Tregear, head of the Labour Department established by Ballance, said on its unveiling that it was 'hideous beyond words; it is very good style for a cemetery but is no more like our dear dead chief than I am like the Apollo Belvedere — and that's "a far cry". . . . Such a statue adds a new terror to Death.'[1]

Further down the hill, in the paved area leading to the steps and main doors of Parliament, stands Seddon: tall, defiant, with a flag placed at his feet and pigeons on his head.[2] Richard Seddon succeeded Ballance as Premier and Leader of the Liberal Party on the latter's death in 1893. The subsequent long reign of 'King Dick' effectively overshadowed the significance of Ballance and his government. In the eyes of New Zealanders and their historians, Ballance became a mysteriously unknown nineteenth-century politician. It was almost as if Ballance had never lived; as if Seddon, not Ballance, had brought the liberals to power in that watershed year of 1890.

In fact, when erected, the Ballance statue stood in the centre of a circular lawn, directly in front of what was then the Parliament Building but now houses the General Assembly Library. Ballance was the first New Zealand Premier so honoured. It was testimony to the enormous respect and affection that surrounded him by the time of his death, and to his remarkable achievements after just two years in office.

Ballance was a spectacularly successful political leader. He led the first reforming, Liberal Administration through its very difficult early years. The conservative oligarchy had been beaten at the polls in 1890 but had by no means entirely given in to the radicals. The Tories fought Ballance every inch of the way yet it was he who came out on top. Reeves said of him:

He had to build up a party which his critics said at the time had no basis or solidarity, hardly even existance; he had to carry a policy which, alike in finance, land law, and labor reform, was so bold and innovating that it was certain to provoke extraordinary and bitter opposition . . . Nearly all the larger and abler newspapers were angrily against him, and though he had a faithful majority in the Lower House, he was utterly without a follower in the Upper. In these straits you know what he did. He turned to the people and used the platform against the press.[3]

This was Ballance's greatest contribution. He established party government and secured it through constitutional struggle, smashing the old political mould once and for all. He made things much easier for reformists who followed him. He posed the crisis presented by an Upper House refusing to pass his government's key legislation in terms of the right of the people to govern themselves. By promoting economic and political self–reliance he inspired a progressive nationalist sentiment and fresh confidence in New Zealand. His premiership brought a new mood of optimism to the country and marked a significant step along the road from colony to nation. Ballance encouraged people to see themselves as New Zealanders rather than Britons of the south seas. He remains one of this country's great nationalists.

The personal qualities Ballance possessed fitted him well for the task he faced. He was kindly, courteous and considerate and had enormous patience. He was a man of honesty and integrity. 'Even those who differed from him acknowledged his sincerity of purpose. Some of his opponents . . . really loved the man, as his friends undoubtedly did.'[4] As a result Ballance attracted extraordinary loyalty amongst his cabinet and party; an asset that was particularly valuable in times of trouble. Stout talked of Ballance's 'magnetic power of attaching people to him'.[5] Many viewed his mild temperament as a sign of weakness as a leader. This was quite wrong. Ballance possessed much political toughness, though it was often hidden and seldom acknowledged. Reeves described him as 'absolutely the most unassuming and unpretentious' of all the successful and able men he had known. But, he added, 'as a Premier — and I say it emphatically — he knew how to be master in his own house'.[6] Ballance showed great political courage as he steered his government through two very stormy years in office; and great personal bravery as he fought against the illness that was gradually killing him.

Ballance had real ability as a politician. He was shrewd and a good tactician, and understood the workings of the political system well. If at times he appeared to lose confidence, or to gain office through events and conditions well beyond his control, this is perhaps truer of many more successful politicians than would admit it. He found power stimulating, exciting and, most important, constructive; out of government he could be unenthusiastic and listless. The purpose of politics was to improve society through beneficent legislation. Politics was not, for Ballance, an end in itself.

Although he was not a great public speaker, as Ballance gained experience he became an increasingly impressive and effective one. He brought people with him through reasoned argument and the obvious sincerity of his words. Most often he spoke in a matter-of-fact way: clearly, precisely and unimpassioned. On occasion, however, he genuinely moved his audience — usually through what he said rather than the way he said it, though in his latter years he did deliver some fine, fervent speeches, when his words came forth 'like a perfect tornado'.[7] Ballance was also a good judge of ability and surrounded himself with a team of very competent men. And he managed his cabinet well, allowing each member considerable freedom yet retaining firm overall control.

Only ill health and financial problems ever caused Ballance to question pursuing a political career, once he had embarked upon it. He stood at every general election from 1875 until his death, and in this time suffered just one defeat. He thrived on politics and was ambitious. His ambition was simply to gain power so that he could achieve particular ends. Ballance entered Parliament not, like some nineteenth-century politicians, to further business or personal interests, but to promote and give effect to principles and beliefs he held strongly to. He was a professional politician in that he engaged in politics for political reasons. It was what he most wanted to do.

Like all successful politicians, Ballance was a pragmatist rather than an idealist. He was impatient with theories too obviously divorced from political reality. Nevertheless, his actions had a strong philosophical base. Above all, he was a most modern thinker. On a vast range of issues — race relations, education, religion, prohibition, the franchise, New Zealand's role in the world — he held advanced views. He had a strong faith in the value of knowledge and the ability of society to progress and determine its own future. He believed that the liberty of the individual should be as great as possible, but recognised that for this to be so state intervention would sometimes be essential. Ballance was a comprehensive radical and thorough democrat who sought to make the political system responsive to the needs of ordinary people rather than powerful interest groups.

Land reform was at the centre of Ballance's philosophy. This was because his experiences had shown closer land settlement to be the key to the prosperity of the individual and of the state. He regarded land monopoly as the greatest evil in the country of his birth and its avoidance vital in the country of his adoption. His views on religion were strongly coloured by the part the established church played in this monopoly in Ireland. In New Zealand, he increasingly saw the need for state intervention to counteract the accumulation of large estates, to preserve remaining crown lands and promote small farm settlement. His approach to unemployment and poor social conditions in the towns during the 1880s was to move people out onto the land through a range of special settlements. When Premier, he set up the Labour Department under Reeves and fully supported new factory legislation and the growth and protection of trade unions. Yet when it came to the 'labour question' in general, Ballance's interest lay in rural solutions such as the state farms that were to provide for and train the unemployed. Underpinning all of this was, perhaps, a rather romantic and idealistic view of the blessings of rural life; of the self-sufficient, independent yeoman farmer engaged in healthy, productive work in an environment far removed from the noisy, cramped and stressful conditions of city living.

In stressing the importance of land reform, Ballance was typical of the liberals who won the crucial election of 1890. As their chief he clearly represented the liberalism that was to be the driving force of his reformist government. That liberalism sought broad rather than sectional support, from the working and middle classes alike. It emphasised land reform aimed at benefiting the country as a whole, providing rural solutions to urban problems. And it emphasised the desirability of co-operation between classes, at the same time denying the inevitability of their mutual antagonism.

Ballance led New Zealand at a pivotal point in its history. He was probably somewhat surprised to find himself in that position. Self-effacing and unassuming, he was in many respects an unlikely leader. Yet he turned out to be one of the country's finest.

Plans for a statue of Ballance began to be made within weeks of his death, although it took some years for the money to be raised, the design to be finally agreed upon and the work to be carried out. The Wellington Trade Council initiated the fund-raising whilst the miners of Cape Foulwind donated the granite for the tiered base of the statue. A committee of both Houses of Parliament, meanwhile, agreed to its being located in so prominent a position. Fifty meetings had been held and over 600 letters written on the matter by the time the statue was finally unveiled.[8] All those involved wished there to be a permanent memorial to 'Ballance, the Rainmaker' — to 'New Zealand's Santa Claus' whose premiership had seen the return of prosperity and hope to the country after long years of depression.

CHAPTER 1

From Belfast to Birmingham

While in religious devotion the people of Glenavy will never be accused of wasting their powers of soul in barren ecstasies, they are most reverential, and the fear of God exercises over them a healthy influence. There is almost an entire absence of the superstitious; fairies are never seen, the banshee never cries, and not a house is said to be haunted.[1]

THE PARISH OF GLENAVY lies on the eastern shore of Lough Neagh in the north of Ireland, and to the west of the Lagan Valley. The gently undulating landscape on the edge of the Antrim plateau is occasionally accentuated by a small hill or a mound, the result of glacial activity or evidence of a Celtic past. Much evidence of early settlement has now disappeared (including the ancient cemetery at Pitmave called the Giant's Grave), though Crew Hill, upon which the kings of Ulidia were crowned, still stands.

Four kilometres east of Glenavy village is the townland of Ballypitmave and here John Ballance was born on 27 March 1839, in a stone house set back from the road to Lisburn (see map 1). His father, Samuel, was a reasonably prosperous tenant farmer, in his thirty-ninth year. The previous April he had married Mary McNiece, a woman in her early twenties who came from a well-known local family. Her uncle Conway McNiece owned property in the area, including the nine-hectare Ram's Island in Lough Neagh which he had bought in 1804 for one hundred guineas.[2]

The Ballances had come to Ireland in the wake of Cromwell's rule. They were of English Puritan stock rather than of the more populous

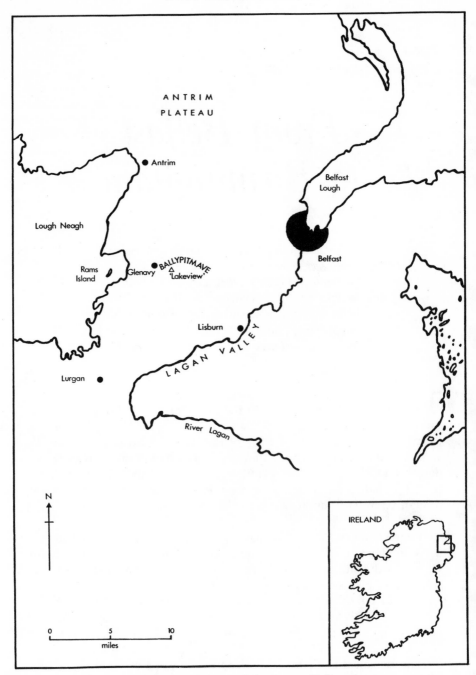

Southeast Antrim and the Lagan Valley

Scottish Presbyterians who dominated the counties of Down and Antrim. Settling first in Lurgan at the south-east corner of Lough Neagh the Ballances later moved north to Ballypitmave,[3] to an area where Anglicans, and English influence, remained dominant when elsewhere in east Ulster they gave way to the Presbyterian influx. The land about Glenavy, originally part of the considerable possessions of the O'Neils, was taken by the English in the early seventeenth century, passing to Sir Fulke Conway (who introduced English and Welsh settlers) and in 1683 to the Hertford family, being handed down until the death of the fourth Marquis of Hertford in 1870.[4]

The house the Ballances lived in was substantial for its day; a single-storied dwelling with a thatched roof, white mortar walls, small windows and a huge open hearth.[5] From the front door Lough Neagh could be seen in the distance, if you looked westwards across the plateau that sloped gently down to the lake shore. The building, 24 metres long and six metres wide, was in good repair. There was plenty of room. Samuel's father, John, had not long died and the 1835 valuation noted that the family had more accommodation than was necessary.[6] Samuel took over his father's tenancy of about 11 hectares of good land, most of which was given over to crops (predominantly wheat) with the remainder grazed. This part of Antrim was the major wheat-producing area in Ulster and served the growing town of Belfast down in the Lagan Valley.

At 11 hectares, the Ballance farm on the Hertford estate was well above average in size, the majority of holdings in the area being below six hectares.[7] The region was agriculturally advanced in eighteenth- and nineteenth-century Ulster since English colonists had improved farming techniques and landowners were relatively liberal and progressive. And farm incomes, at least until the 1830s, were frequently supplemented by weaving. Thus the Ballances were comfortable, even if there was not much left over for luxuries. They were also more secure than their peers elsewhere in Ireland. By the first half of the nineteenth century the 'Ulster Custom' was firmly established, giving tenants a right of occupancy with leasing largely abandoned, compensation for improvements and, subject to the landlord's approval, the right to sell a holding to the highest bidder.

Mary had ten further children before her death in 1864. After John came Jane, then Samuel, Isaac, James, Anna, Rebecca, Isabella, Robert, Henry and Mary.[8] So the once spacious house was soon filled to overflowing, though all 11 children never lived there at the one time. Of the fortunes of most of these people we know little. The family scattered to other parts of Ireland and much further afield. Some followed John Ballance to New Zealand, no doubt encouraged by his success there. Isabella became a teacher and (as did Mary) remained unmarried, while Rebecca died at the early age of 11. Anna (born 1850) married a man called Knox and went to live in Lisburn. Jane (1841–1880) married John McKnight at Magheragall Presbyterian Church in 1862. Their son Robert later settled in New Zealand.[9] Isaac (born 1845) left Ireland also bound for New Zealand but was never heard of again. Family rumour has it that he died en route in Australia. The fate of Samuel, two years his senior, is equally mysterious. Samuel ran the farm at Ballypitmave for a while, living in the family home that became known as 'Lakeview'. Then, in middle age, he too left for New Zealand and according to one account did reach it, though in an exhausted and ill condition. Apparently he was discovered, by his older and now famous brother, lying beside the Wellington to Wanganui road. Travelling home to Wanganui John Ballance had seen a man in distress and instructed the driver of his carriage to pull over to see if they could assist. Only then was the identity of the man, who sadly died soon after this reunion, revealed.[10]

Of the remaining brothers James (1847–1927) took over the family land whilst Robert (1855–1936) emigrated to America where he purchased a dairy farm near Santa Fe. Today the farm at Ballypitmave, including the old home, currently being restored, is owned by James's grandson, John. Finally, Henry Ballance (1857–1932) succeeded to Crew Mount, the property of his grand-uncle Conway McNiece. With this inheritance, a marriage to the daughter of James Smith, agent for the Hertford Estate, and undoubted ability, he established himself as an influential local figure. He was at various times Magistrate, Chairman of Lisburn Rural District Council and Chairman of the Board of Governors of Lagan Valley Infirmary.

John Ballance attended the local National School from which he was rarely absent. His parents saw to it that all their children received a good basic education and all were avid readers. In any case the alternative to school was farm work which held no interest whatsoever for John, who was physically lazy and had a remarkable propensity to do nothing all day but read.[11] No doubt he was the subject of many complaints and a fair bit of ribbing about his mediocre contribution to the endless tasks required to be done. Yet Ballance was certainly not a weak-looking child. The earliest photograph we have of him was taken at age 14 and shows a solid teenager mature for his years, with large hands, a full moderately handsome face and piercing eyes. It would have been difficult for him to plead a frail constitution.

Ballance's father was an Anglican with 'strict evangelical tendencies'[12] and belonged to Glenavy Parish Church, where John was baptised soon after his birth. Mary, however, was a Quaker and on marriage to a non-member would have been subject to expulsion. Whether in fact she was expelled is unclear, but the nearest Quaker meeting house was some distance away in Lisburn and for practical reasons at least Mary associated instead with the Methodists in Glenavy. The affiliations of both parents could be catered for under an arrangement common at this time, whereby on a Sunday the family would attend the parish service in the morning and chapel at 5.00 pm.

Though Anglicans were predominant in the area, there was a large Roman Catholic minority. Little sectarian conflict resulted, however, and Glenavy village, lying on a ridge above a river running through a wooded valley, was generally quiet and orderly.[13] Aside from the occasional riot on market days in the early 1800s the last major excitement had been during the 1798 Rebellion, when the village found itself sandwiched between the rebel United Armies of Antrim and Down. Ballance's grandfather, one of many 'orangemen' recruited to the Yeomanry by the English authorities, had been wounded in the fighting.[14] The Orange Order was a Protestant political organisation established among the tenantry in 1795 to counteract rising Catholic resistance to English rule. It was named after William of Orange, a Dutch Protestant who in 1690, on Irish soil at the 'Battle of the Boyne', ended the Catholic James II's chances of retaining the English Crown. The order aimed to maintain the Protestant ascendancy and the continued subjugation of the Catholic majority.[15]

Ballance grew up in a family and culture of tenant farmers whose greater security and relative prosperity placed them at a considerable distance from the majority of Irish peasantry. English influence could be seen everywhere; in vegetable and flower gardens, neatly trimmed hedges and apple orchards. There were few agricultural labourers and only a handful of semi-skilled and unskilled men worked in local bleach, cotton and flour mills. The famine which struck Ireland before Ballance was ten years old, affected Antrim and Down least of all[16] and his experience of the Hungry Forties would largely have been through newspaper accounts and stories passed by word of mouth, rather than at first hand. An agricultural depression in Ulster at this time did weaken the position of tenants in their relationship with the landlord, but the Ballances appear to have survived without too much difficulty.

As eldest son, Ballance would have been expected eventually to take over his father's farm. Yet we have seen that he had not the slightest interest in farming and even if he had, his father was fit and well and unlikely to hand it over in the foreseeable future. In fact Samuel lived to his eightieth year, remarrying in his sixties following Mary's death in 1864. So it was agreed that John would go to Belfast to continue his education at Wilson's Academy there. He left home in 1853, at the age of 14, and went to stay with his uncle Robert McNiece who lived in the city.[17] The academy had a good reputation and no doubt there were high expectations of John. However, despite his apparent academic bent he soon quit school and went to work as an apprentice to an ironmonger (a seller of hardware). We do not know the circumstances involved but this must have been a disappointment to his parents for the job, in which Ballance remained until he left Ireland in 1857, held no real prospects.

Belfast was within easy reach of home and Ballance's parents continued to influence his development. From an early age politics fascinated him. His father, like his father before him, was an Orangeman and involved in local politics, often proposing the nomination of Conservative candidates for Belfast. John read, watched and listened. His knowledge and understanding of politics grew into a precocious keen political sense and awareness. By the age of 16 he was helping Samuel write his speeches.[18] Yet if it was his father who brought Ballance into early contact with political life it was his mother who influenced the direction of his own political philosophy. She took, in Ballance's own words, 'an all-absorbing interest' in politics and was considerably more liberal than her husband.[19] From her he drew a dissenting belief that culminated in agnosticism and free thought; from her also came concern for the welfare of others. In the meantime, any scepticism the young Ballance might have had of organised religion would have been reinforced by events in Belfast.

Belfast began as a village near the mouth and a crossing point of the River Lagan. The settlement gradually expanded west to the slopes of the mountains that mark the edge of the Antrim Plateau, east towards the Castlereagh Hills and, particularly, south along the Lagan valley floor. Growth had been modest until the Industrial Revolution and Belfast took very much second place to Dublin, which was older, larger and the capital of Ireland. Belfast was to come of age as (in many respects) a typical industrial, Victorian city — and had the utilitarian architecture of that era to match. It generally lacked the elegant Georgian buildings and squares that were commonplace in Dublin. At the time Ballance lived in the town it was booming. Rising prosperity was based on a rapid expansion of the linen industry made possible by the new technology of power looms, and on shipbuilding, now on the eve of a great expansion. People flooded in from the countryside in search of a share in this prosperity: between 1851 and 1861 Belfast's population increased by nearly 40 percent.[20] It was becoming a crowded place to live in and, surrounded by hills, somewhat claustrophobic. Yet if the physical conditions and public amenities were falling behind population growth, the very presence of so many new arrivals meant that there was plenty going on.

The town, like the eastern counties of Antrim and Down that it linked, was predominantly Protestant. Presbyterian influence on its political development was particularly strong. In the past this influence had had radical, anti-English elements but by the mid-nineteenth century politics was already beginning to polarise along religious lines: Protestants wishing to remain under the British Crown, Catholics seeking some form of independence. Political and religious debate was intense and lively. People tended to hold strong views and were not slow in expressing them.

Tension between the two groups rose as Belfast industrialised and drew in growing numbers of Catholics along with Protestants. Particular areas of the town began to be dominated by one side or the other; Ballance would have been very aware of distinct Catholic and Protestant streets, at least in the poorer parts of town. And the developing sectarian divide already affected social activity and intercourse. So with economic expansion came also the 'Age of Riots', though the town had shown a propensity in this direction as early as 1813.[21] Ballance witnessed a succession of sectarian riots that climaxed in 1857, when the inflammatory anti-Catholic preaching of the Reverend Thomas Drew led to a particularly serious series of clashes lasting between 12 July and 6 September. The protagonists were ably fuelled by the Orange Order and another anti-Catholic preacher, the Reverend Hugh Hanna. 'Three hundred ship's carpenters, Protestant to a man', joined in the fight.[22] Ballance later wrote:

> Much bloodshed was caused by street preaching, and though the offensive practice of shouting on a highway that all papists were on the broad road to destruction was naturally objected to by those who were said to be doomed, the practice was persisted in even after it was found that riot had ensued. One character, 'Roaring Hanna', the pastor of a Presbyterian Church, obtained much notoriety by his open air effusions in critical times, and found immortality in Punch. 'Allow', said this divine on one occasion vividly [remembered] ... 'a small passage for the papists to pass along, and it shall be known hereafter as the Pope's Pad!'.

Contrasting the rising prosperity of Belfast at that time with continued rioting he concluded:

> The truth is that the Protestants of the North have long considered themselves the dominant class and cannot to this day tolerate the religious or political equality of the Catholics. The remembrance of the days of the yeoman and the rebellion of 1798 are still faithfully preserved, and Protestant ascendancy is still a principle and a sentiment in the breasts of the descendants of those who put it in practice in many questionable ways.[23]

In the autumn of 1857, soon after this rioting petered out, Ballance left for Birmingham. It may have been that he just wanted to find out what was on the other side of the Irish Sea and was simply in search of new and better things. But a split with his family may also have been involved, with his parents bitter at what they saw as wasted opportunities and his father in particular angry at John's refusal to return to the farm. There is no hint in existing correspondence of family contact being sustained after

Ballance moved to New Zealand and though lack of personal papers makes this by no means conclusive, the absence of any mention of John in his father's will lends credence to the likelihood of a permanent rupture.

On leaving Belfast Ballance's attitude to the Irish question may already have been at some variance with mainline Protestant opinion, in that his mother's liberal influence and his own somewhat bookish and sensitive disposition combined to make him unsympathetic to the aggressiveness of the conservative Orange majority. This attitude probably made life increasingly uncomfortable for him. There were other Protestant liberals around and he may have got to know some Catholics, but the social circle he would have found himself in would not have welcomed pro-Irish views. Both at work and outside it, Ballance was locked into the dominant Ulster Protestant culture of his birth. Yet while he had witnessed sectarianism on the streets of Belfast and had a good idea of what politics in that city was all about, his family and personal circumstances did little to acquaint him directly with the fundamental problems of Ireland as a whole. In many parts of the country outside the north-east, an impoverished peasantry struggled and sometimes starved on small plots of land under a system run for landlords and backed by English force. Ballance knew of what was happening largely second hand and his views on the evils of landlordism developed as a philosophical assessment of these facts. Thus his position on the Irish question hardened with absence from the island as he matured intellectually and came under the influence of various writers and politicians.

Initially Ballance hoped that loyalty to the English Crown could be restored through removing rural poverty which he saw as the basis of dis-content.[24] Later he advocated Home Rule, arguing that Ulster Protestants were by no means solidly against the idea and pointing to their leadership of the rebellions against the English in 1782 and 1798. Ulster had 'suffered just as much from landlord tyranny and from castle government as any part of Ireland'.[25] In 1881 he moved a resolution at a 'monster' meeting in Wellington in support of the Irish National Land League and in sympathy with evicted tenants, whom he described as 'victims of misgovernment, persecution, and tyranny'.[26] A few years later he wrote in the *Evening Herald* that the Irish Church and the land laws were 'the foremost evils to be grappled with' in Ireland.[27] Finally, Ballance rejected totally the Orangeism of his father. The Orange Order was for him an anachronism, engendering a bitterness and violence that could only alienate the Catholic minority and be inherently damaging to the Protestant faith.[28] He attacked the basis of religious and cultural sectarianism by denying the existence of an exclusive and pure Ulster race. Rather, 'the men of Ulster, to their glory be it said', he wrote, 'are hybrids, and they possess the characteristics of the nations with whom they claim kindred. The industry and perseverance of the Saxon, the proud spirit of the Norman, the fervency and enthusiasm of the Irish, and the endurance and purpose of the Scotch, have been beautifully mixed up by nature in this race.'[29]

When he arrived in Birmingham in late 1857 Ballance began a job as commercial traveller for a large hardware firm called McLennan Brothers. Most likely he got the position through connections of his Belfast employers. It was hard work, with a lot of travelling throughout the region and constant pressure to make yet another sale.[30] Ballance later described McLennan's as a firm that 'thought of nothing but making money'.[31] Yet he must have been reasonably happy and successful in the job for he stuck at it for nearly all of the eight years he lived in Birmingham.

Where Belfast was just beginning to expand as it took advantage of the possibilities held out by the Industrial Revolution, Birmingham had been at the very nucleus of change. The Midland city was a major techno-logical and manufacturing centre; leading, for example, in the development of the steam engine. There had been a settlement in the area from before the Norman Conquest and by the thirteenth century it had become a fair-sized market town, focused on the 'Bull Ring'. Rapid growth occurred in the early nineteenth century, and particularly after the establishment of rail links with London and Liverpool — the town spreading out haphaz-ardly and absorbing many of the surrounding villages in the process. In appearance, Birmingham was essentially an early Victorian city that retained some Georgian elements (for example, around St. Paul's Church). During the time Ballance lived there, however, major new projects were initiated which began to change the face of the city. Sanitation was improved, parks established, roads widened and large new buildings constructed in the central commercial and shopping district. As in Belfast, progress was in the air.

Birmingham was an ideal place for Ballance to develop his interests. It provided good facilities for study and a fascinating environment, being at the centre of important political and philosophical movements of that time. Intent on furthering his education he joined the Midland Institute, which had opened in the same year as his arrival in the city, studying at night history, biography and modern politics.[32] His fellow students would have included schoolboys, manual labourers and craftsmen as well as other representatives of his own lower-middle class.[33]

Birmingham's Midland Institute was an integral part of a mid-Victorian culture of self-improvement. Similar Mechanics Institutes had been estab-lished elsewhere by Henry Brougham and were 'in the vanguard of the utilitarian effort to enlighten the working classes'.[34] *Self Help*, the title of the influential book by Samuel Smiles (published in 1859), was a central theme emphasising industry, thrift, orderliness and the ultimate goal of upward social mobility. It had its roots in the earlier Chartist and Co-operative movements and in religious dissent (especially Methodism). Though organisations such as the Mechanics Institutes can be seen as a means of brainwashing the working classes with the social philosophy of the middle classes, popular education was 'a vital article of faith' in the radical creed:

> An educated populace knowing its rights would resist oppression; the spread of knowledge would lead inexorably to progress. The radicals envisaged a society in which educational opportunities would no longer be restricted to the propertied classes. They had in mind a real education, not charity-school training in deference; nor were they willing to accept middle-class indoctrination in political economy.[35]

So Ballance joined the ranks of many young men bent on a moral and intellectual growth that would form the basis for social and economic betterment. 'All for books',[36] he joined a debating society attached to the Institute, became secretary of a Birmingham literary society, played chess and wrote articles for the local newspapers.[37] He attended lectures and meetings of well-known figures such as Faraday,[38] Bright and Chamberlain. It was part of an all-encompassing religion of improvement and self-help. Mechanics Institutes aimed not only at providing information but were intended also to 'form the character, to enlighten the mind, to soften the manners, to refine the taste, to enlarge the views, and to improve and civilise the whole man'.[39] Physical activity was not neglected in this comprehensive programme and Ballance learned to box, sparring with a friend called W. M. Charles who later became a successful businessman.[40]

Life was busy for Ballance as he tried to fit into the hours outside work all the things he wanted to do. Birmingham provided more and better facilities, more entertainment and a wider range of formal occasions to attend than did Belfast. One's impression of Ballance at this time is of a person following a fairly rigorous regime of self-improvement; a serious, single-minded man determined to get on in the world. He worked hard at his job and acquired some business skill. But the effort he put into his other activities is more significant. He was not going to remain where he was, and even his leisure pursuits had purpose in developing his self. There can be little doubt that he enjoyed the evening classes and the political and literary debate he became involved in a good deal more than his paid employment.

Coming from Belfast where politics was dominated by sectarian issues Ballance must have found the political atmosphere of Birmingham new, exciting and stimulating. It had a history of popular radicalism based on middle-class leadership. The Birmingham Political Union formed by Thomas Attwood figured largely in the agitation for reform in 1832 and soon afterwards promoted a national petition which marked the beginnings of the Chartist Movement.[41] In the year of Ballance's arrival the great English liberal John Bright switched his parliamentary constituency from

Manchester to Birmingham, opening his election address with a recognition that he had come to a city with a well-established radical tradition. The movement headed by Bright and the like-minded Richard Cobden sought as priorities free trade and an extension of the franchise. It was hoped that the former would boost industrial development and with the latter increase the clout of the business class at the expense of the landowners.[42]

Whereas Belfast was expanding on the basis of heavy industry and large-scale enterprise, Birmingham's growth depended upon finished metal goods produced in small workshops. McLennan Brothers sold items typical of those being produced in the city, which by the 1850s was servicing the Midlands area and beyond:

> 'Made in Birmingham' was the characteristic mark on ironmongery, household goods, ornaments, jewellery, buttons, trinkets and general bric-a-brac which littered Victorian homes. . . . It also contributed materials more basic to Britain's industrial pre-eminence — nails, screws, staple items in railway construction, and a small-arms trade which flourished in an era of colonial expansion and European insecurity. More civilised needs were catered for by the Cadbury family's flourishing chocolate business.[43]

The smaller scale of enterprise engendered close contact between employer and employed, and trade unionism was weak. Expansion took the form of increased numbers and diversity of small units, where relatively well-off skilled artisans worked alongside masters and interdependence was emphasised by both. There was considerable social mobility and opportunity for self-improvement. As a London journalist found in the early 1850s, household trades existed that 'gave the inmates independence, and often led — if the trade continued good — to competence or fortune'.[44]

Concomitant with artisan independence and political radicalism was a tradition in Birmingham of religious dissent.

> Long-established as a refuge of religious freedom in the Anglican dominated rural Midlands, its manufacturers and ministers had forged the Protestant ethic and the spirit of capitalism into a dominant ideology of progressive dissenting radicalism, despite the numerical equality of Anglican congregations to those of non-conformity combined.[45]

Into this tradition Ballance fitted easily, for as we have seen he had shown a preference for his mother's non-conformity over the established religion of his father. In Birmingham he joined and took an active part in the young men's association of the Presbyterian Church.[46] We can only guess at why Ballance chose the Presbyterians rather than the Methodists or Quakers. It is unlikely that intellectually he would have felt a great attraction to the rigid philosophy of John Knox. Perhaps it was simply that the Presbyterians were particularly strong in the area where he lived and offered a good range of social activities.

Ballance was in Birmingham during the crucial formative years of early manhood. There he underwent intellectual and personal experiences that helped develop and underpinned much of his later political creed. From Cobden and Bright came a liberalism that emphasised the co-operation of the working and middle classes in a common fight against landowners. Also, Ballance's own efforts at self-improvement, in a society pervaded by a philosophy of self-help, left him with a strong belief in the value of education.

In 1863 Ballance married Fanny Taylor, 20 years old and four years his junior.[47] Soon after the marriage the Ballances decided to emigrate. Fanny suffered from poor health and it was hoped that a more salubrious climate would aid her condition.[48] She had a brother living in Wanganui, New Zealand, and for this reason the Ballances chose that destination. Aside from concern to improve his wife's health Ballance must also have believed that his own career prospects would be better in New Zealand than Birmingham. Towards the end of his time in England he quit his job as commercial traveller and went into business for himself. He formed a partnership with a friend but it did not turn out a success and differences of opinion between the two men led to its dissolution.[49] Given that he did not wish to return to a dead-end sales job, Ballance had little to lose in leaving Birmingham.

There seems to have been some talk of taking up sheep farming in the new country but lack of sufficient funds for such an enterprise quickly ruled this out.[50] Ballance had some money saved but little idea of what he would do when he reached New Zealand. In these circumstances the couple travelled to London where, on 6 April 1866, they boarded the S.S. *Ruahine*, a ship bound for Wellington via the Cape of Good Hope and Melbourne. The Ballances had paid their fare only as far as Melbourne, intending to stay in Victoria for two months in order to break up the long sea voyage to New Zealand.[51]

[CHAPTER 2]

Wanganui and war:
frontier politics and
insecurity

THE PASSAGE OF THE *Ruahine* was a rough one, particularly the leg from
the Cape to the Australian coast. A series of strong gales carried off the
mainyard, staved in two lifeboats and did considerable damage to the
bulwarks.[1] The ship was large and comfortable, however, and when the
Ballances were not being pitched to and fro in their berths in the fore cabin
they no doubt took advantage of the facilities provided, which included
a library and piano in the 23-metre saloon, and plunge and shower baths.
On 12 June 1866 the *Ruahine* docked at Port Phillip, Melbourne. During
his stay in the town Ballance bought a large collection of jewellery with
the intention of re-selling it at a profit in New Zealand. This plan to set
up shop in the colony must have been formulated during rather than before
the voyage out, for these items could have been bought at keener prices
in Birmingham. Perhaps one of his fellow passengers, or someone he met
in Melbourne, pointed out just how much more expensive finished goods
were in New Zealand than England or Australia.

The Ballances left Melbourne on the evening of 2 August and, travelling on the *Albion* (the crack ship of the intercolonial service that ran between
Wellington and Melbourne by way of Hokitika and Nelson), reached the
deep harbour of New Zealand's capital nine days later. They had light winds
and fine weather all the way[2] and it seems to have been an enjoyable last
stage of their long journey from England. Captain Kidney of the *Albion*
had favourable memories of the trip and later recalled his impressions of
the young Ballance on board his ship. 'Pleasant, genial, well informed, ready
at all points, above all things original, he made the time pass remarkably

[17]

agreeably for all, and was the centre of attention in consequence.'[3] After a stay of only a few days in Wellington the Ballances travelled on up the coast, arriving at their final destination on 18 August.[4]

Wanganui lies on the northern bank and seven kilometres from the mouth of the Wanganui River. It was a frontier town of about two thousand inhabitants and had a reputation for rowdiness and drinking. At a temperance meeting in 1867 one speaker said 'that of all the places he had ever been in, Wanganui was the most drunken'.[5] The settlement was concentrated in a hollow between two hills on which Governor Grey had built the Rutland and York stockades, and through which Victoria Avenue ran towards the river. A gravel road ran in the opposite direction to St. John's Wood, all other streets consisting of sand and swamp. There was no shortage of hotels (little more than public houses, they included the Steam Packet, the Wanganui, the Rutland and the Exchange) and breweries which with some shops, offices and a few private residences made up the nucleus of the town at the lower end of Victoria Avenue and along Ridgeway Street and Taupo Quay.[6] There were also four churches, one each for the Anglicans, Presbyterians, Roman Catholics and Methodists.

The tiny, isolated settlement was vastly different to Belfast and Birmingham. Everyone knew everyone else, at least to recognise on the street. New residents could not go unnoticed, and indeed their arrival was made something of an occasion. Wanganui had been established in 1841 by the New Zealand Company, essentially as an offshoot of Wellington. Since then its position had been somewhat precarious. The development of the flatter land beyond the hills that surrounded Wanganui was vital to the town's future. Pakeha (European) efforts to acquire this land from local Maori had led to tension and sometimes open fighting between the two groups. Maori and European both felt insecure. Maori saw their land being threatened as the settler population grew. The settlers meanwhile were restless, stuck in the claustrophobic Wanganui River valley with hills and thick bush on three sides and the ocean on the fourth. They knew that for the town to succeed much more land suitable for farming had to be acquired. And roads had to be built to connect the new farms with Wanganui, and to connect Wanganui with other major settlements. In these early days the main link with the outside world was by sea.

Eager to see a return on his Melbourne investments, which must have taken care of a large proportion of his savings, Ballance wasted little time in organising his affairs and opened his jewellery business on Taupo Quay on 19 September, just four weeks after his arrival in town. Taupo Quay (known more accurately as 'The Beach') ran alongside the bank of the river and was the centre of commercial activity in the town. Here Ballance advertised for sale 'a splendid collection of Gold & Plated Jewellery, Electro-Plate and fancy goods. Gold watches from 6 guineas, Silver do., from 2 guineas, warranted. Gents' and Ladies' finger rings, earrings, &c., in great variety'.[7] Unfortunately the enterprise was not a great success since the town proved too small to provide enough consumers for his limited range of goods. In December, with many of his Melbourne purchases unsold, Ballance decided to travel further afield in search of business. At that time Isaac Featherston, as Superintendent of Wellington Province (of which Wanganui was a part), was engaged in the purchase of the Rangitikei-Manawatu Block.[8] Realising that with £25,000 being handed over to the Maori owners there was a market for his wares of considerable potential, Ballance rode out to the meeting at Parewanui and offered his goods to a number of chiefs. On showing a gold watch to Featherston one chief was advised to return it to Ballance. It was impossible, said the Superintendent, to tell whether or not it was genuine. Walter Buller, the Resident Magistrate at Wanganui, was present at the meeting and later recalled the incident:

> Presently the Native came back with a courteous note from Mr Ballance . . . protesting against this interference with legitimate business and offering to guarantee in writing the quality of any watches he might dispose of. I do not think Dr Featherston pressed his objection any further; but Mr Ballance shortly afterwards withdrew . . . and made no further attempt to do business with the Natives.[9]

Despite displaying this kind of ingenuity and determination Ballance was unable to make much headway and soon afterwards ceased trading altogether, his remaining stock no doubt being disposed of at some loss. However, aside from being financially unsound the business would never have satisfied Ballance's ambition and intellect and it is unlikely that he ever regarded it as anything more than a stepping-stone to more interesting ventures. Nor, perhaps, did he have the personal characteristics necessary to succeed in the business world. He was neither hard-nosed nor extroverted and aggressive. The pursuit of money was of no particular importance to him.

Ballance's activities at this time were later criticised by political opponents who viewed this sort of lowly occupation as disqualifying a person aspiring to political office. Salesmen were not gentlemen. Buller recorded the above incident in order to defend Ballance from a speech made by an ex-Governor, Lord Onslow, describing Ballance who was Premier at the time as having been 'an itinerant vendor'. At the very start of Ballance's political career the *Wellington Independent* mischievously reported that he had 'made his appearance in the colony as a travelling vendor of Birmingham jewellery among the Maoris'. Ballance's response gives a clear impression of a man somewhat desperate and down in luck. At that time, he wrote, he was keeping for the first time in his life, and as a kind of *dernier res-sort*, a small jeweller's shop in Wanganui — an event which has been tortured into something which is considered a little lower in the scale of trades . . . [But, looking back] there is not one circumstance in his life he would refer to with more pride than that, in the chequered periods which come to most men, he battled with adversity in a strange country by engaging in a humble but respectable business. If this is to disqualify a man who may have the necessary qualifications in other respects from aspiring to sit in the councils of the people, many of the best statesmen in the colonies would be doomed to political ostracism, and the unfortunate countries would have been left to be ruled and ruined by Foxes![10]

With the failure of his jewellery business Ballance turned to other sources of income. One of these was writing occasional articles for the *Wanganui Times*, a bi-weekly newspaper established in 1865 and backed by the local merchants T. B. Taylor and W. H. Watt.[11] Another was a partnership with a man called Aitken in a brewery, but this proved even more unsuccessful than Ballance's jewellery business.[12]

Meanwhile Ballance was making his mark on the cultural life of the community. An able debater with a wide-ranging knowledge, he spoke at meetings of the town's Literary Society on such varied topics as 'Phrenology', 'Moses and Egypt' and the extension of the franchise.[13] He became known for a 'racy and eloquent' style and according to one melodramatic account spoke 'until he considered that he had made a sufficient breach in his opponent's battery, and then rushed to the assault with such a perfect phalanx of fact and argument as to compel any cidatel [*sic*] less ably defended to surrender at discretion'.[14] At a weekly meeting of the Literary Society Ballance met Archibald Duddingston Willis, a man who was to become one of his closest friends as well as business partner and political supporter.

Willis was born in Middlesex in 1842 of English and Scottish parentage. When 12 years old he began a job with Eyre and Spottiswoode, the Queen's Printers, and on the death of his mother emigrated to New Zealand. Working his passage he arrived penniless in Auckland in 1857, soon afterwards leaving for Napier, having been offered employment as printer on a new paper to be started there called the *Hawke's Bay Herald*. Before finally settling in Wanganui (about 1864) he worked as a compositor on the *Wellington Advertiser* and later the *Canterbury Press*, as well as spending six months on the goldfields at Gabriel's Gully. He brought a newspaper plant with him to Wanganui intending to start a journal of his own, but sold it on being persuaded by J. U. Taylor, then editor of the *Wanganui Chronicle*, to work for him.[15]

In early 1867 Ballance began planning to start a daily evening paper in Wanganui. There was a clear opening for such a venture in that the two existing newspapers, the *Wanganui Times* and the *Wanganui Chronicle*, were both morning bi-weeklies. The evening paper's strength would lie in being able to provide the day's news on that day. Willis was an ideal partner for he was now an experienced printer and could provide the necessary technical expertise while Ballance wrote the editorial material. The partnership was equally appealing to Willis, who had earlier hoped to found a paper on his own. Willis had been impressed by Ballance's 'logical and clever arguments in debate, and was invariably on the same side with him'. So when asked to join Ballance he readily accepted — a decision, he wrote many years later, that he never had cause to regret.[16] Pooling their resources they bought a second-hand printing machine from a man in Wellington, had it transported to Wanganui and set it up in rented premises on Market Place, in the centre of town.[17] This accommodation was cramped and temporary, however, and Ballance soon moved the office and print room to a more suitable building nearby in Campbell Place.[18]

A prospectus for the *Evening Herald*, aimed at attracting both advertisers and subscribers, was issued and on Saturday 4 May the town was placarded with the announcement that publication would commence on 3 June. The *Wanganui Times* unconvincingly welcomed the new paper on the grounds that it would assist the *Times*'s 'advocacy of local progress', something its rival the *Chronicle* simply sneered at. It also rather discreetly mentioned that it would move to tri-weekly publication (on Tuesday, Thursday and Saturday) as from 1 June.[19] Soon after the *Herald* appeared the *Times* admitted that it had been approached by the *Chronicle* with the suggestion that they match up their publication days, the *Times* appearing on Tuesdays and Thursdays and the *Chronicle* on Wednesdays and Saturdays. This would have avoided the need by both to publish three times a week but the *Times* declined the offer, forcing the *Chronicle* into tri-weekly publication as well.[20] Thus the *Herald* was a considerable threat to both papers, though they reacted differently to its appearance. The *Times* took the opportunity to lecture the *Chronicle* on the proper role of the press[21] while the *Chronicle* simply ignored the *Herald* completely for months and pretended that its extra edition was being produced for no other reason than a great demand for advertising space.[22]

Costing one penny, the first issue of the *Evening Herald* (only the second daily evening newspaper to be published in New Zealand, the other being the Wellington *Evening Post*) appeared as promised on Monday 3 June 1867. In his opening editorial Ballance sought to justify a third paper in Wanganui and laid down the ground rules for its future policy. Political issues would be discussed (though he claimed that he would nevertheless be tied to no party) and up-to-date information provided:

> We make this our first appearance as a member of the Fourth Estate, with the strong assurance that, not only our friends, but the general public, whom we hope soon to include in the ranks of the former,

will hail our advent with special favour, and bid us welcome to that position, which we desire to take up, as the representative of independent thought and action in Wanganui. Is there not room? The Herald . . . takes its stand upon the justness of its principles and the intelligence of the community. Two important duties lie before us — to place before our readers all information of local and general interest, and the advocacy of such measures as may tend to the prosperity of the place. It is an easy matter to have news . . . but old news is unpalatable, . . . it loses its freshness and flavour and we read without zest that which otherwise would give relief to the monotony of life . . . Much of our claim to public support rests upon our giving late news, which will be up to half-past two o'clock on the day of publication . . . Some kind friends have suggested that we should abstain from discussing politics — why the thing is impossible — they might as well cancel the constitution. The political concerns of the Colony affect everyone in it in the most direct manner; our rights, taxes, national defences, and liberty, are all in the hands of politicians, and we cannot defer to the wishes of the timid when such principles are involved, while we are aware that all controversy should be carried on with calmness and moderation, as the best way to advance the interests of a cause, if it be just. We are bound to no party and are unbiased in our opinions by such influence; our colums [*sic*] are open to all and we shall report without suppressing, or by altering to suit a purpose, what we may not agree with. Let the public, therefore, be our censors — the impartial, neutral public — and we shall await with feelings of confidence its verdict.

Journalism was much more to Ballance's liking than running a jewellery business and it was a role for which he was particularly well equipped. He was well read, intensely interested in politics and daring, especially on paper. Though his editorials were in the main well thought out and of considerable perspicacity and sophistication, he never forgot that sensational news, forceful views and a touch of audacity sold copies and advertising space. He fully realised the central, influential role a newspaper played in a small town, and later the use to which it could be put to further his own political career. Above all else the *Herald* aimed to inform and therefore to convert — it was didactic and proselytizing from the start and never apologised for being so.

With two shaky business ventures behind him Ballance cannot have been over-confident of the survival of the *Herald*. There were numerous risks involved and many newspapers at that time had only an ephemeral existence. Indeed it became clear that Wanganui could sustain no more than two newspapers (what town today of just 2000 people can boast even a single regular paper?), though equally apparent that it would be one of the morning papers that would go. The *Herald* was in less direct competition with the morning papers than they were with each other and it was the *Times* that soon went under.

Given an able editor, efficient economic management and the requisite technical skills, the success of a newspaper such as the *Herald* depended ultimately upon the prosperity of the community it served. Circulation and especially advertising were extremely sensitive to the vagaries of the local economy. A slump in trade would very quickly be reflected by a reduction in advertising as businesses contracted. It is of crucial importance for an understanding of Ballance's personal and political career to realise that his own financial security rested directly upon the wealth and development of Wanganui. His insistent campaigning for the expansion of the town's port facilities and the opening up of the hinterland to the east was more than mere politicking. On the town he depended (he had no independent source of income) and upon the new land depended the town. Wanganui's future rested upon its ability to act as a supplier to, and exporter for, farming communities being established on the undeveloped, flat, rich land beyond the hills that surrounded the town. Though these tiny settlements stretching from Patea in the north to Bulls in the south were never critical to Ballance in terms of additional circulation or advertising, as the basis of Wanganui's expansion and prosperity, and therefore that of the *Herald*, they were vital.

After one year the paper was boasting impressive weekly sales of over 2200 copies.[23] A photograph taken about this time shows Ballance and Willis with a staff of seven standing in front of the *Herald* office, a small building that, were it not for a ladder leaning against its side, would seem two-dimensional and straight out of a Hollywood set. The *Herald*'s employees would probably have comprised two compositors–cum–printers (Willis plus one other, to make up the type and operate the press afterwards); two learner compositors (who would work almost full time 'dissing' or breaking up the used type and putting it back in the print cases, and also do a limited amount of typesetting); a 'printer's devil' (a boy who traditionally did all the dirty work like inking the press); a reporter to assist Ballance on the content of the paper; a man in charge of distribution; and, finally, a delivery boy. There would have been no one specifically in charge of advertisements. Advertisers simply approached the manager, reporter or compositors direct.[24] Though the paper claimed a readership from Patea to Wellington few copies got further than the town's immediate hinterland. Owing primarily to problems of distribution the *Herald* never broke successfully into the rural market and remained essentially a paper of Wanganui town. This failure to achieve a significant rural readership was a major reason for the launching of the *Weekly Herald* a few years later.

Ballance soon established a consistent political line in *Herald* editorials and reinforced his commitment to these views through increasing involvement in a range of local organisations. He saw all the major issues as revolving around the removal of obstacles to Wanganui's progress and vigorously promoted any venture that might assist in the development of the district; that might, quite simply, bring more people into the area. He was not alone in this. There were very few people who did not have a personal economic (and perhaps also a social) interest in more rapid population growth. Ballance judged their mood well and no stone was left unturned. The possibility of discovering gold excited the town for much of 1868 and Ballance chaired a meeting that sent out a prospecting party to the wild and mountainous country between Wanganui and Taupo.[25] None was found.

More productive was the establishment of the Wanganui and Rangitikei Land and Building Society. A similar society existed when Ballance arrived in Wanganui[26] but he soon realised the greater contribution these bodies could make in providing finance for new settlement. Within two weeks of the first issue of the *Herald* Ballance was lecturing his readers on the potential of these organisations.[27] He became a director of the Wanganui and Rangitikei Building Society[28] and was a founder-director of the Wanganui and Rangitikei Land and Building Society, which held its first meeting in January 1868.[29] The addition of the word 'land' was a significant indication of the broadening role of such organisations. Ballance unashamedly promoted the society through the columns of the *Herald*, pointing out how advantageous it was for both investors (who would receive monthly compound interest on even small sums) and borrowers.[30] Money was lent only on the security of existing property but Ballance was soon suggesting that societies might buy up land themselves and then dispose of it to members over a period of time.[31]

Aside from land and building societies the other major method of promoting local settlement was through the establishment of small farm associations. The idea behind such associations was that a union of small investors could compete with large capitalists and squatters in the purchase of land. By no means all the members of the association would ultimately farm the land but those who did would do so much more intensively than a single squatter. When, in September 1867, the Wellington Provincial Council purchased the 16 200-hectare Parakino Block from its Maori owners, Ballance urged that a quarter of it be immediately set aside for a small farm association. Earlier in the year he had argued that by placing unemployed men and those of limited means on the land, small farm associations would extend trade, help end depression and stem the flow of population out of Wanganui to the goldfields on the West Coast.[32] A Wanganui Small Farm Association had already been formed,[33] but there was great demand for another. Ballance now regarded such associations as not only the best means of bringing prosperity to the district but as essential to a successful contest with monopolists over land:

The natives will shortly have a large quantity of land in the market which will be speedily swallowed up by the capitalist, and the plan we propose would neutralise such monopoly.[34]

The industrious man, of even small means, going upon his 200 acre farm will make it more productive than the squatter with his thousand acres. He will cultivate every rood, and by his own industry turn the fern-covered hill, and flaxy marsh, which are now desolate, or with a sheep to the acre, into a garden, with fields of waving corn and hedgerows that ever remind one of old England . . . Small Farm Settlement appears to us the best way of *possessing* the country and we have the strongest grounds for asking the Government to comply with our request.[35]

A spirit of self-reliance underlay Ballance's vision of progress:

Wanganui, in the midst of a large and fertile district, cannot remain stationary with 2000 inhabitants. Every new township will become another feeder; every farm occupied will minister to her resources. Extraneous assistance is not to be despised, but true prosperity is only to be found in our inherent power — in the capability of promoting our own greatness, without that uncertain aid which is derived from adventitious circumstances.[36]

This view of growth as dependent primarily on the efforts of the townspeople themselves arose in part because Ballance doubted the Provincial Council's will to promote the welfare of any settlement outside Wellington. In this he was not alone. With some justice many people in Wanganui regarded their town as a neglected satellite of Wellington (which seemed far away), and there had been periodic campaigns for separation ever since the province's formation under the Constitution Act of 1852.[37] In only the second issue of the *Herald* Ballance urged the abolition of the provincial system.[38] Specifically, his opposition to the council centred on its economic unviability, unfair distribution of a dwindling land fund and inability to secure loans to promote Wanganui's development.[39]

Of immediate concern to Wanganui was the need to build a bridge across the river to secure the town's position as a vital link in communications along the west coast. There was considerable ill-feeling about the inaction of the Provincial Council on this matter. Money had been voted for the bridge's construction but it was under threat of misappropriation for alternative uses. Ballance argued that if the town could raise the money itself this would remove the means by which the council was forcing Wanganui to maintain its connection with Wellington.[40] He instigated a meeting called to raise a petition for local self-government and discuss the question of financing the bridge. For the first time publicly he laid claim to speak on behalf of the working man:

He saw before him men of all classes who had come forward that night to maintain their rights, and he held that it was not alone the wealthy man, or the man with high position, whose views were to be considered, but that the man who toiled for his daily bread had likewise an important stake in the welfare of Wanganui, and should also have a voice in managing its affairs. Local Government was loudly called for, and the sooner a system that eats up £22,000 of revenue in departmental expenses, in a community of 21,000 souls, is done away with the better for the district.[41]

On wider political and philosophical issues raised in the *Herald* Ballance depended largely upon the ideological baggage he had brought with him from Birmingham, though often adapted to New Zealand conditions. For example, he welcomed the extension of the franchise in England and wrote with some passion and more than a little grandiloquence of his optimism for the future:

> The principle embodied in every extension, is the individuality and responsibility of the person. The world cannot be governed by a few, mounted on a kind of promontory, and looking down upon and controlling the masses by a ubiquitous power, especially if those masses are capable of thinking . . . The art of government is to understand the spirit of the time, and to mould the institutions in accordance . . . The world is growing older and wiser, and the spirit of the present age is more enlightened than the spirit of any preceding age in human history.[42]

As for the present, he was not blind to the operation of the class system in England, which he pointed out was maintained only because sufficient wealth percolated downwards, and the possibility of self-improvement was sufficiently alive to induce some contentment among working men.[43] Opposing the view of many conservatives at the time, he argued that franchise reform stemmed rather than created 'mob rule' by admitting for the first time artisans and labourers, as well as the lower strata of the middle class, to the political system. And no country could be great where power rested in a single class.[44] Finally, if reform was possible in a traditional society such as England, how much easier it would be achieved in a new land:

> They would have no more compunction in some of the Colonies about changing the entire constitution than the people at home would have about a simple extension of the franchise. Nations that have neither history nor tradition, are governed by expediency — the convenience of the greatest number, and are always subject to sudden changes and fluctuations of popular opinion.[45]

This pragmatism, arising from the notion that the political ground rules were different in New Zealand than in the old country, became fundamental to Ballance's philosophy.

The *Herald* was hardly off the ground when Ballance was struck by personal tragedy. In March 1868 Fanny died. Her general health had for a long time been suspect; as we have seen it was a major factor in their decision to emigrate to New Zealand, though since arriving she had been fully active in the town's affairs. She died after an illness lasting only a fortnight.[46] Ballance moved out of their house on Ridgeway Street and went to stay for a while with Archie Willis, who was his closest friend and offered consolation and support. Enormously impressed by Ballance's personal qualities as well as his intellectual abilities, Willis found him kind and compassionate and as a result often imposed upon by others. On one occasion there arrived at the Willis household a newcomer to the town for whom Ballance had found a job and to whom he had lent some money. However, the man had wasted the opportunity and, now destitute, was returning to his benefactor for another handout. On seeing him coming Ballance felt it necessary to assure Willis that he would deal with the man firmly and send him packing, but when he came face to face with the downcast and dejected fellow he rapidly softened and handed him a five-pound note.[47]

Back at his desk at the *Herald* office Ballance was soon in the midst of new controversy. Wanganui was a frontier town not only economically in being on the edge of an undeveloped hinterland but militarily as well. Land disputes with local Maori continued to develop occasionally into armed conflict and with the spillover effects of a war in Taranaki added to the townspeople's sense of insecurity. Recently the area had been quiet and in a series of editorials Ballance had urged the abolition of the locally raised Militia and Volunteers, on the grounds that their 'playing at soldiers' entailed unnecessary expense and needlessly disrupted everyday life in the town.[48] However in June 1868 the murder of three Europeans marked the beginnings of a fresh crisis. The settlers were occupying land south of the Waingongoro River that had been recently confiscated by the British authorities from Ngaruahine Maori. Little by little, more land was being brought under European control and its loss by Ngaruahine was threatening their very survival. Titokowaru, leader of a Ngaruahine hapu (sub-tribe), had tried peaceful means to persuade settlers to leave the area. The murder of the three settlers signalled the failure of this passive approach and the start of armed resistance.

Titokowaru was a fierce warrior, an able general and a charismatic leader with a complex personality. From his base at Te Ngutu-o-te-Manu ('The Beak of the Bird') he began a campaign against the European forces which was to have remarkable effect.[49] On 12 July a small band of Ngaruahine successfully attacked a constabulary redoubt at Turuturu-Mokai, not far from Waihi (see map 2). It was a significant strategic victory for Titokowaru; a defeat for the colonists that Ballance put down to a combination of a 'wily and desperate enemy' displaying some courage and strategy and military incompetence on the part of the commander of the colonial forces. Yet he was confident that the Patea forces would successfully counter-attack and saw no reason for panic in the town nor cause for calling out the Militia.[50]

Despite the *Herald*'s low-key approach Ballance personally was not slow to take precautionary measures. Three days prior to the attack on Turuturu-Mokai he chaired a meeting that formed the Wanganui Cavalry Volunteer Corps, which on its first parade had a strength of two officers and 26 men.[51] The protection of the district was dependent upon these volunteers along with the Kai Iwi Cavalry Corps and a few members of the Armed Constabulary. In addition there were Imperial troops stationed in Wanganui, part of the 2nd Battalion of the 18th Regiment and the only British force remaining in the country, but they had strict instructions on no account to take to the field, their role being purely defensive. In emergencies the town's adult males could be called upon for service in the Militia.

Lieutenant Colonel Gorton, commander of the Wanganui District, put a brave face on the defeat at Turuturu-Mokai, but he was well aware of the imminent danger of an uprising of local Maori encouraged by Titokowaru's success and decided to call out the Militia, issuing orders that it parade on the morning of 23 July. While Ballance fully supported the formation of volunteer corps, he resented the compulsory nature of the Militia and failed to attend the parade. Many followed Ballance's example; at the appointed time hardly a man had turned up and additions over the next half-hour brought the total to only 16. 'I was perfectly aware there was a great feeling against the Militia here,' Gorton complained to Haultain, the Defence Minister in Wellington, 'but this feeling has been greatly encouraged by the scurrilous articles which have lately appeared in the *Evening Herald* when the Militia have been positively recommended not to come forward for duty.'[52] Having identified Ballance as the ring-leader, Gorton decided to make an example of him and wrote him a personal order to attend parade. Ballance refused to obey and having sent an insubordinate reply to Gorton's demand for an explanation was promptly placed in jail, in preparation for a court martial. The *Herald* that evening carried the banner headline 'Military Tyranny: Editor in Gaol'. The town was in uproar as a future premier was locked behind bars.[53]

The specific disagreement between Ballance and Gorton was the legality of the proclamation calling out the Militia. Under the terms of the Militia Act of 1858, Gorton was required to serve each militiaman individually with a notice. With a staff of only two this created considerable practical difficulties so Gorton hoped to entice the whole of the Militia onto parade and then give separate notices for active service.[54] Technically he was acting illegally and knew it; Walter Buller, Resident Magistrate in the town, advised

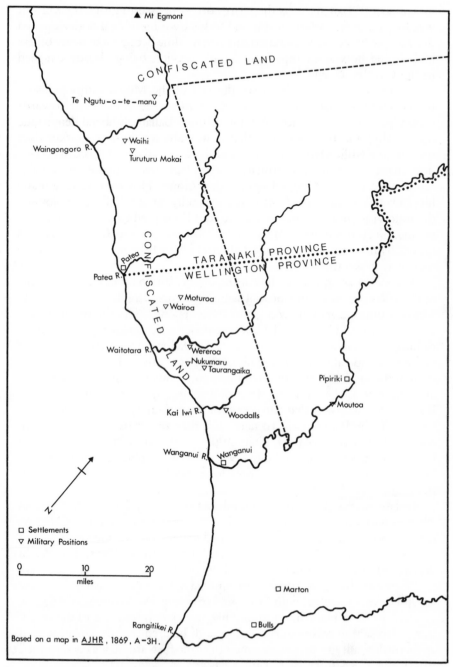

▲ Mt Egmont

CONFISCATED LAND

Te Ngutu–o–te–manu ▽

Waingongoro R.

▽ Waihi
▽ Turuturu Mokai

C O N F I S C A T E D L A N D

TARANAKI PROVINCE
WELLINGTON PROVINCE

Patea □
Patea R.

▽ Moturoa
▽ Wairoa

Waitotara R.

▽ Wereroa
▽ Nukumaru
▽ Taurangaika

Pipiriki □

▽ Moutoa

Kai Iwi R.
▽ Woodalls

Wanganui R.
Wanganui □

□ Settlements
▽ Military Positions

0   10   20
miles

□ Marton

Rangitikei R.
□ Bulls

Based on a map in AJHR, 1869, A–3H.

The Wanganui district and the war against Titokowaru

him as such.[55] Ballance was therefore correct in asserting that the call-out was illegal but his failure to respond to his own individual notice opened the way for his arrest. He refused this second time because like many others he believed he was exempt from Militia service, being already enrolled in the Cavalry Corps.[56]

Behind these technicalities lay the fact of the Militia's unpopularity. In the *Herald* Ballance had voiced the widespread resentment towards compulsory military service (coercion ill-fitted Ballance's liberal democratic philosophy) and the complaint that it was always the town rather than the country Militia that was called upon. He had focused this dissatisfaction on the somewhat unfortunate Gorton and now, in prison, personally represented the town's stand against the colonel. However, having made his point and realising that Gorton was in deadly earnest, Ballance apologised the following morning and was released. He claimed to have been let out because Gorton was afraid of him, which was in part true. Given Ballance's influence in the town a court martial would have been much more trouble than it was worth.[57]

Ballance was undaunted by the experience and only five days after his night of confinement an editorial went into considerable detail about the Militia's unpopularity in Wanganui. He explained why the original call-up was illegal and how martial law threatened political liberty and his own rights of *habeas corpus* when imprisoned. The failure of the parade he blamed on Gorton's inability to exercise his powers correctly and with tact.[58] Criticism of the local military command was combined with advice on logistics and strategy as the situation deteriorated. A large part of the problem, Ballance argued, was that the economic and military dependence of the colony on the British Government, and thus on British public opinion, restricted the actions of the military at the front. Concessions to the Maori had failed, truces had been quickly followed by renewed outbreaks of violence and the time had now come for every Maori to be removed from the disaffected district.[59]

In late August and early September attempts by Lieutenant Colonel Thomas McDonnell, commander of the Patea District, to capture Te Ngutu-o-te-Manu ended in disaster. He resigned in consequence and was replaced by the able Colonel George Whitmore.[60] The northern position at Waihi was abandoned and settlers evacuated much of the area between Patea and the Waitotara River as Titokowaru moved south to establish a new base at Otoia. On 1 October, with Wanganui receiving a steady flow of refugees, Gorton wrote to Haultain outlining his plans for the defence of the town. Immediate action was required and though he predicted that there would again be difficulty in persuading men to come forward he was determined to call out the Militia on a regular basis.[61]

In the meantime Ballance, popular among his peers, had been elected

Chairman of the Council of the Wanganui Cavalry which now totalled about 65 men and was being increasingly called upon for patrols and as escort for ammunition and food.[62] Combining the roles of cavalryman and journalist, Ballance wrote lively accounts of these trips for publication in the *Herald*. One such expedition, described by Ballance as 'as eventful as any immortalised by the enterprising Don Quixote', brought back news that Titokowaru's southward advance had reached the Waitotara River.[63] By the end of October Titokowaru had outflanked Whitmore and established himself at Moturoa, winning over some previously loyalist and neutral Maori on the way.[64] As Whitmore had burnt the settlements deserted by Maori who joined Titokowaru, so too Titokowaru destroyed settler property as he moved south.

Back in Wanganui Ballance continued to plague Gorton, constantly contrasting the efficacy of the volunteers with that of a 'press-ganged' militia. He described one particularly unenthusiastic turnout as follows: 'It was a really lamentable sight to see men, when called on for the protection of their hearths and homes, "creeping like snails reluctantly to school", or being dragged like lambs to the slaughter by an escort of their comrades with fixed bayonets. These are not the men to meet Titokowaru.'[65] New grievances were added: poor pay when on active service and inadequate living conditions. Ballance was certain that the minor concession of issuing a blanket to each militaman would do little to remove the bad feeling.

As the front shifted closer to the town, Ballance was able to provide more detailed information on the movements of the colonial forces and the enemy for his readers. On 7 November Whitmore attacked Titokowaru at Moturoa but was rapidly repulsed. Ballance had got to know and respect Whitmore during the latter's time in Wanganui and generously described the Colonel as retreating 'with great coolness and judgement' to Nukumaru.[66] In fact the position was nothing short of disaster, for Titokowaru now threatened the land immediately to the north of the Kai Iwi stream. A further influx of settlers to Wanganui testified to the serious state of affairs.[67] The Militia were called out to take their turn at the front, an action Ballance was again critical of, arguing that they should remain to protect the town.[68]

Only when Titokowaru moved to Tauranga-ika, within 30 kilometres and a day's march of the town, did Ballance finally succumb to the urgency of the situation. In a dramatic editorial he called all men to the full support of Gorton:

> TO ARMS!!! The time has come for every man that can shoulder a rifle to arm himself at once, which he can do by applying at the Militia Office. Let there be no panic, but with coolness and determination let *every man* be at the post of duty . . . We are not given to foster false alarms, but when real danger is approaching it would be

foolish not to look it fairly in the face, and prepare to meet it. . . Our townsmen are not poltroons, that would lurk in their houses when the enemy was at their doors. If they objected to march out and leave their families, it was because the latter wanted protection, and because there was neither right nor justice in the demand. They will now fall in to a man, if it is for the immediate protection of Wanganui.[69]

Ballance, who seems to have been almost enjoying the emergency (which was all 'grist to the mill' as far as material for the *Herald* was concerned), accompanied this with reports and advice on the steps being taken by Gorton to defend the town. Wanganui had never been in such imminent danger, he wrote, with 'Hannibal approaching the gates of Rome' and a distinct possibility of a rising of Maori up-river. The town was at fever-pitch, especially when the news arrived of a raid made by a Maori called Te Kooti on Poverty Bay. People speculated about Titokowaru's and Whitmore's next move, rumours flew and the place was believed to be swarming with spies. Ballance said that if the Government did not at once initiate a system by which Maori could only enter the town with a pass, wholesale lynch law would follow.[70]

A defence meeting of the townspeople was held on Saturday 14 November, the day following Ballance's call to arms. He was elected to a committee formed to draw up a petition to impress upon Sir George Bowen, the Governor who had just arrived in Wanganui with the Defence Minister, the immediacy of the threat and suggest practical steps that might be taken to protect the town. In the heady atmosphere of deep crisis he called for the resignation of Haultain and urged the Government to pursue more vigorously the war between civilisation and 'cannibalism'. Block-houses were needed and a price should be put on the head of every rebel as a means of securing the loyalty of kupapa.[71]

The committee presented its petition to the Governor on 17 November[72] and when no satisfactory response was forthcoming organised a second public meeting. Ballance again took the lead and, arguing that the town fall back on its own resources, organised a subcommittee to co-ordinate, patrols and other measures of self-defence. The *Herald* that evening carried some rousing poetry:

TO THE MEN OF WANGANUI

The time for action has arrived,
* You must your battles fight;*
Relying on your own strong arm
* To aid you in the fight.*
Then forward all with one accord,
* United heart and hand;*
Go forth to meet the rebel foe,
* and sweep him off the land.*
The blood of slaughtered countrymen
* for vengeance calleth loud;*
For vengeance on the treach'rous foe
* Who slew them in cold blood.*
Then quickly gird your weapons on,
* And hasten to the fight;*
And let this be your battle cry, —
* For God and for our right.*[73]

The necessity for self-defence and the town's nervousness were heightened by the departure of Whitmore's main force to the East Coast to deal with Te Kooti. It is doubtful that Titokowaru would have risked a direct attack on the town but the inhabitants clearly believed this possible. What was likely, however, was a tightening of Titokowaru's siege, and if prolonged this would have been a real threat to the town's economic viability.

Ballance continued the hectic life of soldier, war correspondent, editor and town spokesman on the military situation. The Wanganui Cavalry had been on pay since October and by January 1869 had a strength of more than 80 men. Promotion was by election and under this very unmilitary democratic system Ballance rose from corporal to cornet, third in command, after Captain Finnimore (his future brother-in-law) and Lieutenant Day.[74] With Whitmore gone there was little the cavalry could do save some minor skirmishing, patrolling and escorting supplies and men to Kai Iwi.[75] They were nevertheless extremely jumpy. Ballance was in one patrol that returned to town with the news that Titokowaru's men were at a farm about five kilometres away. Finnimore reported this to Gorton who then informed Haultain. However, it turned out to be a false alarm, the warlike cries heard by the patrol having emanated from a group of rather drunk Maori shearers.[76]

In late November Ballance saw some minor action in a sortie connected with a failed attempt by Whitmore to retake Nukumaru. None of the cavalry was wounded and only one member of the Armed Constabulary was killed. Eager to make the most of every report from the front, Ballance wrote of it as a gallant affair, though reluctantly but honestly admitted that the 'object was slight and the results impossible to be great'.[77] A week later he commanded a party that sought to capture a pa (or stockade) on a hill opposite Woodhall's Redoubt (where the cavalry was stationed). Ballance described it as yet another daring cavalry exploit, studiously playing down the fact that the pa was empty.[78]

More significant was a three-day skirmishing expedition north towards Patea, which left town in mid-December.[79] The Wanganui Cavalry was formed into three divisions, one each under Ballance, Day and Finnimore. They operated alongside the Kai Iwi Cavalry, the exploits of whose commander, Bryce, had gained him a ruthless reputation.[80] In all five villages were attacked, 'growing crops of potatoes, canoes, and about twelve whares were destroyed, two Hauhaus killed, a large quantity of stock recovered, and the enemy laughed at in his very den, . . . all without a loss of a man or horse . . . Although the enterprise was bold, and to some may have seemed rash, yet every precaution was taken.'[81] These killings were particularly shameful for one of the two Maori shot was a woman and neither could with any certainty be connected with the fighting against the settlers. When news of the incident reached Wanganui the town's magistrate, Booth, began enquiring into the affair. In the *Herald* Ballance defended the 'guilty until found innocent' approach:

> The cavalry have always professed that they would kill every male Maori they came across on the other side of the Kai Iwi, unless there was some proof that he was a kupapa, and it is impossible at times, as it was the other day, to distinguish between the men and women. Let Mr Booth get up an inquiry — who cares? — the thing will be treated, so far as the cavalry is concerned, with absolute contempt. War is not made with rose-water, and the cavalry do not live by war, and have no interest in seeing it prolonged. Indeed, it is every man's direct interest to put an end to the war as soon as possible. We question whether it is so with many officers and men in the 'regular' constabulary service. It appears that some are jealous of the cavalry, or disappointed that it has rendered services to the colony.[82]

Having pointed out that desperate measures were sometimes required if the war were to be brought to a speedy conclusion, Ballance went on to make an unveiled threat on a Maori named Ngahina who, Ballance alleged, was a spy for Titokowaru. 'A Maori in the enemy's country is,' he wrote, '*prima facie* one of the enemy and that is sufficient evidence until the missionaries prove the contrary.'[83] In fact, what was more significant was that Ngahina had been influential in getting the Pokaikai Commission set up to investigate alleged acts of cruelty by McDonnell, Commander of Patea District, in August 1868. Ngahina was an obvious target for settler animosity.[84]

Unfortunately for Ballance, Booth passed a copy of this editorial to

Haultain in Wellington who shortly afterwards wrote to Colonel Lyon (commander of the Wanganui forces in Whitmore's absence) instructing him to cancel Ballance's commission.[85] Ballance was told that this action was being taken 'as no person who can publish language threatening the lives of friendly natives who are in the service of the Government can be allowed to hold a commission in the local forces'. Concerned not to alienate Maori whom the Government hoped would at least remain neutral and at most join the kupapa force, Haultain added that Lyon was to 'inform the Wanganui Cavalry and other forces under your command that if any outrages are committed on the native Ngahina or his family, the perpetrators, if known, will be immediately proceeded against by the civil authorities'.[86]

Unrepentant, Ballance launched a fierce attack on Lyon, saying that although it had been an honour to have held command in the cavalry he had a duty to speak out, and that his independence 'could not be purchased by so cheap a thing as a commission'.[87] Yet despite the high dudgeon there was something farcical about the whole affair, and Ballance did not take his loss of rank very seriously. On 6 January the *Herald* published, in a number of acts, an imaginary scene of a court martial held in an 'ancient store' on Taupo Quay. Part of the proceedings included an exchange between two cavalrymen, one pointing out that the Wanganui Volunteer Cavalry were now such bad riders because they had lost their Ballance.[88] Ballance remained in the cavalry as a private and, after Whitmore's return to Wanganui in late January and the critical but somewhat mysterious desertion by Titokowaru of his pa at Tauranga–ika, was involved in the early skirmishes that followed the chief's retreat north.[89] Whitmore reached Nukumaru by 6 February and continued on in pursuit, sending the Wanganui Cavalry back to town.[90] Ballance and the cavalry saw no further action.[91]

In the *Herald* Ballance continued to pull no punches, arguing that peace would only come about through the extermination of all 'rebels':

> Benefits conferred on the native race will at the present time pass for nought, and the whole consideration of Government must be for the colonists. If one colonist is killed, let there be exacted the lives of two aboriginals; if a tribe rebel, stamp out the rebellion by extermination. Transportation will answer the purpose . . . Let the confiscated lands be immediately occupied with white military settlers.[92]

These harsh views were in line with attitudes common at this time. And being what many wanted to read, they were also good for sales. Ballance was bound by the Victorian preconception of British racial superiority over the Maori, including the inevitability of a white military victory. In explaining British defeats he emphasised the failings of individual commanders rather than crediting Titokowaru with any significant military skill or strategy.[93] His comments on racial issues reflected a belief that the basic philosophical premises underlying the conduct of European affairs ought not to apply to an uncivilised race. For example, on the question of Maori political representation he wrote that there was scarcely a member of the House of Representatives who was not 'conscious of the folly of placing natives among Europeans to deliberate on the affairs of state. The native is a failure in every respect . . . The Maori representatives in the Assembly have failed to throw any light on the problem of governing the natives . . . What is their use, then?'[94]

The outspoken and vehement views Ballance expressed in the *Herald* in this period are in stark contrast to his sympathetic and enlightened approach to race relations when Minister of Native Affairs in the 1880s. The explanation for this is threefold. First, this severity came with the unusual and desperate circumstances of war, where the *Herald* was the mouthpiece of a town under siege and dangerously defenceless. With the war over and the threat removed Ballance moderated his views. Second, at this time Ballance's knowledge and understanding of the Maori was very limited. Later, as he came into more contact with Maori people in peaceful conditions he quite simply changed his mind about their problems and the solutions to them.

Finally, there is evidence that *Herald* editorials by no means tell the full story of how Ballance felt about the fighting and in particular his own participation in it. Soon after Ballance's death Archie Willis wrote some personal reminiscences of him which included a story told to Willis by members of the Wanganui Cavalry. It concerned the incident referred to above when shots fired into a whare killed two Maori:

> On the bodies being dragged out it was seen that one of the victims was that of a young girl. Mr Ballance came up shortly afterwards, and when he saw the dead body he was so overcome by the sad spectacle that he burst into tears. His companions, however . . . railled him on what they thought his weakness, not sufficiently appreciating his finely-strung organisation and deeply sympathetic nature. He only once spoke of the subject to me, and said it was one of those sad incidents he should never forget.[95]

The extremism of the *Herald* may have been an attempt by Ballance to compensate for his own sensibility when confronted with the realities of war. His 'sympathetic nature' involved a sensitivity not only to the welfare of other people but also to what other people thought of him. And the reality of war was that much more difficult for Ballance to cope with because his approach to the whole affair tended to be intellectual rather than practical. Clearly, when he finally came face to face with death he was deeply disturbed. (Violence in the form of riots was common in Belfast but the ground rules, acknowledged by both sides, were such that the fighting did not too often result in deaths.) Ballance's reputation for 'calling a spade a spade'[96] arose entirely from *Herald* editorials. He was not bellicose by nature and his participation in the fighting never produced such accusations of brutal pugnacity as clung to men like Bryce and McDonnell for the rest of their lives. The paradox remains: Ballance's aggressiveness on paper alongside the revelation at times of, in Willis's words, 'the softness of heart of a woman'.[97]

Whatever Ballance's own personal feelings, he undoubtedly saw that the war could do the *Herald*'s prospects a lot of good. As a journalist and newspaper owner he made the most of the emergency. The paper outflanked the *Chronicle* (which was milder and much less willing to criticise the authorities) as the medium for the town's discontent[98] and through his first-hand accounts of the fighting Ballance gained a reputation in and beyond Wanganui. *Herald* articles were reprinted in Wellington newspapers, at times providing Haultain with the first information available on the activities of forces ultimately under his command. Precisely how Ballance reacted to the developing situation was not a simple matter, for as we have seen the interrelationship between peace and prosperity posed a basic dilemma. He deprecated any overreaction on the part of the authorities or the people themselves to the possible danger Wanganui was in, since this tended to disrupt lives and was, for Ballance himself as well as the town, frankly bad for business. On the other hand, if there came a point when the town was genuinely in danger, action would clearly have to be taken. In this case Ballance saw a ruthless and above all short campaign as crucial to a successful return to normality. Thus vehement editorials in the *Herald* criticised government weakness, attacked incompetent local military commanders and threatened chiefs of suspect loyalty.

Through the *Herald* and his own clashes with authority, Ballance achieved a personal notoriety that never damaged the prospects of a political career. Indeed it was of positive benefit. He was now well-known and in the eyes of many people in Wanganui had faithfully represented their needs and fears in critical times. Above all, these early experiences of the fragile nature of Wanganui produced in Ballance an almost religious conviction that only the comprehensive settlement of the land could guarantee, for himself and the town, peace and economic prosperity. In general the threat posed by Titokowaru in late 1868 and early 1869 to the town's very existence meant that physical security remained an important issue in Wanganui after it had ceased to be one elsewhere. By the early 1870s, pushing back the frontier through public works and the purchase or confiscation of Maori land reflected the desire for permanent peace as much as that for economic development.

[CHAPTER 3]

The politics of progress

ON 19 MAY 1870 at St Peter's Church in Willis Street, Wellington, Ballance married Ellen Anderson, second daughter of David Anderson and Ann Thompson.[1] Before emigrating to New Zealand in 1849, David Anderson had travelled widely with the British Army. He married Ann in 1828 when he was 22 and she just 14, and they had a large family born in various parts of the world including England, Ireland, the East Indies, Gibraltar and Jamaica. Anderson intended to settle in Ireland but with the onset of the famine decided to emigrate to New Zealand. On arriving in Wellington he bought a store on the beach front, setting up business as a general merchant. The firm was very successful (he may well have been the first trader in New Zealand to use mail order) and he soon established a second store in Molesworth Street.[2] In 1870 'Paddy' Anderson was living with his family in 'Rhyme', a large house in Hankey Street.

Ellen was born in County Down, Ireland, in 1847. At just two years old she left with her parents for New Zealand, enduring a voyage that took seven months, including eight weeks when the ship was becalmed. Her childhood was privileged, though she had her fair share of troubles. She had been born with a slightly lame leg and in addition, after inoculation for smallpox in England, developed an infection that permanently affected one eye. Growing up in Wellington Ellen attended a private school run by Jane and Florence Spinks, daughters of a businessman and member of the Provincial Council.[3] Lessons were held in the Spinks's home in Dixon Street and attended weather and health permitting. Ellen's older sister Ann had married William Finnimore of Wanganui and it was through him that she met Ballance. Finnimore was a businessman who performed a classic 'parasitic' role servicing country districts. He was a government auctioneer, valuator, licensed custom house, shipping and commission agent, stock and cattle salesman and land and estate agent. A second sister, Margaret, married Samuel Griffiths and a third, Jessie, Stephen Foreman, both also Wanganui men.[4]

With Ballance now a figure of some standing in Wanganui and David Anderson a successful Wellington businessman the match was socially suitable. Much more important, as far as one can tell the marriage was to be basically happy and fulfilling for both partners. The couple were the closest of friends and confidants as well as husband and wife. Ellen shared Ballance's interest in politics and was herself thoughtful, intelligent and politically astute. Temperamentally, she was kindly and amiable like her husband, though at the same time could be determined and strong-willed. Her father was a tough, quick-tempered Irishman with a wife as meek as a doormat. Tight-fisted and hard-nosed in business affairs, Paddy ruled his family with a rod of iron. His daughters had a lot to put up with and of necessity developed characters of considerable resilience.

The couple spent their early married life in a two-storied house on the corner of Wilson and Guyton Streets. Ballance bought the land from a woman who ran a private school and may have had the house built himself. The dwelling was simple but roomy, set back from the road on a good-sized section and only a short distance from the *Herald* office in Campbell Place.[5] Some of the money for the new home may have come from Ellen, but the purchase was also made possible by a marked improvement in Ballance's own finances. The *Herald* was doing very well and in July 1869, eager to expand, he had announced a new weekly paper to be launched on 7 August. Called the *Weekly Herald*, it would contain articles and news already published during the week in the *Evening Herald*, as well as new material especially tailored to meet the needs of country readers.[6] It was an attempt by Ballance to reach outlying districts that could not be served on a daily basis and at 2d per copy was cheaper than equivalent weeklies in the colony.

Established on the eve of an economic upturn and an expansion of settlement, the *Weekly Herald* got off to a good start. Its very first issue surpassed Ballance's cautious expectations, the *Evening Herald* reporting that as demand had exceeded supply only previously paid-up subscribers would receive a copy.[7] Both papers flourished and a little over a year later Ballance was able to buy a new printing machine direct from England. At the same time both papers were enlarged, the *Evening Herald* from five to six columns across and the weekly to a total of 60 columns.[8] Ballance's claim that the latter's circulation quadrupled in two years may not have been too exaggerated, and as readership rose so did the chances of attracting new advertisers.[9]

With the war over and prospects bright for major new settlement, Ballance believed that the colony should combine military self-reliance with economic and political independence. He deplored attempts by the Fox Ministry to obtain new military assistance from the British Government[10] and wrote a series of editorials overflowing with a kind of crusading, visionary nationalism:

> The interests of the colony point to independence . . . This country, if an independent state, would command the moral support of every nation in the world . . . The energy that is implanted by noble aspirations would enable the nation to triumph over internal difficulties, and to treat lightly those sacrifices which it would have to make before attaining the goal of unity and peace. Independence will come to us sooner or later. Is the time not opportune?[11]

Yet although the fighting was, apart from minor skirmishing, at an end, Ballance insisted that the threat was still sufficient to justify government assistance in the form of military settlers. He rationalised the confiscation of Maori land by arguing that their rebellion had forfeited their right to occupy it. And in any case 'natives can make no use of the land'.[12] Placing on the land soldiers who had served in the war made military and economic sense. However Ballance soon realised that the military settlements had serious flaws. The settlers were often ill-equipped as farmers and frequently sold their rights to speculators, with land aggregation as the result.[13] At the same time Ballance's stance on confiscation itself also began to change. While he continued to view settlement as essential to peace and economic development, he increasingly saw that extensive alienation of land created discontent and disorder and threatened the very survival of the Maori race.[14]

As land became available through confiscation and purchase, communications were extended to the growing country settlements to channel goods to and from Wanganui town. Until the construction of the railway to Wellington in 1886 Wanganui was the closest, most accessible and therefore the cheapest route for the increasing amount of Waitotara and Manawatu wool and meat sent out through the port. Harbour facilities and shipping capacity responded to the expansion in trade,[15] and the opening of the bridge across the river in 1871 ensured not only Wanganui's position as a vital link in communications along the west coast but also the growth of settlement on the river's south bank. The nature of the town changed as it began to have an economic existence in its own right, beyond simply supplying imports to local settlers and exporting farm produce. By the mid-1870s small local industries had been established such as breweries, soap works, an iron foundry and a rope factory.[16] Nevertheless the town continued in a symbiotic relationship with its hinterland, for local industries needed internal as well as export markets, and its expansion remained dependent on the success of land settlement. Between 1867 and 1874 the population of the surrounding countryside grew at a faster rate than that of the town itself.[17] The future lay in the land.

Despite these encouraging developments Ballance was frustrated by a lack of vitality in the town. He was getting bored and wanted some action, something new and positive, to write about.

> The river bank is crumbling . . . There are no public institutions, except the hospital, and it has neither accommodation nor comforts of any kind. The signal-station is supported by shilling subscriptions; the gaol has so little room that 'justice has to be tempered with mercy', the police, like rats, are leaving the rotten hulk.

The fault lay with the provincial system:

> Look to Wellington, and what do we see. Tottering imbecility *represents* us . . . We might wait until oxidation had removed the semblance of the bridge before one note would rise from the nocturnal labors of our representative. He perhaps works in secret . . . Although ours is the sixth port in the colony, it has not a place even in the inter-colonial time table. Politically, it is absolutely nowhere — deserted, forgotten, even hated, it has surely attained its nadir, its lowest depths . . . The people are apathetic . . . The atmosphere of provincialism is miasmal, the waters stagnant, and both are acting on the system, causing depletion and enervation. We implore anything different from the present system; we cannot be worse governed, and any change will be received with a welcome only to be measured by the intensity of the desire to part with what we have.[18]

Ballance was unremitting in his condemnation of the Provincial Council. The town was simply not interested in the council at Wellington, he said. Local representatives had to be persuaded to stand for election to the council,[19] which was spending nearly all the income of the province in Wellington[20] and performing functions that could be much better carried out by either central government or a local body.[21] The justice of the complaint of inequitable distribution of revenue is difficult to assess, since statistics produced by the provincial government did not break down expenditure regionally. Separate figures were given for Wanganui's gaol, harbour and hospital, and a comparison with Wellington shows that funding on these items was roughly in proportion to population served. Nevertheless, irrespective of the rights and wrongs of specific grievances, establishing direct control over local spending remained the reasonable basic aim of Ballance and Wanganui.

Not only did provincialism inhibit local development but it positively encouraged speculation in land. The Provincial Council in Wellington controlled a vast area of confiscated land and set the terms of settlement. Ballance was well aware that simply selling this land off to the highest bidder would lead to speculation and aggregation at the expense of the small, genuine farmer. In 1869, when 89 000 hectares of the Manawatu were acquired by the council, Ballance demanded that the 'interests of the working classes be considered' when the time came for the land's disposal. Specifically, he wanted a portion of the land sold on deferred payment and at the same time urged that the Wanganui Small Farm Association be revived. Both would promote bona fide settlement. 'Shall this large area of country be absorbed by the Wellington plutocracy, and shall the man of limited means, the small farmer, reap no benefit therefrom? . . . Shall we have to witness the sacrifice of a splendid estate among a select number of monied monopolists?'[22]

Ballance pointed out examples of speculation elsewhere in New Zealand. In Otago, for example, a Melbourne speculator named Clark purchased 16 200 hectares with the intention of selling them at a considerable profit, once roads and railways had made them accessible to settlement. It was the fault of a reckless provincial government, said Ballance, and the sooner the control of land was in the hands of the General Assembly the better.[23] But even with central government control over land there were dangers. The Legislative Council was dominated by wealthy landowning interests and could throw out legislation from the Lower House with ease. Thus Ballance urged either its abolition[24] or at least the appointment of new councillors to counteract the 'clique of large capitalists', so that those 'few men alienated from public opinion and sympathy will not be permitted to usurp the functions of Government and direct the policy of the country'.[25]

The somewhat drab political scene did not remain drab for long. On 28 June 1870 Julius Vogel, the Colonial Treasurer, stood up in the House of Representatives and announced a daring public works and immigration programme. He proposed to spend £10 million (some of which would be borrowed overseas) over the next ten years to facilitate a rapid expansion of settlement in the colony.[26] Ballance was impressed, very impressed. The scheme was bold and imaginative, a grand design that struck a chord with Ballance's sense of New Zealand's destiny. It would see New Zealand come of age. Here at last was a man of vision. The colony had 'come forth from its pupilage, buckled on its armour, and is prepared to take its stand among the nations'.[27] Ballance was even more enthusiastic once the details of the works to be carried out in the Wanganui district became known. Roads were to connect the east and west coasts, and to link with a trunk route running north–south from Foxton. However over the next two years he modified his opinion. He accepted that borrowing was necessary for development but thought that money was being misapplied. Also, it soon became clear that railway construction was slow and expensive and brought much less revenue than Vogel had predicted.[28] Most important, Parliament's refusal to adopt Vogel's plan to set aside land as a guarantee on the borrowed funds wrecked the scheme's finances.[29] Vogel had seen that land beside the new railways would rise rapidly in value, and argued that the central government ought to take control of much of it and use the proceeds from its sale over subsequent years to help pay for the loan.

Still, Ballance could not help admiring the plan and was reluctant to attack it. Instead he found in the problems of its implementation a useful stick with which to beat the provincial system and mentality. He complained that the predominance of provincial interests meant that alliances were being formed simply on the basis of the distribution of borrowed money, deploring pork-barrel politics where each representative fought for his own district without considering colonial interests as a whole.[30] He was right. Politics in this period amounted essentially to a scramble for money for development projects. Politicians acted primarily in the interests of their provinces whilst ministries differed only in the extent to which they were prepared to borrow. Some were more cautious than others.[31]

Ballance also moaned that with the house 'full of speculators . . . of the worst possible political characters', not only would provincial interests dominate but the small farmer, the genuine settler, would be ignored.[32] In fact there was a considerable amount of new 'genuine' settlement going on, particularly once a decision on the positioning of railway lines in the province had been made.[33] Ballance himself applauded the announcement in early 1872 that the provincial government was to set aside 18 200 hectares for sale on deferred payment, under the Wellington Special Settlements Act of the previous year:

> The boon of obtaining land on deferred payments has been strenu-
> ously struggled for by a large section of the working men in this
> province for several years, and its realisation now will be a source
> of unalloyed satisfaction, not only to them but to those who believe
> that the settlement of the country can best be carried out in aiding
> the frugal and industrious, through a generous and liberal system of
> legislation, to occupy and cultivate the lands.[34]

Meanwhile Ballance was becoming increasingly involved in political activity in the town. He supported the candidature of his brother-in-law, William Finnimore, for the superintendency of Wellington Province[35] on the basis that if elected he would make every effort to have the Provincial Council abolished.[36] Finnimore (who with Watt, Hutchison and Morgan represented Wanganui on the Provincial Council) was the local abolitionist candidate and polled well in Wanganui, but was convincingly beaten by Fitzherbert, who supported Featherston (the retiring superintendent) and gained most of Wellington town's votes.[37] Ballance also backed John Bryce for the Provincial Council and Parliament.[38] Born in Glasgow in 1833 Bryce had come to New Zealand before Ballance and farmed land at Brunswick just outside the town. He had been Wanganui's representative in the council, with a gap of two years, since 1862 and was elected to the General Assembly in 1866. Bryce was a tough, uncompromising individual (particularly when it came to dealing with the Maori) whose adherence to principles he was convinced were right made a virtue of stubbornness. He was therefore temperamentally quite different to Ballance, yet appears to have had a basic integrity that attracted the latter's personal loyalty (and that of others who got to know him well) even in the face of later fundamental political disagreements. For the time being they were at one on the unsatisfactory position of Wanganui within the provincial system, the major issue of the day.[39]

Ballance was also at the fore of a campaign to bring a greater degree of local government to the town, through the acquisition of powers exercised by the Provincial Council. This could be done by constituting Wanganui a borough under the terms of the Municipal Corporations Act of 1867. As soon as the act was passed he urged that a petition be drawn up,[40] although it was not until early 1871 that one was ready for signing.[41] There was some opposition to the idea, but a second petition was successful and on 1 February 1872 Wanganui became a borough.[42] In supporting this extension of local government, Ballance at the same time made it clear what the limitations on the functions of the borough ought to be. On the eve of the Town Board meeting expected to discuss the question he specified what he saw as the division of responsibility between local and central government. Matters of local concern included paving, lighting, water and gas supply, parks and the provision of free libraries.[43]

This was all fairly small-scale stuff. Interest in town politics was limited, the issues hardly breath-taking and the stakes pretty low. It never took long to count votes on election day and candidates were wise to make sure they remembered to vote for themselves. Still, Ballance and the *Herald*, with able assistance from the *Chronicle*, tried their best to raise enthusiasm and present political issues as matters of life and death. Failing that, derogatory, highly partisan remarks about some prominent figure could at least hope to elicit a response from a sluggish readership.

The *Herald* was frequently used by Ballance to organise, promote and explain the purpose of, local organisations. One, called the Political Reform Association, had only an ephemeral existence. It was formed on 4 May 1871 at a meeting chaired by Bryce and on a motion proposed by Ballance.[44] The association met again three weeks later when its political principles were outlined. They were general and included the economic administration of the colony, the abolition of the provincial system and the support of candidates sympathetic to the association's views. Perhaps because of this very generality the association disappeared without a trace. There are no accounts of its activities in subsequent issues of the *Herald*.[45]

Much more significant was Ballance's involvement in the Odd Fellowship Society, formed in Wanganui in 1867. Though not strictly a political society, the philosophy of Oddfellowship reflected Ballance's own beliefs and his personal experiences. The Ancient Independent Order of Odd Fellows (with 'lodges' or branches in New Zealand, Australia and the USA) emulated its parent organisation, an English friendly society called the Manchester Unity of Odd Fellows. This latter body was the largest of its kind in England with over 400 000 members in 1872. Like other friendly societies it aimed to provide sickness and life insurance through regular subscriptions of members, but the Oddfellows had extended these benefits to include such things as widow and child relief, and assistance for sickness in old age. Membership was drawn disproportionately from artisans in building trades and traditional handicrafts. The society represented upward social mobility, the success of self-made men who aspired to the ranks of the middle class.[46]

Ballance participated in the Wanganui society from its inception. He was Noble Grand Master of the Lodge[47] and later Deputy District Grand Master of the North Island, which was not quite as grand as it sounds since the society was restricted to the Wanganui area (lodges were opened in Marton in 1872 and Bulls in 1873)[48] and to Dunedin in the South Island.[49] The Oddfellows epitomised Ballance's belief in self-help and self-reliance for it showed that, by organising, working men could provide for their own material wants and, through education, raise their position in society. Indeed it was the 'great leveller of civil society':

> We view its spread as one of the most indubitable signs of the advance of civilisation. Propagating and diffusing principles of the highest ethical standard, and intended to promote a universal brotherhood among all classes of men, it commands the attention of political and social reformers, not in the way of legislation, for it does its own work without interference, but to give a more sudden and marked prominence by the influence which men of elevated station can import.[50]

Aside from providing insurance and charitable relief, the Wanganui society spent its early years constructing a new building for its meetings and for a reading room, to be made available, free of charge, to the public. Ballance opened 'The Institute' in July 1874, delivering a witty speech that having dealt with the history of the Oddfellows in New Zealand turned to the controversy that surrounded the building's design:

> The site (it is said) is not the best; it will suffer the fate of Nineveh from the sand; the door is too narrow; the ventilators wrongly placed; the lower pillars too small, the upper ones too large; and the heavenly bodies on the ceiling tawdry in appearance and not like real luminaries. One gentleman suggested that the balcony was a weakness, on the ground that a sailor might climb the pillars and obtain a peep into the Lodge room where outer barbarians were not permitted into the sanctuary.

No doubt with his own debt to the Midland Institute in Birmingham and his own efforts at self-improvement in mind, Ballance emphasised the society's provision of a public reading room, which he hoped would soon become a well-stocked library, promoting technical and general education. He concluded:

> We suffer from the evils of defective laws and bad administration, or we should have had before now our technical school of art and science supported out of endowments and educational revenue. But . . . we should not remain satisfied with what we have already achieved. All progress depends on the desire to accomplish greater results than what have gone before. Besides, the mind is in the healthiest state morally and intellectually, when it is braced for action. The principle of 'rest and be thankful' has been exploded; there is no finality in any work of man or in nature.[51]

On 6 September 1872 the Fox Ministry, which was dominated by Vogel and had been in power since June 1869, resigned. It was defeated after a long debate on the administration of the Public Works and Immigration Policy, but replaced by a government bent simply on a more prudent continuation of that policy. Stafford, an abolitionist who headed the ministry, had been Premier twice before. With him, somewhat incongruously, were the superintendents of three provinces, Fitzherbert, Curtis and Gillies.

Meanwhile William Gisborne, who had been Colonial Secretary under Fox, resigned his Egmont seat on being appointed commissioner for the Government Life Insurance Office. Ballance made up his mind to stand at the by-election. Precisely when he came to the decision we do not know, but it was on the cards for some time in that he had long been interested in politics and must have become increasingly convinced that a political career was the only way in which he could significantly influence events. It would have been little surprise to his close friends.

The Egmont constituency was based around New Plymouth and far from ideal for a Wanganui man, but Ballance was clearly impatient and reluctant to wait until the next general election for a shot at a Wanganui seat. He was also ambitious, never interested in standing for local government or the Provincial Council and satisfied with nothing less than a position at the centre of political power. From a practical standpoint a political career could be easily fitted in with editing the paper. He was not tied to his desk all day and the *Herald* was doing well enough for him to be able to employ an editor when he was required in Wellington.

As for his chances, Ballance had established his political credentials and was certainly now well known in Wanganui. Journalism was an ideal springboard into political life and ownership of the *Herald* gave him great advantage in self-promotion. Above all it gave him influence that many other politicians gained through wealth and position in society. The roles of editor and politician dovetailed nicely and had been combined successfully by a number of men including James Fitzgerald (a Christchurch politician who brought out the first issue of the *Lyttelton Times* and later owned and edited the *Christchurch Press*) and Vogel (who started the first daily newspaper in New Zealand, the *Otago Daily Times*). However Ballance's big problem in 1872 was that he was not fighting on home ground. He could not realistically expect much support from New Plymouth though Patea, the other major settlement in the constituency, was closer to Wanganui and offered more hope.[52]

Ballance published his address to the electors in the *Herald* on 13 September, saying that he felt justified in coming forward because of his promotion over the last five years of bona fide settlement. He welcomed the change in government since now prudence would replace recklessness. Development should continue and great prosperity was possible but there were grave dangers that excessive borrowing would lead to 'financial ruin and dishonourable repudiation'. His second plank concerned the constitutional position of the provinces where he argued that gradual reform of the provincial system should begin at once, without waiting until the whole system might be abolished at one go.[53]

Ballance's campaign lasted ten days and inevitably concentrated on attracting the Patea vote, exploiting its position as an outlying district of Taranaki Province and playing on the suggestion that the town's future interests would be better served in association with Wanganui rather than New Plymouth. It was at Patea that he found himself on the hustings for the first time. The meeting, on 18 September 1872, was held in an old corrugated-iron shed, hardly glamorous surroundings for his maiden effort. Yet despite the informal, grim and cramped conditions Ballance was very nervous, and said later that 'he was glad he was speaking in a dimly-lighted room, because the people could not see his knees knocking together when he rose to speak'.[54] Did he feel a great sense of occasion, that this was the start of a promising political career? The speech lasted over three hours and was described by the *Herald* as 'wonderfully good'. Its length (though unimaginable today) was not uncommon, for it was expected of a speaker that he painstakingly cover all current political issues — both national and local — in considerable detail. Entertainment was limited and any form of social gathering welcome. The crowd wanted value for money. Two days later Ballance addressed the Hawera electors who were, again in the opinion of the inevitably immodest *Herald*, 'surprised and delighted' with his performance.[55]

The Hawera folk who turned up at the meeting may well have been impressed by Ballance, for he was a competent speaker who sounded as if he knew what he was talking about. Yet despite the optimism brandished through the pages of his paper he soon realised that election would be difficult to achieve. There were two other much more experienced candidates. W.S. Moorhouse had been Superintendent of Canterbury Province and was a personal friend of Fox and consistent advocate of Vogel's public works policy. Harry Atkinson had served in the Taranaki Provincial Council and General Assembly, and (like Ballance) supported Stafford. It was likely that Moorhouse would win with Ballance and Atkinson splitting the pro-Stafford vote. Atkinson had been present at Ballance's Hawera meeting and their campaigns were closely linked.[56] Through pressure from Stafford and having discussed the matter with Atkinson, Ballance decided to withdraw in the latter's favour.[57] Retirement was facilitated by a face-saving formula which pointed out that the rejection of about 80 freeholders in Patea and environs from inclusion on the electoral roll ('through despicable conduct on the part of someone') meant that Ballance could not hope to be successful.[58]

As it turned out Stafford, Atkinson and Ballance were right. Atkinson won by the slim margin of 24 votes and it was his majority in Patea (46 to 17) that was the critical factor.[59] Once in the House, Atkinson asked for a return of the rejected claims to be produced.[60] This may well have been a part of his agreement with Ballance, who was far from pleased at the upshot of events and continued to publicise his grievance through the *Herald*.[61] The return showed that 58 claims had been rejected (compared to only 15 in 1871), a significant number in a total roll of 266.[62] What appears to have happened is that Ballance made a desperate effort to have prospective supporters enrolled but in the haste mistakes were made in the applications and by the time claims had been returned to the electors for correction it was too late to have them included on the final roll.

Over the next few months the political scene was quiet, and there was little to excite Ballance's interest. A Wairarapa sheepfarmer, G. M. Waterhouse, was Premier though it was clear that Vogel, the Colonial Treasurer, was still very much in command. In early 1873, however, a revived separation movement in Wanganui livened things up at the local level and at the same time helped Ballance sustain the momentum of his incipient political career. This resurgence of separatist feeling reflected Wanganui's belief that it was being unfairly excluded from the rapidly increasing revenue of the province.[63] It was not now a matter of overcoming stagnant economic conditions inherent in provincial finances, so much as the town seeking to obtain its fair share of rising prosperity. Ballance pointed out that of the proposed expenditure of £210,000 on public works, the area between northern Wanganui and southern Rangitikei, containing at least one third of the province's total population, was to receive only £5000:

We can only tolerate provincialism when we find it attempting to scatter the gifts with which our constitution has endowed it, with an impartial hand. When it appropriates them for its own aggrandisement or upon a system of favoritism, we look upon provincialism as a thing which should be reformed out of existence by short, sharp, and decisive means . . . Let us again demand separation from Wellington, with the formation of a cheap and economical county government, embracing the district from the Waingongoro River to the Rangitikei . . . A united and earnest attempt to obtain from the legislature the political independence which we consider necessary to our prosperity and growth, is most likely to be favorably received in the Assembly.[64]

Ballance was at pains to make it clear that the separation committee, formed at a meeting in the Oddfellows Hall on 5 May 1873, wanted neither a new province nor a county on the Westland model (a half-way house to full provincial status), but rather a shire. Most important, land sales and revenue would be administered by the general government.[65] Ballance was a leading figure in the campaign and spoke at all the meetings held. Wanganui, he said, could survive on its own. In fact it was going to become the centre of the foremost district in the country.[66] In late May he travelled out to Marton and, speaking there for the first time, emphasised how closely the interests of that settlement were tied to those of Wanganui.[67] He repeated the theme of local independence in Wanganui in June, at a meeting called to question the town's provincial councillors.[68]

A petition of 1108 signatures was gathered and presented by John Bryce (Wanganui's Member of Parliament) to the House on 31 July.[69] Shortly afterwards Bryce moved the second reading of the Wanganui, Rangitikei and Patea Shires Bill, arguing that since Wanganui was already a corporate council and so few powers remained with the provincial government, there would be little difficulty in legislating for complete separation.[70] Vogel, now Premier, though accepting that it might not be the mover's intention, warned that the bill would lead ultimately to the creation of a new province. He would by far prefer to see Wellington and Taranaki provinces combined. More vigorous opposition came from Wellington city members, from Fox (Member for Rangitikei but closely identified with Wellington) and others. The supporters of the bill, including the members from New Plymouth, Egmont, Wairarapa, and Bryce himself from Wanganui, were finally outnumbered 11 to 25. Vogel abstained.[71]

Ballance was well aware of Vogel's increasing frustration with the provinces and in particular their interference in his public works and immigration policy.[72] Soon the question of Wanganui's position within Wellington province became submerged in a general movement towards complete abolition. When in August 1874 Vogel suggested that the North Island provinces be abolished, Ballance pointed out that provincialism had been created in the first instance only in response to the limited communications imposed by the geographical features of the colony, and that with those restraints no longer applicable provinces in both islands should be scrapped.[73] As the localisation of the land revenue was part of the Government's proposals, Canterbury and Otago need have nothing to fear.[74] (Land revenue accounted for a considerably larger proportion of total revenue in Otago and Canterbury than elsewhere. Indeed it was at times larger than the other major source of income, customs duties. In Auckland the situation was the reverse, revenue from land sales making up only one-tenth of the total.[75])

It was clear that Vogel's bill to abolish the North Island provinces was the thin end of the wedge.[76] Ballance stressed that with abolition control of the land must pass to the central government, though the appropriation of the revenue would remain the same, part going to general revenue, part returned to local bodies for public works.[77] He saw maladministration of the waste lands by the provincial governments as a major reason for abolition. The reckless sale of land should cease and genuine settlement be encouraged by central government.[78] 'Genuine settlement' meant small farms for the working classes. Payment should be deferred and the terms easy. Why should the working man 'with little more than his labour . . . pay a greater price than the grazier or the mere speculator. Why indeed? . . . It is high time the barriers which favor capitalists in the Wellington province were broken down, and that the working man had a chance.'[79]

The Government promoted settlement of the less well-off not only through a system of deferred payments but also through 'special settlement' schemes. Special settlements originally consisted of groups of immigrants from the same country, whose passage and establishment on the land was at least partly funded by the Government. Many of the early schemes, a means of clearing land heavily covered with bush, were in Wellington and Hawke's Bay provinces.[80] Ballance was concerned that these and other immigrants should have some capital and be determined and equipped to become genuine small farmers, and not end up in the towns looking for work.[81] He knew how keen England was to use emigration to lessen the effects 'of its own pauperization' by shipping off her surplus population.[82]

In this period between his withdrawal from the Egmont contest and election for Rangitikei in 1875, the broad base of Ballance's liberalism became apparent. The *Herald* followed closely events in England and praised Gladstone's Liberal Administration (1868–74) as probably the best ministry England had ever had.[83] Using Gladstone's arguments, Ballance urged that taxation should be reduced (by lowering *ad valorem* duties) rather than increased.[84] He favoured government assistance for colonial industry, though in the form of direct bonuses rather than protection, since increasing the price of imported goods would be 'taking money out of the pockets of one class and putting it into the pockets of another'.[85]

Ballance continued to read a great deal. He frequently mentioned Mill, for example, in support of his own belief in granting women equal political rights:

> Mill . . . reasoned that not until women had equal political rights would many of the grosser evils which afflict society be removed, and that higher civilisation obtain, to the future realisation of which all the writings of the philosopher tend. The enfranchisement of women was no mere sentiment with him, and it should not be so either with us . . . In every sense the interests of civilisation seem to demand that women shall be placed on a perfect legal equality with men. This equality should proceed to the holding of property in her own right, the exercise of the electoral franchise, and the practice of the learned professions.[86]

Finally, Ballance placed great emphasis on education. 'Every child of poor parents ought to have its education free, and of the best to be had in any country in the world,'[87] he wrote. His views on the subject were set out at some length in a *Herald* editorial in February 1875:

> The hereditary stock of wisdom is not a thing to be locked up, and transferred as idle capital from generation to generation. It must be traded with and increased, so that our children, when they succeed us, may find the edifice of civilisation a storey higher than their fathers found it.

The state had a duty to provide all children with a liberal and popular education, an education

> of the culture of the masses who subsist by physical toil of various kinds, and whose poverty places beyond their reach those educational advantages enjoyed by the wealthier classes . . . The hands of the labourer's child were not made for the sole purpose of manipulating yard-measures and tapelines, ploughs, and pick axes. They could trace forms and hues of beauty, and produce sounds of rapture, as skilfully as those of his aristocratic neighbours, if . . . taught to do so. His eye could do higher and nobler things than scan the pages of legers [*sic*] and day-books, if it were taught to do so.

And the education provided was to be progressive:

> To speak of the Greek and Latin classes as a *sine qua non* of a good education is now only usual with a few old-world folks, whom nothing but the fear of ridicule prevents from appearing in pig-tails and powder, if not in togas and sandals.[88]

It was also to be secular. Ballance believed that religion had no place in schools, though religious liberty would permit Catholics to maintain instruction of their own children.[89] Obstacles to a non-sectarian, state system of education would have to be overcome. 'The intemperate opposition of religious partisans or the groans and grumbles of irritated taxpayers, should not be allowed to impede the progress of education. At the most, their grievances are inferior to the real interests of the State.'[90]

At the beginning of 1875, William Fox resigned his Rangitikei seat in order to pay a visit to England. Ballance, undeterred by his false start three years earlier, immediately declared his intention to stand at the by-election.[91] He was the youngest candidate and was opposed by W. H. Watt and George Hutchison. William Hogg Watt had come to Wanganui in 1842 and with T. B. Taylor set up a shipping business along the coast. Later they built a large store on Taupo Quay and Watt became wealthy and his firm the centre of commercial activity in the town. He was rewarded with the mayoralty in 1872.[92] A provincialist and member of the Provincial Council, Watt was supported by the *Herald*'s rival, the *Wanganui Chronicle*. However, he soon realised the extent of anti-provincialist feeling in the town and declared himself an abolitionist part way through the campaign.[93] Hutchison, a lawyer whose loyalties were divided between business in Wellington and Wanganui, was from the first an outsider.

The campaign brought the *Herald* and the *Chronicle* into closer combat than ever before, and a good time was had by all. The *Chronicle* doubted that Ballance possessed a single qualification entitling him to the seat[94] and criticised the dubious character of his supporters. 'We know full well that the froth of the district is very loud spoken on Mr Ballance's side, but unfortunately for their candidate they have few votes, and can do him no greater good than such tap-room politicians can be expected to render so fitting a representative.'[95] The *Herald* responded in similar vein. Commenting on Watt's meeting at Bulls it described his speech as 'a weak attempt to answer Ballance, [which] ended in a ludicrous fiasco. Four held up their hands for a vote of confidence, two of them being the candidate's sons. He dwelt largely on the insinuations about the honorarium. Impossible to describe either speech or scene.'[96] There was always a problem in deciding whether it was better to criticise your opponent at length or simply ignore him as being irrelevant.

Ballance's election platform was more sophisticated than it had been in 1872. Abolition of the provinces remained a major plank, with revenue to be divided between the central government and local bodies. He favoured an educational system funded by the state and supported the public works and immigration policy so long as economic conditions in the colony could sustain it. Finally, he argued that special facilities should be provided to encourage bona fide settlement.[97]

Ballance pursued a high-profile campaign, seeing his chances in portraying himself as the go-ahead newcomer pitted against the staid figure of Watt. He delivered election addresses in all three polling areas, Marton, Bulls and Turakina. The *Herald* reported that his painstaking canvass of the upper part of the Rangitikei district, that closest to Wanganui, met with a good reception. Settlers dreaded the idea of having a representative (i.e. Watt or Hutchison) whose interests were connected with Wellington.[98] His speeches enlarged on the policy outlined in his published address; criticism of the provincial government for its neglect of the district and the need for central control of land if settlement were to proceed apace. Education was the responsibility of the state, though somehow taxation should be kept to a minimum.[99] At Marton, where Ballance held his most successful meeting, he spent most of his time defending himself against a libel case being brought against him by Fox, whom the *Herald* had called 'an old fool'.[100] The *Chronicle* described Ballance's Turakina speech as having contained 'an even larger amount of bunkum' than generally belonged to election addresses. Neither the *Herald* nor the *Chronicle* reported the speech in full but the latter took particular exception to Ballance's opposition to knighthoods.[101]

Though by the eve of the poll all candidates were agreed on the major issue of abolition there were important differences between them. The *Chronicle* regarded Ballance as a *parvenu* and stressed Watt's political experience and position in the town as an old and respected settler. Yet Ballance's liberal views were well known and in an attempt to divert some of the obvious appeal they had for the recent working-class settler the *Chronicle* argued that it was 'men, not measures' that counted. Ballance believed the reverse, that measures, not men, ought to be the decisive factor in the contest.[102] Watt deplored Ballance's rowdy meetings and the *Chronicle* (as it played the game over attendance figures with the *Herald*) said they reflected Ballance's 'philosophy of bounce and balance'.[103]

The election was held on Saturday 24 April 1875 and the results showed a narrow victory for Ballance, owing to his majority at Marton:

	Marton	Bulls	Turakina	Total
Ballance	70	22	20	112
Watt	47	23	35	105
Hutchison	18	4	5	27[104]

Undoubtedly Ballance polled best among the working class and artisans of the three settlements, and among those who wished to get onto the land. His platform had been geared towards these groups. The *Herald* suggested that were it not for plural voting (large property owners coming into the district from elsewhere to vote) Ballance would have won in Turakina.[105] Outside Wanganui there was little interest in the election. In Wellington the *Evening Post*, which according to the *Wanganui Chronicle*[106] had initially favoured Watt, welcomed Ballance's victory on the grounds that he 'at least knows his mind, and is consistent'. The *Post* was not impressed by Watt's weak campaign.[107] Ballance now packed his bags for the capital.

The New Zealand Parliament, known as the General Assembly, was bicameral. The House of Representatives was elected for a five-year term on a minimal property franchise while the upper chamber, called the Legislative Council, was nominated. Councillors were appointed for life. Power rested with the Government and the House of Representatives, although the Legislative Council could throw out non-financial legislation that came to it from the House for approval. Also, the Governor retained considerable influence, particularly on constitutional matters. The men who sat in the General Assembly came from the colonial middle and upper classes — merchants, large farmers, runholders, lawyers and doctors — and governments drawn from these groups were predominantly conservative. Despite rapid changes in the personnel of ministries there had been much continuity in the essential features of government and administration.

The General Assembly stood just above the shore of Wellington's deep harbour. Most members arrived by sea for the new session, which began usually in June or July and could run as late as November. Travel by ship was slow and regular commuting from constituencies during a session impossible for the vast majority of members. Wellington was therefore home for much of the year. The capital of New Zealand was a rather bleak, though dramatic place — a town packed tight on the little flat land that there was between sea and steep hills. Some houses clung to the gentler slopes and their occupants were afforded fine views across the harbour for their trouble. Much of the native bush on the surrounding hills had been cleared; before being replanted they presented a barren backdrop to the settlement running along the shoreline. Life in the town revolved around Parliament, and to a lesser extent also the small civil service and judiciary. Wellington was, and remains, the political, administrative but not the business centre of New Zealand. Things were quiet when the House was not sitting and many looked forward to the gossip, political intrigue and social functions attendant on a new session. Yet despite being the political capital of the country, there remained in Wellington a feeling of isolation from the other (equally isolated) main centres, some distance away. And perhaps also because it was the political capital, Wellington could be inward-looking, focusing on the trappings of the House and only with difficulty on what was happening elsewhere. Nevertheless, it was a place where ideas and opinions were traded, and to which many people travelled, though usually with a return ticket secure in their pockets.

Ballance first entered Parliament on the eve of a constitutional and political crisis. When the General Assembly opened on 20 July 1875 the Government immediately announced its intention to abolish the provinces of the whole of New Zealand, not simply in the North Island. Vogel had gone to England during the recess, but though Pollen became Premier it was Atkinson, as Colonial Treasurer, who was the leading figure in the ministry and who piloted the Abolition Bill through the House. Ballance made his maiden effort during the debate on the bill. It was well prepared (though paid due attention to key points made by previous speakers), well argued and reasonably concise — features to become characteristic of the many speeches he was to deliver in his political career. He was happiest and at his best when he had had time to plan diligently what he wanted to say, and particularly in the early years tended to be weak in the extempore cut-and-thrust of debate. Ballance spoke when he felt he had something constructive to offer, and only rarely simply for the sake of speaking. Until practice made him more fluent he much preferred to express himself on paper. The *Hawke's Bay Herald* later described his speeches as 'set orations, carefully thought out, elaborately constructed, and ingeniously worded. His voice is bad and weak; he is not an orator, but a reciter of carefully prepared essays. These essays are always adorned with copious quotations from great writers, which give to many of his speeches an air of philosophic thought and culture which they do not possess.'[108] Certainly Ballance's speeches were worth listening to for their content rather than for any marked skill in delivery.

The members of the House gave Ballance a good reception for he rose to speak on Thursday 17 August amidst loud applause. He supported abolition not only because of financial convenience but since it would make the political system more democratic. As a liberal he was especially sensitive to Grey's insistence in an earlier speech that removing the provincial governments would involve a fundamental attack on the democratic constitution. 'If by abolishing provincial institutions,' said Ballance, 'we destroyed our landmarks of liberty, or did anything whatever calculated to curtail the liberties of the people, I think this House should seriously pause before it took any step in the matter.'[109] Eager to display his knowledge of constitutional affairs and the intellectual basis for his argument, he quoted Creasy's *Constitutional History* and De Tocqueville's *Democracy in America* in suggesting that as the councils were already defunct this would not be the case:

> It appears to me that provincial institutions have not got within them that vital principle of liberty which would be a loss to us in case of their abolition. Liberty depends entirely upon power — that is to say, liberty will be reposed in the representative body which has the supreme power in the country . . . This House is the seat of liberty, and not the Provincial Councils.[110]

Ballance, in the unusual position of being a liberal in favour of abolition (other liberals such as Grey and Macandrew opposed it), related the issue to broad political principles. Abolition meant the democratisation of the

New Zealand political system in the expectation that Parliament would then pass liberal legislation.[111] Though he saw the existing franchise as sufficiently generous he believed that the Legislative Council should be reformed so that it fairly represented the people. Finally, greater democracy would also result if important functions were given to the local bodies. Decentralisation was for Ballance an essential prerequisite of abolition.

On the specific economic advantages of abolition, Ballance drew on Wanganui's experience as proof that provincial institutions did not respond to the needs of the people. Especially with regard to the settlement of the land it had been shown that the general government, not the Provincial Council, encouraged bona fide settlement. He repeated the point that he had made many times in the *Herald*, that local bodies should retain a portion of the land revenue, though he disagreed with the section of the bill that allowed part of this revenue to be used for immigration purposes. There was no guarantee that immigrants would remain in the provincial district to which they had been brought.[112] He concluded: 'I believe [this bill] will make this a united colony. I believe the day of provincial institutions has passed; and that no measures whatever, however skilfully framed, can rehabilitate a system which has become degraded and useless in the eyes of the people.'[113]

The speech went down well both inside and outside the House, and Ballance instantly made his mark on colonial politics. Stafford, commenting on the fact that his old rival, Fox, was no longer in the House, lauded the new member for Rangitikei as a worthy recipient of 'the mantle of Elijah', adding that 'there could not have been any speech more openly and conscientiously spoken, or one that has been better received, than that which has just been addressed to the House'.[114] The *Herald* printed the speech in full and was not slow to quote other papers' praise of it.[115] In Wellington the *Evening Post*, though critical of what Ballance actually said, admitted that the House had rarely listened to a better maiden effort.[116] Similar eulogies came from Auckland[117] and Christchurch.[118]

During the remainder of the session Ballance concentrated on promoting the interests of the district he represented, though he did so through legislation embracing principles that he wished to see applied to other parts of the colony.[119] He moved the Municipal Corporations Loans Bill which gave local bodies the power, given the approval of ratepayers, to contract loans.[120] The bill was defeated though Atkinson supported it and promised to have its provisions included in a consolidating measure to be introduced in the following sessions.[121] Ballance was no more successful with an amendment to the Abolition Bill making hospitals and charitable institutions the responsibility of municipalities rather than central government. He argued essentially that assistance should aim to keep people in the community and out of institutions, and that local bodies would be much more in touch with what was needed at grass-roots level. Wellington control would be the 'thin end of the wedge of poor laws and State workhouses'.[122]

When Ballance arrived at the General Assembly he already knew personally some of the other members, especially those from Wellington province. Harry Atkinson was there and so too was Ballance's Wanganui friend John Bryce. Many politicians had heard of Ballance, even if they had not yet met him; he was by no means entirely an unknown quantity. Of the new acquaintances he made in his first few months in the House one was to become particularly special. Robert Stout, like Ballance, had just entered Parliament through a by-election. He was an intense-looking, kindly, optimistic and exceptionally able 31-year-old lawyer who represented Caversham near Dunedin. Son of a Shetland landlord and merchant, Stout had arrived in New Zealand in April 1864. He settled in Dunedin, Otago's main town, where he began a career in schoolteaching. Ambitious and hard-working, he later got a job as articled clerk in a law firm, and after three years of studying passed the professional examinations and was admitted to the Dunedin Bar. Stout rapidly built up a substantial practice and at the same time pursued his passion for learning at the University of Otago, where he was later appointed that institution's first lecturer in law. He entered the Otago Provincial Council in 1872, and there cut his political teeth and made his mark as a liberal who saw the future in a 'nation of small holdings, secured by the state'.[123] Again like Ballance, he delivered his maiden speech during the abolition debate, though argued strongly against the bill.

Despite their disagreement on this issue the two men were quickly drawn to each other and became close personal and political friends. They shared many fundamental beliefs. Both were liberals who emphasised land as a central political issue and sought new laws that would make it much more accessible to the ordinary working man. Both were concerned with the political power of large landowners (Stout had seen the operation of harsh land laws on Shetland crofters) and wanted reform of the Legislative Council. They had in common an ideology of individual self-help and saw in the New World a great opportunity for the creation of a society facilitating self-improvement. Writing after Ballance's death, Stout told of how 'their reading followed similar lines, and their views, except with regard to provincial questions, were in accord. A friendship . . . was formed that remained firm and mending till the last. They were, when both were in the House, continually together; and after the House rose, at whatever hour, they would be seen walking together.'[124] Their greatest personal political loyalty was, ultimately, to each other. And their wives too became close and spent much time in each other's company when in Wellington.[125]

The Abolition Bill passed its second reading by 52 votes to 17, though on condition that it was not to come into effect until after the general election due at the end of the year. The members from the poorest provinces and the outlying districts of Auckland, Wellington, Canterbury and Otago all voted in favour, while representatives from provincial capitals (for example, Grey, Sheehan, Fitzherbert, Rolleston, Macandrew and Stout) made up the bulk of the opposition.

In late October Ballance returned to Wanganui. During the session he and Bryce had successfully lobbied for an extra member for the town and when Ballance arrived home speculation was already rife as to who might take the second seat. He had been asked by the Government to assess the likelihood of Vogel's filling the vacancy and after speaking to a number of people about the matter telegraphed Wellington to say that he thought that if Vogel stood he would be elected. However, he sought on the electors' behalf an assurance that if Vogel (who was still in England but was expected to return to New Zealand soon) were elected for other seats, he would sit for Wanganui. A meeting in the town agreed unanimously that Vogel be requested to stand. Ballance said that Vogel's election would be of great benefit to Wanganui, for his powerful influence would be used to promote new settlement throughout the region. In any case he was much preferable to the alternative, most likely a provincialist and opponent of the Government.[126]

Ballance's own campaign for the Rangitikei seat largely repeated that of the by-election nine months earlier. He looked forward to the abolition of the provinces with part of the revenue from land sales being distributed by the general government. Significantly, he did not oppose Grey's suggestion that the duties on tea, sugar and other necessities of life be completely removed. Taxation should be such that all contribute according to their means and any new tax be on large estates and land monopolists rather than on incomes across the board. Again he emphasised the importance of a state system of education. Finally, land was for bona fide settlement and should not be viewed as simply a means of raising revenue. Small settlers on deferred payments must be encouraged rather than speculators.[127]

James Bull was Ballance's only opponent. Watt, who had given Ballance a close run in April, decided that he had a better chance of taking one of the two Wanganui seats. Bull was a long-established settler in the Rangitikei; indeed he had given the town of Bulls its name. He was a sawmiller, builder, storekeeper and hotel-owner, businesses that formed the commercial centre of the district.[128] But with no political experience he was not a strong candidate. In its lukewarm support for Bull the *Chronicle* could only emphasise that he, unlike Ballance, was a local resident.[129] Though it tended to criticise Ballance personally rather than his policy, the paper's description of him as flashy, dangerous and unsafe signified also his political unacceptability:

We have from the first steadily and consistently opposed his return; and we have done so — because, notwithstanding the command of language which enables him to charm a friendly audience, and the possession of ability sufficient to enable him to dilate pretty freely upon public questions generally — we esteem him to be an eminently unsafe man, who is all the more dangerous because of the flashy nature of his political accomplishments.[130]

What made Ballance's victory more certain were the doubts carefully sown by the *Herald* as to Bull's eligibility to take his seat if elected. His firm of J. & C. Bull was involved in a government contract for the building of the Oroua railway bridge, a fact that might well have forced him to resign under the terms of the Disqualification Act.[131]

In a turnout of around 75 percent, considerably higher than at the earlier by-election, Ballance won with a majority of 74. Bull was only just able to beat Ballance at Bulls, his home town:

	Marton	Bulls	Turakina	Total
Ballance	124	34	43	201
Bull	59	41	27	127[132]

Electors elsewhere returned a substantial majority of abolitionist candidates. Only in Otago and Auckland were provincialists at all successful. None of the new Wellington City members had stood on a provincialist platform.[133]

Before the opening of the session Ballance made some changes to the *Herald*. His biggest problem was that he needed a permanent arrangement for someone to assume editorial control of the paper when he was in Wellington. John Notman had joined the *Herald* staff in 1870, two years after coming out from England and having spent some time on the Thames goldfield, but later went back to his London home.[134] Notman was an able journalist whose politics were similar to those of Ballance. Ballance was therefore keen to have him and pursuaded him to return to Wanganui to take on the job. When in Wellington Ballance would frequently send Notman material for inclusion in the *Herald* and until the appointment of a full-time editor in 1891 always resumed the chair on arriving home from parliamentary duty. In this way he retained a firm grip on the paper.

Meanwhile Archie Willis withdrew from his partnership with Ballance and was replaced by Notman. It was a perfectly amicable parting. Willis had done well out of the *Herald* and was now able to set up his own printing and bookselling business. The two men remained close friends and Willis continued to print both of Ballance's papers.[135] The profitability of the *Herald* allowed them to keep up with technological developments in the industry and they imported a new labour-saving machine that was the first to use water power and to self-deliver the papers when printed. The final change

Ballance made to the paper was a minor one, altering its name from the *Evening Herald* to the *Wanganui Herald*.[136]

Vogel resumed the premiership on his return from England in February 1876. With the abolition of the provinces now a certainty, Ballance devoted the session to making the new constitutional arrangements as favourable to the settlement and development of his district as possible. Of especial interest was the Municipal Corporations Bill which though largely a consolidating measure contained loan-raising powers Ballance had sought to introduce in his bill of the previous year. For Ballance it was a matter not simply of enabling local bodies to pursue public works of their own, but it also involved an element of redistribution of wealth.[137] Granting borrowing and rating powers would clearly hit the pockets of property owners and this fear had helped defeat his earlier bill, so he agreed with Stout that local referenda on special rates should be on the basis of one man one vote. Finally, he objected to that part of the bill that laid down that public meetings might be held only after a licence had been granted by the Municipal Corporation,[138] and carried an amendment that extended the obligation of a corporation to promote local education.[139] The only other issue of the session that Ballance felt strongly about was Stout's Local Option Licensing Bill. Ballance opposed the bill because he did not believe legislating for temperance would work. Combating drunkenness was 'a matter of education and of providing for the comforts of the people'.[140]

In August the question of abolition was finally settled. The provinces were replaced by counties and boroughs, subsidies and obligations being laid down in the Financial Arrangements Act and the Counties Act. With relatively limited revenue-raising powers it was clear that local bodies were to play a very minor role in developing the country and that centralisation was to be almost complete. Fighting a rearguard action Grey proposed that the two islands be separated. Ballance admitted that the House was to assume complete control over the land fund (though money would be expended in the districts where raised) but argued that the new system could be altered to adequately meet local needs. In one of his visionary set-pieces he was adamant in his opposition to separation in any form, seeing the future in a united, democratic, independent New Zealand:

> It matters not whether we remain an integral portion of the British Empire or not — we should so lay the foundation of our Constitution, and lay it so broadly, that whatever position we occupy in the future we may be able to take our stand as a great nation. That is the dream of my ambition — that is the hope and goal which should be in the mind of every New Zealander . . . We are now a united colony; we are pursuing the path of constitutional government, one of the first principles of which is that whoever may sit on [the Government] benches . . . will remain there only so long as they command the confidence of this House.[141]

Grey's motion was lost 32 to 47. Ballance had performed well. The following speaker, De Lautour, said, 'I recognised at once, when he [Ballance] spoke, that we had as able a statesman before us, advocating the cause he believed in, as had arisen in this House for many a long day.' And Vogel sent Ballance a personal letter congratulating him on his 'splendid' speech.[142]

Ballance's participation in the 1876 session was limited, in part because the main concern of the assembly, abolition, was a *fait accompli* and he saw numerous members only too willing to devote time to firmly nailing the lid on the provincial coffin. As well as this, Ballance was pursuing other interests at grass-roots level and spent a considerable amount of energy promoting small farm associations.[143] There was a limit to the role these organisations could play during the sponsorship of special settlements and public works under Vogel's scheme, but by 1876 the growing demand for land could not be met by government promotion alone and a new batch of associations came into being, for example at Bulls, Masterton and Hutt.[144]

Through the *Herald* Ballance outlined how associations might be set up and the methods to be employed to obtain grants of land, and in June 1876 he helped form the Wanganui Small Farm Association.[145] It wanted the Government to make a suitable block of land near a market available for settlement on deferred payment terms, with certain improvements being stipulated.[146] The Government was unresponsive, arguing that the association would have to compete for land on the open market.[147] This was precisely the unrealistic view Ballance had been fighting against. Free competition in land meant that the ordinary settler would be excluded since only the large capitalists and speculators could afford the high prices that were inherent in a competitive system. It was for this reason that associations were seen to be necessary in the first place.

The Wanganui Association disbanded in February 1877, its members annoyed and frustrated at their lack of success. Ballance, too, was disappointed and angry at the Government's attitude, but he urged the association to be patient.[148] At the same time he launched attack after attack on what he saw as the increasing alienation of land by monopolists and speculators:

> In a few years in many if not all of the Provinces the open agricultural land will have passed into the hands of the monopolist and the land-shark. Then will arise a great democracy demanding the bursting up of the large estates, the abolition of the nominee Chamber of the Legislature, and the enactment of all articles in the democratic creed. Would it not be wiser to prevent this by a patriotic effort to secure the available lands for actual settlement?[149]

This early vision of a rising 'great democracy' is fascinating since it was in many respects to be fulfilled in his own premiership, when the large estates were subdivided, the Legislative Council tamed, the franchise extended to include women and the property vote abolished. In the meantime it was the Government's lack of sympathy for organisations that epitomised Ballance's idealisation of New Zealand as a land of small, independent, yeoman farmers that, combined with the political realignments inherent in the settling of the abolition issue, laid the basis for his break with Atkinson.

Looking back on the politics of this period one is tempted to conclude that it was marked by a distinct lack of real issues. Since October 1872 a single 'Continuous Ministry' had, in spite of a number of personnel changes, held on firmly to power. Few politicians could afford to oppose Vogel's public works programme (particularly in the early 1870s when it coincided with rising export prices) and all to a lesser or greater degree had to face their constituents on the basis of their ability to attract government expenditure for local development projects. Equally, politicians from the richer provinces opposed abolition because they feared the loss of their land revenue to central government, whilst those from poorer provinces and outlying districts that felt neglected by their provincial capitals, could only hope to gain out of it. Through different means both abolitionists and provincialists aimed primarily to bring as much money to their locality as possible.

Yet to argue that politics was determined solely on this basis is too simplistic. The desire for economic growth and development has always been central to the functioning of political systems. Given this, the method by which it is achieved and, especially, whom it is to benefit are more discriminating and pertinent questions. Although Ballance and Stout disagreed over abolition their ultimate objectives were very similar. Both were concerned with the distribution of political and economic power, Stout believing abolition would hand over Otago's considerable land fund to a central government dominated by squatters, while Ballance saw in it a more just distribution of expenditure in favour of the genuine settler of limited means rather than the large landowner. For both men the determination of the social groups that would benefit most from development spending was more fundamental than the issue of abolition *per se*. Abolition for Ballance was never an end in itself. Rather it was a constitutional reorganisation essential to establishing a more equitable system of central and local government which would be more responsive to the needs of his electorate. This necessarily affected his attitude to the public works and immigration programme.

Under the provincial system Ballance, and Wanganui, were unable to influence significantly the direction of development funds. Members from each of the provincial capitals could act together and wield much greater power. Ballance saw abolition and Vogelism in terms of what they could do for Wanganui and in particular for the town's poorer settlers who saw their future on small farms in the hinterland. His attacks on provincialism were more often than not combined with criticism of squatters and their hold on the political system. From the start he sought to combat the political and economic power of large capitalists, directly through Parliament and at grass-roots level through a number of class organisations, the most important of which were the small farm associations.

An early
taste of power

IN AUGUST 1876 VOGEL resigned the premiership to go to London as Agent General. Harry Atkinson led a reconstructed government whose numerical majority in the House belied the lack of real enthusiasm of its followers.[1] Sorry to see Vogel go,[2] Ballance was unimpressed with the new ministry generally and particularly unhappy at the appointment of Frederick Whitaker, Auckland businessman and archetypal land speculator, as Attorney General.[3] The *Herald* was soon attacking Atkinson, a change of heart the Wellington *Evening Post* put down to Ballance's disappointment at not being asked to join the cabinet.[4] In fact it was later rumoured that Ballance had been offered a place.[5] If this was true he had clearly turned it down, which was inevitable given his widening split with the conservative-dominated 'Continuous Ministry'.

In his end–of–session speech to his constituents at Marton, on 16 January 1877, Ballance indicated that he was a far from committed government supporter. High public works expenditure plus interest on loans and the costs associated with the abolition of the provinces would produce a deficit in the current financial year. To resolve this problem, Ballance suggested further taxation rather than retrenchment. Given rapidly rising land prices, he felt that this should be in the form of a land tax, which was anathema to Atkinson.[6] Ballance was also concerned about the sale of 32 000 hectares of the Piako Swamp to the Auckland speculator Thomas Russell. The law required that land should be sold for at least five shillings per acre but in this instance the Government disposed of it for less on the grounds that it was largely swamp and of poor quality, intending to legalise the sale by proclamation. Grey objected and though a select committee upheld the Government's action it admitted that there was a technical error to be corrected the following session.[7]

Ballance had talked about a land tax before but now gave it much more emphasis. The *Herald* noted that a general election in Victoria was being fought on the question of a progressive land tax as a means of breaking up the large estates, and suggested that the efforts of people there 'to plant and maintain a yeomanry population' would find many sympathisers in New Zealand.[8] A land boom had begun and with rising prices ordinary settlers were increasingly at a disadvantage.[9] Land was 'either being swallowed up in the rapacious maw of the land shark, or passing into the hands of large proprietors.' The *Herald* also complained that small farm associations were impotent while government policy (for example, the Waste Lands Act of the previous session) encouraged 'speculative settlement associations' such as the Manchester Corporation at Feilding.[10]

This last accusation sounded good but was unreasonable. The *Herald*'s argument here was that the wrong type of settlement was being promoted. There were 'village residences and small suburban plots' where there should have been productive small farms. Given the favourable conditions (government concessions, good-quality land and a rail connection with Foxton), more land ought to have been brought under cultivation. The *Herald* pointed to the Hutt Small Farm Association's Rangitikei settlement at Sandon, where the land was less suitable, as a greater success. In fact the 1878 census shows that Sandon (including the town of Sanson) had a population of only 536. The Manchester block (purchased by the Corporation in late 1871) contained 1700 settlers. Even if the rate of new land cultivation in the former was greater, the value, scale and success of the latter project was undeniable.

The Manchester Corporation was philanthropic rather than speculative. Indeed, in 1872 Ballance had welcomed the scheme, believing it would result in a 'population of hardy and industrious settlers . . . who as "producers" [would] add to the material wealth of the country, and as "consumers" augment its customs revenue'.[11] What lay behind the later charge was Ballance's political preference for land settlement by local small farm associations rather than under English schemes linking settlement to immigration. It was true that in the latter case the Government's emphasis was on immigration (free passages were given and a certain amount of paid employment guaranteed) rather than land settlement. Yet Ballance's suspicion of a private venture that undoubtedly contributed to settlement appears inconsistent given his own connection with another similar enterprise, the New Zealand Land and Loan Company (see pages 84–85).

Three factors help explain this ambiguity. The Manchester Corporation was competing for land with organisations from Ballance's own district (and with people who were his constituents). What prompted Ballance's criticism was the Government allowing the corporation to withdraw a 'large and valuable block of land from all occupation other than that promoted by itself'. There was resentment at privileges being given to strangers.[12]

Secondly, scattered small farm settlement was preferable to concentrated settlement around a town such as Feilding which might come to rival Wanganui. Neither of these considerations was applicable to the property of the Land and Loan Company in the South Island Waimea Plains. Finally, Ballance was undoubtedly suspicious of the organisation's aristocratic patronage. The corporation's ideals looked very similar to those of the Wakefield colonisation companies of the 1840s, the aim being to establish settlements whose social structure mirrored that of England.

Disillusioned with the performance, policy and personnel of the Government and by the frustration of settlement in his own district, Ballance could not but be exasperated when Atkinson opened the new session of Parliament saying that the country needed a time of 'political rest'. The notion of 'standing still' ran contrary to Ballance's inherently progressive nature. Charles Woolcock, the independent member for Grey Valley, was also unimpressed and shortly after the Financial Statement moved that the incidence of taxation be changed. This was a fundamental challenge to a government already weakened by personnel changes (Vogel had stayed in London, Richardson had retired and McLean had died) and disintegrating as the resolution of the abolition issue broke what was often the sole bond holding its supporters together. In the debate that followed Sir George Grey specified in an amendment to the motion that the proposal was to tax income and property and reduce customs duties.[13]

Ballance spoke on 22 August. He was in an uncomfortable position for though he saw that there was no future for him with the Atkinson Government he was eager that his withdrawal of support look convincing and take place when the alternatives to Atkinson were clearer. It was too early to make a formal move; best to sit on the fence for a while, rather than leap over it in one abrupt, reckless bound. Thus he talked of a 'new era of legislation', made possible only now with abolition settled and the House able to consider fundamental questions in an unbiased light.[14] Struggling to find an acceptable compromise between the Government's position and that of Grey, Ballance said lamely that political rest was 'to a certain extent' necessary.[15] Yet despite voting with the Government he spoke in support of a change on the grounds that the existing system was too hard on the working classes and too easy on the wealthy.[16] He favoured a moderate property tax but was particularly eager to see the more specific land tax:

> I have no apprehension of the future of this colony if a tax, fairly adjusted and widely considered in the first instance, is put on the land. It will discourage the creation of those large landed estates, than which nothing can be more destructive to the welfare of a young community. The monopolist will be checked in that land-greed which causes him to take up the best land of the colony, and to hold it without

improving or using it in any way. . . . Our Land Fund is our capital; and, when that is exhausted, what are we to fall back upon? . . . The small-farmer class must be encouraged. The great runholders are not the basis of colonial prosperity. . . . Above all, we have a right to see that in the alienation of new territory it should not be alienated to monopolists, but should be conserved for the benefit of the people.[17]

Two important considerations prevented Ballance's wholehearted support for Grey's amendment. Both foreshadow later liberal attempts to secure an urban-rural alliance and are worth stressing for that reason. Ballance saw that duties served both protective and revenue purposes and that lowering them would harm local industries as well as reduce government income. On the other hand bolstering home industries and maintaining revenue at the expense of high prices for basic commodities was for him and other liberals politically undesirable. The solution was to switch the burden of taxation away from essential goods onto large property owners and capitalists. In this way revenue could be sustained while reducing prices on daily necessities such as sugar and tea. Protection could perhaps take the form of direct bonuses to import substituters rather than high tariff barriers.[18] However, unlike Grey, Ballance wished to tax land as a distinct form of property. He believed that the working classes, along with prospective and existing small farmers, would eagerly support a lowering of food prices made possible through a land tax that promoted settlement, penalised large estates and discouraged land monopoly. Ballance's second point was that Grey had entirely ignored the plight of small farmers who, Ballance argued, were struggling hard to stay on the land. He did not propose any specific relief measures but simply wanted to emphasise just how important it was that this group of people be looked after.[19] Ballance's concern had a lot to do with the fact that he represented a country constituency, but it was also a clear indication of the extent to which he saw the need for a liberal policy that could accommodate rural as much as urban interests.

Grey's amendment was lost by ten votes and the Government, though now beginning to lose other divisions, was temporarily reprieved. As for Ballance's speech, though his style was somewhat cramped by his reluctance to break completely with Atkinson, his advocacy of a land tax caused 'quite a flutter amongst the lords in the gallery'.[20] Ballance's attitude to the Government became clearer with his criticism of the Native Land Court Bill. The bill was initiated by Whitaker and removed the remaining restrictions on free trade in Maori land. Beating simultaneously the humanitarian and anti-monopolist drums Ballance had already voiced his objections in the *Herald*:

Next to the fallacy of 'free trade' in Native Lands is that of the policy of getting the land from the natives without regard to the use to which it is applied. . . . Let [the Native estate] remain in the hands of its

... owners until in the first place the colony can acquire it for settlement, and, in the next, until, the first condition being satisfied, the native shall obtain a fair and reasonable price for the land he desires to sell. Depend upon it that there is no distinction between the interests of colonisation and fair play to the Maori. It is the speculator or monopolist who wishes for laws to wrest from the native his land by fair means or foul; and it is the distinguishing character of the Native Lands Bill . . . that it is framed to serve that purpose . . . Has it then come to that deplorable result that the party of abolition is governed and largely composed of the members and friends of land rings?[21]

In August Ballance moved an amendment to the bill using arguments along these lines. He said that the bill should be withdrawn as it was immoral. Maori ought to get the highest price possible for their land, a policy which was quite consistent with the work of bona fide settlement.[22] More blunt, as it could afford to be, the *Herald* said the bill was produced at the instigation of land sharks and suggested that with increasing support for Ballance's amendment both inside and outside the House, the Government was in danger of being defeated.[23]

In fact the bill was dropped. Less than a year later Ballance said that he had been told by Atkinson that seven government supporters, 'intimately connected with land speculation' had threatened to put the Government out if the amendment passed.[24] The *Herald* explained that Ballance's action was 'direct and simple':

Speculation in Native lands must be stopped; and not only in Native land, but all other [land] must be protected against speculators and monopolists. The present Government are chiefly supported by a landed aristocracy and a landsharking horde of vultures outside the houses of Assembly . . . The time has come when we must wring from the Government a liberal land policy, and if they resist, they must be at once, for the welfare of the country, destroyed. He [Ballance] has commenced on the Native Lands Bill, but he will not end until the land of the colony shall be used for the settlement of the people, nor until the class now ruling the country shall have no privilege above the man of 40 acres.[25]

Ballance now saw his role as fighting for a class of small farmers (and prospective farmers) against the power of a government backed by large landowners. The political party system was being realigned along this fundamental division of interests. Speaking just prior to his formal break with Atkinson, Ballance said he believed that there would soon be two clear parties in the House:

They will be formed, not upon temporary or fleeting questions or principles, but upon principles that will endure — namely, the principles of conservatism and liberalism. Why, those principles are now

embodied in this House — all round it . . . I must give [Grey] credit
. . . for being the advocate of those principles which, in my opinion,
should govern the country. I may say that I have done all I possibly
could to prevail on the Government to adopt those principles . . .
The people of this colony will rule this colony. I believe that to a
large extent in the past it has been ruled by cliques. I believe that
now the first man who appeals to the people will obtain the victory.[26]

This was a major statement of Ballance's own position and of the development of party politics in general. His judgement was good, for subsequent
events showed his analysis to be fairly accurate. Such a view also suited
his own purposes; he, like others, would have to choose one of two camps
being established as the structure of politics changed. It could plausibly
be argued that the system, rather than the individual, was being inconsistent. The *Lyttelton Times* said that Ballance's effort was undoubtedly the
highlight of the debate and recognised that although his vote was given
to the Government 'his speech was the most telling one against them'.[27]
As always, he would have talked the matter over with Ellen, who watched
the developing political situation closely and keenly. He 'votes with the
government' she told Sarah Jane Spinks, 'but cannot agree with them'.[28]
On 3 October Ballance finally wrote to Atkinson saying that he should
no longer be considered a government supporter.[29] It was no great surprise.
Atkinson knew how Ballance felt and had condemned a number of anti-
government articles that appeared in the *Herald* during the recess.[30] 'No
one could have listened to his strong and emphatic denunciation of the
Ministry,' said the *Evening Post*, 'without asking how long he would support
a government in which he had no faith, and to which he accorded no
respect.'[31] Ballance was expected to bring over others with him and indeed
John Bryce and W. W. Johnston followed days later. It was a fatal blow
to Atkinson. On hearing of Ballance's switch the *New Zealand Herald* was
certain that the ministry was doomed.[32] The *Evening Star* complained that
Ballance ought to have made the move much earlier and, making the
inevitable pun, pointed out how opposition hopes had 'risen with the
oscillation of the balance'.[33]

In later years Ballance, by nature particularly sensitive to charges of
disloyalty and inconsistency, stressed that this switch was not a sudden
impulse but the consequence of thought and events over a long period of
time. He emphasised his repeated opposition to the Government's legislation of the session and realisation that Atkinson, increasingly the 'puppet
of the most powerful combination of the hour', would be unlikely to pursue
a liberal policy that he (Ballance) had always pressed for.[34] Yet though
Ballance's alienation from the ministry had indeed been apparent for some
time his final break was clearly calculated for maximum effect. Six days
after his defection, Atkinson was defeated in a no-confidence motion moved

by Larnach. Despite Ballance's later claim that at the time he believed the Government to be secure, it was clear that his change of sides, followed by others, was going to be critical.[35] More important, as instigator of these desertions he was placed in a crucial position when the manoeuvrings to form a new ministry began. A 'middle party' of ex-Atkinson supporters had already emerged, including Montgomery, Gisborne, Fitzherbert and Rolleston, and only after he had dismissed the possibility of a government being formed from this group did Ballance commit himself to Grey.[36] At the opposition caucus meeting following Atkinson's defeat, it was Ballance who nominated Grey as leader.[37]

Having proposed Grey it is curious that Ballance did not take up the invitation of a place in the cabinet when Grey came to form his administration. The offer of the Colonial Treasury was certainly made, most likely on 12 October. Larnach was not appointed Treasurer until 15 October.[38] Yet Ballance did not join the ministry until early January 1878 and as late as 10 December he was telling his brother-in-law, David Anderson, that he still refused a cabinet post.[39] This initial reluctance needs some explanation. The Grey Ministry was dangerously weak. Grey had asked the Governor to grant a dissolution, confident that he had strong support in the country, but Ballance wisely kept his options open. The middle party had split on Grey's accession to power and an election might have actually strengthened the non-Greyite liberal faction sufficiently to make it the basis of a viable ministry. An election would also have removed the possibility of an Atkinson comeback in coalition with the other wing of the middle party.[40] Not until the end of the year did the Governor finally refuse Grey's request for a dissolution and so the possibility of an alternative liberal government disappeared. Secondly, Ballance was worried about a revival of provincialism. Though he argued in the House that Grey was committed to centralised government, only after Larnach's Financial Statement of 20 November announcing that the Government was to take complete control of the land fund, was the separation bogey finally laid to rest.[41] Ballance and other abolitionists such as William Gisborne were now able to feel more comfortable in their support of Grey, and the ministry was as a consequence substantially strengthened.

A third factor was Robert Stout. Ballance and Stout were now confidants and doubtless conferred on their responses to offers which Grey made for them to join his ministry. With an election ruled out and the Government stronger, the remaining condition was that the one would only join if the other were also asked.[42] This desire for mutual inclusion, alongside the earlier hope of an alternative liberal administration, reflected not only their personal and political friendship but suggests that both men foresaw personality difficulties in a ministry led by Grey.

Sir George Grey was a liberal from a privileged background. After a good education he went to Sandhurst, the British military academy, and was soon afterwards serving as a captain in the Army in Ireland. From the military it was just a short step to the Colonial Service. Grey excelled and held posts as Governor of South Australia and Governor of Cape Colony. He was twice Governor of New Zealand where, in the face of considerable Maori resistance, he managed to extend substantially the boundaries of European settlement. During his second term he had been the major influence in the drafting of the Constitution Act of 1852. In 1871 Grey returned to New Zealand and his home on Kawau Island. Three years later, at the age of 62, he emerged from retirement to fight for the provincial system he had helped establish. Grey is perhaps New Zealand's most fascinating nineteenth-century political figure. A man of great intellect, he was also cunning, shrewd, ruthless and devious. As he grew older he became increasingly dogmatic and intolerant; his advocacy of liberalism in defence of the masses was matched by an arrogant reluctance to listen to those who disagreed with him. An aristocrat and autocrat, Grey made a curious popular leader indeed.

When Ballance was appointed Commissioner of Customs and Minister of Education on 12 January 1878 it was on the understanding that he would take over the Treasury when Larnach left for England to negotiate a loan.[43] In fact Ballance was acting-Colonial Treasurer from the start.[44] As there was a constitutional limit to the number of salaried portfolios, Stout was not appointed Attorney General until Larnach resigned on 18 March.[45] Ballance had been in the House less than three years and his appointment to a key cabinet position was remarkable. Press comment on his suitability was largely predetermined by political bias. His youth, inexperience and desertion of Atkinson were serious flaws to the *Dunedin Herald*, while the *Hawke's Bay Herald* suggested that as Ballance was poor as well as ambitious he had gone after a cabinet post right from the start. But the Napier paper did admit that he had gained a reputation, inside and outside the House, through his few 'set orations, carefully thought out, elaborately constructed, and ingeniously worded'. The *Canterbury Press* was sure Ballance, who had 'theories of his own', would only 'encourage the most flighty and impracticable fancies of his chief'.[46] However, most papers were prepared to wait and see how he performed in office. Vogel was pleased. 'I cannot say I am surprised,' he wrote, 'for since I first met you I have been firmly persuaded [that such a] distinction awaited you.'[47]

In the following 18 months Ballance gained invaluable political and administrative experience. He learnt a number of lessons that were to critically influence his later premiership and in this respect his time in the Grey Government was much more significant than that in the Stout-Vogel Ministry of 1884 to 1887. The period also reveals important traits in his character. Above all else, Ballance found that the exigencies of colonial finance placed considerable restraints on his ability to pursue liberal policies. The instability of the land revenue and dependency on overseas borrowing and prices negated any impact he might have hoped to make on the direction of policy. Liberal ideology was surrendered to economic necessity. The financial position of the colony deteriorated drastically between 1878 and 1879 and the surplus which Ballance had inherited became a large deficit. In the short term this experience was discouraging but ultimately it simply confirmed Ballance's belief in the need for greater economic and political independence. Speculators at home and financiers abroad had both to be tamed if liberal legislation were to be viable. Revenue needed to be placed on a broader base. Ballance was to become almost paranoid about deficits and in later years would time and again explain how the 1879 shortfall had arisen. It was not just that he was a conservative financier. He hated deficits because they made him dependent upon factors beyond his control, factors that could therefore undermine liberal policies.

The most important measure of Ballance's term as Colonial Treasurer was the land tax. Theoretically desirable, it was shown (despite some initial technical difficulties) to be politically and administratively workable. It placed the burden of taxation upon those capable of bearing it and encouraged genuine settlement through penalising aggregation. 'The Land Tax had been carefully thought out by him,' Stout wrote later, 'and to him belongs the main credit of its introduction. He arranged the details, formed the estimates, and thought the system out.'[48] A land tax was to be a central feature of the 1890 Liberal platform and the 1878 tax the precedent.

Ballance also learnt that political reform required support from below not merely initiative from above. Grey led the way with a country-wide 'stump' during the recess of 1877–78 which strengthened the Government and shook its opponents. Organisation at grass-roots level was essential if a liberal party were to survive. In addition, Ballance discovered the extent to which internal dissension and conflict at cabinet level could prove fatal. Together with changed economic circumstances this was the major cause of the fall of the Grey Government. It was a matter of both personality and policy clashes. Grey's dictatorial leadership, his touchiness and inability to compromise with strong-willed colleagues, were disastrous.

Finally we see new sides to Ballance's character. His passion for politics was matched by a great capacity for hard work and considerable administrative ability. A man of great energy, he liked to get things done rather than talk about them. Ballance enjoyed office and power, and thrived on the demands they made upon him. He also showed flexibility when possible but strength of will when it mattered, a major characteristic of his later premiership. Following his appointment the *New Zealand Times* recognised that he had 'ideas and a tolerable amount of combativeness' and prophesied that Grey would 'find it a hard job to have it all his own way with him'.[49]

Ballance began his task with great vigour and enthusiasm. He delayed his annual address to his electors until May, remaining in Wellington absorbed in administrative duties and in acquainting himself with the state of the colony's finances.[50] In March the *Evening Post* reported that he was 'running the Government of New Zealand single-handed. All the other members of the Ministry are scattered north, south, east, and west . . . He is 'Monarch of all he surveys, and his right there is none to dispute.'. . . To his great credit . . . Mr Ballance appears to accomplish wonders, and to get through an enormous mass of work.'[51] He was cheerful and optimistic. Support was growing in the country with reform associations springing up advocating liberal land laws, changes in taxation and an extension of the franchise.[52] A political revival had begun. In Wanganui the *Herald* argued that the division between conservatism and liberalism was clearer than ever. Discipline and organisation were essential not only with the coming election in mind but as a means of setting up a more permanent party.[53] Two great parties have been formed, echoed the *Post*, and 'day by day men are joining either one or the other'.[54]

Ballance's immediate concern was preparing his financial statement to be delivered at the start of the coming session. Customs duties and the proceeds from the sale of crown land made up the bulk of colonial revenue. The former had been fairly constant over the preceding years but the latter varied considerably. Deficits in 1875 and 1876 had been financed out of borrowing for public works while a large increase in the land revenue the following year had produced a surplus.[55]

The sale of land was therefore critical to balancing the books. Some property, for example in Canterbury, was already in the hands of the Crown and only awaited opening up. Yet much land in the North Island had still to be purchased from its Maori owners. For Ballance there were important political as well as financial considerations — above all that land should be sold to genuine settlers. The Land Act of the previous session had extended the system of deferred payment existing in a number of provinces to the whole country, but it also increased the price of land on deferred payment by 50 percent. In the open market and with land prices rising rapidly the prospective small farmer remained at great disadvantage. The situation was made worse when Sheehan, Native Minister in Grey's cabinet, stopped government purchasing of Maori land on the grounds that it encouraged 'jobbing' and gave Maori a lower price than they could expect from private purchasers.[56] For Ballance it was a grave error. 'The purchase system has been abandoned,' he wrote to Vogel, '& I fear the sharks will gorge more than ever.'[57] However the Cabinet soon reversed its policy, and the Government recommenced purchasing and through proclamations excluding private capitalists virtually restored Crown pre-emption.[58]

In his first few months in office Ballance had reason to be optimistic.

There were few signs of trouble to come. After sluggish growth from 1871 onwards, exports jumped from £5.5 million in 1876 to £6 million in 1877. Some export prices had begun to fall, but this had been more than offset by increased quantities and Ballance could announce a surplus on the current account. With major new land purchases to be made conditions were thus favourable for liberal experiment.

Ballance's Financial Statement of 6 August 1878 was the most important one delivered since Vogel announced his public works policy in 1870. Part of it dealt with the re-organisation and simplification of accounts following abolition. For us the more important part set out the basic tenets of a liberal programme. 'This year has been looked forward to with more than ordinary interest by the people of the colony,' said Ballance, 'as one in which large and extensive reforms are to be inaugurated, especially in questions of finance and taxation, when inequalities are to be removed and grievances redressed.'[59] His analysis of the state of colonial finance was logical and straightforward. He detailed the previous year's revenue and expenditure. There was a surplus of £120,468. Exports had risen and the loan authorised successfully floated. (Vogel had been keeping Ballance in touch with events in London and had advised him that despite the successful floating of the loan there should be no new borrowing for 15 to 18 months.[60])

Next Ballance announced his proposals. The tariff was to be reformed with ad valorem being replaced by fixed duties. Imposing duty on the value of goods had been a failure since fraudulent undervaluation was common, and so duty would be levied on quantity instead. Some duties were to be removed altogether, in particular those that 'clogged the wheels of local industry'. Ballance believed that industry would be fostered by removing duty on raw materials.[61] Other duties were to be abolished as a means of changing the incidence of taxation, the most important being those on two basic necessities, tea and sugar. Ballance acknowledged the justice of the demand for a 'free breakfast table', given 'the immense proportion of the taxation which these articles yield, and that the labouring classes are the principal consumers'.[62] The duty on Australian wine was also reduced in the hope that some reciprocity towards New Zealand exports might follow, though that on sparkling wine, which Ballance regarded as a luxury, was raised.

Having eased the burden of taxation on the 'wages class', Ballance announced that to further equalise its incidence he would impose a new tax on the landowning class. Greater equality would reduce rather than increase hostility between the classes. Land values had been rising largely as a result of government expenditure on immigration and public works, and so a tax of a halfpenny in the pound on land over £500 in value was reasonable. Improvements would be exempt so that industry was rewarded and speculation, 'which thrives only upon the labour of others,' discouraged:

'We believe that no form of wealth is more legitimately called upon to contribute a portion of the public revenue of the colony than the value of land *minus* improvements.'[63]

The removal of duties on essentials and the imposition of a land tax were for Ballance the core of a liberal policy. Defending the interests of the urban working class through protection was not yet a major issue. Ballance's top priority was to change the basis of taxation. As well as a land tax he proposed a tax of 3d in the pound on the net profits of joint-stock companies. He also recommended a beer tax of 1½d a gallon, on the grounds that concessions had been made to brewers through the halving of sugar duty and in an attempt to recover revenue lost elsewhere. Compared with the duty on beer in England, he said, this was a modest rate.[64]

Ballance calculated that the effect of these changes would be a gain of £24,000 and, after deducting administrative costs, predicted a surplus for the current financial year of £15,273.[65] In conclusion he said that the proposals, as well as being just, would accelerate the prosperity of the colony:

> To maintain . . . those inequalities of taxation which we propose to remedy would benefit no man who intended to remain and make his permanent home in the colony. It would be vain to expect that all interests can be blended in mutual compromise, or to suppose that human nature can be changed to break down the lines of demarcation between the allies of resistance and the advocates of progress; but we can easily imagine a progressiveness arising from the constitutional conflict of both elements . . . [These proposals] will show a country inviting labour as well as capital from all parts of the world by the justice and liberal character of its legislation. It cannot be doubted that the colony possesses inexhaustible resources: it is true that Nature has bestowed upon it the most lavish gifts; but the bounty of Nature must be matched by the beneficence of our institutions, and the equity of our public policy.[66]

The speech, delivered in his now characteristic slightly monotonous style, lasted one and three-quarter hours. It was well received for what it said, rather than for any great skill in the way Ballance said it. Ellen, as often the case, was in the Ladies Gallery to hear her husband. Beside her sat her sister Jessie. They listened throughout, then left for the nearby home of their brother, David, now married to Sarah Jane Spinks (who in the 1860s had run a school attended by Ellen). The couple lived in a house in Hawkestone Street, beside the store David managed for his father. Ellen was happy, arriving at the Andersons in high spirits and telling Sarah Jane that the statement was a great success.[67] Press comment was eagerly awaited and when it came was not disappointing. The proposals were 'moderate and just' wrote the Auckland *Evening Star* and opinion throughout the

colony favourable.[68] The *New Zealand Herald* viewed it as the best financial statement for years, all members admitting 'that Mr Ballance has made
a great hit, both on principle and detail'.[69] The *Evening Post* and *Lyttelton
Times* eulogised Ballance. The former called the statement the 'most masterly
production . . . ever laid before any New Zealand Parliament' and said
Ballance had established a reputation as a leading figure in the House that
would last as long as his political career.[70] 'The first thing that strikes one
about it,' declared the latter, 'is the amount of ability which it shows. It
is evidently the work of a clever, thoughtful man, master of his subject.'[71]

It was not simply Ballance's ability that produced such favourable
reaction. He gained reflected glory from the healthy state of the colony's
finances and this optimism helped make his taxation proposals more palat-
able. Everyone loved a winner. The statement was also well received because
Ballance had carefully prepared in advance public and politicians for its
major provisions. Speaking at Marton in May he had mentioned both a
land and company tax. 'The great principle the Government had in view
was the distribution of land,' he had said. 'If the aggregation of great estates
was allowed to go on, the prosperity of the colony would soon cease.'[72]
Ballance urged that land over 130 hectares be taxed but, when Stout pointed
out that this would exclude many wealthy properties, changed the basis
to over £500 in value.[73]

What made the land tax central to Ballance's philosophy was that it
killed three birds with one stone. It involved a change in the burden of
taxation from those who could least afford it to those who could afford
it most; it provided a more stable, predictable and permanent source of
revenue than that from land sales; and it promoted genuine settlement
through penalising aggregation and rewarding improvements. Above all
he believed it would guarantee the prosperity of the colony:

> We have over and over again written of the small farmer as the life
> and soul of the industrial element of the colony . . . It is by him the
> continued growth and prosperity must be maintained . . . This colony
> should be made a country specially of yeoman farmers and peasant
> proprietors. Much has been done to make it *not* so. The public estate
> has been, and is being, wasted, in order to meet the necessities of
> empty treasuries, and to aggrandise the power and influence of
> monopolists and speculators. If further taxation be required this is
> the class that should yield it.[74]

Within a year Ballance was being held responsible for a major depression
in the economy as indiscriminately as he was currently being applauded
for its prosperity. Within two months considerable opposition had arisen
in the House to a number of his proposals.

Now a cabinet minister, Ballance led a life busier than ever. Social as
well as political demands on his time grew. There were important balls

to attend — the Governor General, Lord Normandy's, an assembly ball, an artillery ball and for Ellen an 'at home' of Lady Fitzgerald's. When not in the House herself, Ellen was often in the company of Sarah Jane Anderson, or looking after the Anderson children while their parents went out. As the year progressed, the Ballances and Andersons were increasingly frequent visitors to each other's homes. They got on well together. David Anderson was interested in politics and Ballance supplied him with tickets for the House. Sarah Jane enjoyed the contact with the high life of Wellington. Before the Governor General's ball, the children were allowed to visit their aunt at her Tinakori residence to see her dressed in all her finery. It was all go.[75]

The debate on the Land Tax Bill opened by Ballance on 30 August covered the whole of the Financial Statement. There was some criticism of the land tax and especially of the company and beer taxes, but most members were content to wait until the committee stage before proposing amendments.[76] Not so Edward Wakefield, a nephew of Gibbon Wakefield. He believed that there should be a general direct tax and then only when the Government ceased to use taxation revenue to subsidise local bodies. According to E. C. J. Stevens (the conservative member for Christchurch who also opposed the land tax), the hot-headed Wakefield, apparently now having given up drinking, had 'conceived an intense apathy for Ballance' and was 'resolved to smash him'.[77]

When the bill returned for its third reading there were grumblings that insufficient time had been allowed for alterations to be made. One amendment considered, excluding leaseholders from taxation, had been defeated by only two votes. Nevertheless the bill passed, in essence unaltered, by 42 votes to 19.[78] It had been agreed by both sides that the debate should be on the financial proposals in general and the confusion that resulted, rather than specific acceptance of the principle of a land tax, produced the large majority. Ballance's reply to the debate consisted of a defence of the beer and company taxes and of the reduction of duties as much as of the land tax. 'There was a multiplicity of theories, a confusion of ideas, and a cross-fire of arguments which gave the debate an appearance which may be described as "considerably mixed". Conservatives and liberals mingled together in undistinguishable groups.'[79] Quoting Mill, Ballance had argued that the state had a right to appropriate the 'unearned increment' — that is, the increase in the value of land owing to factors (government expenditure and rising prosperity) independent of the owner's own efforts. But few speakers accepted this as a fundamental principle and many simply saw the land tax as part of an irresistible movement towards a general property and income tax.[80]

In practice the tax worked reasonably well. Valuations were made on 1 February 1879 and returns showed that Ballance's estimate was very accurate, though the cost of collection turned out to be greater than expected.[81] For the nine months to March 1880 the tax raised £92,803, almost the same as revenue from stamps.[82] Ballance was determined to avoid an income tax which he regarded as difficult to administer (self-assessment produced fraud) and inequitable. It could not be imposed 'with anything like fairness or consideration for the large number of people earning small incomes'.[83] As for the company tax, Ballance argued that the firms affected could well afford it. It would be a tax on profits from investments made in the colony, an appropriation of surplus capital which would not seriously damage the companies involved: 'By this tax we shall reach the great monetary firms which derive large profits from their investments. We shall reach the great capitalists in this colony who are now reaping large profits from joint-stock companies, which are springing up every day.'[84] However, there was considerable opposition to this tax. Some thought it unjust to penalise companies that furthered the prosperity of the colony.[85] Others said that ordinary people, not just wealthy capitalists, were affected and the 'walls of the House rang with heart-rending accounts of aged widows who had invested their small savings in a joint-stock company and were now to be unfairly penalised'.[86]

Similar objections were made to Ballance's beer tax — that it would hit the ordinary working man as much as the wealthy brewer. In fact, brewers would simply pass the tax on to consumers, as was pointed out in 'Ballance's Beer Bill', a piece of political doggerel published at the time by the *Auckland Evening Star*:

> *T'was said by Ballance in his speech,*
> *'The beer-tax none will grudge it',*
> *And spite of brewers not one foot from*
> *His budget will he budge it.*

> *'Three half-pence on a gallon is*
> *Not much to any man;*
> *The publicans can stand it if*
> *The Auckland public can.'*

> *The brewers, howsoever, view*
> *This new tax as an ill,*
> *And 25 per cent. stick on,*
> *To balance Ballance's Bill.*

> *Should publicans their price advance,*
> *The working men will fear*
> *That Ballance's beer tax has brought*
> *Their barrel to its bier.*[87]

Ballance recognised this but argued that beer was not 'altogether' a necessity, that consumers would reduce their consumption and that this would not be a bad thing. However unlike Stout, Ballance was not a temperance reformer. Ultimately he viewed the beer tax as a means, alongside the land and company taxes, of avoiding an income tax. Revenue from duty on English beer had consistently dropped as the consumption of the protected local product rose. Removing protection would restore revenue, though Ballance much preferred the alternative method of taxing all beer consumed since this would not encourage imports at the expense of colonial producers.[88] Surprisingly, Fox and other teetotallers in the House voted against the bill. Having previously argued in favour of increasing taxation on beer as a temperance measure, Fox now declared that a new tax would only make the Government more dependent upon sales of alcohol. An unusual alliance of Foxites, brewing interests and those who genuinely felt that the tax would unjustly penalise the working man defeated the bill by two votes.[89] Ironically the succeeding Colonial Treasurer, Atkinson, proposed a beer duty of 6d a gallon, but after opposition from Ballance was forced to accept a tax half that amount.[90]

A cabinet meeting was hurriedly called to discuss the reverse, at which Ballance and Stout urged that the Government resign.[91] Grey, Sheehan, and probably Macandrew, disagreed. The following day, 4 October, Grey announced that both the Beer and Company Tax Bills were being withdrawn. He recognised that this would 'embarrass the finances' of the Treasurer but said that as there was such great feeling against the taxes he had no choice. According to a later account he had always opposed the taxes. Ballance and Stout, however, had earlier given the impression that the ministry would stand or fall on the taxes and members were quick to notice this division in the ranks of the Cabinet.[92] After the defeat Stout was seen leaving the chamber 'burning with rage' and 'declaring that he would resign next moment'.[93] But for Ballance in particular it was a major upset, for as well as principles being lost the finances now needed reorganising.

The situation was especially serious as the Government had already been defeated on Stout's Electoral Bill. This bill extended the franchise to all men who had been in the colony two years and in the one district six months. In May Ballance had said the intention was to exclude only recent arrivals, to 'prevent the flooding of any roll by the importation of immigrants by Government aid'. He defended the retention of the property vote as 'it was held that any man should have a vote for property wherever that property existed' but in general terms argued that to be secure the constitution needed to rest on a broad base. Under the bill women ratepayers were to be permitted to vote and Ballance said that personally he would go further 'with respect to the equality of the sexes'.[94] For those who knew the Ballances well, this was a rather indirect public acknowledgement of John and Ellen's firm private convictions in favour of the female franchise.

Grey, however, wished to see the property vote abolished and supported an amendment to that effect. Ballance and Stout stuck to the provisions of the bill and the amendment failed.[95] At this stage Ballance viewed franchise reform as some way down his list of liberal priorities. The extension of manhood suffrage from its present level would, he said, have no great political effect. He was insistent that 'political power should not rest in the hands of a few,'[96] but it was not until 1881, with his own electoral defeat by the narrow margin of four votes, that he fully appreciated the consequences of plural voting. The bill passed through the House but was withdrawn by Grey when the Legislative Council, in angry mood having been unable to dump the land tax (because it was a supply measure), excised the rights of Maori to vote as ratepayers. It was a politically immature act on the part of Grey since a bill extending the franchise through a residence qualification, albeit retaining the property vote he detested, would have been better than nothing. The coming election had now to be fought on the existing, limited franchise.[97]

Ballance put a brave face on the rejection of so many of his key measures. Along with the beer and company taxes the House had refused the duty on timber, though Ballance said later that this was not originally part of his proposals.[98] He announced that he would use funds from the public works account, originally meant for harbour defences, to make up the loss.[99] Since demands on the land fund were already great, new public works would be financed out of a loan to be floated the following year. 'There is no fear, barring extraordinary circumstances,' he said as the session drew to a close, that 'if the prosperity of the colony continues . . . we shall not obtain the money we require. I believe our financial position is sound in every part.'[100] Nevertheless when Ballance and other ministers deserted Wellington for their respective homes, leaving only Fisher (the Postmaster-General) behind, it was to lick their wounds after a bitter and disappointing session.

In 1879 the land boom burst. The price of agricultural land was halved while export prices continued their downward trend (the wool index fell from 103 to 90 and wheat from 122 to 105; 1870 = 100). The failure of the City of Glasgow Bank sparked off trouble in Australasia, where it had financial interests. There was a rapid contraction of credit and in New Zealand bank advances and discounts, which had increased £10 million from 1872 to 1878, now fell by £2 million in a single year. Banks were reluctant to enforce the sale of unprofitable mortgaged properties when the price of land was so low, yet despite this bankruptcies rose from 2.4 to 4 per thousand.[101] 'All the loan money of the place is gone and the Banks are drained,' Stevens wrote from Christchurch; 'the price of wheat must also operate powerfully in discouraging purchases of waste lands to say nothing of the fact that the land especially in Canterbury has gone . . . The prospects of Land Sales is very poor.'[102]

Ballance's attempts to deal with the worsening financial situation and his deteriorating relationship with Grey were connected. A series of disagreements with Grey culminating in one particularly well-publicised incident gave Ballance a pretext for resignation and ultimately allowed him to avoid at least some of the blame for the deepening depression. Personal differences in turn rested in part on what Ballance saw as Grey's refusal to accept measures that would help restore government revenue. Ballance's hopes of avoiding a large deficit rested initially on the sale of land on the Waimate Plains and when that fell through on an extension of the land tax.

Many Maori actively opposed the sale of confiscated land on the Waimate Plains, which lay to the south of Mount Egmont in Taranaki, and Sheehan, Grey's Native Minister, had stopped its survey in December 1877. In May 1878 Ballance and Macandrew (Minister of Public Works) urged the Cabinet to resume the survey, backed up with sufficient armed constabulary support. Macandrew, who was spending every farthing he could collect, believed that the land would fetch nearly £500,000.[103] The survey began again in August, only to be interrupted in December and February. By March 1879 Titokowaru and Te Whiti had turned all the surveyors off the plains. A deputation of concerned local Maori went to see Sheehan, who promised them that adequate reserves of land would be made for their use.

Meanwhile Ballance desperately needed the revenue (financial considerations overriding all others) and telegraphed the Commissioner of Crown Lands instructing him to convene an emergency meeting of the Taranaki Land Board (which under the 1877 Land Act was the medium for land sales) 'to arrange for the sale of the Plains within the next few weeks'.[104] He then left with Macandrew for the area. Though Ballance's telegram gave the impression that the Cabinet had agreed to push on with the sale, this was not the case. When Grey heard of what had happened behind his back he sent a message to Ballance ordering him to return, and when he did proceeded to give him a 'good dressing down'.[105] The sale of the land was postponed indefinitely shortly afterwards.

There was a brighter side to the retention of land by the Crown in that it would at least not pass into the hands of speculators.[106] The *Herald* gleefully reported that government proclamation had removed about 20 000 hectares at Waitotara from a 'knot of speculators', a 'fatal blow to Mr Land-shark' on that coast.[107] Yet in the short term it placed Ballance's finances in serious straits:

> The great discrepancy between the amount which the Colonial Treas-
> urer estimated to receive from Land sales and the amount actually
> collected . . . is, doubtless, a source of much trouble to the Govern-
> ment. The inconvenience of the deficiency has been alleviated, to a
> certain extent no doubt, by the excess in other branches of revenue;
> but the fall-off in the Canterbury land sales, and the abandonment
> of all hope of any return at present from the Waimate Plains, must
> have caused Mr Ballance many anxious hours of thought how to make
> ends meet.[108]

Ballance wrote of the situation to Vogel. 'By rigid economy I am trying
to come out with a surplus, but it is hard work to make up for a deficit
in the land estimate of probably £300,000.'[109]

Imposing a higher land tax was another means of increasing revenue.
During the recess Grey 'talked wildly of raising the ½d land tax to 4d or
5d in the pound, and of breaking up the large estates'.[110] More realistic,
Ballance was by June believed to be intending to increase the tax on properties over £2500.[111] In Wanganui the *Herald* carried on its own campaign,
saying that the existing tax was only the thin end of the wedge. A graduated
tax would break up the large unimproved estates as well as simply raise
revenue:

> A class of land monopolists is always a source of danger, and there can
> be no doubt that political power necessarily follows and remains with
> such a monopoly until . . . the pressure becomes intolerable, and then
> a violent popular upheaval shakes the very foundations of society. For-
> tunately the evil here is only in its infancy, and it can easily be nipped
> now. A graduated land tax . . . will render it impossible even for
> wealthy men to indulge in the luxury of locking up from profitable
> occupation broad acres of land, on which people are hungering to
> settle . . . The State has a right to impose such taxation upon land
> so held, that the owner will be obliged to part with it . . . We regard
> a land tax as far more valuable in this direction than as a mere means
> of raising revenue.[112]

However, the *Herald* concluded that there would be a struggle, a party
struggle for political power. Ballance undoubtedly agreed, though when
it came to specific measures he had to be more circumspect. In politics,
especially in government, he could not always afford to be as radical as
his own paper.

There is some evidence that Grey's extreme proposals aimed to destroy
the tax entirely through stirring up strong feeling against it. Ballance later
said he believed this to be the case.[113] Certainly the financial plans of Grey's
Ministry, reconstructed following Ballance's resignation, included a new
income tax (which Ballance at this stage opposed) but made no mention
of increasing the land tax.[114]

Although Ballance was to resign prior to the new session and the announcement of the budget deficit, for years afterwards he felt obliged to explain how it had come about. He was very sensitive to suggestions that the shortfall was his own fault and constantly pointed out, with much justification, that had the land revenue not unexpectedly collapsed the financial situation would have been satisfactory. He insisted that he could not be held responsible for circumstances, in particular the failure of the City of Glasgow Bank, over which he had no control.[115]

These problems over policy were reflected and in turn reinforced by serious personal conflicts within the Cabinet. Splits were already apparent by January 1879 and eagerly reported from the opposition benches by Stevens:

> I think that the failure of the Ministry to either keep promises or perform any acts of utility either administrative or legislative has materially shaken Grey in the country. It must, however, be observed that he cares nothing for his government and loses few opportunities of holding himself up as something altogether distinct from them in sentiment and motive . . . His colleagues are insubordinate and both contradict and vote against each other . . . Grey continually puts forth one set of views whilst his colleagues clip his wings in Cabinet and propose to the House measures often diametrically opposed to Grey's statements.[116]

Over the following four months two disputes in particular deepened the rift between Ballance and Grey. While opposition papers had a field-day, pro-government journals were forced to take sides. Ballance had become a director of two Wellington papers formed a year earlier to promote the liberal cause. One was the morning *New Zealander* and the other the *Evening Chronicle* (neither survived beyond 1880).[117] The *Chronicle* in particular was used by Ballance to defend himself against Grey, and to this end he seems to have supplied the paper with inside information on the details of the growing number of cabinet rows.

The first incident concerned the appointment of D. M. Luckie as Government Insurance Commissioner. Luckie was a journalist and editor of the *Evening Post*. The appointment was a political one, for the *Post* had been a consistent supporter of the Government and Ballance, though Ballance genuinely thought Luckie able and as good a man as he could get.[118] Ballance wrote to Luckie on 10 January 1879 offering him the position at £800 per annum, confirming a verbal arrangement they had made earlier.[119] This salary was a good deal higher than the £200 laid down by Parliament and Grey objected to it, insisting on the lower figure.[120] Whitmore, an old friend who was now Colonial Secretary and a member of the Legislative Council, wrote to Ballance that Grey's advocacy of reduced civil service salaries would be very popular with the public. Luckie would accept £600 and on that basis they could 'stand by him'. Ballance agreed to the compromise.[121] On 26 February the *Evening Chronicle* reported that Grey had not opposed the appointment when it first came before the Cabinet and the following day it seemed that he had accepted the £600 concession. Only Sheehan had joined him in pressing for £200, with Stout, Whitmore and Macandrew all siding with Ballance.[122]

However, in April Grey renewed his objection and the issue broadened into the right of one minister to intervene in another's appointment. Ballance argued that there were many precedents for the higher salary and proposed that the difference be charged to unauthorised expenditure but Grey refused to shift from £200.[123] The dispute then became simply a part of the widening gulf between the two men. Relations were so strained by April that Whitmore, who was leaving for New Plymouth to see Macandrew and trying desperately to keep the peace, advised Ballance to 'avoid any contact' with Grey until he returned. Ballance wisely left for Wanganui the following day.[124] Ironically Luckie's salary was finally fixed at £800 by Parliament in December.[125]

An important cause of Grey's irritation with both Ballance and Stout was their participation in the New Zealand Land and Loan Company. The company had been formed in 1878 to finance the settlement of the Waimea Plains, land just north of Invercargill that was to be sold by a second Agricultural Company, to be floated in London. The land was infested with rabbits and only by selling it in London, where this fact might not emerge, could the speculators involved hope to receive a high price. Though Grey knew about the loan company, of which Ballance and Stout were provisional directors, he had no idea of its connection with the Waimea Plains and the Agricultural Company.[126] When Vogel announced in early 1879 that he had joined the board of the Agricultural Company, Grey insisted that it was incompatible with his position as Agent General and told him to resign from the former. Vogel procrastinated and in the ensuing correspondence it became quite clear that Ballance and Stout both knew of his association with the company. In an official letter of 26 April Ballance informed Vogel of the Government's decision to require his resignation.[127] A day earlier he had written privately, congratulating Vogel on the success of the company and regretting that he was being asked to retire. It was a cabinet decision, said Ballance, and personally he had no objection to Vogel's position.[128]

In January Ballance visited the South Island and at a banquet in Invercargill made a speech emphasising how crucial railways were to the development of the land. The only reproductive railway finance was that which directly promoted settlement.[129] On 27 January he turned the first sod of the Waimea Plains Railway, the construction of which was an integral part of the Loan and Agricultural Companies' plans to dispose of the land and was being financed by a third, auxiliary company. Ballance telegraphed

Vogel in London: 'Line through magnificent country waiting settlement by proposed Waimea Company. Success must contribute prosperity colony, and remunerate proprietors.'[130] The telegram could not have arrived at a more fortuitous moment, for in London *The Times* had found out about the rabbits just as the company was to be floated. Larnach had Ballance's telegram published and the company was successfully launched.

There was some criticism of Ballance for using his position as government minister to promote a private undertaking, but it was minimal. Most attention focused on Vogel and in any case the facts took some months to emerge.[131] There were mitigating circumstances. When sending the telegram Ballance could not have known that events in London had reached a critical stage since the *Times* article revealing the presence of rabbits was not published until four days later. Also, although Ballance was a provisional director of the Land and Loan Company (most likely brought in by Stout) there is no evidence to suggest that he had any personal financial interest in the Agricultural Company. He referred to it as 'your company' when writing to Vogel.[132] More important, Ballance quite simply saw nothing wrong with such a venture promoting settlement. When Fox brought up the matter at the election in September, Ballance had the prospectus of the company printed in the *Herald*, saying that he was not ashamed to be associated with it and applauding in particular one of its chief objectives of subdividing large estates. A branch of the company in Wanganui would, he continued, be of great benefit to the district. Land belonging to the local firm of Taylor and Watt might be cut up into 50 farms and disposed of on deferred payment.[133]

Ballance and Stout's involvement with the company saw their relations with Grey deteriorate still further. The Premier felt betrayed and insisted that they resign their directorships, which they did.[134] Stout said later that they did not resign, rather they were not asked to let their names go on the new prospectus of the company when it was transferred to London, but this was just face-saving and amounted to the same thing.[135] Aside from contributing to the bad feeling already existing in the Cabinet the issue had no effect on Ballance's later decision to quit Grey. He realised that it could be politically embarrassing but maintained that as the company promoted closer settlement it was a legitimate exercise.[136] There were much better reasons for resigning.

By March 1879 disagreements within the Cabinet were being openly paraded. The *Evening Post* urged that differences be patched up:

> Knowing what we do of the autocratic idiosyncracies of Sir George Grey, we are quite prepared to believe that he is entirely in the wrong, and that he does not treat his colleagues with the consideration which they have a right to expect; but even if this be so, he has a right to expect loyalty from them while they remain his colleagues.[137]

Meanwhile the *Evening Chronicle* called Grey a coward for rushing off to his retreat on Kawau Island when trouble erupted on the Waimate Plains. Sheehan was Grey's last remaining ally in the Cabinet and the paper was keen to drive a wedge between them. The Premier had from the start tied the Native Minister's hands, it said. He was a stumbling block to progress whose conduct the country could stand no longer.[138] Echoing this, the *Herald* in Wanganui pronounced Ballance the 'mainstay of the Ministry', he and Stout pulling together while Grey went alone.[139] When John Murray of the Bank of New Zealand wrote to Ballance about the worsening economic situation he also expressed concern at Cabinet disunity and reported that 'Grey makes no secret of his intention to "put Ballance out" '. Murray hoped that if anyone were to go it would be the Premier.[140]

By the beginning of May Ballance had decided to resign[141] and began looking round for a convincing pretext, something more substantial and immediate than the Luckie affair.[142] Meanwhile cabinet meetings ceased altogether[143] and Stout's remaining in Dunedin fuelled rumours of his resignation.[144] It came in mid-June and on the grounds that Stout's law partner was ill and his own health not good. The *Wanganui Chronicle* was rightly sceptical and saw the plea of private affairs as simply a useful 'loophole for escape' from a 'blundering' Ministry.[145] Ballance as always stayed in close contact with Stout, whose advice he regularly sought. Frequent consultation ensured foreknowledge of each other's public actions; and more often than not they acted in the same direction. Like Stout, Ballance too needed an excuse to resign, and quickly. The Financial Statement was due and with the economy still in recession it was all bad news. 'No one on the outside of a lunatic-asylum could view [the] finance without amazement and loathing,' Stevens had written to Stafford, and he added gleefully:

> Report says that Stout will resign his office in the public interest. I shall not be sorry for it in the public interest . . . I expect great fun from Wakefield this session. Last session he flew at nearly everybody and would have flared up even more if he had not been next to a sober animal like myself but this year there will be no holding him and indeed I think I shall set him at Ballance.[146]

Grey was now ruling by decree, 'seeing Ministers individually, telling them what he had decided and thinks should be done'.[147] One such summons gave Ballance just the type of escape route he was seeking. He was called to Grey's office on Friday afternoon, 27 June. Grey had the Treasury Department draft estimates, prepared by Ballance, in front of him and said he was unhappy that the salary of the Private Secretary to the Treasurer, E. Fox, had been removed from the Treasury estimates and placed elsewhere. In fact, Fox was Secretary to the Cabinet and the Premier, and had long ceased to have any connection with the Treasury. Ballance tried to explain that the estimates were only a draft and that if the Cabinet chose to charge Fox's salary to a department with which Fox had no connection, so be it. Intent on a showdown Grey told Ballance that if this sort of thing were to happen he would take over the Treasury himself, at which point Ballance said that he had better resign. Grey refused to listen to further explanation and ordered Ballance to leave the room. Ballance, 'excited but calm' as a later report put it, countered that as long as he was a minister he had a right to free discussion with all his cabinet colleagues, from the Premier down. Grey next threatened to have him physically ejected, Ballance replying that he wouldn't move 'if all the messengers in the building were summoned'. Sheehan, the only other person present, tried to quieten things down but Grey left the room 'in a most excited state, crossed the passage, and entered Mr Fox's room opposite, slamming both doors after him'. Ballance then emerged 'trembling with suppressed excitement' and restrained by Sheehan's hand on his shoulder.[148]

Three days later Ballance tendered his resignation. Grey asked him to reconsider but this was perfunctory.[149] The rift was too deep and it was inconceivable that relations might be patched up, primarily because at heart neither man wanted them to be. Grey had brought their conflict to a climax and Ballance was not going to let the opportunity slip. The specific issue was unimportant, though it angered Grey who had consistently advocated retrenchment in the civil service. In removing Fox's salary from the Treasury estimates Ballance revealed that Fox was in fact acting as Grey's personal assistant.

It was a remarkable incident, not because it occurred but because it was so widely publicised afterwards. Ballance's version appeared in the *Evening Chronicle*, which said that the whole thing had been pre-arranged by Grey. Apparently, half an hour before Ballance was sent for by Grey he received a telegram from Whitmore in Auckland, saying that the papers there had just published an 'extra' containing news of a cabinet disruption.[150] No copies of this paper seem to have survived but it is most likely that it referred to cabinet disputes in more general terms. Papers had for weeks been speculating about splits in the ministry. The *New Zealand Times* noted that rumours of Ballance's resignation had been reaching it from Auckland since mid-June.[151] Ballance's departure may have been predicted but it does not follow that Grey stage-managed the whole affair. As it turned out, Ballance emerged in a more favourable light than the Premier and those papers that did criticise him (and they were in the minority) said simply that he should not have allowed the details of the dispute to have been made public. The facts themselves were not questioned.

Opposition papers were content to watch over the collapse of the ministry. The *New Zealand Times* wrote that Grey 'quite forgot himself, and used language such as no colleague' could condone.[152] The *New Zealand Herald* recognised that the dispute over Fox reflected more fundamental differences between the men and that Ballance had no choice but to resign.[153] Pro-government journalists split, with the *Lyttelton Times* in Christchurch and the *Evening Star* in Auckland continuing to support Grey. The *Times* said that Ballance had been a drag on Grey and so his departure was the best thing for the Liberal Party. Details of the incident ought not to have emerged and those that did were distorted. Politically Ballance was finished, for the Liberal Party would not forget his efforts to supplant Grey. As for the Opposition, they viewed him 'with scorn for reasons best known to themselves. One of its organs . . . lately informed him, in effect, that he is so black that the very sight of him drives the imagination of his critics into the contemplation of all that is most white and most beautiful, in order that his unpleasant figure may be quickly lost sight of'.[154] He had not, recalled the *Times*, been a great success as Treasurer and his ability on paper had never been matched by his performance and influence in the House.

However, in Wellington the *Post* agreed with the *Evening Chronicle* that the whole incident was orchestrated by Grey. The former thought Ballance's version of the quarrel 'so entirely consistent with the course of action generally pursued by Sir George Grey that it may fairly be accepted as accurately representing what took place'.[155] The *Otago Daily Times* meanwhile urged that the party be reorganised to the exclusion of Grey.[156] In Wanganui the *Chronicle* suggested Ballance had long been trying to split the Liberal Party in his favour but that having been found out people now spoke of him as a 'solemn humbug, and laugh at his finance with its ridiculous land tax, and no less ridiculous reduction of duties on tea and . . . sugar'. And he had deserted his post at a time of need.[157] The *Herald* responded by reprinting all those accounts favourable to Ballance that had appeared in other papers.[158]

Ballance's resignation sealed the fate of the Liberal Ministry. Parliament opened on 11 July with the Government promising a new £5 million loan to further public works and an increase in income tax to make up for the deficit in land revenue. The opposition leader William Fox moved a no-confidence motion almost immediately whilst rumours flew that Ballance's resignation from the ministry would also involve his defection from the government benches.[159] In fact, his remaining loyal to Grey was of less importance than the effect his resignation had on the disintegrating Liberal Party. Supporters of the Government who were already concerned about Grey's radicalism or failure to carry through policies now lost all remaining confidence in him. The 'middle party' re-emerged and on 23 July its leader, J. C. Brown, claimed that it commanded 17 votes which would be given to the Government only if Grey were replaced by Macandrew.[160] In the event Brown voted with Grey but the middle party, evidence of the disunity amongst ministerial supporters, had done its damage. The situation was very confused, said the *Post* on 22 July, and political parties 'scarcely exist'.

The Ballance-Grey episode of 1879 (NZ Observer, 1892)

A week later Fox's motion was carried by 47 votes to 33 and the Governor acceded to Grey's request for a dissolution.

Throughout the debate Ballance remained quiet. Indeed he did not utter a single word in the House the whole session. According to the *Evening Star* he was annoyed at criticism of his actions in the press and was actively plotting against Grey. 'Official life has apparently agreed with him. He has grown very portly, and has a habit of placing his hands behind his back, and inclining his ear in a condescending style. He has been busy lobbying this afternoon, and prophesies a coup by the opposition. He inclines to the belief that the session will not last more than a month.'[161] There is no evidence to support this allegation that Ballance, to the extent of joining the Opposition, was working against the ministry. Though he could never again join a government led by Grey, it was vital that his credentials as a consistent liberal remain intact. He had, after all, left Atkinson for Grey less than two years earlier. Ballance was a leading liberal in the House and wished to remain so. In this he was helped by the circumstances of his break with Grey, which could with some plausibility be put down to personal rather than policy differences. In fact Ballance remained quiet quite simply because he had nothing constructive to offer. He was certainly not prepared to join the Opposition in the condemnation of a ministry of which he had been a member. Believing defeat inevitable he looked to the coming election as the only means of resolving the situation and soon left Wellington to commence preparations for his own campaign. According to the *Wanganui Chronicle* he was the first member to do so.[162]

Grey never forgave Ballance. Their public reconciliation in October when Ballance, speaking at an opposition dinner, said he wished bygones to be bygones, was never matched in private.[163] For Ballance, Grey was a stumbling block to securing another liberal ministry. Especially in Auckland Grey continued to have a personal following and influence that for a number of years made the formation of a liberal government without him impossible. Even when Premier, Ballance had difficulty maintaining the support of liberals in that city. Looking back on the whole episode a few years later, Ballance said that had it not been for Grey's deviousness he might have continued leader of a liberal party. Instead he had destroyed it:

> Not by want of talent, but destroyed by want of consistency, by want of political honesty and straightforwardness. This is what wrecked the Liberal party, and the honourable gentleman [Grey] as the possible leader of it . . . There never was a man who came into this House more endowed with all the intellectual qualities and gifts to become a leader of a great party in this colony than the honourable gentleman . . . [But] we want something more as a test of statesmanship than the making of great speeches before large masses of people, without any attempt in the slightest degree to give effect to what is uttered.[164]

There was no posturing in this — it was the honest opinion of a pragmatic politician who by nature was quick to forgive and slow to condemn.

Depression
and defeat

IN THE 1879 ELECTION BALLANCE decided to stand for Wanganui rather than Rangitikei. The move made sense. He lived in the town and his liberal platform was much more suited to it than to the country constituency. There had been signs of growing opposition to Ballance in Rangitikei and his promotion of the land tax inevitably stiffened it. The tax offered much more to urban interests and to prospective rather than existing farmers. All things being equal, Wanganui was better ground for Ballance although the outcome of the 1879 election was by no means a forgone conclusion.[1]

In Wanganui three candidates, all with national political reputations, fought for two seats in a contest that contained the same ambiguities as appeared elsewhere in the country. There was one Liberal (Ballance) and two Conservatives (Fox, Leader of the Opposition, and Bryce). Yet the latter two did not combine to oppose Ballance; rather, Bryce joined Ballance in an alliance aimed solely at excluding Fox. It was a classic case of personal friendship overriding political differences. Bryce could sympathise with, support and advise Ballance in his split with Grey, especially to the extent that it involved what Bryce regarded as Grey's fundamental weakness over native affairs, but beyond this there was now no common political ground between the two men. Bryce voted for Fox's no-confidence motion while Ballance remained loyal to Grey. Bryce, too, had all along expressed doubts about the land tax.[2] Writing to Ballance in May, he thought Fox to be 'gaining popularity' and believed (wrongly) that Watt would be standing with him.[3] Bryce calculated that an alliance with Ballance was the best means of defeating both. Ballance preferred to see Bryce rather than Fox elected alongside himself and his election committee ran both their campaigns. He emphasised how together they had supported abolition in the interests of Wanganui and simply ignored their more recent political differences.

Meanwhile Bryce claimed to be an independent and appealed to the middle ground between Ballance and Fox.[4]

In his campaign Ballance was in the awkward position of having to defend the Grey Ministry and his own role in it while opposing Grey himself as party leader. Thus he praised Grey's liberalism but at the same time insisted that Sir George lacked the qualities necessary for leadership. Ballance did not, however, specify who should replace him. In Wellington the *Chronicle* was much less circumspect and said that the party should ditch Grey for Macandrew.[5] The *Evening Post* urged on the split in liberal ranks by drawing the distinction between 'true, honest liberalism' and the 'Red Republicanism gone mad' of Grey. It argued that the city's Liberal Association was a sham as its proposed candidates, Hutchison and Fisher, were simply Grey nominees.[6]

With three such prominent personalities involved in the Wanganui election interest ran high. Nearly 500 people squeezed into the Oddfellows Hall on the evening of Tuesday 19 August to hear Ballance speak at one of the largest meetings to have been held in the town.[7] Ballance began by saying that he had decided to stand for Wanganui in order to fight Fox, whose articles in the *Rangitikei Advocate* had consistently attacked him. As we have seen, the real reason was simply that Wanganui was a safer bet. The most significant part of the speech concerned Ballance's views on land settlement and the land tax. He argued that the tax was the 'salvation' of bona fide settlers as only the monopolist, whose aim was to 'drive the small holder to the towns, and so retard the progress of the colony', would be penalised. Improvements were exempt, so that as the property was being developed, tax liability would fall. During the campaign Fox had made the important point that 'mechanics' and tradesmen had no interest in a liberal land law. Ballance replied that 'there was not an artisan in the colony who did not strive to get his little bit of freehold, even if it was only a quarter-acre section. Did not every man endeavour to provide for his family by leaving them a little property?'[8] This was unconvincing, and at most only a small part of the answer. What was there in a land tax for the urban working class who wished to remain in the town and had not the slightest intention of becoming small farmers? Ballance would say simply that the tax encouraged closer settlement and therefore meant a larger rural population for the town to service. Not for another five years would he be much more explicit than this on the specific advantages to urban labour of a liberal land law.

Recognising the need for finance to carry out improvements, Ballance proposed that an Agricultural State Bank be established to provide loans for small farmers. The colony's trust funds in savings banks would be transferred to the agricultural bank and money advanced on freehold security at six percent. On the mechanisms to make land available Ballance said that he had already drawn up an amendment to the Land Bill due next session, allowing for the establishment of village settlements alongside the railways. He also wished to replace the auctioning of land on deferred payment by a ballot system. Auctions meant that land went to the highest and often wealthiest bidder. Finally, Ballance returned to the old idea that closer settlement would help solve the 'native difficulty'. Where land was bought up by speculators and 'scattered with a few shepherds' there could be no guarantee of peace. 'Wherever the Government had a block of land with a good title' they should settle it. 'Never mind the price so much as planting settlers. They would repay the country by establishing peace, and also through the Customs.'

In speeches at Waverley and Waitotara Ballance repeated these themes. He also reiterated his statement in the House that politics had now split into two fundamentally distinct parties, Liberal and Conservative, and that it was to the former he belonged. Indeed throughout the country liberal supporters of the Grey Ministry were fighting the election along liberal versus conservative lines. Liberal associations were being formed in the major centres to promote candidates and policy. The Wellington associ-ation established by Grey outlined a 16 point programme, which included a progressive land tax, the abolition of plural voting at local government elections, redistribution of seats according to population, manhood suffrage, the promotion of village settlements, encouragement of local industries and the abolition of the legislative councillors' honorarium.[9] The election was undoubtedly the closest the country had come to such a clear political cleavage. A major source of opposition to the liberals, for example, came from conservative businessmen and landowners unhappy with Ballance's land tax. However, as in Wanganui, so too elsewhere alliances were made that cut across these 'party' lines. There were opponents of the Grey Ministry, for instance, who were distinctly more liberal than some of its supporters.[10] Nevertheless it remains true that Ballance himself fought the election first and foremost as a liberal. His own political platform was in this respect unambiguous.

The *Wanganui Chronicle* inevitably sided with Fox and daily attacked Ballance and his rowdy supporters.[11] It brought up his involvement in the Land and Loan Company,[12] and argued that his 'sensational programme of reforms' would, if he were returned to office, mean an impoverished exchequer.[13] On the eve of the poll a minor issue entered the election. In Otago and Canterbury associations had been formed to press for Bible reading in schools. Ballance was not opposed to religious instruction but had said that its proper place was in church and at home. Introducing Bible reading into schools would also force Catholic children to leave. The *Chronicle*, however, suggested that Ballance had actively wooed the Catholic vote by promising state aid to private schools, and it noted that a meeting on 31 August of the town's Catholics had indeed decided to support him and Bryce.[14] In fact the *Chronicle*'s allegation was unjust. The *Herald* pointed out that Ballance had always supported a state secular system and denied that he had made a deal with the Catholics. The *Chronicle* withdrew its claim.[15] Ballance's opposition to Bible reading in schools was sufficient reason for Catholics to support him rather than the unsympathetic Fox, but it was a small part of his programme and sprang from a liberal philosophy rather than expediency aimed at the Catholic vote.

The key note of Ballance's campaign was a view of politics as essentially a contest between the landless poor in the towns and wealthy monopolists. Shortly before polling day a revealing piece of doggerel appeared in the *Herald*:

Oh, Paddy dear, and did ye hear,
The news that's going around,
The Land Sharks claim thave a right
To all New Zealand ground.
So pluck that fond wish from your heart,
That brought you out from home;
You'll never own a sod of land
In all the time to come.

I met with Bryce and Ballance, and
They took me by the hand,
Says they 'Poor Man;' why don't you get
A little bit of land.
Och thin, says I, 'tis what I want,
But what's the chance for me,
When all the many acre'd sharks
Have said it shall not be.

I came out here because they said,
An honest man was bound,
If he'd work hard and sober keep,
To get a bit of ground.
If Parliament's returned by Sharks,
Without a hope I stand,
Say's they poor man there's more as thinks
That you should have your land.

And though the acred lordings here
Say Fox return you must,
If we but to ourselves are true,
We in ourselves may trust.

So vote for Bryce and Ballance, boys,
Who won't grind down the poor,
You all know well how much you'll get
From Watt and Peat and Moore.[16]

Though Bryce's candidature confused the contest to a certain extent, there can be no doubt that Ballance promoted himself primarily as a liberal who saw politics as a struggle for the control of land and was recognised by electors as such.

The result of the election was close. In a high turnout (80.5 percent compared to the national average of 66.5 percent) Ballance was 13 votes behind Bryce, who headed the poll:

	Ballance	Bryce	Fox
Wanganui	424	426	328
Waverley	72	81	116
Upokangaro	24	24	14
Maxwell	22	24	28
Marangai	5	5	15
	547	560	501[17]

Not surprisingly Ballance's strongest support came from the town. In the main country settlement, Waverley, he polled fewer votes than both Fox (who lived there) and Bryce. In such a close contest the Catholic vote, though small, may have been critical to Ballance and Bryce.

The result of the election nationally put the Government and Opposition on nearly equal terms. The *Herald* noted that although nearly everyone elected claimed to be a liberal, in reality it was possible to distinguish between conservatives and liberals. Parties were becoming more clearly defined, and 'instead of such issues as Provincialism, Separation, and Federation, we have great principles affecting the whole people awaiting decision. This is surely a great gain . . . It must not be supposed that parties have been perfectly organised . . . but a great stride has been made.'[18]

There was indeed to be some further realignment. Shortly after Parliament assembled Grey was defeated in a no-confidence motion by two votes. The vote would have been tied had not Vincent Pyke of Dunstan in Otago decided at the eleventh hour to side with the Opposition. John Hall, who had replaced Fox as leader, then formed a ministry. Meanwhile Grey stood down as leader of the liberals in favour of Macandrew. However, soon afterwards Pyke and Downie Stewart, another Otago member, announced that they would no longer support Hall, and only the desertion of four members of Grey's Auckland party (promised a fairer share of public works expenditure for the city) saved the new Government.[19]

Ballance played a central role in these manoeuvrings, and at the same time made a half-hearted bid for the leadership of the liberals. Before the election there had been some talk of him as a possible leader. The *Evening Star* (surprisingly for an Auckland paper) saw him as a dark horse who aspired to office and was believed capable of holding the party together.[20] In the complicated events that led to Hall's securing of a majority, what seems to have happened was as follows. Ballance and Pyke agreed that the latter would vote against Grey, thus defeating the Government, but then refuse to support Hall. This would leave the way open for the formation of a ministry including Ballance, Pyke and Macandrew. Such tactics would involve little political embarrassment for Pyke (never a firm Greyite) and none for Ballance, who could prove his loyalty and consistency publicly by voting with Grey. Pyke could argue that he simply wished to see greater Otago representation in the Government (which was true as far as it went) while Ballance would accomplish his aim of replacing Grey with an alternative liberal administration.

On the eve of the vote of no-confidence it seemed that Grey was safe: 'Mr Pyke's vote has been secured by the Government. The Opposition had a deputation to the number of twenty prepared to meet Mr Pyke on arrival, with a carriage and pair, but Mr Ballance got hold of him, and marched him off in triumph, to the intense disgust of Messrs McLean and Hall.'[21] Not until Pyke voted against Grey was it at all apparent what had been going on behind the scenes. When the new opposition caucus met following the defeat there were 43 members, yet only 42 had supported Grey. The addition was Pyke. Ballance toyed with the idea of putting himself forward as leader but Reader Wood proposed Macandrew, arguing that only he could unite the party. Macandrew was certainly more acceptable to the Greyite faction than Ballance and he was elected unopposed.[22] Ballance did not press the matter probably because he was reluctant to split the party further and in any case expected Stout to return soon to Parliament and assume the leadership.

Events were going according to the Ballance/Pyke plan and it looked as if a ministry led by Macandrew would be formed. Things went drastically wrong, however, when the four 'Auckland Rats' (including Wood!) changed sides. It was not simply a case of provincial interests reasserting themselves. In fact the four were all from the right wing of Grey's Auckland coalition (all had business interests in that city) and their defection if anything clarified the liberal/conservative alignment.[23] The political reality was that there was inadequate support for an undiluted liberal government. A Grey coalition involving conservative Auckland members was ruled out as past experience had alienated other liberals, and the four Aucklanders knew it. The *Evening Post* persistently suggested a Hall/Ballance/Macandrew combination,[24] but this too was never a possibility. Ballance himself moved a resolution pledging the liberal caucus against an alliance such as this and in the event, of course, Hall did not need it.[25]

With Hall secure, the Opposition (which had held together as long as there was the prospect of power) fell apart. Grey went his own way, speeding the disintegration. Perhaps suffering some reaction from two years of hard work and intense activity, Ballance fell ill for a short time and missed the debate on a no-confidence motion moved by Macandrew. Without the ex-Treasurer to criticise the Government's financial proposals the whole affair was a damp squib.

The Hall Government was a conservative one set on retrenchment as a means of coping with the economic depression that had hit the country. It did adopt some liberal measures of electoral reform, but largely because there was a consensus of opinion in the country and Parliament in favour of them, and because in passing them the Government could neutralise the Opposition still further. There were advantages to be gained in not resisting the popular mood, and in any case retrenchment and the replacement of the land tax by a property tax were more important. From the Opposition benches Ballance did what he could to promote liberal policy — for example, proposing a radical amendment to the Electors Bill and speaking out against a return to the property tax.

The Qualification of Electors Bill gave the vote to all male residents of twelve months, reduced the freehold requirement to £25 and abolished the ratepayers' franchise, but retained the property vote.[26] In committee Ballance managed to put through a revolutionary amendment substituting the word 'person' for 'man' in the freehold qualification, thus in one fell swoop introducing a female franchise. He attempted to do the same with the residential qualification, though this time the amendment failed.[27] In Wanganui the *Chronicle* complained that the time for discussion on the women's franchise was singularly ill chosen. In fact the choice of time and place may well have been deliberate, in that Ballance saw the chance of slipping the measure in through the back door at the committee stage, concealed by the bill's major policy changes. More important, the *Chronicle* voiced the oft-heard cry that the franchise was not sought by New Zealand women. Though the weaker sex were as able as men to take part in political discussions, few would vote if given the opportunity.[28]

Unfortunately for Ballance there were complications. It was soon clear that many conservative members had supported the franchise for women freeholders solely on the grounds of the rights of property. And as a number of his liberal colleagues pointed out, there could well be serious electoral disadvantage in having only property-owning women voting. It should preferably be all or nothing. Ballance would have accepted this limited franchise as a step in the right direction, but he was persuaded by others to withdraw the amendment. In 1890, looking back on these events, he said he was glad he had taken the advice.[29]

The financial policy of the Colonial Treasurer, Harry Atkinson, aimed at tackling the depression through administrative retrenchment, stopping subsidies to local bodies and imposing a property tax. He separated the land account from consolidated revenue in the hope of removing the temptation to make up for lost income by selling land. Ballance, not Macandrew, replied to Atkinson's speech moving the Property Assessment Bill. It was a strong condemnation of the Government's financial proposals as a whole and the high point of what was otherwise a dry debate.[30] He claimed that the principle of the land tax had been accepted in the country because it bore lightly on the 'industrial' part of the community and heavily on the speculators. The property tax on the other hand was unjust in its incidence, since small farmers would pay more under it than under a land tax, even if the land tax were doubled, while the professional class would escape scot-free. If there were to be additional taxation to that on land, it should be on incomes. An income tax, after all, was a tax 'simply on the capacity of the individual to pay it'.[31]

The 1879 session ended just before Christmas. Ballance returned to Wanganui for the holiday but early in the new year was busy back at work. Settling the land was again uppermost in his mind and he produced and had printed at the *Herald* a 'Handbook of the Law Relating to Crown Land in New Zealand'. In the introduction he said that existing law gave the Government sufficient powers to settle the land, but that they were not being used. The key legislation was contained in the 1877 Land Act, which established the system of selling land on deferred payment. Eager to see the revenue obtained from land sales contribute to the development of that land, Ballance had successfully amended the act (section 59) so that one third of the price paid was handed over to local authorities to be expended on new or improved road access to the land. Two years later an Amendment Act introduced provisions for Special and Village Settlements. Under the Special Settlement scheme land was set aside for groups of prospective farmers and sold at an upset price of £1 per acre, with conditions of occupation and improvement attached.[32] It was particularly appealing to the small farm associations that were being formed all over the North Island. Land set aside for village settlements could be sold on deferred payment. Occupants would live on an acre of village land costing £5, and cultivate what was termed a 'small farm allotment' not to exceed 50 acres and sold at £1 per acre.[33] The intention of village settlements was to get working-class men and their families out of the towns and onto the land. Macandrew as the Minister of Lands under Grey had drawn up this act, but similar schemes had earlier been introduced on a small scale by William Rolleston in Canterbury.

Although in his 'Handbook' Ballance thought existing legislation adequate, he did make the sole complaint that the Legislative Council had amended the deferred payment clauses of the 1877 Act to the effect that when there was more than one applicant for a block of land it was to be sold by auction. Ballance had himself inserted the original clause establishing a ballot and it was an important point. Auctions raised the price of land, frequently beyond the reach of working-class settlers, and encouraged speculation.

On a practical level Ballance urged on the efforts of the Wanganui Small Farm Association (which he had helped revive in mid 1879[34]) to obtain land, and chaired a number of its meetings in the first months of 1880.[35] Only when the association came up against an unresponsive Government (in the same way as the 1876 association had done) did he fully appreciate the failings of current legislation. Their appeal to the Government to set aside a block of land under the Special Settlement regulations met with vacillation and then outright refusal. Rolleston, the Minister of Lands, argued that the provisions were aimed at attracting foreign capital and that small farm associations must look to the deferred payment system to obtain land.[36] The Government was not going to form any special settlement in the whole district. Ballance later alleged that the Government had no bona fide intention of using the special settlement clauses of the act. 'These clauses were passed for the benefit of foreign capital, and not for the purpose of securing the investment of the capital which was floating about the country in the possession of the working-classes.'[37]

In a letter to the Wanganui Association Rolleston said that only English capitalists could comply with the conditions laid down for special settlements and cited the Katikati special settlement as an example. This Bay of Plenty town had been established in 1875, with the co-operation of the New Zealand Government, by a bankrupt Ulster linen manufacturer, George Vesey Stewart. The first settlers were all Protestant and included many Orangemen. Ballance admitted that such a scheme might prove beneficial to the colony but he was suspicious, especially when Vesey Stewart called a meeting in the district to persuade its member to vote with the Government. Ballance was probably concerned that Stewart's immigrants were not of the type he wished to see settled in the colony. The second batch that arrived in 1878, for example, included members of the Ulster aristocracy and a number of army officers. Certainly they had capital (believed to be as much as £100,000), but few were experienced farmers. The scheme bore a greater resemblance to the ideals of the Wakefield settlements than to the government-sponsored immigration of the early 1870s. Ballance was also suspicious of Stewart's motives. Stewart had misrepresented the quality of the land to the prospective emigrants in Ireland and stood to make something like £6000 and 1400 hectares of land out of the deal. Yet many would argue that this was fair reward for a good deal of effort.[38] As he had shown in the case of the Manchester

Corporation, Ballance had at times an unreasonable cynicism of private immigration-land settlement schemes.

While the Wanganui association was getting nowhere, economic conditions in the town and throughout the country worsened. Initially Ballance thought that though the depression was 'unprecedented' it was at the same time temporary. He had no solutions to offer beyond halting immigration, removing duties on raw materials used by New Zealand manufacturers, and generally furthering land settlement.[39] Wool and wheat prices continued to fall and did not begin to pick up until the end of the decade. Falling imports reflected reduced purchasing power and lower wages. Heavily mortgaged landowners were unable to meet their commitments. Bankruptcies rose and the marriage rate dropped.[40] Around Wanganui 'swaggers by the hundred roamed the crude coach roads, searching vainly for work'. Food became dearer and soup kitchens were set up; in desperation many people migrated to Australia.[41]

The depression hit the *Herald* in two ways. Circulation declined and advertising became more difficult to attract and sustain, though these effects took some time to be felt. In June 1880 the *Herald* announced that it had the largest circulation in the district. To maintain this position Ballance decided to make some changes. The *Evening Herald*, renamed the *Wanganui Herald* in 1876, had increased in size at regular intervals.[42] Now the *Weekly Herald* was to become the new enlarged *Yeoman*. The paper's politics would remain the same:

> Liberal land laws liberally administered has been our battle cry in the past, and so it will remain until the settlement of the country shows us that the end has been achieved. . . We have never lacked the courage of our opinions, and it is not our intention to learn timidity. Our interests are bound up with the advancement and prosperity of Wanganui, and for that end we shall strive earnestly and zealously.[43]

The first issue of the *Yeoman* appeared on Saturday 31 July 1880. It aimed, as the *Weekly Herald* had done, to reach the country districts not serviced by the daily *Herald*. By increasing the size of the paper Ballance was able to include more material specifically tailored to the needs of farmers, as well as providing them with a fuller summary of the week's news. Every month a 'Farmers' Supplement' appeared, giving information on developments in agricultural science. It was essential, said the *Yeoman*, that farmers kept up with the latest improvements. There were also regular columns on horticulture and gardening, of interest to townspeople as well as country folk. The use of the name *Yeoman* was of course highly significant. It reflected Ballance's ideal of the nature of country settlement: small independent farmers cultivating land to the maximum extent, leading productive, healthy lives far from the cramped conditions of the towns. Political propaganda was an integral part of the paper, for policies had to be changed if this ideal were to reach fruition. More than this, both the weekly and daily papers continued to promote Ballance's political career. Some later editors, and James Duigan (who became editor in 1891) was one of them,[44] thought that Ballance went too far in this and that too close an association between paper and politician was damaging to the paper's interests. The argument was not just that equity demanded a less partisan approach, but also that an obviously party political paper deterred many potential subscribers and advertisers.

The *Yeoman* was to publish many interesting political articles that because of their length would have been difficult to fit into the daily *Herald*. W. L. Rees, a liberal Auckland politician, wrote a series on 'New Zealand Politics and Politicians' less than two months after the paper first appeared. It was a thinly veiled attack on the Government.[45] Later the *Yeoman* reprinted a lecture given by Stout, at Napier, on 'True Democracy'.[46] A third example, in early 1884, was a series on the 'Maori Wars', written by a Maori and translated from Maori into English for the *Yeoman*.[47]

The 1880 session was a frustrating one for Ballance. Atkinson's budget attempted to tackle the depression through the conventional means of retrenchment and balancing the books. He suggested little else and the Government simply kept its fingers crossed in the hope that the economy would soon pick up. The Opposition, however, was in no state to take advantage of this obvious inactivity in the face of rising unemployment and falling incomes. Grey's presence made it impossible for Macandrew to form a united party and no clear alternative to the ministry's policy emerged. A no-confidence motion failed by 30 votes to 45. Ballance's speech in the debate was rambling and unimpressive and dwelt largely on a defence of his own performance as Colonial Treasurer. He criticised individual items in Atkinson's Financial Statement but there was no condemnation of the general direction in which the Treasurer was moving. Unconvincingly, Ballance attempted to make a virtue of the Opposition's disunity by saying that different shades of opinion were inherent in a healthy liberal party.[48]

Over the following months the depression deepened and the political situation remained inert. In May 1881 Ballance wrote a gloomy letter to Stout criticising Macandrew's leadership and stressing the need for a clear liberal programme to 'lift the party from the dead'. Ballance complained that Macandrew, by putting forward a policy including the issue of paper money to pay for public works and Bible in schools, and by not specifying what should replace the property tax introduced by Hall, was failing to represent the opinions of his party. Yet Ballance seemed reluctant to take the lead himself. His pre-sessional speech on 11 May had been vague and indecisive.[49] He now told Stout that he had not put forward a liberal platform because doing so 'would have been interpreted in many quarters as an ambitious effort to become a leader, a position I would shrink from even if I thought I had the qualities, in which I know myself utterly deficient. Grey will advance as far as anyone, but he cannot organise his opinions. This work you will probably be called on by the party to perform, the great majority of which is anxiously expecting to see you in the next Parliament.'[50]

Ballance genuinely felt that Stout would make a better leader than himself. It was true that Stout was the favoured choice of the non-Greyite liberals and Ballance may have been simply acknowledging this fact and declaring his personal loyalty. Yet this could have been done without Ballance confessing the low opinion he held of his own leadership potential. Perhaps it was just false modesty. Nevertheless Ballance was an ambitious man and this rather feeble deference to Stout remains a little surprising. The explanation seems to be that Ballance regarded Stout as his intellectual superior and mentor, and looked to him for advice and sometimes approval. Stout was something of an academic, and Ballance may have envied him this and his legal profession. Their special, dependent relationship inevitably found Ballance underestimating his own qualities when contrasted with those of his master. There is no direct evidence that Ballance had in general some kind of intellectual inferiority complex, though his limited formal education and eagerness to adorn his speeches with quotations from leading writers and philosophers give the proposition a degree of circumstantial support.

Although willing in principle to play second fiddle to Stout, until Stout re-entered Parliament Ballance was not slow to take the initiative on the opposition benches. From the start of the new session in June he conveyed the distinct impression that he was speaking on behalf of others as well as himself.[51] When Atkinson sat down at the end of his budget speech it was Ballance who rose to make the reply.[52] It was a dreary session, however, with little for Ballance to get his teeth into. An election was expected soon and many members looked forward to it in the hope that it would resolve the confused and unsatisfactory political situation. The only measure of any significance was the Representation Bill, and it aroused minimal opposition. Few could deny that boundaries needed to be redrawn so that representation was based more squarely on population and Ballance supported the bill as a move in the right direction. Ideally he wished Maori to be included on the same basis as Europeans and hoped ultimately they would agree to give up their special representation. If they did, he believed that there would be more Maori members in the House. In general Ballance thought that the bill did not go far enough, and he was unhappy that country districts would remain over-represented. He argued that if the political representation of urban areas were increased the interests of the country would not suffer, since both had a commitment to maximising settlement. At the moment, he complained, the opposite was occurring.

Property was being consolidated, large estates formed, and increased political power to large landowners would inevitably follow. Redistribution would assist what should be the first duty of Government, 'the cutting-up of the land, the dispersion of property, and the location of people upon the land'.[53]

Parliament was prorogued in late September and Ballance returned to Wanganui to begin campaigning for the December election. The political platform he stood on was more ambiguous and, in one important respect, less radical than it had been two years earlier. With the country in recession, Ballance advocated caution and conservatism. He did not propose the reintroduction of the land tax, arguing that changes in the type of taxation were damaging to the country. Instead the property tax should be amended to include the 'best features' of the land tax; improvements, agricultural implements and machinery should be exempted, and a progressive tax on large holdings added. Though this amounted to the same thing, there was in his speeches noticeably less emphasis on taxation as a means of promoting land settlement and more on revenue considerations. Like Atkinson, avoiding deficits as the depression hit the Government's income was Ballance's main concern. Ballance also found himself in an awkward position over possible alternatives to the Hall Ministry. He was unhappy with Macandrew, and Grey, too, was ruled out along with Stout, who was not standing at the election. Pressed by Carson, editor of the *Chronicle*, Ballance said that he regarded J. D. Ormond (a large landowner from Hawke's Bay who had become leader of yet another 'middle' party in the House) as a liberal 'in most matters', and that he would be prepared to join him in a ministry. Ormond was a strange bedfellow, but given that Ballance could hardly suggest his own name (and assuming he regarded himself as preferable to Ormond) this was all he could answer. Ballance did, however, break new ground in one important area. Prompted by the depression and rising unemployment, he announced that he had changed his mind on the question of free trade. It was 'most suitable for England' he said, but not for a young country. Local industries ought to be protected 'by every means in our power whether it means by import duties . . . or bonuses or taxation of raw materials'.[54]

This move to protection was a highly significant development in Ballance's political philosophy, but in the short term it made the general charge of inconsistency appear well founded. The *Wanganui Chronicle* talked a lot about 'sham liberals'[55] and pointed out that Ballance had 'recanted' from free trade to protection, and from a land tax to a property tax. He had called the 'acred' Ormond a liberal; in fact, he had 'patted the monied interest on the back'.[56] At the same time Carson somewhat inconsistently wrote that Ballance would 'sweep the large farmer off the face of the earth' and that his views on the land question were 'of such a character that no man owning an acre of land in freehold . . . could feel himself safe if the

Wanganui apostle of Socialism had the power of settling the affairs of the nation according to his will'.[57] Ironically Ballance was being labelled a socialist at a time when he least deserved it.

Standing against Ballance was James Bamber, a dull ex-mayor and owner of a blacksmith's shop in the town. Bamber had little hope of beating Ballance and in mid-November wisely withdrew from the contest without having uttered a single word, though not before the *Yeoman* had had its fun. On 12 November it printed a satirical account of an imaginary Bamber speech, reported by a 'clairvoyant correspondent'. It concluded: 'An elector wanted to know Mr Bamber's views with reference to the inscription of New Zealand Stock? Mr Bamber replied that he believed all stock ought to be branded and ear-marked. (Great applause!)' It looked as if Ballance was to be returned unopposed until his old rival, W. H. Watt, declared his candidature hours before nominations closed. It would be a disgrace to Wanganui, said Watt, if Ballance were to have a walk-over.[58]

Though Watt was mayor of the town and well-known, his entering the contest at such a late stage must have encouraged Ballance's expectations of an easy victory. Recent boundary changes also operated in Ballance's favour. The Wanganui constituency was reduced in size with many country electors who would be less sympathetic to his liberal programme being transferred to a new Waitotara electorate. 'It must be clear,' Ballance stressed in opening one of his campaign speeches, that he was 'more identified with the town of Wanganui than with the country districts.'[59]

What made Watt a much more formidable opponent than he would otherwise have been was the support given him by Bryce. The rift between Ballance and Bryce had become permanent when the latter became Native Minister in the Hall Government. The ending of a political alliance of ten years brought charges of inconsistency and treachery from supporters of both men. The *Herald* accused Bryce of dishonesty in joining Hall after campaigning on a liberal ticket.[60] In fact Bryce had never declared himself a liberal during the 1879 campaign. The December 1881 election came in the wake of Bryce's occupation of the Maori settlement at Parihaka, the arrest of the leader Te Whiti and subsequent breaking of Maori resistance to further European settlement on the west coast. It was a considerable political success to the Government in general and to Bryce, who was elected unopposed for Waitotara, in particular. During the campaign Ballance said that the trouble on the west coast was the result of a history of government mismanagement, inconsistency and weakness. Yet at the same time he fully supported Bryce's decisive action of 5 November, and had to be content with the minor criticism that things should not have been allowed to drift for so long.

Despite this approval there were complaints that Ballance was soft on Te Whiti.[61] Ballance was known to be fairly sympathetic to the plight of the Maori and he had no doubt soft-pedalled his objections to Bryce's policy largely because of its widespread popularity. Part way through the campaign one of Ballance's supporters, John Duthie, defected to Watt, saying that Ballance was 'ungenerous and unpatriotic' in his attitude to Bryce's handling of 'native' affairs.[62] Watt realised the possibilities of attracting reflected glory from Bryce's success.[63] Ballance's supporters were well aware of the danger and managed to prevent Bryce from speaking at a Watt election meeting, but the damage was done. They were throttling the freedom of speech, said the *Chronicle*.[64]

Early on in the campaign rumours circulated in Wanganui of Ballance's 'indifference to his election'. He was certainly pessimistic about the political scenario, with the Opposition split and unlikely to defeat the Government, and Stout unwilling to re-enter Parliament. Perhaps he felt he should be spending more time at the *Herald* office, now that money was getting tight. Was it also that he was getting 'too big for his boots', as some people were saying,[65] and took his election for granted? In any case his lack of enthusiasm had become all too obvious, so much so that he found it necessary to publish a denial in the *Herald*. 'We beg to give the rumour the most unqualified contradiction. Whatever Mr Ballance's private feelings may be, his duty to his friends . . . is to stand to his guns, and he will take all proper means to inform the electors of his opinions.'[66]

The election was held on 9 December. Ballance was defeated by just four votes, polling 393 to Watt's 397. There was only one polling booth.[67] It was later reported that seven of Ballance's supporters had arrived too late to vote after the carriage conveying them into town broke down.[68] The *Chronicle* attributed Ballance's defeat to the 'ill-advised action of his supporters in connection with Bryce at Watt's meeting'.[69] In Wellington the *Post* said that defeat was 'not quite unexpected', except perhaps by Ballance himself.[70] The *Taranaki Herald*, whilst recognising Ballance's ability, pointed critically to his 'plastic political creed'.[71] Stout rushed off a telegram saying he was 'intensely vexed and disgusted at the result'.[72]

Publicly Ballance said that his defeat was merely that of a wing of the Liberal Party, and put it down to Watt's superior organisation.[73] He was in fact one of a number of prominent politicians to lose their seats: Fox, Saunders, De Latour, Gisborne, Reader Wood and Ormond all failed to get re-elected. Privately Ballance was taken aback. He had tended to take success for granted, and having committed himself to the contest was far from pleased at coming out the loser.

During the campaigning there had been allegations of bribery and intimidation of voters. Hoping to overturn the close result Ballance got Willis (his election agent) to bring charges against John Anderson, a cabinet-maker and a leading Watt supporter, under the Corrupt Practices Act. Stout appeared for the petitioners, arguing that there had been two specific acts of bribery and undue influence involving the promise of employment and money, as well as other general cases. The hearing lasted a few days, the evidence closely followed by the *Herald*. At its conclusion the Chief Justice found against Willis and Ballance, mainly on the grounds that the threats were vague and that there was no evidence of them being carried out.[74] The *Herald* disagreed, quoting the *Wairarapa Standard*'s view that the judge must have been 'most obtuse' not to have recognised that intimidation had taken place.[75] So Watt went to Wellington as Member for Wanganui. For Ballance defeat was not as serious as he might at first have imagined. The 'Continuous Ministry' remained in office, led first by Whitaker and subsequently by Atkinson. There was little Ballance could have done.

Philosophy for improvement: state help and self-help

I N 1882 BALLANCE WAS FORCED to re-organise his business as the effects of depression began to be felt. In May his partnership with John Notman was dissolved when Notman decided to set up on his own as a general commission and insurance agent.[1] Ballance either could not find or did not want a new partner, for in September he formed the *Herald* and *Yeoman* papers into a joint stock company. In any case this gave him the security of limited liability. Editorial control, he said, would remain in his hands.[2] Ballance managed to sell just 64 of the 750 shares (each worth £10), buying the remaining 686 himself. The minor shareholders included a reporter and compositor working on the paper, a labourer, storekeepers, solicitors, a commission agent, an accountant, a woman teacher and a 'lady'.[3] There were seven directors. Shareholders had a vote for every share up to ten, and an additional vote for every 30 shares thereafter to a maximum of 15 votes.[4]

Ballance was hard pushed to find the funds to buy the unsold shares. His wealthy father-in-law, David Anderson, had lent him £1700 the previous year and a month before the launch of the company came up with a further £310.[5] In mid-September, when the difficulty of disposing of *Herald* shares became all too obvious, Ballance approached Anderson for yet another loan, this time to be met with a polite decline.[6] The *Yeoman* was meanwhile claiming that its circulation had trebled in three months and that it had now the largest readership of a weekly outside Auckland.[7] However, the general trend was not nearly so good. After peaking in 1881, newspaper deliveries in the Wanganui area began to decline and continued to fall for a number of years.[8] As the economy slumped further and his papers began losing money,[9] Ballance found it an uphill struggle to repay his father-in-law. Anderson viewed the transactions on a purely business basis (Ballance paid ten percent and eight percent respectively on the loans) and was annoyed by Ballance's defaulting.[10] The old man may have been in his seventy-sixth year but he had no intention of letting things slip. He had recently sued a debtor for the grand sum of 2/6d and taken to court a butcher who unwisely blocked Nairn Street with his cart. Still, family was family and in 1884 Anderson lent Ballance a further £1500. From September 1884 Ballance received a salary as Minister of Lands and Native Minister and after three years in government had cleared all of these debts. He was also able to raise some money by gradually selling off some of his shares. They were bought almost entirely by people closely associated with the *Herald*: employees, Anderson relatives, Ballance's nephew Robert McKnight and Ellen Ballance (who inherited some money on the death of her father in 1889).[11]

Competition between the *Herald* and the *Chronicle* intensified as time wore on. Each company remained under the control of a closely knit group of prominent Wanganui citizens. The papers established core, often fiercely loyal, readerships — the one liberal and the other conservative — though the *Herald*'s political bias weakened following Ballance's death. Conflict in the 1880s was political rather than financial. The depression affected both papers, and as circulation fell there was little chance of successfully poaching each other's readership. This would have been less true had the papers been less partisan and both morning or evening papers (thus more obviously alternatives). The only solution to falling revenue, a merging of the companies, was not practicable. So they suffered together.

The rivalry between the papers was on occasion more friendly than it appeared to be on the surface. A story told in Wanganui about Ballance and Gilbert Carson, the *Chronicle*'s editor, shows that they had a certain understanding. The two men had been engaged in one of their frequent and long editorial wars 'when Ballance was called to Wellington on parliamentary duties. He went down to the office of Carson and explained the position, requesting a truce until such time as he returned. "No," came the reply from Carson, "there will be no truce. You may go to Wellington and I'll write both articles." And write both articles he did — until Ballance was back to occupy the *Herald*'s editorial chair again. He castigated the Herald's leader writer in the columns of the *Chronicle* and in the evening he replied to himself, denouncing the vitriolic pen of the *Chronicle*'s leader writer and deploring his sad lack of logic.'[12]

Aside from putting more time into his business, Ballance took the opportunity of an enforced retirement from politics to do some serious writing. During 1882 he wrote a series of articles outlining his views on land policy. Robert Stout may have prompted him, for the articles were published in the Dunedin *Echo*, which Stout edited. Five years later they were reprinted with an introduction as a pamphlet entitled *A National Land Policy Based on the Principles of State Ownership*.

It is not surprising that Ballance's first (and only) publication outside the *Herald* was on land ownership. He had consistently regarded the land question as the most important political issue of the day. In the articles Ballance put forward the case for land nationalisation, meaning the desirability of a programme of compulsory repurchasing of private land by the state. It went far beyond the land tax he had initially favoured, for it involved the state assuming ownership of the land for posterity. A combination of intellectual and political developments in and beyond New Zealand influenced Ballance in this change. His most practical concern was that the state's ability to promote new settlement was severely curtailed by the simple fact of the decreasing amount of suitable crown land.

Land reform became a key issue in England in the late 1870s and early 1880s, largely because of the onset of an agricultural depression which saw Britain begin importing food from the New World. Ireland was worst hit, and the plight of its peasantry led to political agitation that culminated in the formation of the Irish National Land League and a 'land war'. The league was supported by many English liberals and demanded what was known as the 'Three Fs': fair rent, fixity of tenure, and the free sale of the tenant's interest in land. Irish land reform was a major concern of the Gladstone Liberal Ministry that came to power in 1880.[13]

Like many other radicals of his time, Ballance found intellectual support for his views on land reform in the writings of John Stuart Mill. Mill had played a leading role in the formation of the Land Tenure Reform Association in England in 1870.[14] The association aimed to break up the remnants of the feudal system through the abolition of the law of primogeniture, the state acquisition and leasing of land, the encouragement of agricultural co-operatives, and the taxation of the future 'unearned increase of the rent of land'. The notion of the 'unearned increment' was central to advocates of land reform, especially to those like Mill who stopped short of complete nationalisation. It was the 'rent' which the landlord received, not from the application of labour to land but from the land's fertility and its value arising from the development of the surrounding community. Ballance's 1878 land tax attempted to recover, on behalf of the community, part of this rent. During the debate on the tax Ballance made it clear that he did not agree with Mill that the whole of the unearned increment should be appropriated. They may have that right, 'but it would not be wise on our part to claim it, for the reason that it would discourage industry, and would keep people from investing money in that particular class of property'.[15]

However, by 1882 Ballance had moved well beyond this cautious approach. In doing so he was strongly influenced by the immensely popular American 'single taxer' Henry George, whose *Progress and Poverty* was published in New York in 1879. Drawing on his Californian experience, George noted how speculation raised the price of land, which in turn led to its monopoly and under-utilisation. George agreed with Mill that the community had a right to this unearned increment, indeed he went further, saying that the whole of the rent should be confiscated. If this were done speculation would cease and land become more freely available. People would then move onto the land, cultivating it more intensively and at the same time creating a labour shortage in the towns. Industrial wages would rise as a result. Land, in other words, was the key to general prosperity.

For George the solution to depression was simple: to make land common property by confiscating rent through taxation.[16] The advantages were clear. The land tax would be the only tax, therefore removing burdens from other sectors and stimulating production through incentive. The tax avoided nationalisation (and so any 'shock to present customs and habits') and an extension of state intervention. In fact the whole taxation system was greatly simplified. The tax was on value and not on production, and it would increase agricultural productivity through destroying speculative rent. Finally it was equitable, since a tax on rent was one on the development of the whole community: the value of land would grow and be taxed as the community grew.[17]

George's writings powerfully identified a single issue and solution that rang true to the experience of the land hungry of the New World. It was a solution essentially preventative, raising the land question to the forefront of politics (at the expense of all else) in an effort to protect the fundamental capitalist structure from the threat of radical doctrines. For such radical ideas, 'which bring great masses of men, the repositories of ultimate political power, under the leadership of charlatans and demagogues, are fraught with danger'.[18]

Ballance never accepted George's theory in total. He did not believe in a single tax alone and went beyond George by proposing the ownership of land by the state. Yet George influenced Ballance in one particularly important respect. He provided theoretical support for something Ballance already suspected — that the solution to New Zealand's problems lay in the land. Land reform was to be the cure-all for a new country's ills. It was a complete theory of prosperity and stability. Opening up land to closer settlement would relieve pressure on towns and avoid the political consequences of poverty and unemployment.

In his pamphlet Ballance acknowledged his debt to Mill, George, and to Stout, who he said had 'long been the ablest and most eloquent advocate of the Nationalisation of the Land in the Colony'.[19] Ballance emphasised the differences between the concepts of land nationalisation and the unearned increment, noting how George sought to avoid the former through the state's taxing the whole of the latter. Ballance argued that nationalisation was necessary, though it would only come about gradually and in the short term should be encouraged by a progressive land tax aimed at breaking up large holdings. Philosophically he defended the appropriation of the unearned increment through a land tax on two grounds. First, because 'the state has the moral right to declare that no person *in future* shall be entitled to property which others, not the person, may earn'. Secondly, 'if a class enjoy exceptional privileges, it is called upon, under a system of abstract justice, to contribute more than do those classes which are not in the enjoyment of those privileges'.[20]

Land nationalisation was for Ballance a separate goal, requiring a different justification:

> In our opinion the principal reason in favour of the nationalization of the land is that the land of any country soon becomes a monopoly, the possessors being few in comparison with the population. The monopolists without effort grow rich. The landless, continually increasing their number, grow poor, and, having the franchise, live in a state of agitation, and attack the privileged . . . Let us suppose, now, that we have only national land. The phenomena presented in this case would be, on the one hand a body of cultivators paying rent to the state; and on the other a greater body living by wages, mainly in towns, deriving a beneficial interest from the rents, and remaining content in the knowledge that they participate in the prosperity of the agricultural tenant. On the ground of self-interest the more numerous class will cast their votes against the disturbance of a system which works in their favour.[21]

This was Ballance's ideal: a country of small farmers leasing from the state. Wealth came from the land and only its equitable distribution, through nationalisation, would enable the demands of urban wage labour to be met and guarantee political stability. 'The present system of monopoly is fast arraying the landless and landowning classes against each other. This . . . seems inevitable,' he wrote in the *Herald*. 'The ownership of land confers so many privileges not possessed by those who do not own land that it is impossible to secure that the unfavoured shall not cast an envious eye on the possession of what they cannot hope to obtain.'[22] Ballance feared the conflict that would result if the towns did not get their fair share of New Zealand's agricultural wealth. Only state ownership of land could ensure this.

Ballance was optimistic about achieving nationalisation. Though Mill had only attempted to modify the existing system, 'he had to deal with the customs and habit of thought of centuries, and, what he approached with no uncertain step in England, we may surely attempt with some confidence in a country barely fifty years subject to the rule of a civilised power'.[23] Nevertheless he acknowledged that there was 'in the minds of the masses a strong prejudice against leasing'[24] and believed that nationalisation would only come about gradually. Ballance was a skilful chess player and used the game as an analogy in explaining the Fabian tactics to be employed. The 'stronghold of individual property in land' would be attacked through progressive legislation:

> A chess player who understands something about the strategy of the game does not rush right away and concentrate all his forces on the quarters of the King, but operates on many parts of the field at the same time, hoping that the sum of his advantages will render his Majesty's position ultimately untenable. In actual warfare, great victories are won in the same manner.[25]

Cautiously Ballance suggested that the state should begin by purchasing estates above 4000 hectares in areas 'where the capacity to occupy the land was greatest'. Compensation based on the market value of the land would be given, financed through overseas borrowing and internal loans. He thought the country could raise the necessary money, though significantly a later *Yeoman* editorial suggested that nationalisation was limited by factors affecting the colony's credit. Ballance, finally, argued that compulsory expropriation was unnecessary for as long as sufficient land could be bought by the Government on the open market.[26]

In the year following the publication of the *Echo* articles Ballance came up with more definite and more radical proposals. He divided land in the colony into three. Land held by the Crown (4.5 million hectares approximately) was to be retained by the state and leased. The five million hectares of Maori land were to be either retained or leased by Maori themselves, or sold only to the state.[27] That left about six million hectares of land held by private individuals. Of that, four million hectares were in holdings of more than 2000 hectares. These were to be either broken up or repurchased by the state. Only the remaining two million hectares of smaller holdings would be left alone. 'The yeoman farmers . . . are the pillars on which the colony is resting, and it would be a dangerous policy to disturb them.'[28] Essentially therefore, nationalisation for Ballance meant the state holding onto land it possessed and moving to ensure that private holdings were no larger than 2000 hectares.

Ballance was only one of a growing number of advocates of land reform in New Zealand, though not all went as far as he did. There was Stout, of course, but also men like John McKenzie, who farmed part of a sub-divided Otago run and was first elected to Parliament in 1881.[29] In explaining the rising agitation for land reform the importance of overseas and philosophical influences can easily be overstated. Land reformers such as Ballance and McKenzie were not doctrinaire theorists. They sought to fit theory to political reality, rather than vice versa, and the intellectual support provided by George and Mill was utilised only as far as it was applicable to New Zealand conditions. Although land reform was seen as a solution to the depression, it was not adopted with such vigour in New Zealand simply because of its popularity elsewhere. Nor indeed does the sheer presence of the depression explain why that particular solution was sought. Unlike their English counterparts, liberals in New Zealand seized on land reform as the main remedy to depression simply because the colony, unlike England, was essentially an agricultural country. For the same reason land reform was also prominent amongst the demands of early New Zealand trade unionists. For example, two leading unionists, W. M. Bolt from Dunedin and H.W. Farnall of Auckland, were both followers of George.

Throughout 1883 the land nationalisation debate raged in the pages of the *Herald* and increasingly dominated politics in Wanganui. When in March Stout formed a Land Nationalisation Society in Dunedin, Ballance urged that branches be established throughout the colony and that Stout become president of a national association.[30] Momentum gathered over the following months. At a public meeting in October Ballance said that land nationalisation was 'fast becoming a burning question in the colony'. He believed that the towns would soon command the country and in doing so would tackle the political power of large landowners. The state should begin by purchasing estates over 8000 hectares, the money to be borrowed using the land as security.[31] Just before Christmas Ballance and others finally set up a land nationalisation society in the town.[32]

These views came in for much criticism. Some said that they were communistic. Ballance replied that nationalisation would involve greater individualism, not less, and that it was therefore the antithesis of communism.[33] The first number of an Auckland publication entitled *Land*, edited by the liberal politician F. J. Moss, complained that the issue would split the 'Democratic' party.[34] The *Herald*, however, argued that nationalisation would benefit 'all classes except the mere land dealer':

> We have little doubt that public opinion will declare itself in favour of the change, and consolidate the party that has made the nationalisation of the land the chief plank in its platform . . . The nationalisation of the land [will] redress gross inequalities. It will prevent those reaping where they have not sown, and return to the community the profits of its industry. There is no communism in this, but only justice. But even were it communism, it would be preferable to legalised robbery of the many for the sake of the few.[35]

In fact, it was unlikely that land nationalisation as envisaged by Ballance would receive widespread public support. Many people wanted land, or at least wanted to see more intensive settlement and the wealthy landowners dealt with, and would welcome the subdivision of large estates. Yet few thought that land made available in this way should be leased permanently by the state. The desire for freehold was just too strong. Equally, Ballance's proposal to prohibit the sale of crown land and (other than to the Government) of Maori land, ran up against the cultural tradition of private ownership. Ballance was strongly committed to leasing as an ideal. He welcomed the attempts of William Rolleston, the Minister of Lands, to introduce a new perpetual leasing tenure, and hoped that it would be the 'thin end of the wedge of nationalisation'.[36] The lease was to run for 30 years with the right of renewal for another 20, but the Legislative Council added a right of purchase, effectively turning it back into deferred payment.[37]

Ballance knew that the nationalisation of all land was politically a non-starter, even assuming the vast amounts of money required to buy it could be found. He was at pains to emphasise that small freeholders would not be touched and suggested 2000 hectares as the maximum private holding. (This figure may well have been appropriate for North Island beef and dairy farms, but was too low for a viable South Island high–country sheep run.) In his pamphlet he wrote that land nationalisation ought to be the central plank of the Liberal Party platform.[38] What he meant by land nationalisation was neatly summed up in a *Herald* editorial:

> We . . . think that no more of the public lands whatever should be sold, but disposed of on perpetual lease. With respect to private land, we hold that nationalisation should be applied to the lands of absentees and to large freehold areas but that the cultivating occupiers of land, within certain limits as to quantity, should be permitted to retain their freeholds. There is no reason for disturbing the freehold cultivator who wishes to retain that tenure. Nor would it be wise to interfere with a class forming the backbone of the colony.[39]

Cultivating the land more intensively was an obviously attractive solution to New Zealand's woes. This was especially true in Wanganui, whose economy continued to depend largely upon servicing country districts. Many saw moving onto the land as the best means of improving their own economic circumstances, but for the town as a whole the closer settlement of small farms made more sense than trying to establish major industry. For the working classes in particular the answer to depression was seen not so much in tackling unemployment and low wages through trade union organisation and industrialisation, as was beginning to be the case in the larger centres, but rather in removing obstacles to the opening up of the land. Others also saw that moving people onto the land would lessen those social evils well known in the old country to be associated with urbanisation.

Nevertheless, as Ballance wrote, 'a large population cannot be maintained by agriculture alone'.[40] In his election campaign of 1881 he had argued in favour of protecting local industries. Rising unemployment since then saw many more people coming round to the idea, and in mid-1884 Ballance helped form an Industrial Association in Wanganui. The association wanted local businesses protected and developed. In the longer term protection would enable the town to achieve some independence from the country:

> The old idea that the town depended on the country ought to be exploded. The truth is that they are mutually dependent. A large town population, if well sustained by local manufactures, is the best thing the surrounding farmers could desire, for it gives them a market at their own doors, and the highest price for their produce. On the other hand, where there are many producers in the country we have a corresponding population in the towns acting as distributors and manufacturers.[41]

The argument that protection favoured farmers as well as town-dwellers was difficult to sustain. Ballance denied that protection would mean higher prices for manufactured goods.[42] Yet, as farmers were aware, the small scale of production and the high cost of imported raw materials usually made New Zealand manufactures more expensive than imported equivalents.

Land nationalisation was just one of a number of progressive movements that emerged during this period of questioning and change. The mid-Victorian era witnessed a comprehensive ferment of ideas, a ferment in which Ballance was eagerly swept up. Most significant was his advocacy of free thought. Ballance's experience of sectarian feuding in Ireland had made him cynical of religion by the time he arrived in New Zealand. Some early *Herald* editorials reflected this. They criticised, for example, the Anglican Church's ownership of property, emphasising the alliance between clergy ('greedy land sharks') and landlords at the expense of the people. Ballance warned of the 'evils of ecclesiasticism' being introduced into the colony and pronounced religious debate to be backward looking and of little value: 'If the brain tissue that is wasted in unseemly wrangling over religious matters were devoted to progressive knowledge, the state of society would be improved, and man would attain a higher intellectual state in the world . . . There is a higher vocation for the mind than theological speculations.'[43]

By the early 1880s Ballance was a convinced 'freethinker'. That is, he became a secularist, believing in rational thought rather than religious dogma. English free thought had its roots in Thomas Paine's *Age of Reason*, in religious dissent and nonconformity, and later in utilitarianism and the radical liberalism of men like Mill. With the pace of scientific discovery greater than ever before, the arguments of Darwin and others brought science and religion into head-on collision. 'Beneath the surface of respectable religious conformity was a turmoil of doubt and uncertainty. Nearly all the representatives of Victorian thought, nearly all the intellectuals, had to struggle with the problem of belief.'[44]

Like others, Ballance's freethought views were an integral part of a broad philosophical package. The confidence he placed in science (he devoured books on astronomy and medicine) rather than religion as the way forward for man led him to emphasise the importance of education. The acquisition of knowledge meant self-reliance for the individual; dependency on one's own intellectual resources rather than on those of religion and the church. Ballance believed that education should be provided by the state, but he also recognised the role self-improvement through self-help had to play, and therefore the value of societies such as the Oddfellows. Free thought was also a culmination of his own life experiences — of religious scepticism drawn from the nonconformity of his mother, the observation of sectarian riots in Belfast and his self-education in Birmingham.

What brought free thought particularly to the fore in the 1880s was the refusal of a freethinking politician, Charles Bradlaugh, to take his oath on election to the British Parliament. Free thought then left the domain of philosophical speculation and entered the sphere of practical politics. The furore was temporary but it reached New Zealand, where Ballance, Stout and others led something of a free thought 'revival'.[45] Stout promoted his free thought views in the Echo, which was published again in early 1880 after an absence of seven years, and was shortly afterwards purchased by a Dunedin bookseller and freethinker called Braithwaite. Editorials reflected the fusion of free thought and radical liberalism. The Echo published articles by Ballance and others on land nationalisation. It also carried news of both free thought and land nationalisation societies which had been established in Dunedin.[46]

Ballance and Willis formed a Wanganui Freethought Association in mid-1883, and to promote their ideas soon brought out the first issue of the monthly Freethought Review. When the Echo ceased publication in November the Freethought Review became the sole mouthpiece of the colony's associations. Ballance wrote a number of editorials for the Review, as did Robert Pharazyn, an ex-Mayor of Wanganui and minor politician who was to be appointed to the Legislative Council in 1885. Edward Tregear, who later became the first Secretary of Labour, also contributed some material. The first number of the Review declared its aim as the 'happiness of mankind in this life':

> Whatever, in our opinion, may tend to hinder the advance towards this ideal, it will be our duty to assail. For superstition and prejudices, as we feel no reverence, we shall show no regard . . . Obedience to conscience is the highest moral injunction, transcending all creeds. Religious dogma covers over and obscures this sublime lesson, and people wonder that formalised religious instruction does not make them better than they are. The wonder rather is that it does not make them worse.[47]

The Review ran for two years. Aside from reports on the activities of freethought associations, it contained articles on free thought along with comment on the role of the church in New Zealand society.[48] Ballance's editorials sustained the link between free thought and liberalism that had been present in the *Echo*.[49] He attacked Christianity as having always been a persecuting religion and wrote that free thought aimed to undermine the 'enslaving theology' of the Roman Catholic and Protestant churches. Freethinkers had their own creed. It was a higher faith, 'the enthusiasm of humanity — which will give to the world a deeper morality and a loftier conception of duty. Theology can never supply the inspiration, as it cannot afford demonstration of the truth of its own dogmas, and, being based on rewards and punishments, it does not appeal to the highest sense of moral obligation.'[50]

Freethought associations were also formed in Christchurch, Auckland, Wellington, Nelson, Picton and Woodville. They survived at most a few years. In March 1884 Ballance was elected vice-president of the New Zealand Freethought Federal Union, with Stout as president. The Union met only this once. Aside from general sentiments on the promotion of free thought in New Zealand, there was little concrete it could focus on. Its programme included the abolition of religious oaths and it passed a resolution in sympathy with Charles Bradlaugh in his 'arduous struggle against bigotry and injustice'.[51] But that was it. A meeting of minds, but little else.

For Ballance free thought was a critical element in the development of individual liberty and much more than simply a belief in a secular society. Paradoxically his zeal for free thought bore resemblance to a religious crusade. In later years Ballance admitted this, according to a story told by John Macmillan Brown, Professor of English, History and Political Economy at Christchurch University at the time. In his memoirs Macmillan Brown tells of an evening spent with Ballance in Wanganui:

> Our host and I fell into a sharp discussion on his lyceum teaching. I held that he was contradicting his own tenets for he was turning his anti-religion into a religion. So warm was he in defence of his practice that when he came down next morning to see us off, he began the discussion again and carried it on till the train moved off. A few years after, when he was Premier, I met him again when going up the long staircase of the big matchbox [the large wooden building in which the Government Departments are housed] to see Mr Habens in the Education Department. We passed, saying 'good morning'; after a few steps, he turned and came back and said to me, 'Do you remember that discussion we had in Wanganui?' I replied, 'Yes' and he said, 'I have come round to your point of view.' We parted and saw each other no more for in the following year his fatal malady carried him off.[52]

Ballance's freethought convictions did little damage to his political career for they never became a major issue. Religion entered elections in Wanganui primarily in connection with education, and Ballance's advocacy of a state secular system was supported by many members of the Protestant churches. Opponents did of course try to make capital out of Ballance's irreligion, and pointed to his opposition to Bible-reading in schools as evidence of his antagonism to Christianity.[53] Ballance was sensitive to the charge and no doubt lost some (though minimal) support because of his freethought activity. He played down his views on religion and in general attempted to separate religious from political issues. The *Herald* reported meetings of the Wanganui Freethought Association, but editorials never promoted freethinking.[54] On the other hand, Ballance was not cynical enough to make appearances in church just for the sake of a few votes. When guests staying at the Ballance's wished to attend a Sunday service, they went without their host.[55] Above all, Ballance genuinely believed (and his Irish background reinforced this) that his religion, or lack of it, should be a 'matter for private contemplation'.[56]

This desire for the separation of religion and politics was reflected in Ballance's attitude to education. He had long argued that religion had no inherent part to play in education.[57] While a member of the Grey Government, Ballance had briefly held the education portfolio. The Education Department was a minor one, though it assumed greater importance with the passing of the 1877 Education Bill, which established a system of free primary education throughout the colony.[58] Ballance was concerned mainly with overseeing the implementation of the Act. Problems centred on financing the system, and especially on the provision of school buildings and the setting aside of land as education reserves.[59]

Ballance was committed to a free secular state education system as a matter of liberal principle. One of his first actions in the House of Representatives had been to urge the Government to introduce a bill for elementary education.[60] In 1881 he said that despite the difficulties that had arisen in connection with the 1877 act 'there must be education for the people'. Education was liberating as it 'gave the people a great power to work their own ends'. He believed that a free state system beyond primary level should be established irrespective of how much it cost.[61] These views were not inconsistent with Ballance's belief in self-education and his support for lyceums. Self-education was a necessity — especially for the working class — only because of the lack of state provision.

A combination of state provision and individual self-help was also characteristic of Ballance's opposition to prohibition. At various times during the late nineteenth century temperance reform became an important political issue. In the mid-1890s it would assume major significance. Ballance believed that the state should tackle intemperance not through prohibitive legislation but in the provision of the material wants and encouragement of the self-respect of the individual. He had presented a petition signed by nearly 1000 Wanganui citizens against the Local Option Bill of 1877 and successfully amended the bill (which in the event failed to pass) to provide compensation for publicans who would lose their licence.[62] Earlier Ballance had put forward his views on temperance in a paper read at a Christchurch meeting held in anticipation of the Local Option Bill coming before Parliament. His argument was that legislative prohibition would not effect reform and that temperance depended instead upon 'the education and prosperity of the people'. He objected that the Local Option Bill allowed no middle course — it was all or nothing; it attacked the rights of property of public house owners; reversed a basic principle of representative constitutional government by introducing a referendum; and, most important, simply would not work:

> The great hope of diminishing drunkenness must be by stimulating the intellect to find food for its own nourishment. Intemperance and ignorance go hand in hand, and emancipation can only take place when education finds pleasures more attractive than strong drink . . . The cause of intemperance must be discovered in the man, and not in the facilities with which drink is supplied.[63]

Ballance pointed out that public houses served a basic human need and criticised the paternalism and hypocrisy of temperance reformers:

> Nothing appears to my mind more unreasonable than the denunciation of the public house by those who have never done a single thing to establish any other source of enjoyment. Man is a social being, and there is in the public house, apart from any craving for alcohol, much that satisfied his social instincts . . . The system of paternal philanthropy which would reform the working classes by keeping them in leading strings, has never yet succeeded, and is sternly resented by their most intelligent leaders. The attempt to deprive a working man of his glass while the more opulent member of the club can enjoy his at pleasure, or lay in a supply, is a specimen of paternal regard which is fast losing its hold even on the most philanthropically inclined.[64]

This enlightened approach to attempts at social control was not particularly common among liberals. Many liberals (including Stout) and a growing number of women observed the serious consequences of over-indulgence for men and their families, and saw prohibition as a progressive rather than a reactionary step.

By early 1884 the Atkinson Ministry was running out of steam. It was tainted by the deepening depression and its chosen remedies of increased taxation and retrenchment alienated many of its supporters. Higher grain duties, for example, found little favour with Canterbury interests. However neither Montgomery (who had replaced Macandrew as opposition leader) nor Grey could form a viable alternative, and so both sides settled on dissolution and a fresh election. If Bryce's action over Parihaka dominated the 1881 election, it was Vogel's return to politics that formed the backdrop to the 1884 contest. The Agricultural Company was in dire financial straits, and the subsidiary Waimea Plains Railway Company was having difficulty collecting its rates. Vogel hoped to rescue the enterprise by returning to power. The new government would restore confidence, end the depression and raise land values. It would also purchase the ailing Railway Company.[65] Vogel knew that an alliance with Stout would greatly enhance the chances of making such a ministry possible. Stout had interests in the companies and connections with other South Island investors. He played ball, and months before the election they together planned their moves. Politically Stout could defend such ventures as 'patriotic efforts to develop that voluntary co-operation on which he believed depended "real growth and progress in the masses" '.[66]

Ballance may or may not have known in advance of this agreement between Vogel and Stout. His own involvement with the company was minimal and had no bearing at all on his decision to stand again for the Wanganui seat. Ballance was a career politician whereas Vogel and Stout were not. Only Ballance's defeat in 1881 prevented him from being in Parliament continuously from his first electoral victory in 1875 until his death in 1893. He was in politics to promote his political principles, not his business interests. For Ballance, what was important were the political consequences of Vogel's return, independent of the *raison d'être* of the agreement. Vogel was able to attract considerable support through his own personal prestige. The suggestion that he might end the depression through development policies associated with the prosperity of the 1870s was for many irresistible. Given this, Ballance may well have seen, early on, that the only way of defeating Atkinson in the country was through an alliance of liberals and Vogel. The Opposition was disorganised and disunited. Liberals comprised only a part of it, for there had been many independents elected in 1881.[67] It was a question of alternatives, or rather the absence of them. Montgomery, like his predecessor, had not been an impressive leader and his advocacy of separation was anathema to Ballance. Grey was a spent force and there were in any case suspicions that he was seeking a coalition with Atkinson in order to keep Vogel out. On the other hand, Vogel's opposition to leasing and land nationalisation would be an embarrassment to Ballance if an alliance were anticipated. The *Herald* also pointed to the legitimate doubt as to whether depression could be overcome by new borrowing alone.[68] Nevertheless by the election Ballance was predicting that Vogel would become Premier, and saying that 'he would not be sorry for it'. As for himself, he would not accept office 'unless his principles were fairly represented'.[69]

Ballance's campaign reflected this contradiction between his advocacy of a radical liberal programme and his appreciation of political reality. He attempted in part to fuse liberalism and Vogelism (rapid economic development through borrowing for public works) and the alliance required concessions from both. Ballance's liberalism was undeniable, but the necessity to accommodate Vogel forced him to play down the sole claims of a liberal party. Indeed such a party barely existed, and in his speeches Ballance made no reference to it. He foresaw the need for coalition and argued that Vogel was the best the Opposition could come up with.[70] As for Vogel's penchant for borrowing, Ballance admitted that Vogel 'might be inclined to go too fast unless he had a House which could put a drag on. [But] it was better to have a statesman that had a tendency to be a little too fast, rather than one that did not move at all'.[71]

On 8 July Ballance delivered his major campaign speech to a crammed Princess Theatre in Wanganui. He was at his most radical. He opposed Atkinson's suggestion of federation with the Australian colonies on the grounds that it would involve a loss of sovereignty for New Zealand. He criticised the giving and acceptance of colonial titles. The Australian ex-Premier Sir Henry Parkes had suggested the creation of colonial earldoms, and recently the Wellington politician William Fitzherbert had accepted a K.C.M.G. 'Why look to England for such honours as ought to flow freely from the people of the colony,' questioned Ballance. 'It was more noble to reject these honours and die in the possession of the confidence of the people' than to be covered with them. These distinctly republican and nationalist sentiments would emerge with much greater force later in Ballance's career.

Ballance believed unemployment ought to be tackled through restricting immigration to those 'fitted for country life' and those with capital. Local industry should be encouraged through protection. The property tax ought to be replaced by a progressive land tax, for the former was 'taxing industry, discouraging enterprise, and heaping taxation upon the working classes'. Though his advocacy of land nationalisation was not as strident as in his *Echo* articles, it went far beyond the land tax he had proposed at previous election campaigns. He stressed the advantages of leasing and the need to retain crown land in the Government's hands. He pointed out that seven men in New Zealand owned one million hectares, and 20 owned 1.5 million hectares. 'Could the colony progress while these large blocks were thus held?' Ballance did not actually suggest government purchase of these holdings, but the hint was there and his views on this were already well known.[72]

It was with respect to local development issues that Ballance's attempt to utilise Vogelism emerged. Economically Wanganui was stagnating. Ballance had seen the population of the town virtually double, between

1871 and 1881, to 4646, but since then the rate of increase had slowed drastically, and the next decade added just 365 further inhabitants.[73] Businesses that were established and that survived reflected Wanganui's basic role as a distributive and servicing centre for country settlements. The town boasted an iron foundry (producing agricultural implements among other things), flour and bone mills, a bacon factory, sale yards and a large sheep dip, vineyards, an abattoir and preserving factory, and a cheese factory. There were smaller firms producing for the local market, for example a confectionery and biscuit business and a sash and door company.[74]

To maintain and extend this role the transport network needed developing. In particular the harbour had to be deepened. Ballance had led a "progress party" on the Harbour Board that tried to push ahead with dredging work and an extension of the breakwater, but it was hampered by a desperate lack of money. Now Ballance proposed a rating bill to finance improvements.[75] He also wished to see the Wanganui River opened up so that the land through which it flowed might be settled. Ballance said that the £20,000 needed for the work ought to come from the Government and suggested that 'they would not have to ask Sir Julius Vogel twice' to provide it.[76] Yet though Ballance was not slow to pose the advantages for Wanganui in Vogel's return to power, he was cautious on the broader issue of the extent to which a government ought to borrow for development. He said that if elected 'he would insist upon the curtailing of borrowing, except judicious borrowing for railways and roads through native lands'.[77] In general Ballance argued that public works expenditure should be reduced until the properties that would benefit from new spending were taxed. There was no place in Vogelism for this. For Vogel, state intervention was aimed at promoting rapid development and would stop well short of restricting the profits of private capital investment.

At the election Ballance was opposed by the same two men whom he had faced in 1875: W. H. Watt, the sitting member, and the lawyer George Hutchison. Watt's lacklustre performance in Wellington was acknowledged even by his own supporters. The *Chronicle* admitted that he was 'deficient in many of the qualities' that it would wish to see in a representative, but supported him on the grounds that he was a safer bet than Ballance.[78] During the campaign it became clear that Hutchison was the stronger of Ballance's opponents. Politically, Hutchison was much closer to Watt than Ballance and thus would split the anti–Ballance vote.

The campaign was fought on local and national issues. Ballance's advocacy of a rating bill to finance further harbour improvements was popular in the town, particularly the proposal to spread the burden by rating the country areas that the port served as well as Wanganui itself. Watt, fatally, opposed both the bill and Ballance's ideas on developing river communications. Hutchison, in his one major disagreement with Watt, supported the bill.[79] On broader issues Ballance was condemned for his past record and present policy. The *Chronicle* criticised his desertion of Atkinson and subsequent failure as Colonial Treasurer. It argued that his political principles did not run deep, though somewhat inconsistently also attacked Ballance's theories on land nationalisation.[80] There was some criticism of his freethought views, in the form of correspondence to the *Chronicle*: 'As a Freethinker and Infidel Mr Ballance ought to be rejected by every right-thinking Christian in the town. He who assists to pollute the minds of the little ones is not worthy to be trusted with the administration of the affairs of this colony . . . Christians, unite, and drive this infidel once more into private life.'[81] And again, 'not content with denying his Maker, [Ballance] is anxious to teach our children the tenets of a Bradlaugh or a Besant . . . Orangemen, be true to your colours, and refuse to be longer allied to the snake in the grass.'[82] However the *Chronicle* was content simply to publish these letters. Neither it nor Watt or Hutchison raised the issue to any significant extent during the campaign. Ballance's only response was to say that religion and politics ought not to be mixed.[83]

Ballance won the election with 541 votes to Hutchison's 205 and Watt's 154.[84] It was an impressive victory, by a margin that seems to have been unexpected by Ballance and his supporters as well as opponents. There had been suggestions that his majority might be between 50 and 100. As the crowd gathered in anticipation of the declaration of the poll tensions ran high. Some enthusiasts ran out of patience and began throwing eggs and flour. When the result was eventually announced so many Ballance supporters climbed onto the hustings that the platform collapsed under the weight. Ballance was then carried shoulder high to the Court House steps, where he briefly addressed the crowd. The result, he said, completely atoned for his previous defeat. He had never been prouder of Wanganui.[85] He was genuinely moved.

Ballance won so convincingly because although out of Parliament since 1881 he had remained politically active, and had been promoting a number of popular causes. He also benefited from the adverse reaction to Watt's term as Member for Wanganui. But most important, Ballance's platform was more positive, and the worsened economic conditions made it more attractive, than it had been three years earlier. It involved an unambiguous bid for working-class support by advocating land reform and protection as means to restoring prosperity to the town, and to the country upon which the town depended. Explicit, too, was a redistribution of wealth. Labourers and artisans comprised over half the Wanganui electorate in 1884.[86] Ballance's policies were directed specifically at these groups and it was on them that he staked his political future. In addition he attracted support from the town's small businessmen and shopkeepers who welcomed any policies aimed at boosting the local economy.

Ballance's radicalism was channelled primarily into land reform because he believed that closer settlement was the main solution to New Zealand's problems. His only direct reference to labour issues came in answer to a question asked at the conclusion of one of his speeches. It concerned the length of the working day and he replied that he believed in an eight-hour day but that there should be freedom of contract.[87]

In optimistic mood, Ballance left for Wellington on 5 August and Parliament met two days later. When Atkinson resigned, acknowledging that a majority of members opposed the Government, Vogel and Stout set about forming a ministry. Stout persuaded Ballance to join.[88] The *Herald* had said on 6 August that Ballance's decision to accept office would rest 'mainly on how far his well known principles in connection with land administration' were accepted by his colleagues. The use of the word 'administration' rather than 'nationalisation' or 'reform' may have been significant, in that Ballance did not want to put too high a price on his inclusion in the Cabinet.

Ballance was appointed Native Minister and Minister of Defence in the government formed on 16 August. Stout became Premier and Vogel Colonial Treasurer. Ill health and a dislike of administrative chores stopped Vogel from assuming the premiership. Included in the ministry were Macandrew, Montgomery and Richardson, a South Island dominance that could not hope to attract sufficient support from northern (and especially Auckland) members.[89] 'We doubt whether any Government ever assumed office with a more decided public opinion against it,' wrote the *Evening Post*.[90] Many were also astounded at the combination of liberals and 'conservative' speculators, while the *Post* was disappointed that Vogel did not take on the premiership himself.[91] After less than a week in office the ministry was defeated.[92] J. W. Thomson of Clutha then attempted to form a government. His failure was followed by that of Grey, who was unable to entice the necessary support of Atkinson. Next, Atkinson himself tried to assemble a cabinet with Vogel's support. When this too fell through, Atkinson formed a ministry on his own. Without the co-operation of either Vogel or Grey this was also doomed and lasted only six days.

What resolved the impasse was a reconstructed Stout-Vogel Ministry without Macandrew or Montgomery.[93] It survived because it was less radical than the first version and could attract Greyite support through the inclusion of J. A. Tole from Auckland. Circumstances favoured Ballance as a representative from the North Island, and he was now given the important Lands portfolio in addition to those of Native Affairs and Defence. Yet some evidence suggests that for a time he hoped for a different outcome. On the eve of the vote of confidence on Atkinson's 'interim' Ministry, George Fisher of Wellington sent Ballance a note seeking clarification as to the intention of the Opposition. Did they want a return to the Stout-

Vogel Ministry? Ballance replied: 'Not to bring back the Stout-Vogel Ministry. Hope the result will be a combination acceptable to House. But Atkinson's lot must first be defeated.'[94]

The Stout-Vogel Ministry did return, albeit with some important changes in personnel. The question is whether Ballance realistically expected the formation of a ministry excluding Vogel and Atkinson, and including himself, Stout and (if absolutely necessary) even Grey. The *Post* reported on 2 September that Macandrew and Montgomery were seeking to reach agreement with Grey, who had earlier been advised by his supporters to attempt an accommodation with the Stout-Vogel faction.[95] Perhaps Ballance hoped to attract Greyite support without having to include Grey himself, and in a sense this is what happened. A desire on Ballance's part to split Stout from Vogel would be natural. Ballance was well aware of the likely difficulty in persuading a government strongly influenced by Vogel to adopt a radical land programme. Yet was there any preferable, viable alternative? If Ballance believed that there was it suggests (among other things) that he was not fully aware of the commitment of Stout and Vogel to each other or that, if he was, he attached little importance to such an agreement. Was Stout keeping Ballance as fully informed as Ballance would have kept Stout?

In the event Ballance could hardly complain. It was clear eventually that if he wanted office he would have to accept Vogel — a minor sacrifice when he was getting three portfolios, of which Lands in particular was right up his street. As he wrote to Fisher, who looked to Ballance for guidance:

> The time has not yet come in this colony when a pure Liberal party can be formed, and until it does come we can only wait and make the best of the position, yet keeping in view the object we wish to attain. The majority of the House is probably (?) not guided by Liberal principles, and no Govt. can go very far ahead of public opinion. You and others can do a great deal to hasten the time when a distinctly Liberal programme can be put forth by the party from the Hustings, & when such a programme will be honestly given effect to in Parliament. I hope the day is not far distant.[96]

[CHAPTER 7]

A curious combination

IN THE FIRST WEEK OF September 1884 Ballance eagerly took up his duties as head of the Lands, Native Affairs and Defence departments. He worked solidly, with only a short break in October enforced by a bout of illness, until the session ended in early November.[1] His cabinet colleagues were very much a mixed bag, a reflection of the diverse forces that had brought the Stout-Vogel combination to power. Stout and Vogel were co-operating for personal rather than political reasons. There was little political ground common to their supporters, beyond the hope that the Government might end the depression and restore prosperity. Many, including a substantial number of prominent businessmen, merchants and runholders, looked forward to Vogel waving his magic wand. Canterbury in particular had returned a high proportion of Vogelites, those of the 'commercial and landed aristocracy' who had been hit by the collapse of wool and wheat prices.[2] They were excited by the prospect of new borrowing for development projects and were represented in the Cabinet by a Christchurch contractor, Edward Richardson, now Minister of Public Works. The conservative faction could also claim W. H. Reynolds, a Dunedin businessman who became minister without portfolio. The two other members of the ministry were both liberals and lawyers. J. A. Tole, a Greyite from Auckland, was appointed Minister of Justice, while Patrick Buckley became Colonial Secretary.

The disparate nature of the ministry severely limited what Ballance could hope to do during his term of office. Vogel would himself resist any move towards land nationalisation or restriction of the free market in crown or Maori land. He gained the support of the Canterbury members only by assuring them that despite the presence of Stout and Ballance 'all fads and nonsense would be dropped'.[3] Many conservatives, like Scobie Mackenzie,

[126]

recognised the talent in the Cabinet and hoped to 'keep the men in' but their measures out.[4] So from the outset Ballance knew that radical, controversial legislation was a non-starter.

The other major constraint on Ballance's ability to put his theories into practice was lack of money. The Government was unable to make any headway in arresting the economic decline. Vogel's Financial Statement of 1884 reduced the property tax by one half and proposed a new loan for public works,[5] but within a year the optimism arising from these measures had vanished. The depression deepened. Export prices continued to fall and the country's annual deficit rose from £147,000 in 1884 to nearly £500,000 by 1887. Bank credit contracted further.[6] Vogel restored the property tax to its original level and proposed an increase in tariffs,[7] while plans for new loans were shelved with the collapse of the colony's credit in London. It was an admission that Vogelism had failed. The vast majority of the tariffs were rejected by a House increasingly determined to deal with depression through cuts in government expenditure. A motion to reduce public works expenditure by £500,000 was proposed by W. R. Russell, Member for Hawke's Bay, and carried by a majority of 15.[8]

Vogel did not waste any time in trying to rescue the New Zealand Agricultural Company. He wanted the Government to purchase the Waimea Plains Railway, thus giving some relief to the Agricultural Company, which as owner of most of the land through which the railway ran was liable to the Railway Company for a large sum of rates. The Railway Company was itself also in deep financial trouble. The District Railways Leasing and Purchasing Bill passed through the House in October 1884, but was subsequently thrown out by the Legislative Council. The bill allowed the Government to buy any district railway, while the council insisted on separate legislation for each individual purchase. Not until two years later was a second District Railways Purchasing Bill, for the acquisition of the Waimea Plains Railway only, successfully introduced.[9]

As the legislation was debated fresh allegations were made, by Grey in particular, of the involvement of members of the ministry in the railway and agricultural companies. Vogel in fact had mentioned his connection with the Agricultural Company when he moved the second reading of the 1884 Bill. When the Speaker ruled that those with a pecuniary interest in the company should not vote in the division on the bill, Vogel, Stout and Ballance all abstained.[10] Ballance had been a provisional director of the Land and Loan Company, set up to help finance settlement on the Waimea Plains. This company was the New Zealand twin of the London-based Agricultural Company, which sold shares and land to British investors and prospective settlers. During the debate Ballance pointed out that though he had been associated with the Agricultural Company he had no financial interest in it. He had been connected with it, but 'without any prospect

'On the brink': the Stout-Vogel alliance (McIntyre 1886)

of reward and without receiving one penny'. In any case, he said, he was not ashamed of the company. It aimed at cutting up large estates for settlement, which was a 'perfectly legitimate' motive. Grey denied the suggestion of Ballance that as Premier he (Grey) had given sanction to the Agricultural Company. Grey rightly said that initially he had known nothing of it, and that when he did find out about it he insisted on Vogel's resignation from the board of directors.[11]

The Government managed quite successfully to play down the involvement of Stout and Vogel in the companies. There were other district railways in financial straits, so that the idea of government purchase had more general appeal. Also, only Grey and a very few other members had any idea of the past history of the company. And it was difficult for Grey not to appear to be motivated by personal spite. His accusations were inevitably associated with his political estrangement from Stout and Ballance since the fall of his ministry in 1879.

The whole affair was certainly of some embarrassment to Ballance. As a member of the Cabinet he must have been aware of the reasons behind the eagerness of Vogel and Stout to see the Waimea Plains Railway purchased, and would also have known of its link with the Agricultural Company. Ballance can be criticised for keeping quiet about what was going on, though not for any personal involvement he had in the company. As for his role in the Land and Loan Company, in 1891, when he was Premier, the matter was again raised in the House, In a revealing statement Ballance sought to put the record straight:

Some person or persons were good enough to put my name on the provisional prospectus. I declare I never signed my name to that provisional prospectus, and never consented to its being placed there. It was placed there without my consent; but when the real prospectus came out my name was no longer there. I never subscribed to the company . . . The person who put my name on the provisional prospectus did so without my consent. I did not even know my name was on the provisional prospectus until I was told about it some time afterwards, and I never even saw the provisional prospectus which contained my name. I never placed a penny in it, and I had no interest in it whatever. These are the simple facts.[12]

That Ballance did not mention this earlier may well be explained by his wish to protect Stout, who was most likely the person who put Ballance's name on the prospectus.

As Minister for Lands Ballance aimed to place as many people as possible on the land. He encouraged leasing and as a step towards nationalisation reduced the amount of land sold outright. James McKerrow, the Secretary for Crown Lands, wrote rather sourly in his 1885 report that there had been less crown land sold during the past year than in any previous year. This had not been because of a lack of purchasers, he said. Instead extensive areas had been withheld from sale.[13] Over the following three years cash land sales continued to decline, and picked up only after Ballance left office.[14] At the same time, the number of new settlers rose and the average size of holding fell during Ballance's tenure. Settlement more than doubled between 1886 and 1887, reaching an annual figure unmatched by the Liberal Government of the 1890s.[15]

Increasingly Ballance saw land settlement as a solution, along with developing industry and halting immigration, to the growing problem of urban unemployment.[16] He extended existing and devised new settlement schemes with this object in mind. His 1885 Land Act was a major piece of legislation. A consolidating measure that replaced all previous land law, it also established a number of new tenures and forms of settlement. The overall objective of the bill, said Ballance, was to get and keep bona fide settlers on the land. His short pithy speech on its second reading emphasised the advantages of leasing: 'the best of all kinds of bona fide settlement is that which enables the State to retain control over the land, and which enables the people who want land to cultivate and not for speculative purposes to go on the land and hold it so long as they are complying with the conditions of improvement and settlement.'[17] Therefore the freehold encouraged speculation, while 'where the object is to settle down and to make a home . . . there is nothing in the world which will compare with the system of perpetual leasing.'[18]

Under the act land could be sold for cash or on deferred payment, or it could be leased. Leased land was let by tender at an upset price of five percent of the capital value of the land. Owners of more than 260 hectares of land in the colony were ineligible for leasing. There were residence and improvement conditions and lessees were able to acquire the freehold after six years.[19] Ballance would have preferred there to be no freehold right, but political pressure meant that its inclusion was essential to the successful passage of the bill. Nevertheless he predicted that perpetual leasing would become the 'prevailing system in the colony'.[20]

The act introduced four new forms of settlement. The first, the leasing of 'small areas', was particularly important to Ballance. Under this system town dwellers could lease up to 20 hectares of land bordering urban areas.[21] Ballance aimed it primarily at labourers who during temporary unemployment would work and live off their land. 'I maintain that the true outlet for the labouring-classes,' he said, 'is to have small holdings in the neighbourhood of large towns upon liberal conditions.'[22] In fact only 52 settlers on 600 hectares of land were established under this tenure. Ballance recognised the flaws in it, the most serious of which was the lack of available land close to centres of population. He argued that given this the Government ought to purchase the necessary land.[23] Yet even if land was found, settlers could not long survive on its proceeds alone. As the *Yeoman* acknowledged, the success of the scheme depended both on good quality land and the existence of job opportunities near by.[24]

Although the scheme attracted few settlers, it was an important practical application of Ballance's philosophy. It was a qualification of the yeoman ideal, halfway between urban and rural living for the working classes. Advancement would come through working the land, though a settler would remain socially bonded to the town. Significantly, the regulations denied the right to acquire the land's freehold and so discouraged those who wished to become full-time farmers from joining the scheme.

This dual urban-rural employment was a central feature of a second and much more successful type of settlement introduced by Ballance. This was the Village Settlement scheme. Rolleston had formed village settlements on a small scale in Canterbury in the 1870s. Under the Land Amendment Act of 1879 similar schemes could be set up elsewhere, but the provisions were little used, despite such recommendations as the following from the *Evening Post*:

> Working men who live in the large cities of the colony should direct their earnest attention to the system [of village settlement] by means of which they obtain freehold homes for themselves and families. It is a serious evil that so many working men should remain in the large cities, often choking up the labor market, when they would have a far widely [*sic*] scope for their exertions in some of the country districts, besides the opportunity of acquiring a permanent home of their own.[25]

Under Ballance's plan villages were to be established with each settler receiving up to one acre of urban land and up to 20 hectares of rural land. The land could be bought or leased. The act also gave the minister the right to purchase land (with Parliament's approval) for such settlements.[26] However, what was significant was Ballance's amendment, through an order-in-council of 1 September 1886, of the regulations for village settlements on perpetual lease. Leases for these Village Homestead Special Settlements, as they were called, were to run for 30 years, with renewals for subsequent periods of 21 years. There was no right to the freehold. Settlers were to be given loans to enable them to construct a house and clear the land, repayable along with the annual rent fixed at five percent of the value of the holding. Certain improvements had to be made within a given period of time.[27] Ballance's aim here was to establish whole working class families on the land. In particular he hoped to attract the unemployed and under-employed who were crowding the towns.

Village Homestead Special Settlements were the most popular form of village settlement. By 1890, 9530 hectares were held under the scheme; 913 hectares under the ordinary perpetual lease; 2990 hectares sold on deferred payment and 2340 hectares sold for cash.[28] An early rush of applicants reflected the depressed economic conditions of the time and the favourable incentives offered. Between May 1886, when the scheme was announced, and the end of March 1887, 896 settlers took up land under the homestead regulations.[29] As a later report pointed out, the scheme was a useful 'relief measure to absorb the unemployed workmen who had congregated in the towns'.[30]

Of the 1196 settlers established by 1889, 765 were labourers and 103 were carpenters. There were only 40 farmers.[31] Over half the homestead settlements were in the Auckland district. Canterbury and Wellington accounted for nearly all the remainder. That the former figure was so high had a lot to do with the enthusiasm and persistence of John Lundon, whom Ballance appointed to promote settlement north of Auckland. Lundon had been Member for Maunganui and Bay of Islands, and had suggested to Ballance that unemployment in Auckland could be reduced by placing families on land near the gumfields and sawmills of Northland.[32] However, the scheme suffered similar problems to those of the small area leasing tenure. Good-quality land and a nearby source of employment were vital, and both were lacking in many of the Auckland settlements. By 1888, 133 of the 639 Auckland sections had been abandoned and 168 settlers were in arrears with their rent.[33] On the other hand, in Canterbury, where the land was free of bush and markets were easily accessible (for example, at Orari), the schemes fared better.

Ballance visited village settlements in the South Island in early 1885, before the homestead regulations appeared.[34] He was particularly pleased with a 'small farm settlement' (a type of village settlement held on deferred payment) called Beaconsfield, near Timaru. He discovered that its success lay in the fact that all the men, aside from farming their four-hectare sections, had paid employment in town. In general, however, good land was short in Canterbury and Ballance again suggested that the Government ought to acquire what was necessary by compulsory purchase.[35]

The village settlement and in particular the homestead schemes attracted much criticism. Many said that the premises they were based on were unsound, evidence of which was the increasing arrears owed by settlers.[36] Ballance was also attacked for the large amount of money he spent on road works in Auckland to provide employment for the settlers. According to Lundon, only the support of Auckland members (welcoming any expenditure that might lessen unemployment in their city) saved Ballance from a vote of censure in the House.[37] Grey complained that by insisting on residence and limiting holdings to 20 hectares the scheme amounted to quasi-slavery. The land could not be sublet or added to and could only be sold to a purchaser who agreed to the same terms as imposed upon the original lessee.[38] Grey was quite right that 20 hectares was too small an area to support a family. The point was that Ballance did not intend settlers to increase their holdings and become full-time farmers. The land was not meant to be the sole source of income. In this respect the scheme contained a contradiction. It aimed to reduce unemployment but could only succeed where there was an adequate supply of part-time work for the settlers. In other words it was particularly vulnerable in the very depressed conditions it hoped to tackle. Ballance realised this, and thus the need for the £15,000 for road-making in north Auckland.[39]

The Atkinson Ministry which came to power in 1887 halted all advances to homestead settlers and new settlement was brought to a virtual standstill. The scheme was revived, however, by John McKenzie, Minister for Lands in the early 1890s.[40] The 1891 report on village homestead settlements detailed the problems that had been encountered but said that the fault lay with the location of settlements rather than with the plan itself. Good land, sufficient employment opportunities, a near market for the sale of produce, good road access to the settlement and the selection of suitable settlers were all vital.[41] Ballance continued to defend his scheme, especially as a solution to unemployment.[42] He also argued that it had destroyed 'that old bogey, the assumption that people would not improve land unless they held it in the form of absolute freehold'. Indeed many saw the insistence on leasing as an important step towards land nationalisation. Ballance certainly believed perpetual leasing to be a viable proposition. 'Wherever proper conditions have been observed,' he said, 'the scheme has been a success.'[43]

As for the settlers, they were generally content and optimistic. A string of newborn babies were named after Ballance,[44] along with a village itself, just north of Pahiatua on the edge of the Tararua Ranges. In 1888 a meeting of the Hukerenui settlement in the Bay of Islands passed a resolution expressing its gratitude to the Minister of Lands:

> Within the short space of eighteen months a complete transformation has taken place in this district. What was then a comparative wilderness, with only an isolated whare to be seen at intervals along the main road, has now given place to comfortable dwelling houses and well grassed paddocks, in most cases securely fenced, and the condition of the cattle etc., grazing therein is ample proof of the good quality of the land. The settlers are with few exceptions well pleased with their holdings . . . We recognise that the village scheme is the only one which has successfully grappled with the difficulty of placing the people on the land — thereby dealing a death-blow at the iniquitious [sic] system of 'land sharking' so long a veritable curse to the colony. Notwithstanding the fact that the scheme is looked upon with small favour by the present Government and that we are absolutely without roads — we have every confidence in its ultimate success, and appeal to all who claim to be the working man's friend to lift up their voices in favour of its extension.[45]

Two other accounts, both of Northland settlements, were in similar vein. The Pakahue village settlers wrote to Ballance:

> The undersigned village settlers tender you our sincere thanks for the assistance you have rendered in placing us on the land. We hope your efforts will, as they deserve, be crowned with success. Some malicious person, or persons, are circulating the report that the settlers are leaving Pakahue. This, we beg to state, is false. We are all pleased with the place, and feel sanguine of our future prospects. We believe the time is not far distant, when, with ordinary industry, we shall have gathered round us comfortable homes in this most beautiful valley, teeming with the good things of the earth.[46]

And a Herekino settler gave his personal view:

> I like the place well. A few parties have gone back to Auckland. The land is good in general. I have a few acres cleared, and a hut up. I have made it pretty snug. There is any quantity of mullet and other fish in the river. The man that would stop in Auckland looking for work, deserves to starve. I had not a shilling when I reached here, and I am quite satisfied I can make a home here comfortably, and before long the land will grow good crops.[47]

In numerical terms the village homestead scheme made only a minor contribution to settlement in New Zealand. They did not survive in their intended form — that is, involving part-farm work and part wage employment. A few, such as Pahiatua and Te Aroha, merged with other settlements which grew into country towns. Others, for example Ballance itself and Herekino, remained tiny villages. Many more (including Pakahue) disappeared as settlers sold out and the land was consolidated into larger holdings. Their political significance at the time, however, was well out of proportion to their actual success. They pointed to a practical means by which the land hungry in the towns might be satisfied and unemployment relieved. They greatly enhanced Ballance's mana by holding out the prospect of what might be achieved. Finally, though the notion of dual employment proved to be impractical, it was central to the rural myth of urban New Zealand — to the rejection of city and idealisation of country life which to this day finds form in the suburban section.[48]

A third type of settlement developed by Ballance was the Special Settlement system. There had been similar schemes before (for example, Katikati and Te Aroha), whereby the Government granted concessions to organisations wishing to establish whole settlements. Provision for new special settlements had been made in the 1879 Land Amendment Act, but as Ballance had complained it had largely been ignored. Requests from groups such as the Wanganui Small Farm Association for the Government to provide land under the legislation had fallen on deaf ears. Ballance was keen to put this right.

The Land Act of 1885 limited the land that could be set aside for special settlements to 40 500 hectares per year. Land could be sold or (and this was a significant change to the 1879 legislation) leased.[49] Associations would deal directly with the Government, for it was Ballance's aim to cut out the middleman. The price would be fixed by valuation; there would be no auction or tender. Once acquired the land would be distributed by ballot among the association members wishing to settle.[50]

The detailed regulations for special settlements were set out in orders-in-council of November 1884 and March 1885. By the latter date 20 associations of about 2000 members had applied for 82 500 hectares of land. The applications of 12 had been accepted. Associations were to consist of at least 25 people. Full-time residence was required, though a selector was allowed to appoint a substitute.[51] This would enable a working-class man to remain in town, placing a substitute on land (that need not be particularly near by) and using his savings to develop what was essentially an investment for his retirement. Ballance denied that the substitute was simply a middleman and he opposed a motion in the House to reduce the residence requirement from full-time to three months per year. This would encourage speculation, he said, and the land would not be worked to its full potential. He wanted working-class men permanently on the land, not middle-class, part-time farmers.[52] Again through an order-in-council, Ballance reduced the maximum area allowed under the regulations from 130 to 60 hectares in the case of land held on deferred payment, and from 260 to 80 hectares of leased land.[53] This limit on the size of holdings along with the residency requirement made speculation difficult.[54]

Ballance tried hard to persuade associations to opt for the perpetual lease. The Masterton-Mangatainoka Special Settlement Association, for example, was advised that its application for land would be more likely to succeed if it chose the perpetual lease rather than the deferred payment terms it had sought. The secretary of the association acquiesced, but when the other members found out they refused to take up the land.[55] *Yeoman* articles also promoted leasing. The mortgaged freeholder, it said, was sooner or later enmeshed in the capitalist creditor's net. Freeholders suffered years of slavery and high-interest payments, frequently only to have to give up their land eventually to the mortgagor. Perpetual leasing avoided all of this.[56]

However, pressure from Ballance and argument both failed. The hunger for the freehold inherent in man's nature (as Vogel put it in 1884) could not be denied.[57] By 1892 there was only one association on leased land (13 settlers on 778 hectares in the South Island).[58] Nineteen associations, the vast majority in the Wellington district, held 38 888 hectares on deferred payment.[59] The special settlements were for many ideal low-premium, long-term investments. The desire for the security of freehold naturally was strong among the upper working and lower-middle class regular wage earners that the scheme primarily attracted. And these groups, unlike the labourers settled under the homestead scheme, could meet the higher deferred payment instalments. Reporting the formation of a Wellington association, the *Evening Post* pointed out that the regulations were particularly attractive to tradesmen and clerks who wished to get their sons onto the land, but who could not afford to buy the land outright.[60]

For Ballance the objectives of the small area, homestead and special settlement schemes were the same. In the short term they would give immediate relief to the unemployed. In the long term land made available under liberal conditions would provide opportunities for the self-advancement of the masses. Liberalism in land settlement meant gradual land nationalisation, 'removing the land from the control of individuals and placing it under the control of the State in the interest (of) the people at large — giving all a chance of becoming land occupiers under terms conducive to the well-being of all'.[61] Nationalisation was seen by Ballance as both utilitarian and democratic. His settlement schemes were the practical form of the radical liberalism he hoped would head, and at the same time satisfy, the democratic movement in New Zealand. Land would be made available for all, and those who took it up were expected to remain content with the leasehold and politically aligned with the urban majority. Perpetual leasing, mixed urban-rural employment and the restriction to the size of holdings would advance the interests of the many and assure the loyalty of the lessees. The freehold would be seen as undemocratic and inequitable, while the small farmers would share with town dwellers an interest in the provision of generous leasing conditions. Nationalisation would guarantee for the urban population a fair distribution of the country's prosperity. Yet the town was not to dominate the country. Rather there would be an identity of interests. These were the terms of settlement that Ballance said would be 'conducive to the well-being of all'. And this bonding of town and country, involving high-density settlement on nationalised land, was Ballance's ideal.

A fourth form of tenure introduced by Ballance was the small grazing run. Under this system land was leased by auction for 21 years (with the right of renewal) up to a maximum of 2020 hectares. Residence was required for the first six years, during which certain improvements had to be made.[62] This tenure aimed particularly at good but steep hill country suitable only for grazing. Low rent reflected the fact that much of the land had to be cleared of bush before sowing and grazing could begin.[63] Sixty-eight selectors took up small grazing runs in 1887, the first year they were offered. The following five years added over 300.[64]

The promotion of settlement through these various tenures involved Ballance in an immense amount of work. In the first place he had to find and set aside by proclamation suitable blocks of land. A good deal, of course, was done by the Lands Department staff, yet Ballance's initiative and enthusiasm were critical. The *Evening Post* reported in October 1886 that his efforts in establishing new settlement were 'almost universally eulogised', even by the opposition press.[65] Yet Ballance was well aware that the shortage of land was severely curtailing the rate of settlement. Much of the best land was in private hands. He had suggested the solution many times before, but now came up with a specific proposal. In a key speech at Blenheim in December 1886, he announced that he was going to introduce a bill in the following session to allow the Government to expropriate any private estates it might require. The owner of the land would receive a sum equal to the value of his holding (as determined for the purposes of the property tax) plus ten percent.[66] Further details of this radical proposal emerged soon afterwards. Under the Land Acquisition Bill associations of at least 20 persons could contact a landowner and attempt to purchase, after due investigation by two commissioners and with the approval of the Government, a block of land for small farm settlement. If the owner refused to sell the Government could acquire the land compulsorily, provided that the owner's total holdings in the colony exceeded 400 hectares. The land acquired was to be leased to the association's members, each individual receiving no more than 40 hectares. The freehold could not be purchased and only one block of land could be held.[67] Ballance argued that the state had a moral right to acquire land for settlement in this manner, so long as fair compensation were given. The time had come, he said, when the monopoly of land, 'which was impeding settlement and robbing the country at large, should no longer stand in the way of the interests of the colony'.[68]

The Stout-Vogel Government fell shortly after the start of the 1887 session and so Ballance's bill never reached a second reading. In any case he would have had considerable difficulty getting it through the House. Two years later, when Leader of the Opposition, Ballance revived the bill and printed it in full in the *Herald*.[69] The bill's proposals were central to his election campaign of 1890 and it was the forerunner of the subsequent Liberal Government's purchasing legislation.

While Ballance was praised by some for his persistent advocacy of the leasing and nationalisation of land, others regarded him as the devil incarnate. Annie Wilson, wife of James Wilson, the conservative Member for Foxton, described Ballance in 1887 as having 'a big head and a persuasive Irish tongue and Irish tact. He is one with Stout in his atheistic views and follows his lead exactly in stuffing the people with tales against property-holders, only going further, advocating the nationalisation of the land and "bursting up" big estates and so on. He has a wretched little newspaper in Wanganui which pours out his views . . . nothing pays in politics like flattering the mob.'[70]

Many agreed with Ballance's ends but were horrified by his proposed means. A contemporary commentator, John Bradshaw, applauded Ballance's promotion of closer settlement but deprecated leasing and nationalisation. Men would not work for a state landlord, he said, and much preferred the deferred payment system. As for the Land Acquisition Bill, 'a more socialistic measure [had] never been laid by a pretendedly civilised Administration before a civilised people'.[71]

In 1886 a prominent Manawatu farmer, James Bell, wrote a 24-page pamphlet full of vehement criticism of Ballance, land nationalisation and the operation of the Land Act. The premise that underlay Bell's argument came in his final paragraph: 'It would be well if Messrs. Stout and Ballance and other agitators who win the noisy plaudits of a small unthinking section of town residents, would consider well whether really the supposed wants of this class are so all important. After all, the country was not made for the towns, but the towns for the country.'[72] Bell had arrived at the crux of the matter, in the sense that one of Ballance's major aims was to secure an equitable interdependent relationship between town and country. Achieving this through state ownership and control of land would mean that the question of town versus country would no longer arise; neither sector would predominate, for their interests would coincide. Neither could hold the other to ransom.

Land issues were also central to the activities of the Native Department. With an expanding population and contracting amount of suitable crown land there was increasing pressure to acquire Maori land for European settlement. Further, of particular importance during Ballance's tenure was the purchase of Maori land through which much of the proposed North Island trunk railway was to run. The rail aimed not simply at linking Wellington with Auckland, but at opening up new land for settlement, especially that between Marton and Te Awamutu.

Ballance's views on race relations had altered considerably since the days of Titokowaru's siege of Wanganui. This change came with the end of the emergency and as part of the general radicalisation of Ballance's philosophy in the early 1880s. As he came into more contact with Maori his sympathy for, and understanding of, their condition grew. Possibly, also, his personal witness of the killing of innocent Maori during the 1868 war left a deep, lasting impression on him of the realities of the injustices Maori were subject to at the hands of the Pakeha. A *Herald* editorial written by Ballance in January 1873 pointed out that disease, death and crime among Maori had all risen as contact with Europeans increased. The Maori race was being decimated.[73] Two years later he concluded that McLean (the Native Minister) had failed to pursue his declared policy of assimilation, the merging of Maori into the European way of life. Rather the two races had grown further apart, for where Europeans settled Maori vanished.[74] Finally, in a remarkable speech (particularly given the widespread European hostility to the activities of Te Whiti at the time) to the House in 1881, Ballance said that 'with regard to the Native difficulties in the past . . . there has scarcely been a single war in this colony — in which the Europeans have not been more to blame than the Natives'.[75]

Ballance's policy as Native Minister fell between his hope that ultimately the two races would become assimilated and the realisation that in the foreseeable future Maori interests would have to be protected if assimilation were not simply to mean (as it had in the past) annihilation by Europeans.[76] He wished that Maori and European could be treated alike, arguing, for example, that Maori should eventually give up their special representation in the House. He believed there would be more Maori members returned when this happened. Yet it would take time for the Maori population to be 'educated up' to the position where they could take advantage of representation on the same basis as Europeans.[77] Until then Ballance acknowledged that Maori would be under-represented.[78]

This recognition of the need for protection alongside the long-term aim of assimilation was the basis for Ballance's approach to the central issue of Maori land sales. The Crown's pre-emptive right to purchase Maori land contained in the Constitution Act had been repealed by the Native Land Act of 1865. Since then land could be purchased by private individuals once its title had been ascertained by the Native Land Court. As Maori land was held communally this was far from simple. To get around the problem the Native Land Act restricted to ten the number of owners that could be listed in the sale of a block of land under 2020 hectares. In fact it became common practice for this limit to apply to land over 2020 hectares as well, and many Maori lost their share in land to co-owners eager to sell and more susceptible to the ploys of Pakeha purchasers. Throughout the period, 'a predatory horde of storekeepers, grog-sellers, surveyors, lawyers, land agents and money-lenders made advances to rival groups of Maori claimants to land, pressed the claim of their faction in the Courts and recouped the costs in land.'[79] Land sharks proliferated. As the *Yeoman* put it, every 'disreputable trick and debasing agency [has] been freely used by these land devouring gentry, and hundreds of thousands of acres of native lands have been alienated from their aboriginal owners without the latter reaping any real benefit from the sale'.[80]

Ballance appreciated that Maori land was held communally and proposed legislation to allow Maori to retain control over their land in that form. European settlement, however, necessitated the individualisation of title as a prerequisite of sale. Yet individualisation had led to injustices, fraud and monopoly. In his *Echo* article on 'Native Land Policy' Ballance argued that individualisation was wise only when the Government was the sole purchaser. He cited the Taranaki war, sparked off by the purchase of land from a Maori chief whose ownership of that land was far from certain, as an example of the 'practice which places the tribe at the mercy of its worst and most irresponsible members'.[81] This 'dishonest system of bribing individual Natives to sell, and then using these as decoy ducks for their more intractable compatriots' had persisted.[82] Therefore Ballance wanted Maori land to be leased by Maori themselves or bought and leased by the Crown. His concern for the interests of Maori landowners (involving at the same time an attack on European monopolists) was consistent with his policy of closer settlement. It was also paternalistic. 'It is beyond doubt,' he wrote, 'that the Native is in many respects an infant needing a guardian.'[83]

One of Ballance's first actions as Native Minister was to prohibit the private purchase of land alongside the planned route of the North Island trunk railway. Having spoken to a leading King Country chief called Wahanui, he was confident that the land required (about 1.8 million hectares) would be made available by its Maori owners. The Government would administer the land on behalf of these Maori. A board was to be appointed for this purpose, though Ballance hoped that eventually it would be elected by Maori themselves.[84] Speaking on proposed legislation to give effect to these arrangements, Ballance outlined the general principles he would follow in formulating future policy. He recognised that Maori still had to be convinced that they could trust the Government. To gain their confidence he believed that control over Maori land should be vested in the whole tribe. He criticised the Native Land Court for refusing to recognise this fact of Maori custom, attacked those who supported free trade in Maori land, and said he had already discovered many reserves wrongfully alienated from their owners. It was clear that Ballance wished to move towards complete prohibition of private dealings in Maori land, for Maori were able to bring any land they desired under the restrictions of the act. And he suggested that the powers of the existing Native Committees might be greatly extended to enable them to deal with the sale of all land on a tribal basis. Ballance concluded that this policy would differ from that of the past since it would allow settlement of Maori land while also 'contributing largely' to Maori 'welfare and to the stability and prosperity of the colony'.[85]

This linking of a conciliatory Maori policy with the promotion of European settlement was an important theme, and one that Ballance developed in a speech delivered in Wanganui in late 1884. He argued that racial conflict centred almost entirely on land and that its resolution lay in giving Maori greater control over their land. He proposed to stop all private land transactions between Europeans and Maori. It was not a return to crown pre-emption, said Ballance, for that tended to limit the price Maori received for their land. Rather it was a prohibition of direct private purchasing. All land transactions would have to pass through a body containing Maori representatives before being offered for public sale. Under this system the 'natives would see that their interests were identical with the interests of colonisation . . . If they could see that the Government were not encouraging the land sharks, and were not themselves to be a land-shark Government but rather prepared to see the natives utilise their own lands, they would become hearty co-operators in the work of colonisation.'[86]

Ballance faced fierce opposition from hawks inside and outside the House who had little concern for Maori people and judged the effect of his policy as simply locking up Maori land. However, quick success in gaining the co-operation of Maori leaders on the trunk railway project greatly strengthened Ballance's position. Wahanui and Kemp (the Wanganui chief) were persuaded early on and in December the old Kingite leader Rewi Maniapoto agreed to help. Rewi asked to be kept informed of Ballance's intentions and extended to him an invitation to visit. Ballance had in a few months, remarked the *Evening Post*, 'succeeded in doing what his predecessors tried for years in vain to do'.[87] The way of the railway was greatly smoothed by this consultation with chiefs, along with the use of Maori labour in its construction.[88]

As he worked on the new legislation and awaited the start of the 1885 session, Ballance was able to do something in the interim to halt the acquisition of Maori land by private purchasers. When Maori owners were granted title to a block of land, conditions were frequently attached that prevented sale without the approval of the Government. In the past this consent, given the appropriate political connections, had normally been a formality. However, immediately on assuming office Ballance refused to rubber-stamp any sales. The *Evening Post* reported that 'hundreds of deeds, only awaiting an order-in-council to render them valid, have been presented to him, and the strongest pressure has been brought to bear to make him yield, but he has remained immovable, and refused to validate even a single transaction.'[89] Thus the liberal *Post* rejoiced that 'the whole tribe of land sharks and speculators' that had monopolised land purchasing was 'exceedingly angry' and in despair.[90] The *New Zealand Herald*, an organ of Auckland speculators, was furious. 'Things cannot remain as they are,' it said. Ballance had shut up the country by law and was generally making a 'pretty kettle of fish' of the Native Department. His policy amounted to government and native landlordism, and as for his proposal to place control over Maori land in local committees, the *Herald* was sure Maori could not possibly work a representative system.[91]

A variety of government-sponsored Maori bodies had existed since the founding of the colony. In the early 1880s Maori themselves asked that powers be given to local committees to administer tribal land and a bill to this effect reached a second reading in 1882. Ballance welcomed the idea but went further by arguing that the committees should only lease, not sell, the land.[92] A year later an act was passed allowing regional committees to discuss and advise on land claims.[93] Pressure for more significant powers continued. Particularly active in applying it were W. L. Rees, the Auckland lawyer and liberal politician, and Wi Pere, who was elected Member for Eastern Maori in 1884. Rees's 'Memorandum on the Native Land Laws', recommending the election of committees that would have the legal right to deal with land tribally, presented a number of the arguments and suggestions upon which Ballance's legislation was based.[94]

Under Ballance's Native Land Disposition Bill, Maori landowners could elect a local committee to decide on the sale or lease of their land. The committee's recommendations would be given effect by a board of management, consisting of a commissioner and two government appointees. Committees could be dissolved by the Government on the application of at least two-thirds of the owners of the land. In this way Ballance hoped to ensure their continued representativeness and accountability. The Land Court would still investigate undetermined titles. Finally, in clause 62 the Government was empowered to bring any land covered by the act under the ordinary land laws of the colony. The Minister of Lands, in other words, could set the conditions of settlement.[95]

In early 1885 Ballance made an extensive tour of the North Island to gauge Maori opinion on the bill and other matters. He was the first Native Minister since McLean to do so. He met Kemp and Maori of the upper Wanganui River; Te Kooti, the old warrior now pardoned; Tawhiao, the

Waikato chief who had just returned from a visit to England to demand a separate Maori parliament; and Maori of Thames, Rotorua and the East Coast (including Wi Pere). In May he visited Parihaka. At these gatherings Ballance heard much criticism of the Native Land Court, such as the high court fees and tendency for land to be awarded simply to those who were able financially to conduct a case. The plans for the trunk railway, on the other hand, were generally approved.

At each meeting Ballance outlined the main provisions of the Land Disposition Bill. At the same time he warned Maori of the consequences of parting with their land. However, there was little discussion on the bill, as it had not yet been printed and as the Maori needed time for debate among themselves before coming to any conclusions. Ballance was well received, his eagerness to meet Maori on their own territory acknowledged. He made an effort to acquire some fluency in the Maori language, though it was never sufficient to dispose of the need for interpreters.[96] Maori people were soon calling him 'Ngawari' meaning 'soft' or 'sweet' man, as opposed to Bryce whom they pejoratively referred to as 'Maro' or 'hard man'.[97] Though congratulating Ballance on the success of the meetings, Vogel complained that the Native Minister was showing too great a 'concilliatory [sic] disposition' towards the Maori.[98]

Ballance too was confident of the outcome of his trip. At the opening of the new session in May the Government declared that European-Maori relations had 'never been of so friendly a character'. Maori were co-operating over the railway and the proposed bill would do them justice while at the same time promoting settlement.[99] When the Native Land Disposition Bill came up for its second reading he said that the meetings indicated that a great majority of Maori approved of his proposals. He quoted letters he had received from chiefs and officials to prove his point. Through competition, he argued, the bill would give Maori a better price for their land. Direct private purchase would be prohibited, but having passed through the bodies established by the bill land could be sold or leased in the same way as crown land.[100]

In fact there was growing opposition to the bill from Maori and Pakeha alike. The *New Zealand Herald* argued that it was simply part of Ballance's 'mischievous' plan to nationalise all land.[101] This was not far off the mark, for Ballance undoubtedly hoped to use the extensive powers contained in clause 62 (which he described as the 'main feature of the Bill') to impose leasing conditions on as much land as possible.[102] The *Herald* also noted that the Cabinet was split over the matter. It did not mention names but Vogel would certainly have been unhappy with the bill.

Objection to clause 62 was prominent amongst the many criticisms made when the bill went to the Native Affairs Committee.[103] Amendments by Wi Pere and Wahanui placed the power to prescribe the terms of settlement with the boards instead of the Government.[104] James Carroll (a half-caste Maori who was interpreter in the House of Representatives) and F. D. Fenton (ex-judge of the Native Land Court) echoed the common complaint that in general the bill gave too wide powers to the Government. The recommendations of the boards, local committees and Native Land Court were all subject to government approval. This was unacceptable to Maori, they said.[105] Wahanui denied he had written the supportive letter cited by Ballance during the bill's second reading.[106] As well there were problems with the provisions concerning the granting of titles, arising mainly from legal complications but also related to existing grievances against the Native Land Court. Ballance was made particularly uncomfortable by some questioning from Grey; and after an exchange with the highly experienced Fenton, the Native Minister asked rhetorically and with exasperation, what would reconcile the interests of settlement and those of Maori themselves.[107]

In response to some of the criticisms Ballance made a number of amendments to the bill, for example replacing the two government appointees on the boards by two Maori.[108] Further amendments by Wi Pere (which had the sanction of Carroll, Wahanui and others) removed the right of owners to sell or lease land to the Crown without going through a committee and generally placed more power in the hands of the committees and boards. Despite these changes the Native Affairs Committee recommended that the bill be dropped for the current session. Too many problems had arisen and Maori members requested more time to hold meetings to consider the bill and proposed amendments.

These meetings were held during the recess and having attended a number of them Ballance came up with a new Native Land Administration Bill. The change in title was significant. 'Disposition,' Ballance said, implied giving away land. The bill replaced the boards by commissioners, for Ballance had found that many Maori believed that their own representatives on the boards would be too open to corruption. The local committees remained much the same as before, though with greater powers. They could, for example, direct the commissioner in the allocation of money received from the sale of land. The clauses allowing landowners to deal directly with the Crown and giving the Government power to fix the conditions of settlement of land brought under the Act, were retained. The private purchase of land from Maori was, as before, made illegal.[109] The new bill, however, excluded the controversial part of the Disposition Bill concerning the legalisation of leasing transactions made prior to 1883.[110]

Ballance argued that the act would protect Maori from themselves. The 'great danger is, not that the Maoris will conserve their lands and create great estates, but that they will too readily part with them. My own experience is that they will part with their last acre if they get the opportunity.'[111] Opposition to the bill, he said, came primarily from land speculators.[112] Having this time survived the Native Affairs Committee and with the support of Maori members the bill passed its third reading by a majority of 20 votes.[113]

The act was a substantial advance towards the protection of Maori land, the key to which was the legal recognition of communal ownership. The next step, sought by Wi Pere among others, would have been to grant committees the power to determine title; but Ballance was reluctant to interfere with the Land Court and certainly any attempt to do so would have met with fierce resistance in the House.

The act, however, was never brought into operation. Overlooking the powers of the committees, Maori feared to place land in the hands of government commissioners. The history of land-grabbing ministries was too long — there was little trust in the Pakeha. Also, the mana of tribal leaders had eroded so far that ordinary landowners were reluctant to give committees any control over communal land.[114] In fact, the reports of the commissioners for 1887 show that no land at all had been invested with the committees. One application had been made but was withdrawn, apparently because of suspicion between the owners rather than of the Government.[115]

The act was repealed by the Atkinson Ministry in 1888, and with direct purchasing restored a new wave of land-buying (including that of major Maori reserves) began.[116] Three of the four Maori elected to the House in 1887 had campaigned against the act. The defeat of Wi Pere in particular was seen as evidence of Maori opposition to Ballance's legislation.[117] However, the new members soon discovered that the Atkinson Administration was much less sympathetic to their wishes than its predecessor.[118] As Ballance had predicted, the removal of purchasing restrictions resulted in the rapid accumulation by 'companies and capitalists' of vast amounts of Maori land. These groups had a financial stake in land purchasing, he said, and had destroyed his Act because 'it swept away a vast number of Native interpreters and middle-men, who had previously been urging the Natives to sell their land. It destroyed their influence and put them outside the pale, and then we had their enormous influence brought to bear on the Maoris to prevent their taking advantage of the Act.'[119] Thus ended 'perhaps the fairest attempt to balance the interests of settlement and Maori landholders that the Colony had yet seen'.[120]

The other major activities of Ballance as Native Minister also concerned his defence portfolio. They involved the continuing saga of Maori protest at Parihaka and Ballance's approach to law and order and to Maori grievances in general. Ballance's policy on these issues was quite different to that of Bryce, who had led an armed assault on Parihaka in November 1881. Shortly after coming to office Ballance began reducing the paramilitary

Armed Constabulary throughout the North Island, on the grounds that stations with substantial numbers of constabulary only annoyed the Maori.[121] 'I say that the Native race are to be influenced more by a sense of justice and right than by all the Armed Constabulary we can maintain, and that the best policy to employ is a policy such as we propose, and not a policy of repression.'[122] This 'one policeman policy', as it became known, was vigorously pursued by Ballance. By 1885 the number of Armed Constabulary units had been reduced from 428 to only 48 and under the Defence Act of the same year they were replaced entirely by a new, smaller, Permanent Militia Force.[123]

Not long after the release of Te Whiti and Tohu (they had been imprisoned following Bryce's raid) activity began again in Parihaka. Marches were led out from there throughout Taranaki and by May 1885 the Pakeha press were calling for government action to quell the disorder.[124] Ballance visited Parihaka late in the month and was afterwards interviewed by the *Hawera Star*. He said that the reported activities of the Maori had been 'distorted and exaggerated' and that therefore he was not going to station men to Pungarehu (a European settlement near Parihaka) as some settlers had requested. He was quite aware of Maori discontent but argued that the presence of military posts irritated them further. 'We must simply watch the natives, be prepared for anything, and in the meantime do all we can to remove grievances.' Prominent among complaints was the small sum received by Maori landowners once a host of costs had been deducted from the rent paid by European lessees.[125] Ballance did in fact attempt to improve the lot of Maori landowners. For example, he reduced the amount of commission charged by the Public Trustee (which leased the land) and generally gave Maori more control over trusts held on their behalf. Through an annual Special Powers and Contracts Act a wide range of Maori grievances were dealt with.[126]

Back in Wellington Ballance ordered a report on the disturbances in south Taranaki. When published it showed that the threats alleged by Europeans to have been made against them were almost entirely without foundation.[127] A second report, on speeches delivered in Parihaka by Te Whiti and Tohu, reinforced the view that the Maori sought only peace.[128] In the House Ballance said that the whole affair had been 'got up by Europeans for the purpose of bringing back to the place a large expenditure in the shape of Armed Constabulary'. In fact he believed that the Maori were much more content now he had removed the constabulary from the area. If such a policy had been followed in 1881, the 'battle of Parihaka' need never have occurred. Finally, he described a suggestion to bring into force the Peace Preservation Act (allowing government detention without trial) as a cruel attempt 'to keep in subjection harmless people who have not committed any offence against the people of this colony'.[129]

Despite this optimism there was some trouble ahead. It began when a group of Maori, including Titokowaru, moved onto a farm north of Hawera owned by a European named Hastie. Police intervened, scuffles followed and arrests were made. The 'Battle of Hastie's farm' over, Pardy, the local Inspector of Police, obtained Ballance's permission to detain Te Whiti. Te Whiti had been warned that he would be held responsible for any breaches of peace in the area and the authorities had 'positive information' that it was upon his instructions that Hastie's farm had been occupied. He was arrested on 20 July in a lightning dawn raid made by a small group of men led by Pardy. Te Whiti was brought to Wellington and, in contrast to his treatment in 1881, given a trial. He was fined £100 and jailed for three months.[130]

The whole affair had been handled with great success, for Parihaka was quiet and remained so. 'All is silent', said Ballance, because the Maori 'believe the Government of the colony is prepared to act fairly to them, and to reason out questions with them'.[131] Clearly much of the credit lay with Pardy's tact and sensitivity. Yet Ballance's 'one policeman policy' was seen to have borne fruit and his prestige was justifiably enhanced. At the same time, because the arrest had been carried out in a matter of minutes and without violence, his mana amongst the Maori did not suffer. Not long after the incident, for example, Ballance was able to persuade Te Kooti to halt a march to Poverty Bay.[132] Such a visit would, on account of Te Kooti's raids on settlements in the area in 1868, have been fraught with problems. Also at Ballance's suggestion Te Heu Heu, chief of Ngatituwharetoa, gave as a gift land in the central plateau of the North Island for the establishment of Tongariro National Park — one of the world's earliest national parks.[133]

Ballance's approach to race relations was much more sympathetic and enlightened than his predecessors'. The protection he sought for Maori interests was considerable and his views on communal ownership of land remarkably advanced among Pakeha politicians of the time. However, he rejected claims by Maori to any form of political independence.[134] In common with many late nineteenth-century radicals he regarded the European as essentially superior to the Maori and, particularly as a rationalist and freethinker, largely accepted the tenets of Darwinism. His policy was 'qualified assimilationist' and paternalistic, rather than bi-cultural. Maori would ultimately come under European law and institutions:

> We should desire to bring them into the same position as the Euro-
> peans, with the same rights and liberties, to plant in the minds of
> the Natives the same feeling of satisfaction with the laws of the colony
> as prevails in the minds of the Europeans . . . This policy is in accor-
> dance with the Treaty of Waitangi; it is in accordance with the prin-
> ciples of justice.[135]

That Maori might not survive as 'Europeans' was of course the basic flaw to such an approach, and one that Ballance could never really come to terms with. The pervasive ideology of racial superiority was too strong and assimilation, in that it was regarded as inevitable, seemed just. Yet Ballance admitted in the case of land ownership that the retention of Maori custom was necessary if assimilation were not to mean destruction. This was closer to the policy of 'amalgamation', the incorporation of Maori on an equal basis with Pakeha into a European system, espoused by the British authorities in 1840.[136] Experience had shown that, however well meaning, such a policy, under settler pressure, quickly turned into assimilation.

Consistent with his demilitarisation of sensitive Maori areas, Ballance's defence policy in general aimed to reduce the numbers and therefore the cost of the colony's armed forces. Aside from the police these were the Volunteers, the Permanent Militia and the Militia. The volunteer force, which Ballance had joined in Wanganui in 1868, had declined in popularity because it was little needed and offered poor conditions of service. However, Ballance saw that it was considerably cheaper to maintain than an unnecessarily large standing Armed Constabulary, which in any case had been formed to meet the temporary emergency of the war against the Maori. He therefore encouraged the volunteers, raising their capitation allowance and appointing his old friend (now Sir) George Whitmore as their commander.[137] The Permanent Militia (essentially the regular army) replaced the large Constabulary. The Militia remained as before, covering the adult male population and to be called out only in emergencies.[138]

Though Ballance cut total spending on the armed forces he increased that on harbour defences, in response to the Russian 'threat' of 1885. The threat was taken very seriously at the time, though it never actually materialised. It arose from a conflict of British and Russian interests in Afghanistan. Guns were ordered from England and work begun on fortifying the harbours of the four major centres. Meanwhile Whitmore organised mock battles involving the repulsion of Russian attacks by sturdy volunteers.[139]

The crisis brought to the fore New Zealand's dependence upon the British Navy and Stout was soon negotiating with London a yearly colonial contribution to the cost of this protection.[140] Personally, Ballance was reluctant to increase defence expenditure. It had been forced upon him, he said, when bankers came to the Government and said, 'if ports were not defended they would ship their gold away to Australia'.[141] Generally Ballance's views on defence and New Zealand's position in the world were strongly tinged with the nationalism and self-reliance that would feature prominently in his later premiership. At this time the Australian states were moving towards unification within a federal system and there was debate in New Zealand as to whether to join in. In 1885, when Parliament debated the question, Ballance was lukewarm on the proposal.[142] By 1890, however, he had moved firmly against the idea, believing the colony would inevitably suffer a loss of economic and political independence and seeing in federation no advantage in trade or defence.[143] There was also much discussion in the 1880s about New Zealand and other colonies being tied in more closely with Britain in some form of Imperial Federation. Again Ballance was reluctant, largely on the grounds of loss of political independence. Also, he saw no sense in Imperial Federation without the federation of the constituent parts of the United Kingdom. This would be exceedingly difficult to achieve, he admitted, and 'a dream until we get rid of monarchy — until we have a republic'.[144] In any case, as far as defence needs were concerned, Ballance argued that as long as Britain had trade interests in the Pacific the colony would be afforded protection when necessary, irrespective of any formal federation. Nor was he willing to commit New Zealand to any overseas military venture and refused to send colonial troops to assist Britain in the Sudan.[145]

Essentially Ballance's defence policy rested upon the realisation that New Zealand had neither the money nor men, and therefore should not attempt, to defend itself against an attack from a major power. In line with this his nationalism was isolationist, not aggressive. National self-reliance meant developing the country's natural resources while remaining detached from the outside world. It matched Ballance's long-held belief in individual self-reliance, forming a broad philosophy that underlay his approach to the 1890 election.

Ballance's birthplace today

'Lakeview', aerial view, circa *1970s*

John Ballance aged 14 years
(Alexander Turnbull Library)

High Street, Belfast, 1851
(Ulster Museum)

Parliament Buildings, circa *1875 (*Alexander Turnbull Library*)*

Wellington, circa *1870s (*Alexander Turnbull Library*)*

Robert and Anna Stout (Alexander Turnbull Library)

Anderson Family (Alexander Turnbull Library)

Kathleen Ballance aged eight years (Alexander Turnbull Library)

David Anderson's store, corner of Molesworth Street and Hawkestone Street, 1862
(Alexander Turnbull Library)

John Ballance, circa *1884*
*(*Alexander Turnbull Library)

Robert McKnight

Ellen Ballance, circa *1890*
(Alexander Turnbull Library)

'The Knolls', circa *1890*

Wanganui, circa *1890s (*Alexander Turnbull Library)

Kathleen Ballance and Sarah Jane Anderson in the garden of 'The Knolls'
(*Alexander Turnbull Library*)

Kathleen Ballance beside the Ballances' pony and carriage (Alexander Turnbull Library)

Premier's residence, Tinakori Road, circa 1890
(Alexander Turnbull Library, courtesy Mrs K. M. Foster)

John Ballance, circa *1892 (*Alexander Turnbull Library*)*

*Ballance Cabinet, 1892 (*Alexander Turnbull Library*)*

Ellen Ballance in old age
(Alexander Turnbull Library)

*Ballance's funeral, Wanganui,
April 1893 (*Alexander
Turnbull Library)

Unveiling of the Ballance statue (Alexander Turnbull Library)

Ellen and Kathleen Ballance's house in Wicksteed Street, Wanganui
(Alexander Turnbull Library)

CHAPTER 8

Leadership

THE FUNDAMENTAL IDEOLOGICAL DIFFERENCES between Ballance and Stout on the one hand and Vogel on the other surfaced regularly during the life of their ministry. Ballance was considerably more cautious than Vogel on the question of further borrowing. Vogel was equally unenthusiastic about Ballance's land policy. In the 1885 session the Government suffered a number of major defeats, for example on tariff increases and public works expenditure. In January 1886 Ballance told his constituents that the Government ought to 'formulate their policy, announce it to the country and dissolve before the session commenced'.[1] There was widespread talk of dissolution over the following weeks,[2] though not until the close of the session was Stout's request for one turned down by the Governor.[3] Vogel resisted an election until the purchase of the Waimea Plains Railway was finalised (the bill did not pass until August 1886), a fact which gave Ballance and Stout (who in this respect had less to lose by dissolution) some leverage on him.[4] Yet the splits within the Cabinet were clear for all to see. Ballance and Stout voted for the Government's Representation Bill while Vogel and two other ministers, Larnach and Richardson, opposed it. The bill, which redistributed seats in favour of the under-represented North Island, failed to pass by just three votes.[5]

For Ballance the advantages of dissolution were ambiguous. His Land Act had already been passed and by 1887 he was arguing that an election would be necessary to test the feeling of the country on his more radical Land Acquisition Bill.[6] On the other hand his settlement schemes required careful administration and vigorous promotion if they were to achieve any success. He was also keen to see his Native Land Administration Bill go to the House and was confident that it would get through. Finally, there was always the chance that an election would only make the political situation worse.

Dissolution came willy nilly in May 1887 when, following a pessimistic financial statement, the Government was defeated on its proposed tariff increases. The triennial election was in any case due in August. The protection of New Zealand businesses through higher tariffs on imports was now a major political issue. Encouraging local industry broadened the base of the country's economy and at the same time increased employment opportunities in the towns. Also, raising customs duties boosted government revenue and was an alternative to cutting expenditure as a means of reducing the budget deficit.

The election was fixed for September 1887, the delay allowing for the passage of the Representation Bill before the session's end. The act reduced the 'country quota' (the artificial addition of population to country electorates in order to over-represent them at the expense of the growing cities) from 25 to 18 percent and established a commission to redraw electoral boundaries.[7] The campaign was fought in the midst of the worst depression the country had seen. Government revenue and expenditure were falling and trade slumped to an all-time low. The excess of immigration over emigration (a good indicator of the level of economic activity) was down to under 1000 and over the following year a staggering 9000 more people left the colony than arrived.[8]

Ballance had been convinced of the need for protection for some time and the matter assumed a greater urgency as the depression deepened. Import prices were falling, making it increasingly difficult for local producers to compete. Speaking at Lawrence in Otago in February 1886 he argued that protection was vital to the survival of the country's industry. Without it manufacturers would be 'crushed by an influx of shoddy goods' imported by wealthy merchants.[9] Ballance rode the rising demand for protection and in early June 1887 proposed at a Wellington meeting the establishment of a New Zealand Industrial Protection Association. In a highly significant speech he attempted to bring together the interests of manufacturers, the working classes and small farmers. He quoted statistics to show that more farm produce was consumed within the colony than was exported, concluding that farmers needed the large market and manufacturers of the towns as much as the towns needed country customers. 'Create a population in the country and in the towns,' he said, 'and they create markets for each other. The two interests are inseparable.'[10] So Ballance proposed the protection of all industries, linked to a policy of closer settlement. The only people hit would be the importers and large landowners who had been doing so well under free trade.

Despite Ballance's efforts to persuade farmers that protection was in their interests (even if initially it meant higher prices, this was far outweighed by the long term advantages of industrial expansion), it was primarily an urban policy. In his first significant comments on the colony's incipient trade union movement,[11] he said that unions as well as employers should be represented in the Industrial Protection Association. If free trade continued it would result in the 'degradation of colonial labor'. Therefore,

> every artisan should join in this movement and assist in the estab-
> lishment of an association where employers of labor and the employed
> could meet on an equal footing, and where all classes of the industrial
> community might be fairly represented ... What the working people
> wanted was organisation, without which they had accomplished
> nothing in the past, and would accomplish nothing in the future. What
> they wanted was a patriotic and national policy ... Too long they
> had been accustomed to rate their comfort on the wealth of the few
> and not the prosperity of the many.[12]

This was a populist appeal which looked to agreement rather than conflict between classes. Ballance said that strikes brought the two classes into collision when they should be 'combining to oppose the common enemy' of free trade. 'There need not be any irreconcilable difference between employer and employed on this question,' he concluded.[13]

Ballance opened his campaign at the Princess Theatre in Wanganui on 22 June. His speech placed great emphasis on village and special settlements which, Ballance argued, were essential if the unemployed working class were to be settled on the land and 'congestion of labour in the towns' avoided. Where land was in short supply, large estates ought to be bought by the Government and split into small farms, along the lines of his Land Acquisition Bill. On retrenchment he said that any reductions must be made all round; large salary-earners ought to face cuts as well as low wage-earners. He was reluctant to see the school age raised as a means of reducing Government expenditure on education. Finally, Ballance argued that protection was necessary to establish new industry and new jobs. Having repeated many of the points made in his Wellington speech, he concluded:

> It was not everyone who could go on to the land, and they must
> provide for the people in the towns, and Protection was the only way,
> as far as he could see, by which it could be brought about. The farmers
> might be hostile to Protection for a time, but he could assure them
> that Protection was their best friend, and that they would find a home
> market more profitable than a foreign one.[14]

While Ballance raised protection as a major issue at the Wanganui election, his opponent Gilbert Carson was deliberately vague on it.[15] The expression of strongly anti-protectionist sentiments would have been politically unwise in an urban constituency. Carson was manager and editor of the *Wanganui Chronicle* and the paper's longstanding opposition to Ballance naturally hardened when Carson himself entered the political fray. The *Chronicle* regularly published Carson's letters, which reinforced a stream of tendentious editorials.[16] The *Herald*, of course, was equally partisan in Ballance's favour.

Carson was a respectable establishment figure in a sense that Ballance was not. A total abstainer and ex-Baptist lay preacher, he was prominent in the Y.M.C.A. and supported the Bible in schools. He had been Mayor of Wanganui. One of his leading protagonists referred to Ballance's followers as the 'scum of Wanganui'.[17] Other Carson supporters pointed to Ballance's 'antagonism to Christianity' and the holding of meetings of the Freethought Association on Sunday evenings 'apparently with the view of stultifying the work of the Christian church'.[18]

During the election Carson advocated major cuts in expenditure, criticising the extravagance of the Stout-Vogel Government and of Ballance in particular. He queried Ballance's travelling expenses and the money spent on village settlement, schemes he described as 'miserable, poverty stricken affairs'.[19] Towards the end of the campaign the *Chronicle* brought up Ballance's involvement in the Land and Loan Company ten years earlier.[20] Carson was desperately looking for mud he could sling and make stick.

The constituency of Wanganui had been enlarged since the 1884 election. It now included Aramoho, Eastown, Castlecliff, Westmere, Campbelltown, Putiki and Durietown, all nearby settlements previously part of the Wai-totara electorate. The addition of Aramoho, a working-class district where the railway terminus and workshops were located, would act in Ballance's favour. Speaking there in July he made his first reference of the campaign to the Liberal Party, and said that he expected it to win a majority of seats at the elections. Again he saw land settlement and protection as 'two of the most vital questions of the day'.[21]

The paucity of references to the Liberal Party was understandable given the position Ballance was placed in. He had to defend a government whose composition and support included both liberals and conservatives. Ballance was able to emphasise the liberal nature of his own legislation, and to a certain extent sidestep the obvious political inconsistencies of the Stout-Vogel alliance. As the election drew near, however, rumours abounded of splits within the ministry. Candidates were allying themselves behind individual cabinet members, reported the *Post*, the main division occurring between supporters of Ballance and Stout and those of Vogel and Larnach.[22] Certainly the Ulster-born storekeeper Felix McGuire, whom Ballance was assisting in the Egmont election, had publicly stated his opposition to Vogel; and the same was true of J. A. Tole in Auckland and of George Hutchison, who was standing against Bryce in Waitotara. Though Ballance denied that there was any plot afloat[23] he did all he could to put his political weight behind the more decidedly liberal government candidates. For example, in Wellington he supported Robertson, an iron manufacturer who was a protectionist and strong advocate of Ballance's land settlement schemes.[24] Never before had Ballance made such efforts to influence elections out-side Wanganui. They were testimony to the fact that he was now regarded, and regarded himself, as a leading political figure.

The Wanganui election was fought almost entirely on national issues rather than local ones. One exception was the question of harbour improvements. The matter had been raised in 1884 when Ballance promised, if elected, to promote a rating bill to provide finance for river development. True to his word he introduced the Wanganui Harbour Board Rating Bill soon after the opening of the new Parliament. The bill, which had the support of the vast majority of the town's ratepayers,[25] passed a second reading but was nullified by a Legislative Council amendment requiring any rate to be sanctioned by two-thirds of the electors on the roll, rather than simply two-thirds of those who voted.[26] The *Yeoman* immediately proposed that the council be reformed.[27]

Ballance's subsequent efforts to have similar bills passed also failed. The main problem was the fixing of the rating area; that is, how much of the country surrounding Wanganui should be included and thus (assuming a favourable poll) made liable for rating. These country districts had little sympathy for the board's financial problems,[28] and certainly did not feel obliged to dip into their own pockets to help it out. Their cause was championed by John Bryce, who opposed Ballance with as much persistence as the latter showed in repeatedly bringing the bill before Parliament.[29] The 1887 bill, even after Rangitikei was excluded from the rating area, was again rejected by the council. This time Bryce 'walked out during the second reading, saying he preferred to be neutral'.[30] During the election Ballance countered criticism that he had failed in his promises by simply pointing to his numerous attempts to have the bill passed and said that he had certainly more chance of getting it through than had Carson.[31]

Ballance romped home at the election with his most convincing win yet, polling 865 votes to Carson's 423.[32] His victory contrasted starkly with the performance of government candidates elsewhere. Stout suffered a shock, and for a Premier a particularly humiliating, defeat. Tole, the Minister for Justice, also lost his seat. McGuire and Lundon (who was standing in the Bay of Islands) both failed to get elected, though Bryce was beaten by Hutchison and Rolleston defeated in Canterbury. When Parliament assembled, the Stout-Vogel Government tendered its resignation and the Governor called for Harry Atkinson.[33]

Ballance did so well because unlike the other members of the ministry his personal reputation had been greatly enhanced by three years in office. His campaign emphasised real practical achievements in the fields of land settlement and race relations. In a town close enough to feel vibrations from Maori unrest further to the north, and where Bryce's political influence was always a consideration at elections, Ballance's greater success in dealing with Parihaka was an important factor. At the same time these personal accomplishments helped to obscure the Government's failure to reverse the deepening depression.

In general, Ballance's political platform was well tailored to Wanganui. His land settlement and protection policies drew support from many businessmen as well as from the town's working class. Closer settlement offered social and economic benefits for both groups. As for protection, raising tariff duties helped balance the nation's books while at the same time encouraging local industry and stimulating employment. The Opposition proposed dealing with the depression through wholesale cuts in government expenditure, but these would clearly hit the working class and struggling small businessmen rather than the wealthier importers and more self-sufficient farmers. This alliance of the land-hungry working class and small businessmen attempting to expand local industry at a time of economic stagnation was achieved much more easily in 1887 than three years later. In 1890 it would be threatened by industrial unrest and trade union activity which alienated many of the town's employers.

Lack of a viable alternative brought Atkinson and his 'Scarecrow Ministry' to power. The House was split into a number of groups, Atkinson drawing support from rural free-traders led by W. R. Russell and Ormond as well as from those who saw the need for limited protection alongside retrenchment. Atkinson's Cabinet was inexperienced, 'makeshift' and 'doubtfully reliable',[34] and little emerged from three years of the Scarecrow Ministry aside from a few financial measures and a Representation Act. It survived because the Opposition, now led by Vogel, supported Atkinson's tariffs and was in any case in even greater disarray than the Government itself. The Opposition included followers of Vogel, 'Stout-Ballance' liberals and a collection of junior members including Reeves, Ward, Perceval and Seddon, who formed the ephemeral 'Young New Zealand Party'.

From the start of the new Parliament Ballance attempted to gather around him a group of like-minded liberals. In October he was 'busy among the remnants of the Stout wing in the late Stout-Vogel array', and appeared 'determined to form a little cohort under his own leadership to act independently but generally with the Vogelites'.[35] Ballance saw no future in Vogel and so with John McKenzie, Cadman and others from this liberal group held aloof from a Vogel caucus meeting.[36]

However, these manoeuvrings were halted when Ballance became seriously ill. In the last months of 1887 he made few appearances in the House. He had in fact been unwell since before the September election.[37] He had worked hard and travelled far over the past three years and the exertions had clearly placed a great strain on his weak constitution. Though energetic in his younger days, he had since then led a sedentary but busy life that allowed little time for leisure, and by 1887 was a somewhat portly, middle-aged man. The hobbies he did find time for were mentally rather than physically demanding. His great passion was for chess, at which he was extremely competent.[38] In the late 1870s he had started a chess club in Wanganui and a weekly chess column in the *Herald*.[39] This, reading and discussions with his friends on political, social and philosophical questions were his greatest delight. Years ago, Ballance had been a good horseman and the exercise would have helped to keep him fit. He attended race meetings and himself owned a racehorse called 'Lough Neagh' (he had not forgotten home). The animal was later sold and re-named 'Fishhook', and became one of the most successful of its day.[40] But now he travelled in carriages and on trains.

The nature of the illness that struck Ballance at this time is unclear. The *Yeoman* rumoured that it might be fatal and the annual Christmas gathering of the Anderson family at 'Rhyme' in Wellington was cancelled because of the seriousness of the situation.[41] Fortunately, however, Ballance was soon on the mend and after a recuperation period of some months appeared to have made a full recovery.[42]

While Ballance's health was improving, his financial position worsened. He no longer received a ministerial salary and had resumed full editorial control over the *Herald* in January 1888.[43] That year the economy sunk to an all-time low and by May the *Herald* company was in dire straits. The directors cut back where they could but told Ballance that they needed a loan of between £500 and £700 to survive. When he heard just how bad things were Ballance proposed a number of remedies, such as reducing wages to a maximum of £30 per week. He also offered to take over day-to-day management of the paper from an existing employee who was reluctant to carry the responsibility. In addition both he and Ellen were willing to pledge all their shares in the company as guarantee for a loan. Ballance believed that the *Herald* would survive:

> We must not be beaten, but we must at the same time face the position. The paper will soon recover itself, if we give it the chance . . . Personally I am quite willing to make any sacrifice on behalf of the shareholders who have invested their capital in the concern, & begin again. But I firmly believe the loss will be quickly recouped. There is in our favour the fact that the paper has a large circulation & hold on the people, & consequently commands the advertising. And even a great reduction of reading matter will not affect it prejudicially.[44]

Ill-health and money worries dampened Ballance's enthusiasm for advancing his political career. There was also the consideration that the political auspices were not good. Vogel had left the country during the recess and Opposition Members were, in the words of the *Evening Post*, 'like sheep without their shepherd'. And the *Post* thought that it would 'be very difficult to find any one capable of mustering the flock and guiding it out of cold shades to the pleasant pasture which lies behind the Treasury benches'.[45] Ballance recognised that skilful husbandry, to continue the quaint pastoral analogy, had been lacking. Writing to Stout he lamented that Vogel's poor leadership had 'almost broken up the Opposition as an organised body'. It was a depressing scenario. The ministry's Land Bill and encouragement of cash sales involved a complete reversal of Ballance's settlement policies; though Ballance unrealistically thought that 'so glaring an attempt to play into the hands of the capitalists & runholders [would] tell its tale' and soon destroy the Government. A Representation Bill reducing the number of European members from 91 to 70 in order to save money would, if passed, said Ballance, be a 'terrible blow to the democracy. This is the Reactionary Parliament, & the question is, where is it going to stop?' He hoped that Stout would return to politics as soon as possible and resume the fight.[46]

By May 1888 Ballance was considering quitting politics for good. He wrote from Wellington to his friend John Notman in Wanganui: 'I am thinking of retiring from politics at the end of the session & devoting myself entirely to business. This is very confidential for the present.'[47] The session had just opened with the address-in-reply being adopted 'without a single word uttered'. 'The reason is that there is no leader of the Opposition,' said the *Post*, 'nor indeed, an Opposition party.'[48] Ballance was the obvious choice as leader on the grounds of experience, ability and national standing, but he let it be known that he was not willing to take on the job.[49] His recent illness and financial problems were the main reasons he turned the offer down. The Opposition appointed instead a committee (including Ballance) to co-ordinate its activities. It was chaired by J. D. Lance, an ex-army Canterbury runholder, and comprised also John McKenzie, Oliver Samuel (a New Plymouth lawyer), Richard Seddon from the West Coast, the journalist W. J. Steward and Aucklander F. J. Moss.[50]

Yet Atkinson was also in difficulties. A gloomy Financial Statement concluded with a proposal for increased tariffs that immediately exposed the fragile nature of his support in Parliament. Further duties would help the towns at the expense of country property-owners who had until now supported the Scarecrow Ministry. 'The Government could easily be put out of office if we had a leader,' McKenzie wrote to Stout.[51] Only with the Opposition's assistance was Atkinson able to get the tariffs through the House. 'It is a great victory, and it has completely disintegrated the Ministerial party,' Ballance reported to Stout:

> The Govt. have lost the cream of their party in the Freetraders, whose severance is complete & whose bitterness will prevent a reconciliation. I believe we can carry a vote against the Govt. if we think it prudent to do so this session. It must be admitted however that there is a kind of demoralisation in the Opposition ranks . . . If we cd only get rid of the Representation Act we might hope for liberal legislation in the future. It is proposed in a week's time to move in going into Supply that the Representation Act be not brought into force until after the

next census. We want time to enable the country to swing back again. I think it will be carried . . . The Govt. have now about 30 followers & no more. The Opposition number 39, and the Freetraders 25. Macarthur says 15 of these are prepared at any time to turn the Govt. out.[52]

In fact, the motion on the Representation Act was lost by the substantial margin of 20 votes to 41[53] and there was no challenge to the Government during the session. Ballance was clearly reluctant to force an election. He knew that the Opposition was in no position to face one and reckoned that the country was not yet ready to dump Atkinson.

Ballance's end-of-session speech made it quite clear that he assumed considerable responsibility for the actions of the Opposition. For example, he defended its support for the Government's tariffs:

> It appears to me the true functions of the Opposition are to accept all that is good and reject all that is bad, and that, when the Opposition found the tariff exactly suited its views, it acted on that principle . . . We believe that Protection will be for the benefit of the country ultimately; we believe that almost immediately it will be beneficial so far as the artisans of the towns are concerned.[54]

Ballance also said that the Opposition's success ought to be measured by the number of bills that had been thrown out, as much as by the passing of the tariff.[55] Looking back, it had indeed been a barren session. A Native Land Bill, restoring private purchasing, was the only major non-financial measure to survive.[56] And as far as that Bill was concerned, Atkinson admitted that settlement would be encouraged best by Government rather than private initiative.[57]

Political developments during the recess were as confused as ever. The *Post* predicted that Stout would return to politics and form an alliance with Atkinson.[58] This was wishful thinking. Such a coalition was most unlikely. Stout supported the Government's tariff measures but so did much of the Opposition. And in any case he was doggedly refusing to re-enter politics. Along with the more conservative journals, the *Post* much preferred to see Stout back rather than have Ballance elected as opposition leader. Ballance was regarded as distinctly more radical. 'Mr Ballance would be a capable leader if it were not for his extreme views on certain questions.'[59] He would not be able to gather and lead a party that could seriously threaten Atkinson, it was argued. 'On many of the points which a large number of members most differ from and distrust the Premier upon, Mr Ballance holds even more pronounced and advanced views. They distrust him still more, and would rather keep Sir Harry Atkinson in power than assist Mr Ballance to office.'[60]

The *Herald*'s financial problems continued into 1889. Ballance borrowed another £100 from his father-in-law and later sold him 3000 shares in the

Mokihinui Coal Company, in lieu of the loan repayment.[61] Paddy Anderson was not unsympathetic. In February 1889 he let one of his properties in Willis Street and credited the rent to Ellen.[62] A month later he died, leaving a substantial sum to be divided among his children.[63] All this helped the *Herald* survive the crisis and by mid-1889 the Ballances' finances were significantly healthier than they had been a year before. Ballance's earlier optimism was justified. By 1891 the *Herald* had turned the 'large overdraft . . . and heavy outside liabilities' of 1888 into a profit of £480. Twelve months later profits increased to £600, the debt owing to the bank was repaid and a dividend declared for the first time in a number of years.[64]

The way was now clear for Ballance. He was physically and mentally restored, and his business affairs were showing marked signs of improvement. Also, Stout had made it plain that he would not be returning to politics. Ballance took the initiative and in his pre-sessional address delivered at the beginning of June staked his leadership claim, suggesting that 'there was a very solid party in the House' who agreed with his views.[65]

Parliament opened on 20 June 1889 and in early July a caucus meeting of 32 opposition members elected Ballance leader. W. C. Walker, the only other candidate mooted, made known his support for Ballance and the vote was unanimous.[66] Ballance said that he took on the task 'not without much hesitation' but felt it his duty.[67] This was largely posturing. It did not look good to be too eager for the job.

Though Ballance publicly lamented Stout's absence from the House,[68] having come this far he did not welcome continual suggestions that it might only be temporary. Ballance respected Stout's intellectual ability, looking to him for moral support and acknowledging his superior claims to leadership of the liberals, but his persistent presence in the wings was irritating. It was difficult for Ballance to establish himself as leader when many viewed him as 'only the nominal head of the party, a kind of *locum tenens*' while Stout was away.[69] Not until Ballance had firmly secured his position as Premier did he finally shake off Stout's shadow. As for Stout, he enjoyed being regarded as the person 'pulling the strings' behind the scenes,[70] content to theorise and philosophise from a distance for as long as Ballance held centre stage and got on with practical politics.

Critics of Ballance naturally over-emphasised the influence Stout had on him, interpreting it as a sign of Ballance's weak, dependent leadership. It did not help matters that Ballance was known to be 'a nice guy'. Many saw him as too conciliatory and courteous, and not abrasive and forceful enough, to make a strong leader. Stout's significance was also exaggerated by liberals who wished to see the Dunedin lawyer moderate the 'dangerous' Ballance.[71] They were much more comfortable with the respectable Sir Robert (he had been knighted when Premier) than the radical Ballance, the first distinctly lower middle-class leader the country had seen.[72] In general Ballance's opponents thought that though he was 'too original, too much of a thinker,' he was also 'too fond of trying to reduce fine theories to practice . . . to be a safe man'.[73]

There was a more difficult problem for Ballance in conveying the impression of convincing leadership. By nature he disliked the negative aspects of the job. He suffered from the honourable, but for a political leader unfortunate, failing of being reluctant to criticise for the sake of criticism. Ballance was happiest when in a position to initiate, legislate and administer practical measures. This was not true of all politicians, as it might at first sight appear. Grey revelled in attacking the party in power with the rhetoric of defending the working class against the might of the establishment. On the other hand he was weak as an administrator and broker between divergent cabinet colleagues. With Ballance the reverse was the case. He found the role of Opposition leader frustrating and at the same time deplored the lack of activity, the barrenness, of Atkinson's Ministry. Having been congratulated by the Premier on his assumption of the leadership, Ballance told the House how he intended the Opposition should operate:

> I am confident the Opposition will pursue no factious course in this House, recognising as it does that its chief function is to promote the despatch of public business. Where we have to dissent from the honourable gentleman and take exception to his measures of policy and acts of administration, we hope to do so according to well-established custom and upon purely constitutional lines.[74]

The first major concern of the House was the Representation Bill which, as well as reducing the number of members, raised the country quota, but also abolished plural voting. Ballance argued that the reduction in members was undemocratic, since only the wealthy would be able to afford to fight the larger country seats. He said that the bill aimed to create antagonism between town and country whereas it ought to be realised that their interests were mutual.[75] Welcoming the abolition of plural voting he thought that there should also be single electorates and equal electoral districts. He also announced, 'I want one woman one vote as well, and I want to make, in reality, the family the unit, the basis, of civilisation and of political influence in the country, and not single men.'[76]

The bill passed despite some vigorous stonewalling by city members, and the country quota was fixed at 28 percent.[77] Ballance rejected suggestions to turn the issue into a matter of confidence, believing that such a vote would fail and in any case he was still unsure of the desirability of an early election.[78] Instead he carried out a poll among members to gauge support for the restoration of the number of seats to 91.[79] It was all he could do, especially considering that advocates of the quota included liberals such as Cadman, McKenzie, Seddon and Ward. Also, if a no-confidence vote were carried but a dissolution then refused, Ballance would face the uphill task of trying to form a government from the far from cohesive ranks of the Opposition.[80] An election would be preferable to this, albeit unlikely, scenario.

The Government came under more serious threat over taxation. Atkinson proposed to make minor changes to the property tax, for example exempting machinery in order to give some relief to industry. However, the House was bent on more drastic action. Conservatives favoured reductions in the property tax to be made up by further cuts in government expenditure,[81] while liberals wanted new income and land taxes and lower duties on basic necessities. No sooner had Atkinson sat down after moving the second reading of the Property Assessment Bill, which contained the taxation changes, than the Member for Parnell, F. J. Moss, proposed the amendment that the property tax was unfair in its incidence. The Aucklander thus forced the debate into a matter of confidence.[82] Ballance had to admit that he had had no advance warning of Moss's intentions.[83]

In his speech on the bill Ballance appeared as the epitome of moderation. He simply wished the existing taxation system 'reconstructed' so that it bore 'equally on all classes', and fell well short of arguing for the replacement of the property tax by income and land taxes.[84] Some misread this as recognition of the impracticability of doing away with the property tax.[85] In fact, as Atkinson and others were well aware,[86] Ballance was trying to unite against the ministry conservative and liberal opponents of the tax, and this necessitated the minimum of comment upon what might replace it. When it came, the division was close, the Government surviving by just four votes.[87]

Sophisticated tactics were also involved in an apparent attempt by Ballance to bring down Atkinson. Moving a motion of no confidence, he said that the Government had lost the support of the country and had neither policy nor measures. 'There are periods of reaction in all democratic countries, and this is one we have upon us.'[88] In fact there was no possibility that his motion would be carried, and his tongue-in-cheek plea met with much amusement from following speakers. The point was that he hoped to prevent Atkinson dissolving Parliament when it suited the Premier best. The Governor would most likely refuse any subsequent request from Atkinson for a dissolution on the grounds that the House had already, on Ballance's motion, declared against it.[89] In any case, there was reluctance to force an early election, because with the reduction in the number of members many were uncertain of their chance of being returned.

As the session dragged on the Cabinet began to disintegrate. Earlier in the year George Fisher had resigned over personal and policy disagreements with Atkinson.[90] Now in September 1889 the Colonial Secretary, Hislop, was forced to retire after censure by the Legislative Council for the misuse of ministerial influence. Atkinson, who was becoming increasingly ill, secured a reprieve when W. R. Russell agreed to join the Government and brought the support of the free trade 'middle party' with him.[91] For these predominantly rural conservatives the only alternative to Atkinson was Ballance, a 'self-confessed radical'.[92]

In his review of government policy at the end of the session Ballance returned to old themes. He argued that the rising emigration from the country should be reversed by promoting new settlement: 'We want every man who can to go upon the land and maintain himself upon it, whether he has capital or not.' He accused the Government of administering the land laws for the benefit of capitalists. 'Unless a man is prepared to "dummy" the land as a speculator he is heavily handicapped . . . The yeoman village settler is treated to the cold shoulder.'[93] Ballance also complained of political prejudice against village settlements and criticised the stream of 'improper transactions' involving Maori land that had been validated by the Government. Finally he warned the new Railway Board, set up by Atkinson to take over control of the railways, not to attempt to regulate wages. If the board did it would be abolished within five years: 'I should protest in the strongest terms against any interference with or any attempt to reduce the rate of wages in the colony,' he said.[94]

Criticism of the Railway Commissioners was prominent in Ballance's first public speech as opposition leader, delivered to a large gathering at Napier in late October. It was an important matter. As Ballance pointed out, Atkinson had established the board in the hope of avoiding direct responsibility for a lowering of railway wages that would inevitably push down rates generally. Ballance said that wages should be increased rather than decreased.[95]

Ballance was keen to make a good impression at Napier. Though 'on the warpath' he had been advised by W. C. Walker, Member for Ashburton, to remember that he was 'addressing not only Napier and the hungry democrats of that place, but the whole colony':

> Remember too you have a . . . [reputation] for being somewhat of a dangerous man in relation to certain views and you would triumph over many who doubt you if you show them that you are not what they suppose you to be. What would be all right for a candidate fighting for his own hand . . . would be quite out of place for you, representing as you do a party composed of more than one shade of opinion. Besides criticism is the proper role of an opposition: and it is always dangerous to be too positive as to programme till the time comes for responsibility.[96]

Ballance recognised the need to moderate his radicalism in the interests of party solidarity. His approach to the debate on the property tax took full account of the advantages to be gained in playing for the middle ground. Yet he only partially followed Walker's advice at Napier. Though he talked about achieving a land tax by amending the property tax to exclude all improvements, he also made clear his support for a progressive land tax aimed at the large estates and the 'crying evil of absenteeism'. This graduated tax, with absentees paying double the rate, was the major proposal to emerge from his speech. He emphasised it because he believed that 'the real cause of the depression was without doubt land monopoly, and bad administration of the waste lands of the Government'.[97]

The speech came in for some severe criticism. In Wellington the *Post* complained that it had never met with a 'speech less worthy of a leader of a party . . . It is almost impossible by any form of words to convey an adequate idea of its weakness . . . It is impossible to gather from it what line of policy Mr Ballance would pursue if, by any chance, he succeeded to power.'[98] Certainly Ballance could claim consistency rather than originality, though the *Post's* objection sprang in large part from political opposition to what it terms 'spurious Liberalism, based upon Protection'. Adverse reaction to Ballance's speech also arose because it was only partially reported. The *Napier Evening News* said that considering Ballance's position as opposition leader and the fact that he spoke for nearly two hours before 900 people, it was 'scandalous that such a meagre and misleading report was sent'. The *News* blamed two local pro-Atkinson papers, the *Herald* and *Telegraph*, for failing in their responsibility to provide the Press Association with a full account of the meeting.[99]

There does seem to have been a deliberate effort to suppress Ballance's speech. Stout protested and the *Lyttelton Times* accused the Press Association of being guilty of a 'very stupid omission'. The *Dunedin Herald* said the speech was 'one of the best, the most able, the most statesmanlike' ever to have been made in the colony, and condemned its 'deliberate boycott'. Other press comment, adverse and favourable, confirms the view that it was Ballance's radicalism rather than any personal defects that lay behind much criticism of his suitability as opposition leader. In Auckland the *Herald* described his 'threat' to interfere with the Railway Commissioners as 'cowardly and unconstitutional'. Meanwhile in Wanganui the *Yeoman* went into battle carrying the banner headline 'TAX THE BIG ESTATES' and published Ballance's Land Acquisition Bill of 1887. This was at the heart of Ballance's platform. As the *Otago Daily Times* pointed out:

> It is really round the land question that the whole of Mr Ballance's policy centres, and nothing is plainer than that the country is at present very far from adopting Mr Ballance's views upon this or most other matters. His Radicalism is of a more uncompromising type than has yet been ventilated by any party leader in New Zealand, not forgetting either Sir George Grey or Sir Robert Stout.[100]

Only the tide of events in the unexpectedly critical year of 1890 made such a radical platform hard to resist.

CHAPTER 9

The tide of events: land for the people

LIFE AS OPPOSITION LEADER was for Ballance, particularly as the election drew near, almost as hectic as that during his term in the Stout-Vogel Government. Much time was spent travelling between Wellington and Wanganui, and in January 1890 he journeyed to Dunedin to see and consult Stout.[1] He was accompanied on this trip by his brother-in-law and close friend, David Anderson junior.

The Anderson clan was Ballance's surrogate extended family. The only relative of his own in New Zealand was a nephew, Robert McKnight, who lived in Palmerston North (and who, incidentally, bore a quite extraordinary resemblance to his uncle). Ballance found much friendship and support among his wife's relatives, especially in David and Sarah Jane Anderson. These family ties were all the more important and valuable because the Ballance marriage produced no children. In 1886, however, they adopted the four-year-old daughter of Allan Anderson, Ellen's brother. (Why Allan Anderson gave her up is not clear, though adoption within the extended family was not uncommon in the Victorian era.) The girl was called Florence but the Ballances had her re-christened Kathleen.[2] They loved her dearly and referred to her fondly as 'Kit'. She was a 'typical little Celt' who soon 'entwined herself into the affections of her new father'.[3] Her proud grandfather, David Anderson senior, wrote of her as a 'remarkably fine child'.[4] The Andersons were a close-knit family. On Christmas Day of that year there gathered around David Anderson senior's table at 'Rhyme' 25 Andersons along with John, Ellen and Kathleen Ballance, and Robert McKnight.[5]

In early February 1890 David, Sarah Jane and family travelled to Wanganui to stay with the Ballances. Sarah Jane's diary gives some impression of everyday life at 'The Knolls', the large house and grounds on St John's Hill to which the Ballances had moved from the centre of town.[6] Ballance spent a good deal of his limited leisure time playing draughts and chess with his young nephew Eddie Anderson. On occasion they were joined by Ballance's personal friend but political opponent, John Bryce.[7]

In the evenings Ballance was more often out than in. On 12 February he attended a meeting about the formation of a freezing company in the town. It was an important matter, for Wanganui was losing a lot of valuable trade to the Wellington Works. A Wanganui company opened the following year, with Ballance as one of its directors, greatly boosting the town's economy. Local farmers were able to make a greater profit on their sheep by selling them in Wanganui and saving the cost of rail freight to Wellington.[8] Sarah Jane, however, did not entirely approve of her host's continual absences. 'This is the third evening in succession Mr Ballance has been out,' she complained.[9] Ballance was unrepentant. The following night he was out again, this time at a masonic meeting.[10]

On Sundays Kathleen would go to church, though without her parents.[11] Frequently she would be driven there by Julius Kurth, the Ballances' man-servant and gardener. Domestic help was difficult to come by and for much of the Andersons' visit Ellen had to cope without a girl in the kitchen. When one did arrive she was, it seems, not quite up to scratch: 'we waited some time for lunch,' Sarah Jane curtly remarked.[12] Ellen was known to be soft on her servants.

Political discussion doubtless helped to occupy the time before, during and after meals, though perhaps not all of the Andersons shared the Ballances' complete fascination with the subject. Ellen had views and aired them. She was astute and well informed, and her regular attendance at the House was accompanied by a sophisticated appreciation of political tactics and manoeuvrings. Her contemporaries held a high opinion of her and in 1885 a government steamer had been launched bearing her name.[13] So politics dominated the lives of both Ellen and John Ballance, and 'The Knolls' witnessed many a long debate on current issues and future prospects. Not all agreed with Ballance's vision. On 20 April Sarah Jane wrote:

> At dinner we had a strange conversation; Mr Ballance said that in fifty years all people would travel free on the railways, as he now does; & the expenses of the railways & salaries of the railway officials would be defrayed by taxation; I said Ernest [Eddie's brother and Ballance's nephew] might be alive then, but we older ones, would not, & he should have this book so that if he *should* be alive, he might refer to this date & see if Mr Ballance's predictions were fulfilled: & Eddie said if Ernest were to talk about Mr Ballance's prophecy at the end of fifty years he was to mind & say '& my brother said "Bunkum"[']. Not a very suitable conversation for Sunday.[14]

Impressions of the Ballance family suggest a close, loving relationship between John and Ellen, and now also between them and Kit. Those likeable characteristics that featured in the favourable public perception of Ballance were matched in his private life. It is the lot of politicians that time for domestic activities is frequently very limited. This was true of Ballance, but he did what he could. He was a caring and considerate husband and father, who enjoyed the privacy and intimacy of home life and the company of children.

In May 1890, not long after the Andersons left Wanganui for home, Ballance delivered his first speech to his constituents as opposition leader. Not wishing to suggest that he had actively sought the job, he told his audience that he had been reluctant to take it on because of the adverse effect the extra work and responsibility might have on his health. He only agreed following the Opposition's unanimous request and feeling it his duty to his colleagues. The speech was dominated by land issues but circumspect and deliberately moderate in tone. Ballance knew, as the *Post* remarked, that he had to give the 'party standpoint' and not simply his own.[15] So although condemning the property tax, he suggested that it was too soon to institute a land and income tax. Instead, the property tax should be amended by being graduated and exempting improvements. Depression would remain for as long as land was locked up in large estates. Ballance argued that a progressive property tax was also desirable because it would be more equitable than existing, regressive, indirect taxation.[16]

Ballance's attack on Atkinson centred on the ministry's failure to promote closer land settlement. Government policy, he said, had led to the aggregation of holdings and it would be on the land question that the coming election would be fought. In fact the situation was not as straight-forward as Ballance suggested. Fresh issues had arisen over the past months, largely concerning the position of urban workers. Labour unrest had been growing as the depression deepened and wages fell. A new union organisation called the Maritime Council had recently been formed. More dramatic, a sermon by the Rev. Rutherford Waddell (an Ulster Presbyterian) on 'The Sin of Cheapness', followed by a series of articles in the *Otago Daily Times* on the clothing industry, shocked the New Zealand public with the reality of the poor working conditions in the cities. This 'discovery' led Atkinson to establish the 'Sweating Commission', whose report was now soon to appear.

Besotted with land settlement and underestimating the significance of these events, Ballance made little reference to the 'labour problem'. He welcomed the setting-up of the Sweating Commission, saying simply that working conditions were of concern to both employers and employees. The question of labour and capital was 'one of those things' which had to be solved. Ballance did voice his disapproval of the Railway Commissioners' employment of child labour. But he made no direct reference to the growing labour movement.[17]

In his speech Ballance made much of the Government's recent appointment of Judge Edwards to the Supreme Court. Edwards had been made Chief Commissioner of the Native Lands Court but had insisted on also being appointed to the Supreme Court. The Supreme Court attracted an annual salary of £1500 compared to the commissioner's £600. This caused problems for Atkinson, however, because the Civil List Act only allowed for the payment of salaries for five judges and Edwards' appointment brought the total to six. The Government proposed to amend the act, but in the meantime, though Edwards could be appointed, he could not be given the extra salary. And as Ballance quickly pointed out, an appointment made without first fixing the salary was incomplete and illegal. Atkinson had got himself into quite a tangle. The 'Edwards Case', as it became known, proved an invaluable stick with which Ballance could beat and discredit the Government.[18]

An aspect of Ballance's speech which went largely unnoticed was his very firm stance on the question of further borrowing. People in New Zealand, he said, 'were being made slaves of for the sake of standing well in the English money market'. He believed they should 'release themselves from these bonds of slavery by simply stopping borrowing'. Ballance foresaw the country's dependency on overseas loans placing serious constraints on a future liberal government. Radical measures might be hampered by a loss of confidence in London and subsequent outflow of capital from New Zealand. A policy of greater self-reliance would help resolve this problem, for 'having no intention of borrowing any more, there was no reason to fear the English money lender, and therefore no reason why they should not carry out their ideas as to taxing (the large estates) . . . for the benefit of the colony'.[19]

When Ballance arrived in Wellington for the new session of Parliament, the ministry was in greater disarray than ever before. Atkinson was seriously ill and had been forbidden by his doctors to speak in the House.[20] Politically he was under strong pressure from his right wing (a group that became known as the 'skinflints') to make big cuts in the estimates. In the country there was increasing frustration over the Government's failure to remedy the depression and concern at the consequences of this in the form of growing industrial unrest.

It was all bad news for Atkinson. The Maritime Council was growing daily in membership and in its propensity to intervene in labour disputes. In July it became involved in the protracted quarrel between Whitcombe and Tombs and the Canterbury Typographical Association.[21] Meanwhile the report of the Sweating Commission had been published. It found that working conditions in New Zealand were little better than in the Old Country and recommended the immediate passage of a new Factory Act.

In his opening speech on 20 June Ballance criticised the Government for being out of touch with the country and called for an immediate election. Referring to recent events he argued that the labour movement would 'not find itself arrayed permanently against capital'. Rather there would be a reconciliation. Ballance did not see a class war between employers and the employed as inevitable. He blamed the depression and the exodus of population from the colony entirely on a government land policy that encouraged the accumulation of great estates:

> I attach the greatest importance to this question . . . [because] I think the proper settlement of the people on the land — not merely the alienation of the land in large blocks, but the disposal of it to *bona fide* settlers — is the one great means of restoring prosperity to this colony.[22]

It was true that under Atkinson fewer settlers were taking up larger areas of land.[23] It was also true that putting more people on the land could do something to alleviate the effects of economic depression. However, to argue that close settlement alone would restore prosperity was too simplistic. The causes of the depression were many, not least a long-term decline in the value of the country's agricultural exports. Also, promoting land settlement did little to improve the lot of the working class remaining in the towns. Ballance argued that urban wages would rise when movement onto the land reduced the size of the labour market, and that in general towns would benefit from a more prosperous rural sector. Yet the potential for land settlement intensive enough to significantly affect urban wages was just not there. Farms of the small size Ballance had in mind were not viable propositions. For the same reason, although the economy of many towns was highly sensitive to that of the surrounding countryside, closer land settlement would not necessarily result in greater rural and therefore urban prosperity.

Ballance believed that the labour problem would be resolved only when the land problem had been dealt with. The *Yeoman* told the new unions that land nationalisation should head their political programmes. The monopoly of land, it said, was a source of conflict and a 'sin against society'.[24] Many unionists went along with this, particularly those who were single-taxers and followers of Henry George. When in March George had visited Auckland en route to Australia, he was met by a committee that included the trade unionists R. A. Hould and Arthur Withy. H. W. Farnall, a prominent member of the Auckland branch of the single-tax organisation called The Knights of Labour, was also there.[25] Interest in George's single tax theory was at its peak. Farnall had just told a large meeting of the Knights of Labour that the sole cause of depression was land monopoly and the only cure a single tax upon land.[26] During the previous 18 months groups promoting the single tax idea had sprung up all over the place.[27] Many of the single-taxers were also liberal or union activists. Some, for example W. M. Bolt of Dunedin, were all three.

While Atkinson clung to power Ballance worked to bring the Government down so that it would face the country under the stigma of parliamentary defeat. Even before the House reassembled he was in touch with opposition members[28] and with Stout[29] about an early no-confidence motion. He moved it on 1 July, demanding the abolition of the primage duty (a temporary tax imposed on all imports) and transformation of the property tax into a graduated land tax. In a largely tactical move to woo the support of the skinflints, Ballance said that further cuts in government expenditure were necessary but that they should, and could, be carried out without adversely affecting the efficiency of the civil service. It was a self-assured speech, albeit in Ballance's dry and matter-of-fact style, roundly condemning government policy and ineptitude. Again he focused upon land reform, arguing that the 'growing evil' of land monopoly and absentee landlordism could be tolerated no longer. 'The question of land-settlement is . . . the most important of all questions that can possibly affect the present and the future of New Zealand.'[30] The motion failed by six votes, the skinflints realising that the only alternative to Atkinson was the radical Ballance. Other members saw that it was wise to hold off an election as long as possible, given that the reduction in seats made their chances of being returned more uncertain than ever. Nevertheless, as an effective body the Government was finished. A host of bills subsequently presented to the House fell at numerous hurdles placed in their path.

Over the following weeks Ballance grew in confidence, in large part because of the political advantage gained through government inertia and impotency in the face of growing dissatisfaction and unrest in the country. Events were moving in his favour. With Atkinson incapacitated the *Lyttelton Times* pronounced Ballance 'the best leader in the House'. And it described his speech during the no-confidence debate as follows:

> His suave, easy debating manner and quiet air of moderation are merely the mask which covers the command of much debating and tactical talent . . . Mr Ballance speaks in a soft melodious voice, is exceeding[ly] courteous in manner, lacks excitement or much fire, but is deeply earnest . . . It is plain his speech is logical, and has sequence, argument and continuity. The spectators say a good speech, calm, unimpassioned, without fire, excessively gentlemanly — these are its characteristics.[31]

Ballance's lack of fire as a public speaker helps explain why there were still widespread doubts about his leadership potential. Yet much criticism of his performance so far was politically motivated, many papers complaining that he was unimpressive simply because he was not saying the things they wanted to hear. The *Evening Post* called him a weak leader because he was unreliable:

He is always saying or doing something which surprises, without pleasing those who think they know most of his views and objects. He has not been a success as a leader of the Opposition, and he would, we are confident, fail even more completely in the role of Premier, if by any contingency he became cast for it.[32]

It was quite untrue that Ballance had a tendency to do or say the unexpected. The *Post* itself had earlier complained (and the theme continued throughout 1890) that there was 'nothing new' in what Ballance had said at Napier. If in fact Ballance was, as the *Post* now noted, leader of a 'very disorganised Opposition', it was the diverse political make-up of that body rather than failure on Ballance's part that was the problem. The Opposition had never been organised and Ballance faced an uphill task in trying to represent an amalgam of widely differing viewpoints. Any attempt to force his own particular beliefs upon his colleagues, though it might seem a sign of strong leadership, would have simply broken up the Opposition still further. Ballance was a much more impressive leader when Premier, largely because circumstances allowed him to be.

What also cramped Ballance's style was the continued speculation that Stout might return to Parliament. In July a petition was signed by most opposition members, including Ballance, requesting Stout to re-enter politics and it was expected, at least by the press, that he would comply.[33] Yet Stout was content to remain as Ballance's chief adviser and so again declined. It is unlikely that Ballance would have welcomed Stout back at this late stage. And in fact the petition may well have been a ploy by Ballance to force Stout to come to, and make public, a decision earlier than he might otherwise have done.

The Atkinson Ministry continued in a downward spiral involving what the *Herald* termed a 'shuffle along, wait awhile . . . do nothing' policy.[34] Both Premier and Government were old, sick and weary. Further attempts were made by Ballance to defeat them, usually centering on a motion to reduce the estimates.[35] Then George Hutchison, from Waitotara, made allegations of preferential treatment being given to the Bank of New Zealand by cabinet members who had large personal overdrafts with the bank. A committee of enquiry was set up and only with difficulty was the Government able eventually to bury the affair. It was all grist to Ballance's mill.[36]

Much more serious for the Government was the strike called by the Maritime Council in the dying days of the session. The strike arose from a dispute between the Australian Maritime Council and the Shipowners' Association about the right of marine officers to join a Trades and Labour Council. The Australian conflict spread across the Tasman when the Union Steam Ship Company in New Zealand refused the Maritime Council's request to forgo its Australian trade during the dispute, and instead employed non-union labour in its Sydney operations. New Zealand crews immediately walked off their ships and a general seamen's strike was declared on 26 August. Bodies affiliated to the council followed suit (with the exception of the railwaymen) and so began the country's first general and most bitter strike.[37]

In commenting on the strike Ballance was careful to take into account public concern at the disruption, disorder and economic costs associated with it. His basic sympathies were with the strikers, in that he recognised the right of working men to organise and to withdraw their labour, which largely was what the strike was all about. He was fiercely critical, for example, of the dismissal by the Railways Commissioners of railwaymen who refused to be used as 'blacklegs' to break the strike and pointed out that the commissioners were delighted with the excuse the strike provided to cut labour costs.[38] And he hoped that the unions would not be broken: 'I think that the unions are calculated to do good. The union is a protection to the men; it gives them self-respect, and in every way is capable of benefiting the employees.'[39]

On the rights and wrongs of the original dispute, however, Ballance would not be drawn. Though 'there was a great deal' in the union argument, 'he would not profess to say which [side] was right.'[40] He continually emphasised that strikes were undesirable and would not be necessary if there existed a legal system of conciliation and arbitration. 'I see no difficulty,' he said, 'in establishing tribunals to bring the two classes together on the basis of compromise.'[41] Before the strike Ballance had spoken against a compulsory system,[42] but he was now increasingly convinced that for arbitration to be effective rulings would need to be binding. At the same time Ballance was at pains to stress the positive side to unions, and so try to counteract the public view of them as essentially disruptive:

> I firmly believe the unions are acting from a true spirit of brotherly feeling, and that they are not to be associated with any disorder . . . I look to the unions to preserve order, and not in any way to break it . . . I think many of the charges against the unions are false, and I hope nothing will be done to discourage or discredit this great means of education, of preserving self-respect, and which must tend to raise the working-classes of this country.[43]

Ballance's appeal was populist; that is, he attempted to attract broad rather than sectional support — from the working class, from shopkeepers and businessmen, and from small farmers. This was good political tactics but also a genuine reflection of his political philosophy. The distinctive feature of Ballance's radicalism was the pre-eminence of land reform. He wanted to reduce conflict between classes by encouraging upward social mobility through closer land settlement policies. He wanted a society where self-help produced rewards, and so it was that the monopolists of land and therefore of opportunity were the target for his wrath, not the urban capitalists. The only class war to be waged was on behalf of landless labourers against the political and economic might of the large landowners. The landed gentry were the ideal scapegoat for all the country's problems.

The fact that Ballance came from Wanganui and not one of the four major centres significantly influenced the determination of this political outlook. A populist appeal made sense in a community where Ballance could not afford to alienate the large number of small businessmen and shopkeepers. An anti-capitalist platform aimed predominantly at the working class would have been a recipe for disaster in Wanganui, where it might have been safe in a large city electorate. A broad appeal also made sense because Ballance and others in Wanganui recognised the interdependency of town and country. There was little major industry — and so trade union organisation inevitably lagged behind that in the cities — and for all groups prosperity meant developing the potential of the land.

So though sympathetic to the unionists and to calls for the reform of the capitalist system, Ballance paid scant attention to the 'labour problem' *per se*. In a lively speech at the conclusion of the session he concentrated on attacking the Government's land policy. There had been no attempt to prevent 'dummyism' and the accumulation of large estates, no recognition that closer settlement was the key to prosperity: 'The administration of the land during the last three years has been a total failure . . . There is the greatest possible difficulty in small farmers getting suitable land. Dummyism is an evil, but the greatest evil of all . . . is the aggregation of large estates.'[44] The Atkinson Ministry was in tatters and, sensing victory, Ballance delivered one of his more stirring and impassioned efforts. Now on the offensive, there was no more talk of just amending the property tax. Only a graduated land tax would do:

> A graduated land tax . . . is a plank which every Liberal should have as one of the first in his platform. We shall never have true prosperity in this colony — it is impossible — unless the agricultural lands . . . are occupied by a large population. That must, in my opinion, be the secret of all prosperity . . . The time is rapidly approaching when all difficulties in the way of small settlement must be got rid of, and I believe we must say that no more land shall be disposed of except on perpetual-lease tenure, so that the remaining lands of the colony shall be held as a heritage for the people. That doctrine may not be palatable to some, but I believe it is a growing doctrine among the people generally.[45]

Immediately the session ended Ballance returned to Wanganui and there, on 23 September, opened the election campaign at the Oddfellows' Hall. It was usual for the Premier to do so but Atkinson's illness ruled this out. Indeed his inactivity during the whole contest gave Ballance more than a head start.[46] The election was to take place at the end of October or early

November, though in fact the Government delayed the poll until 5 December.

Ballance's speech was carefully calculated.[47] He attacked the Government where he was sure he could do some damage, and so made a good deal of the Edwards affair and Hutchison's charges about preferential treatment of the Bank of New Zealand. On the labour unrest he sympathised with the unionists, paying particular attention to the plight of the dismissed railwaymen. Many railwaymen from the local workshops and terminal at Aramoho would have been in the audience. They had played a major role in the formation of a Trades and Labour Union in Wanganui days earlier[48] and Ballance now assured himself of their support. Some unionists were helping in Ballance's campaign. A man named Cage, for example, was on both the Trades and Labour Union's and Ballance's election committees. Ballance knew where his strength lay and every so often would take a walk along the railway line out to Aramoho and Eastown to have a chat with the railwaymen there.[49]

Yet in his speech Ballance again stressed that strikes were undesirable and should be avoided by disputes being referred to arbitration. If this were done, he said, the present strike would be the last the country would see. In any case he argued that the question of land monopoly, not of labour versus capital, was the fundamental issue of the election. The land monopolists were the privileged class to be faced by working men, the class to be destroyed by a graduated land tax. 'As sure as night follows day, so sure will it be found that these estates will be subdivided and disposed of, and for every one man at present there will be ten in the future.'[50] Land for the people was what Ballance held out: a means of self-improvement for the working man and his family, and a sharing by all in the wealth of the land.

The programme outlined by Ballance included a graduated tax and a compulsory land purchasing scheme based on his Land Acquisition Bill of 1887. He also said that no more freehold land should be disposed of by the Crown. This was radical stuff indeed from a prospective Premier. In Wellington the *Evening Post*, which had been reluctant to lend its support to either side, was particularly angry at the suggestion to halt freehold land sales and now decided that a switch from Atkinson to Ballance would be a step 'out of the frying pan and into the fire'.[51] Though dominated by land reform, as the press noted,[52] Ballance's speech contained other proposals. For example, on the important issue of retrenchment he said that a liberal government would not reduce any civil service salaries under £200 per annum; only the higher paid employees would suffer.

The election was an exhausting, long-drawn-out affair. Having opened his campaign on 23 September, Ballance did not make his final speech until 4 December, on the eve of the poll. Meetings held throughout the constituency echoed the forthrightness and confidence of his maiden effort.[53] A radical land policy was by far the dominant theme. Emphasis on it helped Ballance divert attention away from the continuing industrial unrest. The strike was unpopular with the general public, who saw it as a conflict that originated outside, and need not have involved New Zealand. It was also running out of steam. With the prevailing high rate of unemployment, employers were able to take on non-union labour at ease. Conciliation conferences failed and the strike collapsed by early November. Politically there was danger for Ballance in being too closely associated with the strike. So he took great care in what he said and was happy just to watch the disruption caused by the dispute place the final nail in Atkinson's coffin. Ballance said enough to bring pro-unionists solidly behind him, without unambiguously supporting the particular actions of the strikers. But he also made it clear that he did not welcome the conflict between capital and labour, and believed that it should, and could, be avoided.

High on the list of issues raised by Ballance was reform of the Legislative Council. When during the past session there had been rumours of new government appointments to the council, Ballance had said that no additions should be made until the total number of councillors fell to under half the membership of the House, which was what Atkinson had promised in 1887.[54] Now Ballance also argued that the tenure of office of councillors ought to be reduced from life to seven years.[55] His concern was that the council's tradition of acting as a brake on reforming legislation would halt a new liberal regime in its tracks. As we shall see, this fear was well founded.

This was all sounding disturbingly ominous to the country's predominantly conservative press. The majority of newspapers soon lined up behind Atkinson, who 'promised no extra retrenchment, no new loans, no changes in the tax system, no machinery to avert future strikes'.[56] Ballance was not known as a rabble-rouser who floated radical ideas just to play to the gallery and without much serious concern as to their practicality. His proposals were well considered and he could be counted on to attempt to carry them out if elected to power. Ballance was viewed as distinctly dangerous[57] and more extreme than other prominent liberals such as Reeves[58] and Stout. Stout, indeed, was trying to moderate his more radical friend and differences between the two men began to be commented upon by the press. In July Stout had expressed his confidence in Ballance, saying that the opposition party was 'quite competent to deal with political questions without any suggestions or assistance from him'. Yet he shortly afterwards proclaimed there should be a renewal of overseas borrowing, embarrassing Ballance who had declared a policy of self-reliance.[59] And the following month, Stout sent Ballance a telegram 'expressing strong disapproval' of the Opposition's tactics in trying to defeat the Government through attracting 'skinflint' support for severe retrenchment motions.[60] Stout's plea that he was only speaking for himself, not the party, did not make things any easier.[61] As a prominent and respected ex-Premier his opinions carried much weight.

The divergence of opinion between the two came to a head in October, when in Napier (a long way from his base in Dunedin) Stout announced that the country was not ready for a land and income tax, and that instead change should come about 'gradually and carefully'.[62] At the meeting the local liberal candidate proposed a motion calling for Stout's return to politics, yet he again declined. This was all very awkward for Ballance but, significantly, he stood his ground. The *Herald* took the offensive by pointing out how much Stout, who had 'finally made up his mind not to stand', was being praised for his 'cautious words' by the colony's Tories. It then reprinted Ballance's end-of-session speech condemning outright the property tax.[63]

Indeed, throughout the campaign the *Herald* and the weekly *Yeoman* regularly and unashamedly churned out Ballance propaganda, and in consequence were closely watched by other journals.[64] As both journalist and politician Ballance knew well the crucial role the press could play in an electoral contest. He had in fact just established a newspaper in Stratford called the *Settler*. The timing was no coincidence. Ballance had to borrow £300 to set up the paper, which immediately put its weight behind McGuire's attempt to unseat Atkinson.[65] The money came (not surprisingly) from McGuire himself and also from George Hutchison, who was standing for the liberals in Waitotara.

In Wanganui the *Herald* followed Ballance's daily activities. It defended him from attacks by other newspapers and expanded and explained points made by him at the many meetings held in and around the town.[66] All but one of what it saw as the main planks of the liberal platform concerned land:

1. The arrest of the exodus of population by greatly increased facilities for occupying the crown lands.
2. The compulsory acquisition of agricultural land out of the big estates for small farm settlement.
3. The nationalisation of the remaining crown lands.
4. The taxation of land, minus improvements.
5. A graduated tax on the big estates.
6. The abolition of taxation on the necessaries of life, which cannot be produced in the colony.
7. The settlement of labour disputes by means of national tribunals.
8. The restoration of the pre-emptive right in respect of native lands.[67]

With the reduction in the number of seats in the new Parliament, constituencies had been enlarged. Wanganui now included the surrounding settlements of Fordell, Mosstown, Okoia, Turakina and Brunswick, and had nearly one-third more electors than in 1887.[68] The *Yeoman* was careful to explain to the farmers in these outlying areas that they would not be expected to pay both a land and an income tax. Indeed small farmers would pay less under the land tax than the current property tax.[69]

The Wanganui contest was fought on national issues. Ballance's opponent was again Gilbert Carson, editor of the *Chronicle*. Carson supported Atkinson and was totally opposed to land and income taxes.[70] The issue was the major source of conflict between the two protagonists. Carson attracted a much higher proportion of farmers to his meetings than did Ballance[71] and his paper voiced their fears.[72]

Although there was no national party organisation and Ballance remained in Wanganui, he made some attempt to co-ordinate the country-wide campaign. He wrote to leading liberals in the main centres advising them on tactics and in return received progress reports on how the party was doing.[73] Coming from Wanganui gave Ballance some political advantage as a leader. He was able to avoid accusations of favouring a particular city and could act as broker between regional rivals — rising above the discredited provincialism of the past. On occasion he put his own weight behind favoured candidates.[74] Ballance was very concerned at the prospect of vote-splitting in constituencies where there was more than one anti-government contender,[75] but had only limited success in persuading people to stand down. He publicly supported A. W. Hogg's selection for the Masterton seat and was able to pressure the other liberal candidate into withdrawing.[76] However on election day in Timaru, the liberal W. Hall-Jones competed against J. M. Twomey (who had labour backing) and in Wairau S. J. Macalister and T. L. Buick both sought to defeat the sitting government member, A. P. Seymour. Fortunately for Ballance, in these instances one of the opposition candidates was victorious, but the same was not true elsewhere. At Palmerston the conservative J. G. Wilson received 1055 votes to the liberal Pirani's 994. Pirani may well have been elected had a second opposition candidate, J. Stevens (who polled 396 votes), stood down.[77]

In general, as in previous elections the selection of candidates remained a predominantly local affair and there was often little Ballance could do to sort out squabbles between factions. There were candidates supported by liberal associations, labour candidates and self-appointed hopefuls with largely personal followings. Many liberals failed to appreciate the growing political ambitions of the trade unionists, with the result that 'amicable relations between liberals and labour were the exception rather than the rule'.[78] For example in Invercargill the lack of diplomacy of the liberal Henry Feldwick led to the Trades and Labour Union putting up a candidate, who emerged the victor, against him.

Despite these problems Ballance was optimistic. In mid-November he wrote to Stout on the progress of the campaign:

> In Wellington we are in a bad way with too many Liberals, & may only win one seat . . . In Auckland we must gain heavily. Canterbury looks well, & your account of Otago is very encouraging. This is the greatest organised effort the Liberals have ever put forth, and it will show what they can do against the classes.[79]

Of his own election he held great hopes. 'The election here is going on as well as possible, my Committee giving me a large majority, but we are not boasting for fear of creating over-confidence.'[80]

As far as policy was concerned liberal candidates generally followed Ballance in seeing the land question as of paramount importance. And it was the question of land, not labour reform that saw the greatest divergence of opinion between the supporters of Ballance and Atkinson. Even for those opposition candidates who had union backing, labour reform was often of only secondary concern.[81] H. S. Fish, for example, speaking on a platform with the other 'labour' candidates in Dunedin, William Earnshaw and William Hutchison, said that the future success of New Zealand would depend on the resolution of the land question.[82] On the eve of the poll the *Yeoman* stressed that the working class in particular had a great deal to gain from a liberal victory. 'One of the first duties of a Liberal administration,' it promised, 'would be to introduce legislation to provide land for the location of the working classes.' And, 'The purchase of land near to towns where there are no crown lands, and the settlement of it in small areas so as to give every man a chance of acquiring a homestead, is necessary to restore prosperity and retain our population.'[83]

The election was held on 5 December. After the polls closed Ballance and his supporters gathered at the Court House in the centre of town to wait for the results to come in. The first return, from Fordell, gave him a lead of 14. This was followed by a narrow win at Mosstown, bringing his majority over Carson to 16. Then came a shock, for Ballance was defeated at the main booth by seven votes. It was a real cliff-hanger, which had Ballance more than a little worried. He was reported to have fainted three times during that stressful evening.[84] Then Aramoho gave him an overwhelming victory. It was to prove critical, for his overall majority was whittled down to just 27 votes after defeats at Turakina, Okoia and Brunswick:

	Ballance	Carson
Fordell	54	40
Mosstown	25	23
Court House	542	549
Aramoho	95	30
Okoia	20	31
Turakina	44	76
Brunswick	28	32
	808	781[85]

The small farmers of the surrounding district clearly disagreed with Ballance's argument that his closer land settlement policy would favour them, and not only the landless in the town. Ballance fared worst in Okoia, Turakina and Brunswick, where the proportion of farmers was highest.[86] They were new to the enlarged constituency and their hostility to Ballance explains in part his poor showing in 1890 compared to three years earlier.[87] As well as this, however, the sizeable town vote for Carson indicates that many professionals, businessmen and shopkeepers must also have been unhappy with Ballance. Some voters were doubtless perturbed by Ballance's obvious sympathy for the strikers, and were unconvinced by the stress he placed on co-operation between labour and capital and the need for a mechanism that would resolve disputes before they led to industrial action. Also, the turnout was down by ten percent compared to 1887 and an over-confident Ballance campaign might have resulted in his supporters, rather than Carson's, remaining at home. What is certain is that Ballance drew his main strength from the working class. Nearly two-thirds of the electors at Aramoho were labourers or artisans[88] and here Ballance received 70 percent of the vote.

Elsewhere in the country the results were pleasing. Although Atkinson improved on his 1887 majority (ironic considering Ballance's poor showing and subsequent events), government candidates in general fared badly. Most devastating was the opposition victory in the major centres. All three seats in Dunedin and Christchurch had been captured, and two out of the three in Wellington and Auckland. And most noticeable and significant in the cities was the success of the labour candidates. The closest contests were in the country towns, where a number of liberals achieved narrow but crucial wins. Ballance's majority had been 27; next door in Waitotara Hutchison clung on by 22. A. W. Hogg took Masterton by 18 and E. M. Smith New Plymouth by only 23. In the South Island opposition candidates won by more convincing margins, for example T. L. Buick by over 70 at Wairau, William Hall-Jones by 52 at Timaru and Thomas Duncan by nearly 500 in Oamaru.[89]

Historians have stressed how in 1890 labour issues and trade unions for the first time played an important role in a New Zealand election.[90] While this is correct, the fact remains that the opposing parties disagreed more over land than labour reform. Labour politics was still in its infancy. Also, the effect of the 'labour factor' varied from place to place. In the cities it aided the liberal cause. In Wanganui, Ballance won despite the strike and his views on labour reform, rather than because of them. He had lost support since 1887 and the labour question, the major new issue of 1890, must be held in large part to blame.

Still, it is clear that differences between Ballance and Carson during the Wanganui campaign centered around land, and that Ballance won primarily on a programme of radical land reform aimed at broad rather than sectional support. He had written to the liberal candidate for Akaroa, John Joyce:

> With respect to what is known as 'labour candidates', I think that the people generally will make a mistake if they are led away by a cry of that kind. What is wanted is a broad Liberal programme, which will protect the rights of labour and promote wholesome reforms of every description. A member of Parliament ought not to be a mere delegate from a particular class, but should be a representative pledged to principles. This kind of representative will do more good for the working-classes than a one-idea'd man sent up to Wellington to speak by the card.[91]

Once all the election results were known, the *Herald* concluded that there had never been 'so decided a victory gained by the Liberal party on clear and defined principles. There is absolutely no doubt whatever that the Government have sustained a smashing defeat.'[92] Yet though the ministry was now in a minority, it was not immediately apparent that Ballance could form an alternative administration. A number of independents, albeit most with liberal leanings, had still to declare their loyalties.[93] In Wanganui the *Chronicle* optimistically argued that the Government had actually been victorious, since all ministers but one had been returned, [94] while in Wellington the *Post* gave Ballance only 28 seats, well short of a majority.[95] But within a few days the picture became clearer and the prospect of a Ballance administration greater.[96] Yet Atkinson clung on, advice 'pouring in from all sides' as to how Ballance might be kept from office.[97] In an interview the Premier said that though the election had gone badly he was not sure that the Opposition had a majority, and was certain that not all of them were followers of Ballance.[98]

While the Cabinet planned its strategy in Wellington, Ballance stayed in Wanganui and spoke from 'The Knolls' of his confidence in being able to form a ministry. He was at last in control and was enjoying it. Press and politicians rushed to him to seek his opinion. He simply reminded them of an agreement he signed with Atkinson in August, aimed at avoiding an extra session, whereby the Government promised to resign immediately if the outcome of the election were clear.[99] Ballance said that there could be no doubt about the result. Stout and Patrick Buckley (a liberal who sat in the Legislative Council) hurried to Wanganui to advise him on the construction of a cabinet.[100] Although Stout later said that Ballance himself selected the ministry and that it was formed in January, not December, this early consultation was clearly decisive.[101] The *Otago Daily Times* suggested a Ballance cabinet including Buckley (Attorney-General), Seddon (Mines), McKenzie (Lands) and also Cadman, Perceval or Reeves.[102] It was to prove a very accurate prediction.

Meanwhile, though there was some talk of a reconstructed ministry under Rolleston,[103] Atkinson decided to face the new House on 23 January himself. His resignation was imminent but the delay allowed the Government, scared stiff at the prospect of Ballance in power and pressed hard to act by leading conservatives such as Hall and Bryce, to pack the Legislative Council against the inevitable Liberal administration. 'It will . . . be a serious disaster if the Council is not strengthened before the Reds get into the saddle,' wrote Hall to Ormond.[104] The plan had been suggested months earlier and had the full support of the Governor, Lord Onslow.[105] Many people anticipated a Ballance victory (in spite of the propaganda of the conservative press) and the question of appointments to the council had been aired during the election. So the announcement of seven new councillors (including Atkinson himself) when Parliament met on 23 January came as little surprise.[106]

In fact, Atkinson's ploy proved much more trouble than it was worth, for by the time the appointments were gazetted Ballance had made out a very strong case against them. Weeks earlier he had presented Onslow with a persuasive list of reasons as to why new appointments would be unconstitutional. First, they would be contrary to the wishes of the people, for Atkinson had been rejected at the general election. Second, as the leader of a minority ministry, Atkinson had no right to nominate new councillors. Third, the election had shown a majority in favour of reform of the council and so nothing should be done until Parliament met. Fourth, the appointments ought not to be made since the number of councillors was still greater than 35, the size Atkinson had promised to cut back to in 1887. Finally, in a neat point, Ballance said that Atkinson's claim to recommend the appointments as the right of an outgoing ministry contradicted his persistent refusal to admit defeat.[107] All this intricate, technical debate was something Ballance thoroughly enjoyed indulging in; though of course there were at the same time critical issues at stake.

The force of these arguments was widely recognised, even by those who were otherwise unsympathetic to Ballance.[108] Onslow was handed a petition with 5000 signatures against the appointments and began to doubt the wisdom of agreeing to them. As William Rolleston now realised, the creation of 'such a batch of Peers' could gravely damage the fight against 'Neo-Radicalism, Pseudo-Liberalism and socialist violence'.[109] It was a serious tactical error. In the short term the affair discredited Atkinson and pushed liberal independents over to Ballance, who was able to pose the issue in terms of democracy versus privilege. In the long term Onslow's approval of the appointments not only strengthened the case for reform of the council, but also brought into question the position of the Governor himself. 'We cannot believe,' said the *Yeoman*, 'that His Excellency, in the face of Mr Ballance's protest, which put the whole question most forcibly and conclusively, will comply with the wishes of a Government that has been so plainly condemned by the country. To do so would bring the Governor into unnecessary antagonism with the people, and greatly imperil his usefulness, as it would savour of partisanship, a thing no Governor should give any grounds for.'[110]

Christmas for the Ballances must have been full of eager and perhaps also anxious and seemingly endless anticipation. But at last the time came for Ballance to leave Wanganui for the capital. He arrived in Wellington early in the new year and the opposition caucus met the evening before the opening of Parliament. There were 30 members present, with eight others said to be accounted for, and they unanimously elected Ballance to the chair. As was the convention the meeting gave him a free rein in choosing his cabinet. It selected Major Steward as the party's nomination for Speaker and formed a committee to draw up a further petition against the council appointments. Ballance knew that he led a caucus of widely differing viewpoints and personalities. In a short speech he emphasised the need for party unity, at the same time encouraging his followers by suggesting that this was the first occasion when a 'solid and united Liberal party had been constituted on clearly defined party lines':

> Their business would be the sinking of individual ambitions for the good of the party and to work as a party for the happiness and good of the country as a whole. This would be the best reply that could be made to the ridiculous charge that they were a set of revolutionists anxious only to tear down, burn, and destroy.[111]

The following day the government nominee for Speaker, Rolleston, was beaten by 36 votes to 29 by Steward. Mitchelson then announced Atkinson's resignation.[112] Next, Ballance stood up from the front row of the opposition benches and said, deadpan and with 'not a trace of triumph' in his voice, that he was in the process of forming a ministry.[113] Since most of its personnel had been chosen a month before, a new cabinet was ready to be sworn in within 24 hours of the Government's resignation.[114] Shortly afterwards the brief session, held out of season because of the special circumstances created by the December election, ended. Business would begin for real in June.

Though caucus had given him a free hand, Ballance had to be careful to select a team that could command the confidence of both the party and the House. Important political and geographical factions had to be represented. Like Atkinson, Ballance reserved for himself the Treasury and Trade and Customs, but added Native Affairs. The Wellington lawyer, Patrick Buckley, who with Stout had closely conferred with Ballance following the election victory, became Attorney General and Colonial Secretary, and represented the Government in the council. The young William Pember Reeves, recognised as 'one of the coming men of the colony',[115] was appointed Minister of Education and Minister of Justice. Reeves had a legal background but was also, like Ballance, a journalist, becoming editor of the *Lyttelton Times* in 1889. First elected for a Christchurch seat in 1887 he had just been returned, with labour support, at the top of the poll of the multi-member constituency. A liberal of longer standing, Richard Seddon, received the Public Works, Mines and Defence portfolios. Seddon, whose power base lay with the miners of the rugged West Coast, had known Ballance since 1876.[116] The other important posts, Lands, Immigration and Agriculture, went to John McKenzie, an Otago farmer who had been in the House since 1881. McKenzie was a big man (he stood six feet four inches high and had a circumference to match), determined, intelligent, honest, outspoken and subject to the occasional burst of hot temper. Having an active farmer as Minister for Lands would be an advantage when the sensitive question of a land tax came up. His appointment was particularly pleasing to the *Yeoman*. He 'knows the wants of the farmers,' it wrote 'and the tricks of the land sharks and monopolists'.[117] There were two other members; Joseph Ward, an Invercargill businessman, was Minister without portfolio but soon became Postmaster General and A. J. Cadman, from Thames, took on Stamp Duties.

The strength of Ballance's cabinet was just the first surprise for those who had all along questioned his ability to form a stable government.[118] The presence of the South Islanders, Reeves, Ward, McKenzie and Seddon, helped remove one of Ballance's weaknesses, that outside the North Island he was relatively unknown. It also admitted to the fact that it was in the South that the liberal victory had been secured. Ballance's party won a majority of South Island seats but only a minority of those in the North Island. Auckland was represented by Cadman and Wellington by Buckley. Politically, Reeves would help secure the support of the new labour faction.

It was recognised that Ballance had selected men of considerable talent, even if most of them were untried in administrative ability. The apparent speed and ease with which he had formed a cabinet likely to satisfy the main factions within the party was also noted.[119] If there were doubts expressed they tended to centre on the choice of Seddon, who had a reputation for 'uncouthness' and as an 'obstructionist' in the House. However, this tendency to 'talk a great deal' could, as the *Post* pointed out, be put to useful effect by the ministry.[120] In any case Seddon was an experienced, leading member of the party. The Ballances certainly thought him rather vulgar and did not rush to mix with him socially, but his inclusion in the Cabinet made too much sense to be seriously questioned.

There was a strong feeling at the time that the December election and now Ballance's cabinet marked a distinct break with the past. These were new men. Aside from Ballance only Buckley had any ministerial experience. Reeves and Ward were barely in their thirties. Ballance was the first Premier whose background could be described as decidedly lower middle class and only Reeves and Buckley had had a secondary education. It was something of a shock for the establishment, already reeling from the thought of the newly elected working-class members sitting in the House. The Continuous Ministry was gone forever.

Ballance's mild nature and temperament would largely determine his approach to the premiership, and indeed would have an important influence on how successfully he held together his lively and forceful cabinet colleagues. Commentators were already pointing out how his personal style would see another change from the past:

> Mr Ballance may not perhaps be as good a driver as his predecessor. He will use other means than those of the bullock-puncher to ensure progress, and although he may require an equally large hat as Sir Harry Atkinson is wont to wear, there can be no doubt that his boots will be found several sizes smaller and destitute of the hobnails which have now became [*sic*] historic.[121]

Politically the Cabinet was the most radical the country had seen, and a fair reflection of the forces that had overthrown Atkinson. If Ballance's populist appeal had only partially succeeded, in that support from businessmen and especially farmers was shown to be limited, the nature of that appeal was clear. What frightened conservatives at the prospect of Ballance in power was his land policy. And it was believed that the attempt to 'burst up the land', rather than any labour reforms, would be the cause of his ultimate demise.[122] Although the labour question and trade unions played important roles in the Liberal victory, the most contentious issue between the two sides concerned the land tax and nationalisation. Land reform was the central feature of Ballance's political platform. 'It is not my policy to sacrifice the public estate,' he said the day after announcing his ministry.[123] Instead the state was to lease land on easy terms to the working class. Ballance promised to attack absentees, those who blocked opportunities for upward social mobility and who were 'public enemies standing in the way of progress'.[124]

New Zealand for New Zealanders: self-reliance and nationalism

It was largely because Ballance's ministry was an unknown quantity that there were doubts concerning its ability to survive. It was not clear just how radical it would prove to be and whether or not Ballance would be able to retain control over the forces that had brought him to power. He was not regarded as a strong leader: 'He does not inspire confidence or attachment amongst his followers, or the respect which comes of dread amongst his opponents. He is a first rate lieutenant but not a good general,' said the *Post*.[1] However the paper conceded that it was really a matter of Ballance being untried and added that there was a 'strong suspicion' that as Premier he would 'surprise expectation and develop qualities of practical steadiness with which he has not hitherto been credited by many'.[2]

Despite heavy rain there was a large crowd at the railway station to greet Ballance on his triumphal return to Wanganui on 12 February 1891. He was accompanied by McKenzie and Reeves. At a banquet that evening he received the congratulations of local dignitaries and then outlined his government's legislative programme. He promised a radical change in the incidence of taxation, the taxation of large estates and the conservation of crown land. A return he had just requested indicated that there were only 1.1 million hectares of crown land remaining for settlement, not 1.5 million hectares as had been believed. Therefore the Government would purchase additional land for small farm settlement and, at the same time, institute a system of perpetual leasing of Maori land. Ballance also promised that the Government would draw up a bill to establish boards for the 'reconciliation of Labour and Capital', so that strikes 'could not occur'. And finally, he confirmed that overseas borrowing would cease.[3]

While Ballance and his cabinet began work on the details of these proposals the Government received a fillip from a by-election victory at Egmont. The seat had been vacated by Atkinson who was now in the Legislative Council, and in a close contest Felix McGuire, Atkinson's opponent at the past two elections, defeated the conservative R. C. Bruce.[4] It underscored the outcome of the general election and, particularly coming so early on in the Government's life, was a valuable and encouraging win. Ballance believed that it 'had a marked effect in strengthening the hands of the Government throughout the country'.[5]

The Government's commitment to encouraging genuine settlement and discouraging speculation was quickly apparent. A new Land Bill was being drafted that would insist upon improvement and residence conditions being fulfilled before a person buying land would be given its freehold title.[6] Also, McKenzie tightened up the special settlement regulations by revoking the right to convert leaseholds into freeholds. McKenzie said that the aim was to 'prevent associations selling their allotments, as soon as improvement conditions are complied with, thereby frustrating the object of association to get [closer] settlement'.[7] In addition, he announced that the Government was to institute proceedings against a well-known reactionary Wairarapa landowner named Coleman Phillips, who was accused of dummyism.[8] After lengthy proceedings Phillips eventually escaped with a caution, but the Government had made its point.

Ballance travelled between Wanganui and Wellington a number of times in the months prior to the opening of the new session. He also visited and spoke at New Plymouth. There was much work to be done and a good deal of consultation with others necessary. Though parts of the Government's legislative programme had been hinted at in advance,[9] his Financial Statement was eagerly awaited. When it came, just five days after the Governor's speech, Ballance announced a package of major reforms. The property tax was to be abolished and replaced by land and income taxes. The land tax, of one penny in the pound, would grant exemption on improvements up to £3000 in value and land up to £500 would be tax-free. Mortgages would be deducted from the taxable value and the tax paid instead by the mortgagee. There would also be a graduated tax on land valued at more than £5000, rising from $1\frac{1}{8}$d, $1\frac{5}{8}$d in the pound on land over £100,000. The income tax, of one shilling in the pound, would commence on salaries over £300. Companies were to be taxed at the same rate (on profits) though with no exemption. Other proposals included the complete cessation of overseas borrowing, the reduction of postal charges

'Liberal Ministers and the Good Work they are doing' (NZ Observer, 1891)

to a uniform 'penny post', cutbacks and reorganisation of the civil service, and the establishment of a new 'Labour Bureau' to collect statistics on unemployment and help the unemployed find work. There was a small surplus from the past year, which would be used to pay off the 1888 deficit and to compensate for the lower postal rate. Finally, £30,000 was to be spent in the coming year on opening up land for settlement.[10]

This budget was the most significant yet presented to a New Zealand Parliament. The graduated land, income and company taxes, and the recognition of government responsibility for unemployment, broke entirely new ground. The House discussed the document over the following weeks. Bryce, now opposition leader, said that the cuts in the civil service would be a sham and that the new tax would scare capital from the country, an accusation made by many other conservatives.[11] In an entertaining speech Scobie MacKenzie doubted that Ballance seriously expected to get his radical proposals through the House. He also noted that there was no mention of the promised absentee tax.[12] Other complaints surrounded the supposed practical difficulties in assessing and collecting the taxes, and of the problem of fraud. Ballance had heard it all before. Similar objections had been raised when he introduced his land tax in 1878. And much more recently he had received Vogel's warning from London that a land tax would 'deter the investment of foreign capital, which the colony has hitherto so much depended on'. Vogel also pointed out that even with an income tax, the land tax would not bring in the same as the property tax.[13]

The 'great debate' came to a close on 10 July when, 'at 7.30, with crowded galleries and benches,' Ballance rose to deliver what some thought 'one of the best and most statesmanlike speeches' ever heard in the House.[14] He made a not unimpressive sight. A political satirist later described him as:

> A tall, but not very tall man. Physically, a large man — large all over. Head, well developed; hair, smooth and iron grey; eyes of pale or neutral tint, eyes which look out cautiously, sometimes suspiciously, at times timidly, from beneath pent-house brows; features, massive and marked, Hibernian in cast; shoulders, large and round — rounded, may be, by the cares of State or the burden of leader-writing when there was nothing to write about; arms, long; hands, small and, seen from a distance, delicate. Garb these proportions in seemly broadcloth, tweed, and fair linen, and you have, roughly speaking, the Premier of New Zealand.[15]

Ballance said that the land tax was a matter of justice, for it would make the large landowners pay their fair share of taxation. At the same time, the tax would encourage the disintegration of large under-worked estates and promote closer settlement. It was more than simply a fiscal measure. He quoted the English economist Newman in explaining why the land question was the cornerstone of the Government's programme:

> If the trades-unions could but open their eyes to facts, they would see that the constant pouring of population out of the country into the towns (which become sinks of misery) is their great grievance. This not only affords cheaper labour to employers, but fills lodgings, raises rent, pollutes air and water, lowers the standard of decent living, causes beggary, vice, and disease, and degrades the working-classes. The first political aim of the artisans ought to be to effect such a change in the laws of land-tenure as shall secure that the country shall feed all its new births, shall be so fully tilled as to make farm-products cheap in the town market after well feeding the producers, and shall facilitate an emptying-out of the unwholesome density of the towns into the vacant rural areas. All this would tend immeasurably to the comfort, health, and affluence of the artisans.[16]

This was exactly Ballance's view. Closer settlement was the cure for the colony's current ills, in particular the continuing high level of unemployment, urban poverty and the exodus of population overseas. 'Now,' he remarked, 'will honourable members deny that the first plank in the Liberal programme should be the land-question?'[17] Finally, Ballance disputed that capital would leave the country, as Scobie MacKenzie ('that great economist, that gentleman of lofty principles, a walking dictionary of phrase and fable') and others had predicted. If the 'dangerous' and 'suicidal' policy of borrowing were halted and confidence restored to New Zealand, he said, there would be ample investment in the country, particularly in the productive small farms encouraged under the new tax regime.[18]

Shortly after this Ballance suffered the first attack of an illness eventually diagnosed as cancer of the bowel.[19] Rumours abounded that he would, because of ill health, appoint himself Agent General in place of Sir Francis Dillon Bell, who was soon due to retire.[20] The notion that Ballance might also be desperate to desert the sinking government ship was eagerly played upon by the conservative press, whilst being flatly denied by the *Herald* and Ballance himself.[21] In fact Ballance had already decided to appoint Westby Brook Perceval. It is almost certain that when constructing his cabinet Ballance wavered between Perceval and Reeves, and that he selected the latter on the understanding that Perceval would go to London when the post of Agent General became available.[22] It was an important job and there was much criticism of Perceval's appointment on the grounds of his relative youth (he was 37) and political inexperience; that he would be 'a babe and suckling compared with Sir Julius Vogel or Sir Dillon Bell'.[23] But one of Ballance's great strengths was that he was a good judge of character and ability. Perceval was very capable and confident, and socially very presentable. The *Post* described him as 'a very nice young man of the class supposed to especially adorn small tea parties'. He would cut quite a dash in London. More importantly, Ballance believed him to be well equipped for the vital task of countering the damaging effects of reports being received in England of the New Zealand Government's radical and 'socialistic' measures.[24] Though Ballance had never any intention of taking the job on himself, the press persisted in suggesting that that was what he really wanted. Even after Perceval's appointment the *Post* argued that it was only a temporary posting, allowing Ballance time to 'complete arrangements to abandon political life and go Home'.[25] This was just wishful thinking.

In early August Ballance briefly introduced the Land and Income Assessment Bill, which set up the machinery for the new system of taxation. Fighting his illness he was, as Hansard records, 'frequently inaudible in the gallery'. He stressed that the graduated tax was aimed not merely at raising revenue but also at breaking up the large estates, so directing capital into smaller units and encouraging closer settlement.[26] The effects of his illness were still apparent when he replied, two weeks later, to the debate on the bill.[27] Despite this hindrance, he made perhaps the finest speech of his career. Much was 'off-the-cuff' and as much came straight from his heart. He answered charges that his radical programme would scare capital from the country and thus wreak havoc with the economy by turning from defence to attack, making a virtue of self-reliance out of the necessity:

> I will tell [you] . . . what our policy means. It is a policy I have long had at heart. It is a policy of New Zealand for New-Zealanders. And, Sir, I have not much regard for the speculator. I am not much concerned for those gentlemen who are always talking about sending capital out of the country, and who send their sons to the Argentine Republic, and who are continually shaking the dust of poor New Zealand from the soles of their feet and leaving it altogether . . . Every man should be hardened up to this conclusion: that our policy should be formed and matured to suit the interests of the people in New Zealand and of the people who will not leave New Zealand; that we should make New Zealand a place for New-Zealanders to live in . . . I care little for the mere capitalist. I care not if dozens of large land-owners leave the country, for I tell honourable gentlemen this: that the prosperity of the colony does not depend upon those classes. It depends upon ourselves, upon the rise of our industries, and upon markets being secured in other countries.[28]

This was stirring stuff and Ballance continued the nationalist theme when he drove home the importance of his land policy:

> I say that the State should not part with a single acre more of its land, for I believe thoroughly in land-nationalisation . . . I firmly believe that the greatest, if not the sole, cause of the intense poverty which prevails in old countries is . . . the way in which the lands of those countries are held. I believe in that most emphatically . . . I believe pauperism and poverty depend upon the state of the land-laws of any country. Are we to build up a system of great landlordism similar

to that which prevails in the Old Country, with these facts staring us in the face? . . . We must face the problem, and decide that the land must be held by the people . . . I have every confidence in the future of New Zealand. Some honourable gentlemen are full of despair. My confidence is as great as honourable gentlemen's despair.[29]

The Land and Income Assessment Bill passed by the sizeable majority of 15. As a supply measure it could not be opposed by the Legislative Council. The act was to come into force on 1 April 1892 and the property tax was reimposed until that time.[30] Valuations made for the purpose of the property tax would form the basis of government calculations as to how much revenue the land and income taxes might bring in.

Meanwhile the ministry was running into stiff opposition over its Land Bill. To encourage the development of land and discourage speculation, the bill placed strict improvement and residence conditions on cash purchases. As before, land could be bought on deferred payment. The most significant change, however, was that the act would deny holders of the perpetual lease (the tenure introduced by Rolleston in 1882) the right to acquire the freehold. Ballance was determined to make a start to conserving crown land. He wanted the state to retain permanently good land that it could lease to small farmers. So when the council inserted an optional purchase clause into the bill, he insisted that the whole measure be dropped and re-introduced the following session. The press reported that McKenzie was willing to accept the amendment[31] and at the same time praised the council for halting a measure regarded as the 'thin end of the wedge of Land Nationalisation'.[32] Ballance was adamant, pointing out that a genuine perpetual leasing system was basic to the Government's programme and threatening to go to the country over the issue. 'We could not surrender to another House,' he said. 'They do not represent the people. We represent the people. We stand firm on this question.'[33]

It was not only the Land Bill that fell in the Upper House, for in the 1891 session the council ravaged government legislation on an unprecedented scale.[34] In the past, major conflict between the two houses had been minimal since both tended to be conservative bodies. With a radical Liberal Government in power for the first time, it was hardly surprising that the council became more active than ever before. Ballance's earlier fears were well founded. Twelve bills were either vetoed outright or lapsed following the failure of reconciliation committees of both Houses. Labour bills were particularly vulnerable (for example, the Shop Hours and Workmen's Lien bills), but the council also threw out the Payment to Members Bill, which Ballance regarded as one of the Government's and Liberal Party's principal measures.[35] Speaking during the debate on the bill he argued that realistic remuneration was not only vital to democracy, enabling the working-class majority to be fairly represented, but was the right of public men. 'I know of no man more entitled to receive the respect of the community, no man who renders more valuable service to his fellow-men,' he said, 'than the public man who honestly applies himself to politics.'[36] Two private members' bills (Grey's Friendly Societies Bill and Hall's Female Suffrage Bill) which had much support from the government benches were also killed in the council.

Ballance knew that the council would somehow have to be tamed if his government were to make any significant legislative progress. Yet he did not support a bill moved by William Rees in late July, which would have cancelled the Atkinson appointments to the Legislative Council. He agreed with Rees that the appointments were morally wrong and technically unconstitutional, but argued that once the Governor had made them the councillors could not then be impeached.[37] The Colonial Office, meanwhile, had absolved Onslow for accepting the advice of the Government to make the appointments, but not Atkinson for giving it.[38] The Bill only just failed to pass.

In fact, Ballance knew that even if the Rees Bill got through the Lower House it would most likely be killed by the council. Indeed he had decided to adopt a more subtle piecemeal approach to the problem. He successfully introduced a bill reducing the tenure of councillors from life to seven years, a reform prominent in the party's election manifesto, saying that it would result in a more liberal Upper House in the future. A high turn-over of councillors would allow new governments to appoint sufficient members to ensure the passage of legislation and would also keep liberal members (who, Ballance observed, too often became conservative) on their toes.[39] The Upper House accepted the bill, largely because the measure had considerable public backing and, more important, did not affect the tenure of existing councillors. All this did not, of course, resolve Ballance's immediate problem. The next and much more difficult step would be to persuade the Governor to appoint a new batch of Ballance's own nominees. But there was certainly a groundswell of opinion in favour of making the Council much more representative.[40]

The council's opposition to the Government's land legislation (it would almost certainly have blocked the land tax if that had been constitutionally possible) foreshadowed more widespread criticism. There were genuine fears of the effect the land tax and the move away from freehold tenure would have on the availability and cost of credit. Land in New Zealand was traditionally heavily mortgaged. Often mortgaging was the only way a farmer could raise the cash to pay for the improvements necessary to make the land productive in the first instance. Though the general tax was paid by the mortgagee, there was concern that the borrower would soon suffer through higher interest rates. Money for improvements and the cost of existing mortgages would therefore become more expensive. Further,

*'Preserving the Ballance of Power': Labour Bills and
the Land Tax (*NZ Observer, *1891)*

the graduated tax on the landowners and the tax on improvements over
£3000 would force loan companies to look elsewhere for more profitable
and secure investment. Capital, it was argued, would leave the country.
The London *Times* went so far as to predict that the whole mortgage system
on larger estates in New Zealand would come to an end.[41] Ballance was
also faced with the problem that denying the freehold to lessees would
limit their ability to get credit. It was very difficult to borrow money using
only a leasehold as security. Finance for improvements, particularly crucial
in the North Island where much land had still to be cleared, was for lessees
virtually unobtainable from the private sector. The alternative was for the
state to advance sums to settlers.[42]

Ballance underestimated the force of many of these points. During the

[191]

debate on the land tax he had brushed aside concern about a capital flight from the country. As for the availability of loan money for small farmers, he said simply that he hoped that the necessary finance could be raised internally. He did get an act passed enabling the Government, through loans to local bodies, to provide money for the opening up of the land. But with the maximum amount fixed at £50,000 per annum this was just scratching the surface.[43]

Although Ballance was having to fend off growing hostility from a number of quarters, his proposals were not, of course, without grass roots support. He received many letters congratulating him on his reforms. Some believed that they did not go far enough. For example, while welcoming Ballance's 'Liberal & progressive policy', the Otago Protection League wanted to see changes in the tariff.[44] The Wellington Knights of Labour meanwhile complained that there had been no significant change in the incidence of taxation, since duties on basic necessities remained unaltered.[45] In Auckland the Knights of Labour and the Anti-Poverty Society passed identical resolutions against any exemptions at all to the land tax.[46] Exemptions reduced the revenue that could be raised and were anathema to those organisations sympathetic to George's 'single tax'. Ballance wanted to see both the duty on basic necessities removed and protection given

'The Premier attaches more weight to the resolutions of the Liberal Associations than to those of the Chamber of Commerce (NZ Observer, 1891)

[192]

to local industry, but he was concerned at the effect these changes would have on lowering government revenue. He had certainly no intention of presiding over a rising public debt. For now, he simply pointed out that his taxation reforms would benefit the working classes.[47] On the question of exemptions, to abolish them entirely would harm the small farmers Ballance wished to encourage.[48]

In formulating and putting across his policy Ballance tried to meet the wishes of supporters as well as defuse alarm amongst opponents. The Christchurch Liberal member, W. C. Walker, believed that Ballance had at least achieved the former. The Financial Statement, he wrote, was 'bold enough for the extreme men and ought to satisfy the country constituencies who at all events in the South are cautious enough'.[49] Some in Auckland, however, were not so sure. A fan of Ballance's working for the *New Zealand Herald* wrote that though the paper generally supported the Government (which was quite untrue),[50] it was nervous about changes in taxation driving capital 'still further' out of the country. 'Capital all over the world is frightened, and it will not be good for New Zealand if it gets abroad that it is about to take the lead in putting in practice wild untried notions in respect to land nationalisation &c.'[51]

Though his critics were reluctant to point it out, Ballance was actually a most conservative treasurer. For example, it was largely financial caution that lay behind his willingness to pursue retrenchment — reducing civil service salaries and staffing levels, and cutting back government services. It was not a policy of which the liberals could claim a monopoly; indeed it had been the usual response to economic depression in general and budget deficits in particular. In 1891 the economy remained sluggish. Government revenue, which came mainly from customs duties and land sales, fell slightly between 1890 and 1891, and the need for some cuts in expenditure was widely accepted. Political differences tended to focus upon their extent and where they should be made.

Early on Ballance had tried to make savings without impairing efficiency. The Land and Survey departments, for example, were amalgamated,[52] the customs office at the Bay of Islands closed down[53] and the cost of defence reduced.[54] However Ballance argued that there was a limit to the savings that could be made and he was not prepared to affect services seriously.[55] There was also the very real political danger in retrenching party supporters. Ballance was told that in Nelson one of only two known liberals in government departments had been given his notice.[56] So Ballance trod carefully, and turned down a number of suggestions for the amalgamation of posts.[57] More important, he refused to agree to any reductions to departmental estimates of expenditure and was forced into all-night sittings to get them through the House.[58] Government expenditure was eventually cut by £44,000 but some salaries retrenched by Atkinson were restored.[59]

Linked to the question of retrenchment was reform of the civil service. Reform aimed at a more professional service which would be more efficient and therefore cheaper. Breaking new ground in yet another area, Ballance decided to introduce a system of classification of public servants.[60] His Civil Service Bill also provided for a pension scheme and the establishment of a board to advise the Government on changes that ought to be made. The bill did not get beyond a second reading, largely because of opposition to the compulsory nature of the pension scheme, but it showed the way for later, successful efforts.[61]

Ballance had to battle hard through all of the 1891 session. He was by nature placatory, though often he also found a conciliatory approach to be tactically effective. The satirist Evison wrote:

> In manner Mr Ballance is generally agreeable. When he is having everything his own way he is very agreeable. Many people are like that. When he is nice, he is very, very nice. It has been said of him that his methods are sometimes even saponaceous. Without precisely going so far, I may be disposed to admit that when his audience are favourable and he is trying to get something he particularly wants, and is handling a subject he likes, he becomes remarkably sleek and smooth in tone, caresses his subject with fond little oratorical pats and, metaphorically, exudes butter and honey. The python has a playful, but practical, little habit of lubricating its subject prior to deglutition. I intend to convey by this simile nothing offensive to — the python.[62]

But for much of the session Ballance was not having it all his own way. His government was proposing radical change and inevitably some of the fierce political debate became personalised. It was particularly embarrassing and trying for Ballance when two of his own supporters turned against him. The first to do so was the Dunedin Member H.S. Fish. Though a self–confessed liberal, Fish had a history of political inconsistency, for example voting with the free traders on the 1888 tariff.[63] He had been elected in 1890 with labour support but took umbrage when he was not included in Ballance's cabinet.[64] Fish's ambitions received another setback when he failed to get elected Chairman of Committees and his personal grudge against Ballance grew still further.[65] There followed an exchange of letters, with Ballance angry at Fish's 'incessant attacks' on the party and particularly at one on a labour member, William Earnshaw.[66] Fish then made this correspondence public and intensified his criticism of the Government in speeches during the recess.[67] Although Ballance found it necessary to reply to these charges, Fish was too obviously motivated by personal spite for his actions to receive much support.[68]

A second defection from the government benches also involved dashed expectations. George Hutchison, the Member for Waitotara, knew Ballance well and largely for this reason had been tipped for a cabinet post. But there were much stronger candidates and Ballance had to disappoint him.[69] As Ballance was fully aware, Hutchison's politics were by no means fully in tune with mainline party thinking. This became apparent early in the new session. Hutchison opposed the principle of progressive taxation and so voted against the Land and Income Assessment Bill.[70] He also supported the Legislative Council amendment to the Land Bill which allowed lessees to become freeholders.[71] The creation of a 'state tenantry' without the option of purchase, he argued, was against the best interests of the colony.[72] This was embarrassing for Ballance particularly because of his close association with Hutchison. Politically, Hutchison's stance simply reflected the lack of appeal of the Liberal programme to rural settlers. Hutchison represented a country constituency (which surrounded Wanganui) and was voicing the concerns of established rather than prospective farmers.[73] By August he had crossed the floor of the House for good.[74] Thereafter he tried to collect around him a new 'middle party', including Fish and Fisher, that in alliance with the Opposition might hope to defeat the Government. 'It is a very old game,' Ballance assured Stout, 'and its methods will not take us by surprise, but for all that there is an element of danger in it.'[75] Hutchison remained a thorn in Ballance's side, but little more.[76]

The pressures and strains of the 1891 session saw another of Ballance's long friendships come to an end. In August he was involved in an unfortunate clash with John Bryce, now Opposition Leader. During one of the increasing number of heated debates in the House, Bryce queried a ruling of the Speaker. When Ballance pointed out that this was a breach of parliamentary procedure, Bryce replied that Ballance 'ought to be ashamed of himself'. Bryce then refused the Speaker's request to withdraw these words, saying he was prepared to 'take the consequences'.[77] The House took up the offer and promptly censured him. Bryce resigned in disgust.[78] The general feeling was that Bryce had over-reacted, behaving 'more like a petulant school boy than as a man posing to be a leader'.[79] The censure had been mild and his resignation unnecessary. Ballance certainly did not seek it.[80] It was a sad end to a long career. Ballance later told his constituents that he regretted the incident 'more than anything' that had taken place for years.[81]

The session that ended in late September had been little short of disastrous for the Government. Of the 70 new laws only a few were of major importance. The most significant bills had been rejected by the council and 80 were dropped at an earlier stage.[82] Despite the fact that the ministry's position in the House was very strong (most divisions being won by at least ten votes), the lasting impression was of an insecure and ineffectual administration. A radical government had been tamed, at least for the present, by the upper chamber.[83]

All this encouraged the conservative press in its efforts to kill the new regime. There were fundamental issues at stake. Ballance's policies were said to be based on 'wild and revolutionary political theories';[84] he was accused of making 'indecent' attacks on the Legislative Council,[85] of scaring capital away from the country, and politicising the civil service by appointing people 'of the right colour' (a favourite phrase of Ballance).[86] In Wellington the *Evening Post*, with an eye to a by-election due in the city early in the new year, was particularly virulent: 'The Government policy has gone in the direction of land nationalisation: it has assailed the free-hold tenure, it has truckled to the masses, it has indicated a tendency to the increase of Protection, it has proposed extreme Radical changes in the Constitution, and has embodied rash experiments of legislation towards the realisations of fads.'[87] In the country's commercial capital, Auckland, the *New Zealand Herald* was 'exceedingly hostile'. As Ballance was well aware, the financial interests behind the paper (the Bank of New Zealand and Assets Company) would be affected by the new taxation.[88] Indeed the Liberal programme in general inevitably found little favour with big business. The city's other paper, the *Evening Star*, had in the past favoured the liberals. But local activists now told Ballance that its support for the Government was 'of very weak-kneed character'.[89]

Ballance was fighting for survival. He had strength in the House, but knew that grass-roots support would have to be mobilised if the Government were to get anywhere. In this respect there were two obvious requirements: the conservative bias of the press needed to be countered and a permanent party organisation established.

In late 1891 Ballance received a number of requests for financial assistance from government sympathisers planning to establish new newspapers. Auckland liberals were particularly eager to start a paper and were looking for £100 to ensure its first three months of publication. It was hoped that after that period the paper would attract sufficient advertising to become financially self-supporting. Ballance was told that the new paper would be moderate in tone. A previous liberal journal called *The Tribune* had apparently been so 'violent' and 'revolutionary' as to prove a 'curse instead of a blessing'.[90] There was also talk of a new publication in Wellington.[91] In many smaller towns, however, it was more often a matter of rescuing existing ailing papers than setting up new ones. The *Napier Evening News* was in dire trouble[92] and in Gisborne the *Standard* was for sale.[93] The cities were growing in population and power, and with better communications their newspapers were in turn expanding and gaining in strength. It was this competition, along with the effects of the depression, that hit what was clearly now an over-abundance of local newspapers.

There was little Ballance could do to help, aside from trying to see that pro-government journals received their fair share of official advertisements (some opponents said they got more than their fair share[94]) and giving editors the benefit of his journalistic experience. For example, he suggested that the Dunedin *Globe* should reduce its reporting staff and replace 'heavy' editorials with 'bright and racy' short paragraphs. The paper's expenses ought not to exceed £40 per week (they were perhaps twice that amount) and Ballance argued that this could be done without cutting wages. There was plenty of editorial talent in the country, he said. With this assured, success depended on good management. 'No one has seen more of the internal workings of struggling papers than myself, and I have come to the conclusion that failure in nearly every case is the result of incompetency on the part of the man in control.'[95] The plight of the liberal press came up in cabinet discussions,[96] but so many requests for assistance had been received that Ballance was forced to pursue a policy of turning them all down.[97]

Ballance's frustration at being unable to provide financial support emphasised the fundamental need to establish some form of national liberal organisation. He had proposed a federation at least as far back as May, but not until after the session could he devote time to the project. In November he sent out circulars to prominent liberal politicians to canvass their support for a 'Liberal Federation'. The federation aimed to be 'an effective organisation of the whole liberal forces of the Colony':

> The Federation has been called into existence really for the purpose of providing funds to assist our people in fighting elections etc, etc, without which I have seen great difficulty in keeping the party together, more especially in presence of the fact that the other side are vigorously organising and contributing liberally to a fund for the purpose of securing a Tory majority at the next elections. We propose to engage an organising Secretary at an adequate salary, say £250 a year, with travelling expenses . . . The success of the organisation will depend to some extent upon the activity of local committees, and the assistance which they may be able to give the secretary when he visits the districts.[98]

The local leaders were asked to ascertain the potential party membership in their area. Existing organisations could simply affiliate to the new federation. They would still select candidates, with the federation providing financial and other assistance.

Although formal party organisation was new to New Zealand, Ballance would have had the English precedent in mind. The English National Liberal Federation had just held a conference in Newcastle, at which it outlined the party's political programme. The influence of the federation (established by Chamberlain in Birmingham in 1877) was at its height. The 'Newcastle programme' was accepted by Gladstone as official party policy.[99]

For Ballance the New Zealand federation was vital to the Government's survival and he worked hard to set the organisation upon a sound footing.[100] Originally he had hoped to appoint Thomas Bracken as organiser, a man with a background not dissimilar to that of Ballance. He was a Protestant Irishman who favoured home rule. Settling in Dunedin in 1869 he became a journalist and newspaper owner, and then entered politics as a Greyite. He failed to get elected to Parliament in 1879 but won two years later with the help of the Trades and Labour Council. Retiring in 1887, he next tried to make a living as a poet (he wrote *God Defend New Zealand*).[101] It was in large part financial considerations that led him to turn down Ballance's offer, for he seems to have regarded the post as a risky venture.[102] In any case he had soon left the colony for Australia.[103]

The job eventually went to the Member for Wairau, Thomas Buick.[104] It was a typical Ballance appointment of a bright, 'up and coming' young man. In his mid-twenties, Buick had a working-class background and with labour support had gained his first parliamentary seat in 1890. A great believer in self-reliance he was, like Bracken, an advocate of home rule.[105] Buick's salary and other necessary finance was to come initially from personal donations and then also from annual subscriptions. Ballance tried to arouse enthusiasm for the new organisation by telling those asking for money to set up liberal newspapers that funds would be available if the federation succeeded.[106] He said that their needs had played a major part in his decision to form an organisation in the first place. The task ahead was enormous, and at times seemed almost to overwhelm Ballance. He began also to suffer from spells of depression, which were undoubtedly related to his progressing illness. 'We must have money,' he wrote to Stout, 'the demands that are coming in are enough to frighten any one out of his senses. You never saw anything like it — from all parts for assistance. Were it not for the hopes of the Federation I should be in the depths of despair.'[107]

Ballance appointed an executive council to oversee the federation's affairs. It consisted of nine members: Ballance himself (president of the Federation), Stout, Reeves, Cadman, F. H. Fraser, David Pinkerton, William Tanner, Jackson Palmer and C. H. Mills.[108] The objection was made that the council should have been elected, but as Ballance pointed out, this was impossible until there were people to elect it. 'As we had to make a start, the first body necessarily had to be virtually self-constituted; but we have provided for the election to take place early in 1893, when the Organisation will, we hope, be more than a name.'[109] From then on, the council was to be elected by the federation's members for a two-year term. There were to be various types of membership. Ordinary members paid a subscription of one pound (or if wage earners, ten shillings) per annum. Life membership was a bargain at only ten pounds and the council could elect honorary members. Finally, there were private members who paid an annual one pound subscription, while remaining anonymous.[110]

In setting up the federation Ballance was deliberately vague about its political programme. The federation's function was primarily to select and promote candidates at elections. This was the most urgent need. But more important, policy laid down at national level could not be too specific if the federation were to unite rather than divide liberals throughout the colony. Local prejudices and conditions had to be catered for. For example the radical programme of the Dunedin Liberal Association, formed in May 1891, would be asking too much of the more cautious Aucklanders.[111] The Dunedin 24-point manifesto included the nationalisation of land, mines, railways and coastal shipping, the statutory limitation of rent and interest, and the abolition of the Legislative Council and election of the Governor.[112] So it made a good deal of sense to play down the policy role of the federation. Article Four of the constitution said simply that the federation would advocate 'all such reforms of a liberal character as may be resolved upon at any general meeting of the Federation'.[113]

During the recess Ballance went on a nationwide crusade to defend government policy (in particular the land and income taxes) and at the same time promote the new federation. It was his first major 'stump' of the country. And it was to be the last. Buick simultaneously began his own trip to organise local party committees.[114]

Ballance's regular post-sessional address in Wanganui set the scene for his tour. He emphasised how much valuable legislation had been destroyed by the council, though also pointed to some areas of progress. The new Labour Bureau, for example, had already found jobs for 927 of the 1561 persons registered with it. 'It is the duty of the Government to see that the people are employed,' he concluded:

> The wealth of every State must be measured by the prosperity of the great mass of the people, and if there is a large number of people weltering in poverty and misery, that country is not well governed. It is all very well to measure our conduct by the practice, usages, and experiences of old countries, but I say we are in a new country [and] we are laying the foundation of a new nation.[115]

Ballance's stump proper began when he travelled to the South Island.[116] He spoke briefly (and for the first time) in Christchurch, at a banquet to W. B. Perceval, soon due to depart for London as Agent General.[117] It was Ballance's subsequent speech in Dunedin, however, that was significant. There he confirmed that the Government's new Land Bill would not include provision for granting the freehold to holders of perpetual leases. McKenzie was known to be wavering over this matter,[118] but Ballance was determined to make no concessions on what he saw as a key part of the Liberal programme.[119] Ballance also announced at Dunedin that the Government intended to appoint new members to the Legislative Council before the start of the next session. This was vital to the successful passage of the Ministry's measures and of the Land Bill in particular.

After Dunedin Ballance returned to the North Island.[120] As his tour progressed he gained in confidence. Speaking to the Knights of Labour at Woodville he urged liberals to organise and said that if the Legislative Council 'persisted in defying the expressed wish of the people' it would have to go.[121] The *Evening Post* was horrified:

> Representative and Responsible Government is to be replaced by popular convention and the plebiscite. Thought, reflection, and the knowledge which can only be obtained by study and experience, are to be discarded from public affairs, and the hastily expressed voice of the majority, or those who by violence and vociferation represent themselves as such, is to be accepted as an infallible guide and direction by those with whom the duty of administration rests . . . Mr. Ballance is the mouthpiece of the mob . . . According to him, the multitude must always be right, and those who oppose its demands are enemies of the State. Had Mr. Ballance's lot been cast in Paris a few years ago, he must, with his present views, have embraced the Commune.[122]

Ballance was the *bête noire* of the *Post* as never before. It described his liberalism as bogus, wild and revolutionary, and his assault on the freehold as particularly reprehensible.[123] A by-election was soon to be held in Wellington and the *Post* was backing the opposition candidate, F. H. D. Bell, whom it regarded as the genuine liberal article.[124] Ballance returned to the city eager to speak in support of the Government's nominee, William McLean. Once on the platform the Premier wasted no time in attacking the Wellington press in general and the *Post* in particular.[125]

Criticism of the press was also prominent in speeches Ballance subsequently made at New Plymouth, Patea, Auckland, Palmerston North and Feilding.[126] At each venue he outlined the Government's programme, extolling the virtues of the leasehold and saying that land and absentee taxes would encourage small farm settlement by exempting improvements and penalising undeveloped large estates. The Legislative Council was again stigmatised as preventing the legitimate demands of the democratically elected Government being fulfilled. 'The people should rule,' said Ballance, not 'a few autocratic Tory old fogies' rule the people.[127]

The battle lines had been drawn. Ballance saw himself defending the rights of the people (particularly to land) against external threat from foreign capitalists and internal opposition from entrenched conservative landowning interests in the council. Posing the Government's plight in this fashion had enormous popular appeal, as Ballance was well aware. Land reform had become the touchstone of a new, self-reliant democracy. 'I think that the time has come', he wrote to a liberal in Napier, 'when we should not encourage a Landlord class. The march of democracy is a great and incontestable fact. That it has become a power few will deny; that it is likely to become a still greater power, many will admit . . . I do not in the least fear the outcry raised by people at home or in the Colony, that capital will leave the country. Capital in my opinion ought to be the servant and not the master in every industrial and self governing community.'[128] In fact, democratic nationalism was soon to gain a number of important victories.

[CHAPTER 11]

The Rainmaker

BALLANCE WAS NOT CONFIDENT of the outcome of the Wellington by-election. Bell was favourite to win. The liberal, William McLean, had come next to bottom of the poll at the general election and Ballance thought him a candidate weak 'to the verge of almost certain disaster'.[1] McLean was also a single-taxer, which could seriously limit his political appeal. Bell, on the other hand, was the son of Sir Francis Dillon Bell and had recently been elected mayor of the city. He had been runner-up at the general election and was supported by all three Wellington daily papers.[2]

It was recognised that the contest would be a major test of the Government's popularity and the campaign was fierce and bitter. The *Wellington Post*, for example, carried an advertisement alleging that Ballance employed men in the *Wanganui Herald* office at below union rates. The *Herald* denied this, adding that the wages were similar to those paid by other provincial papers. It also pointed out that the company had not declared a dividend for a number of years, the bulk of its income going to its employees.[3] The election attracted comment from outside the country as well. The *Melbourne Age* saw it in the context of a determined effort of the 'old and privileged classes' to regain control of the state. They hoped to overthrow Ballance whose policy, said the *Age*, was 'directed in its entirety, to making New Zealand, as far as possible, independent of external support'.[4]

Appreciating the election's importance and that the odds were stacked heavily against the Government, Ballance and Reeves took to the platform in aid of McLean. To Ballance's delight their efforts bore fruit. 'Meeting after meeting we carried by storm,' he later wrote to Perceval in a rare moment of self-congratulation, 'completely nullifying the persistent assaults of the press, with the result that we carried the election by some 140 votes. I need not tell you that this has done the Government throughout the Colony some service, and rather alarmed the other side.'[5]

Meanwhile the organisation of the Liberal Federation proceeded apace. It gave £50 to McLean's campaign fund[6] and £20 to Ebenezer Sandford, who was elected for Christchurch City to replace Perceval.[7] Ballance hoped that the federation would tie in to the liberal cause as many sympathetic organisations as possible.[8] Groups such as the Knights of Labour, with their own particular brand of liberalism, could provide valuable financial and organisational assistance. Ballance was in touch with them in Napier,[9] Hamilton,[10] Masterton,[11] Palmerston,[12] and Woodville.[13] These organisations offered varying degrees of practical assistance. The Auckland branch said that though as a body it would not join the federation (it wished to retain its 'individuality'), Ballance could 'rely on the support of its members'.[14]

Liberal organisations themselves had to be persuaded to put their full weight behind the federation. This was Buick's task in the major centres of population, while in the smaller towns he often had to start from scratch. By mid-January 1892 he was in Dannevirke, on his way to Hawke's Bay. He told Ballance that the Wellington victory would do 'enormous good', but was worried about his reception in the conservative stronghold of Napier and suggested that Reeves be sent there to assist.[15] Ballance assented and Reeves obliged.[16] After Hawke's Bay Buick travelled north to Auckland, returning to Wellington via the West Coast.[17] A Taranaki Liberal Association was formed a day after his meeting in New Plymouth.[18] Buick's tour did not extend to the South Island, where outside Dunedin and Christchurch liberal organisation was weak.[19] And in Wellington itself, liberals were well able to form an association without his assistance.[20] Liberals in Gisborne set up a branch there in April.[21]

It was in Auckland that Buick created the greatest stir. In urging Ballance to form a national organisation, the Auckland Liberal Association had told him of the Government's unpopularity in the city.[22] Jackson Palmer, a Belfast-born radical lawyer who had been elected for Waitemata as an independent, detailed a host of local grievances. High on the list was bitter disappointment over the Government's not disbanding the Railway Commission (that 'Tory institution') and complaints that recent Justice of the Peace appointments had gone to 'rank conservatives' instead of government supporters. Ballance had a hard job persuading him to serve on the federation's council.[23] Ballance's difficulties with Auckland had also a lot to do with the persistence of regional rivalries. His cabinet was dominated by members from the South Island and south of the North Island.

As far as government measures were concerned, the city was particularly worried about the effect of Ballance's taxation proposals. Auckland was the financial heart of the colony and there the 'capital scare' was felt strongest. And in a region containing no large estates, few found the land tax particularly appealing, except perhaps to the extent that it might allow a reduction in customs duties. The Knights of Labour was active in the city, but had still to win over the working class.[24] H. W. Farnall, the founder of the Auckland branch, had come bottom of the poll at the 1890 election.

There was also the persistent problem of Sir George Grey and his small but loyal band of followers. The Grand Old Man had more than once let slip his lack of enthusiasm for the Government and rumours abounded of a plot by disaffected liberals to replace Ballance with Seddon, Grey's confidant.[25] In the House the tension between Grey and Ballance was palpable:

> Sir George seldom or never shows sign of vitality while Mr Ballance holds the floor. At the first sound of the Premier's voice the G.O.M. retreats, snail-like, into his shell and closes the door. Thereafter, till the voice ceases, the face of Sir George is as the face of the Egyptian Sphinx. Sometimes he gets up to reply; oftener he says nothing. If he is silent Mr Ballance, after assuring himself of the fact, assumes the expression of a gourmand who, anticipating something unpleasant on his plate, finds something quite toothsome there. If, on the other hand, Sir George, after laboriously disencumbering himself from comforter and coat, rises to address the House, anxious, alarmed and not altogether pleasant are the stealthy glances shot by the ex-lieutenant at his former commander-in-chief.[26]

Ballance had spent a week in Auckland just before Christmas, encouraging the party faithful. This seemed to help matters,[27] although a claim that the Wellington victory had made the northern city safe was much too optimistic.[28] Ballance was finding it exceedingly difficult to gain the loyal support of Auckland's liberals. They were even dragging their feet over paying his expenses. All other associations had with alacrity parted with their money.[29] Grey still had mana and was egged on by the anti-Ballance press. There was considerable truth in the *Post*'s argument that Buick's mission aimed primarily to get the city's liberals to 'accept Mr. Ballance instead of Sir George Grey as the prophet, priest and leader of Liberalism'.[30] But the paper's suggestion that Grey would hold the balance of power in the coming session and might be able to form a ministry of his own, was pure fantasy.[31] He retained a personal following but as a national leader was a spent force.

In fact, Buick's visit did little to improve the party's position in the city.[32] W. J. Napier, an Auckland solicitor and prominent liberal, wrote to Ballance in July that the situation was getting worse rather than better.[33] Appointments were still causing dissatisfaction while the *New Zealand Herald* was trying to drive a wedge between Greyite and Ballance liberals. The estrangement of the two men in 1879 had been dragged up again. The 'Tories' had money to spend, said Napier, and both Shera and Rees (the two Auckland city liberal members) were losing ground:

> We shall have a big — even a desperate — fight up here at the next election and the Tories are moving Heaven and earth to try and carry

the three city seats. You have no idea of the odium one incurs by prominently identifying oneself with the Government. I have been persecuted here by the big financial companies and clients have been taken from me simply because of my political opinions. In social circles too it has been very plainly hinted to me that any devotion to the Liberal cause is regarded as an unpardonable 'eccentricity'.[34]

There was one bright spot, however, for the *Evening Star* was apparently supporting the Government with more conviction than before.[35]

The federation, therefore, was struggling to get off the ground. Auckland was particularly difficult but Buick faced lack of enthusiasm and commitment elsewhere as well. He managed to create interest and controversy but liberal supporters and activists took a lot of persuading before being prepared to sign up for the new national party organisation. Ballance was disappointed at the small number of members who had been enrolled and had paid their subscriptions. Nor was Buick able to attract many major personal sponsors.[36]

Ballance was making more progress on other fronts. For example, there were soon positive results from his efforts to counteract the colony's conservative press. There had been talk of setting up a new liberal paper in Auckland, but with the problems of the press in the capital exemplified at the by-election, and the Auckland *Evening Star* coming round, Wellington's needs were the more urgent.[37] Before the by-election Ballance had been gloomy of a liberal paper's chances. 'The project is not so hopeless as Reeves says you are inclined to regard it,' his old Wanganui friend Walter Buller wrote to him.[38] However, McLean's win and moral support from a number of quarters boosted his spirits. And by the time Stout reported that he had managed to secure badly needed financial backing, Ballance was much more hopeful and enthusiastic.[39] Reeves, who had his experience on the *Lyttelton Times* to draw on, was put in charge of the project. He had promised £750 for the paper himself and also to contribute articles.[40]

The cheapest and easiest method of starting a new paper was to acquire an existing operation. Ballance and Reeves had hoped to buy the *Evening Press*, renaming it *The People*, but the deal fell through.[41] Instead the Wellington morning daily, the *New Zealand Times*, was purchased for £4,500 and turned into a joint stock company.[42] Ballance suggested changing the name to simply *New Zealand*, with (significantly) the motto 'New Zealand for the New Zealander',[43] but it was decided to keep it as it was. Reeves became managing director of the company and its other directors included Ballance, William McLean (the new Wellington member) and three trade unionists, W. Cliff, P. R. Russell and W. Miles.[44] R. A. Loughnan, previously of the *Lyttelton Times*, became editor.[45]

The inclusion of labour representatives in the board of directors reflected the growing prominence of unionists in the Liberal Party. It was also a novelty for such an enterprise.[46] The paper was soon in print but was not without some teething problems. There was a fair amount of political infighting,[47] a high turnover of editors and criticism of the paper's content.[48] Yet as early as March Ballance was reporting good news. 'We hope to establish the paper on a firm commercial foundation,' he wrote to a Dunedin Liberal, 'for unless that is done it is utterly useless to aim at having a political organ. A mere flash in the pan would have done no service to the party, but, on the contrary, a positive injury. There is reason to suppose that the paper can be made a sound commercial concern. It is now showing a respectable surplus.'[49]

Ballance was also taking the initiative on the matter of the Legislative Council. On 16 February 1892 he formally requested Governor Onslow to appoint 18 new councillors.[50] Onslow, however, refused to accept more than eight names, after which Ballance sought a compromise on an 'irreducible minimum' of 12.[51] At this point negotiations were halted, for Onslow was due to leave the colony and wisely decided to let his successor deal with the tricky problem.[52]

Ballance wanted and expected to have some say in the appointment of the new Governor. He hoped that Onslow's replacement might be more sympathetic, or at least not so hostile, to the Government's stance on the council nominations. And he argued that, constitutionally, the Government ought to be told of the candidates for the governorship and so be able to ensure that the person selected would not be 'distasteful to the colonists'.[53] In fact, Onslow did ask for Ballance's view on two possible replacements: Sir Williams Robinson and Sir Robert Hamilton, current Governors of West Australia and Tasmania respectively.[54]

Further information came from Perceval, who had meanwhile been making a favourable impression on the London scene.[55] The Agent General told Ballance that Sir William Jervois, who had already been Governor from 1883 to 1889, wanted the job.[56] Ballance replied that Jervois 'would not do', since he was 'mixed up with money rings and speculators', had been consistently unsympathetic to the Government and was generally 'a thorough intriguer'.[57] Through Perceval, Ballance asked to be informed by the Colonial Office of the name of the new Governor before the official announcement was made. Ballance was promised that he would be consulted 'as far as possible'.[58] Yet he did not realistically expect to be able to do more than prevent a 'very objectionable person' being sent out.[59] And Perceval certainly suspected that he himself was being kept in the dark.[60] In the event, both Ballance and Onslow first read of the Earl of Glasgow's appointment as Governor in a telegram from London published in the colony's newspapers on 10 February.[61] 'I think we have been badly treated by the Colonial Office,' Ballance wrote to Perceval, and that you have a right to complain, that the Press was taken into the confidence of the Authorities before the Representative of the Colony. Have they not broken faith in not keeping their promise to inform you at the earliest possible moment . . . I am told that Glasgow is Sir James Ferguson's appointee. If so we may expect trouble, unless he is a man of great discretion. Ferguson, from a letter he wrote to Lord Onslow, bears the Colony a good deal of ill-will over the absentee taxation.[62]

Unknown to Ballance at the time, Onslow had taken the unusual step of leaving Glasgow a confidential memorandum about the council appointments. In it he told of Ballance's original request for 18 new members and explained why he had declined to approve more than eight: 'I should have been accused of lending myself to a scheme which might alter the complexion of the Upper House in order to enable the Ministry of the day to carry measures upon which the voice of the country had not been directly heard, and without the direct authority of the electors given to the proposal to bring the Upper House into harmony with the Lower.'[63]

Acutely aware of how critical the issue was to his government's survival, Ballance confronted Glasgow just two days after his arrival in the country. The Premier asked that the appointments be made and announced before the opening of the new session.[64] 'It is plain that no Government can carry on the business of the House satisfactorily when in one Chamber they exist

The political card game (NZ Observer, *1892*)

only on sufferance,' he told Glasgow. He suggested that Onslow would have agreed to 12 and was no doubt taken aback when Glasgow pointed to the memorandum he had received from his predecessor.[65]

Glasgow quickly reaffirmed Onslow's view: he would only appoint eight new members, plus an additional one to fill a recent vacancy. The decision of both men was quite clearly political. The argument that the appointments would 'swamp' the Upper House required an assessment of the political allegiance of councillors.[66] (In fact, Glasgow overestimated the effect of 12 new members. As the Colonial Office later pointed out, even with them the Government could still only be sure of 17 supporters in a council of 47.[67]) Further, Glasgow and Onslow deliberately refused to acknowledge the widespread feeling in the country in favour of the Government. Their view that the party's policies had not been 'directly' placed before the people was a highly political interpretation of the 1890 election, and was recognised as such by much of the press and populace. The position of Governor was rapidly losing credibility as being politically neutral. Everyone knew that Onslow had colluded in the Atkinson appointments.

Ballance had predicted that Glasgow would be no more sympathetic to the Government than Onslow. Yet when the new Governor announced his decision it set off in Ballance another spell of depression. These periods of gloom and despondency increased in regularity as illness took a firmer grip on Ballance's body. 'The Government will not have a very long life,' he wrote dejectedly to Vogel in May 1892,

> our Policy tends to make enemies in all directions. We are relying upon the good opinion of the great mass of the people whom we try to represent faithfully. The vested interests are very powerful and use every weapon that comes to their hand to damage the reputation of the Ministry. However it is of no consequence: while Ministries disappear, Parties remain, and I think we have a Party which will not fall to pieces when not in power.[68]

There had been talk of dissolution for some time,[69] in part for tactical reasons. Ballance used the threat of his resignation to try to pressure the Governor into agreeing to all 18 appointments. Glasgow knew that the whole position of the Governor would be a major issue in an election held under these circumstances. Yet the possibility of an election was now very real. Glasgow was standing firm and Ballance saw little point in proceeding with the new session just to have key government measures thrown out by the council for a second year in succession.[70]

As well as the continuing threat of the council, Ballance's government faced howls of protest from business and financial interests at home and abroad. Unfortunately, as in 1878, the 1891 land tax came just when economic conditions were worsening. The Baring crisis of 1890 led many

English investors to withdraw their deposits from the colony and credit was contracting rapidly. Farmers were being hit by a further fall in export prices, while unemployment rose and conditions in the towns remained bad.[71] In 1891 emigration exceeded immigration by more than 3000, the greatest population loss since 1888.[72]

The numerous reports of foreign mortgage companies withdrawing or intending to withdraw their capital from the colony, inevitably blamed the capital flight on the new land and income taxes.[73] Financial journals in London such as the *Times* and the *Economist* brimmed with articles critical of Ballance's measures.[74] Ballance argued that these articles were inaccurate and misinformed, and that they originated with government opponents within the colony.[75] There was much in this latter point: 'Some expression of alarm from your side of the ocean, and a reported disposition to withdraw capital, might do good,' Sir John Hall had written to Richard Oliver in early 1892.[76] It was also true that there were many other reasons for capital leaving the country. From London, Vogel consoled Ballance by saying that some funds would have left irrespective of the tax.[77]

English investors were particularly critical of the absentee tax. This tax had not been part of Ballance's original programme, since he believed that the graduated tax would be sufficient to force absentees to either develop, or subdivide and sell their properties. Instead it had been insisted upon by the Opposition, largely as a means to outbid and embarrass the Government.[78] In any event it was being misinterpreted in London, as Perceval, the Agent General, reported:

> It is most difficult to get people here to understand that this tax applies to land only and it is I fear doing no little harm. I have always advocated an absentee land tax but it brings in so little revenue & is so irritating, that I am sorry it was put in the bill. I quite see your difficulty in altering it now. People are refusing to lend money to N.Z. in any capacity giving the absentee tax as their reason . . . I believe the absentee tax has done more to create this *furore* against the land act than anything else.[79]

Rightly or wrongly, government policy was being blamed for an apparent loss of confidence in the New Zealand economy. The action of the loan companies did not surprise Ballance. 'I never supposed they would take kindly to the New Zealand Self Reliant Policy,' he wrote to Vogel. Yet Ballance was a realist and aware of the limitations to such a policy:

> The assertion of our independence is, of course, subject to many qualifications: We are not independent of the London Money Market, and I am not sure whether we shall be for a generation, if so soon, but what I have been preaching and trying to aim at has been to get rid of that *servile* dependence which has so long operated, in my opinion, to our disadvantage.[80]

[209]

By now Ballance had decided that an early election was inevitable. Less than two weeks after his letter to Vogel he wrote to Archie Willis that he would soon be in Wanganui to prepare for the contest. Ballance outlined a campaign plan involving the cutting up of the town into blocks of 50 to 100 electors, each district thus created being under the direct supervision of a chairman and committee. He also denied rumours in the press that he might seek election elsewhere: 'You need not be afraid of my leaving Wanganui, I shall stand or fall by the old place; I never had any other intention. . . . You know I cannot be responsible for all that is said about me in the papers: especially the Conservative papers.'[81] Ballance thought that his chances of re-election, with a larger majority, were favourable. If he lost he would retire from politics for good.[82]

Ballance's stay in Wanganui was brief. He arrived there in early June but by the third week had returned to Wellington for the opening of the new session. When Ballance met with his cabinet, the arguments supporting an early election were significantly less convincing than they had been a month before. Ballance's colleagues may well have persuaded him that he was being too pessimistic about the situation. And Ballance himself must have sensed that the pendulum was beginning to swing back in the Government's favour. On 24 June he wrote to one of his campaign committee in Wanganui that though an election might come, the Government was 'not going to court it'.[83]

Ballance turns down a knighthood (NZ Observer, *1892*)

One major reason for putting off a decision about dissolution was that the latest economic news was very good. Customs receipts, the major source of government income, had risen significantly, suggesting an increase in economic activity.[84] Further, the land tax was expected to bring in a lot more than had been anticipated.[85] In February a surplus of £100,000 was predicted; by June this had tripled to £300,000.[86]

A second bright spot concerned the Edwards case. The Atkinson Government had appointed W. B. Edwards Chief Commissioner of the Native Lands Court. Edwards also sat as (and received the salary of) a Supreme Court judge. It had been objected that the appointment was illegal, since the civil list only allowed for the salaries of five Supreme Court judges and Edwards's elevation brought the total to six. Atkinson's intention of amending the relevant act had been thwarted when he lost the 1890 election. When Ballance subsequently took office he refused to make provision for Edwards's salary.[87] The case went to the Supreme Court, which ruled three to two (the Chief Justice and Judge Connolly) in Edwards's favour.[88] Undaunted, and encouraged by the Chief Justice and Stout,[89] Ballance appealed to the Privy Council in England, and won.[90]

Throughout the affair, Ballance emphasised the constitutional principle at stake; that is, the obligation of a government to abide by the statutory limitation on the number of judges, rather than the question of whether another judge were needed.[91] As in the debate over the Legislative Council, Ballance put forward a democratic, moral argument that gained him enormous respect in the country.

Ballance's reputation as a leader of integrity and of the ordinary man in the street was growing. And it was secured beyond doubt when it was revealed in June that he had turned down a knighthood. As Premier the offer was a matter of course, but Ballance suggested Buckley instead.[92] Ballance had long opposed the granting of titles. When Vogel received his in 1875 the *Evening Herald* condemned them as 'cheap honours which cost little to the givers and have but a dubious merit with the majority of colonists'.[93] He had not changed his view since then. 'My own opinion,' he wrote early in 1892, 'is that as the Democratic party in the State we should not touch titles — the time is coming when they will be less valued than at present, & when the only title of honor will be that following upon services rendered to the state.'[94] The press acknowledged Ballance as a man of great principle.

The general public now viewed Ballance personally in a very positive light. There was much more to it than recognition of his high principles. His kindness, cheerfulness and consideration for the feelings of others were all-apparent in his dealings with individuals. Inevitably word of this, and of the vast energy and effort he put into his work, spread. Amelius Smith, his private secretary, later recalled:

> He was never irritable, even under circumstances that would have
> tried the equanimity of most men. I have often wondered at the
> patience with which he would brook intrusion upon his privacy and
> lay aside some important . . . work in order to receive and converse
> with some casual visitor; and I have also been struck with the facility
> with which, when the visitor had departed, he could take up the thread
> of his interrupted task. Nothing seemed to put him out.

Ballance was ever accessible and suffered for it, working day and night
with the briefest pause for meals. He was also reluctant to delegate tasks
he felt were his responsibility to perform. Smith was impressed:

> He had a remarkably quick apprehension, grasped the points of any
> subject with the utmost readiness, and retained them in a powerful
> memory, while his capacity for work was so enormous that he never
> seemed to tire. His brain was ever alert and active. He could not bear
> to let any work get into arrear. Everything must be kept up to date,
> and to accomplish that he never spared himself.[95]

The Premier's rising personal popularity strengthened his government. As
for the problem with the council appointments, Ballance tightened the screw
on the Governor by telling him that he intended to reintroduce the measures
thrown out by the council the previous year, and to seek an election if
they were rejected for a second time.[96] There was nothing to lose by this
approach, and always the possibility that the Governor would respond to
the rising public pressure for him to give way.

Just prior to the new session Ballance re-organised his cabinet.[97] On
the suggestion of Cadman, the Native Department was closed down. The
department's role had declined over the preceding decade and increasingly
Pakeha politicians saw it as both desirable and feasible that Maori should
be 'placed upon the same footing as Europeans'.[98] When established, the
department had been regarded as essentially a political device for bringing
Maori under European law and it had not been intended that a separate
administration for Maori continue once this objective had been achieved.[99]
The remaining functions of the department were dispersed. The Land Court
was placed under the Justice Department and the land purchasing activities
of the Native Department transferred to McKenzie at the Department of
Lands. Cadman was to hold the Justice and related Native Department
portfolios. At the same time, James Carroll, the Member for Eastern Maori,
became Native Member of the Executive, responsible for the welfare of
the Maori people.[100]

Reeves had held the Justice portfolio in addition to education, and with
the former passing to Cadman he needed new duties of equal importance
if his position within the Cabinet were to be maintained. He had wanted
the colonial secretaryship but Buckley refused to give it up. Meanwhile
Ballance decided to create the new post of Minister of Labour, and Reeves

eagerly responded to the Premier's suggestion that he take on the job.[101] Reeves had been supervising the Bureau of Industry and Labour established the previous June and was the obvious choice.

In less than 12 months the bureau had found jobs for 2974 men, 2000 in the private sector and the remainder on public works.[102] Under Reeves and his secretary, Edward Tregear, the Department of Labour (as the bureau soon become known) would, with the growth of factory legislation and the passing of the Industrial Conciliation and Arbitration Act, greatly expand its activities. There were to be major improvements in the conditions of employment of workers. Factory inspection had already begun under the 1891 Factories Act. In the House Ballance said that the establishment of the portfolio reflected the great importance the Government attached to the work the bureau was doing. He mentioned its achievements so far and also plans to create a few experimental 'State Farms'. Each farm was to comprise about 400 hectares of good agricultural land and on it unemployed (and particularly older) men and their families would be settled. Ballance believed that the farms could be made self-supporting.[103] Under the supervision of a 'practical captain of industry' the men would erect their own buildings, work the farm and also receive training in trades. The farms were to be 'transit stations', for it was hoped that after a period the men would be able to obtain employment back in the towns. In the meantime they would receive food, shelter and a small wage. There were also

'Ballance, the Rain-Maker' (NZ Observer, 1892)

'Weighed in the Balance and not wanting'
(NZ Observer, *1892*)

provisions for members to share in the profits of the farm; the co-operative
nature of the enterprise was stressed.[104]

With whom the idea for these farms originated is not clear beyond all
doubt, but it was almost certainly Ballance. The proposals have his stamp
all over them, the *Yeoman* published details of the farms at some length,
and towards the end of Ballance's life they were one of his favourite topics
of discussion.[105] Like the village settlements, the state farms aimed to utilise the resources of the land to ameliorate poor social and economic conditions in the towns. The concept was original, practical and remarkably
ahead of its time. Ballance had a strong social conscience and an equally
strong conviction that the state ought to take direct action in improving
the lot of its citizens. In fact only one state farm, 320 hectares of bush-

covered land at Levin, was established. It had considerable early success but without Ballance (when he died the experiment was just months old) and Reeves (who was soon replaced as Minister of Labour by Seddon) the original idea was lost. Also, as unemployment fell there was less pressure and less need for such a venture. The farm became essentially a labour-intensive work scheme for the unskilled unemployed, with little attention to training. And once the land was cleared, sown with grass and fenced, it could no longer provide work for the large number of people that had been placed on it. In 1897, therefore, the department purchased a new block of undeveloped land near Taihape where it could send surplus labour from the towns.[106]

In general terms the alterations Ballance made to the Cabinet simply reflected the changing roles of government. At the same time the work-load among ministers was distributed more evenly. Ballance himself lost Native Affairs and Ward, originally minister without portfolio, now took over as Postmaster General from Buckley. This latter post was to become more important as telephone communication was established throughout the country.

The re-organisation preserved the relative position of key cabinet personalities, amongst whom Ballance continued to achieve a high degree of harmony and consensus. In the House and in Cabinet he led by example; his firm but polite and calm approach to political debate helped greatly to keep the irascible Seddon and McKenzie under some control. Ballance was keen to maintain Reeves' influence and the Labour portfolio was no mere bagatelle. Reeves may well have been offered more, but asked Ballance to be relieved of as much work as possible. 'I felt the strain last session very much and rather fear the coming tax upon a health which has never been very strong. Family and private matters . . . have told on me a good deal. Moreover I have now the *N.Z. Times* to attend to.'[107] Ironically Ballance was dead within a year, while Reeves was to live to a ripe old age.

Ballance brought down his Financial Statement early in the new session, happily announcing a record budget surplus of £330,000.[108] The satirist Joseph Evison described Ballance as he made the most of the good news:

> Then, more especially when the appreciative gentlemen, mostly on Mr Speaker's right [i.e., on the Government benches], howled encomium, he beamed the largest-sized Ballance beam. He made every point with aplomb, and if he halted now and again, and in the proper places, sure his unkindest critic will admit that most Financial Statements require a little condiment of this description to make them go down.[109]

Ballance had reason to be pleased. A surplus of this magnitude (it had been £10,000 the previous year, £126,000 in 1890 and a negative figure for much of the 1880s[110]) convincingly countered criticisms of the Government's financial performance and of the effects of its policies. It was a great morale booster for the party. Aggrieved financial institutions and opposition papers had the wind taken out of their sails. Also, coming after long years of depression, the announcement marked the beginning of the public's association of Ballance 'The Rainmaker' with the return of prosperity. The economy was picking up and improved rapidly over the following years. The balance and terms of trade moved increasingly in New Zealand's favour, as dairy farming — made viable as an export-earner by refrigeration — took off in a big way.

The budget surplus meant that the Government's and Ballance's central policy of self-reliance was seen to be a viable proposition.[111] The London *Financial News* said that the policy, which had been forced on the colony by the depression and the accompanying withdrawal of capital, was a great success. The surplus indicated an 'inherent prosperity', enabling the people to 'put their trust in themselves'.[112] Specifically, Ballance was able to transfer over two-thirds of the surplus to the Public Works Account so that further settlement, traditionally financed through overseas loans, could be funded directly out of revenue. For Ballance this was how things should be, although he well knew that such a favourable situation might not last, as he explained to the editor of the *Lyttelton Times*:

'New Zealand Santa Claus': Ballance brings prosperity (NZ Observer, 1892)

It is true that in future years we may not have a surplus, and yet be compelled to carry on certain necessary works for the opening up of lands and the settlement of the country, but there are at the same time great possibilities, if we continue to prosper and carefully guard the revenue on one side and the expenditure on the other, that we shall have a surplus, I hope, for several years. If on the other hand the people of the Colony say that they are determined to have the surplus disposed of by remitting the duties upon the necessaries of life, and reducing taxation, then one of two results must follow. Either we must cease to colonise, or resume borrowing operations: I do not see any other alternative, and it would be well to make this clear to the people.[113]

Ballance opposed borrowing not simply because of the financial burden of debt repayment. Certainly one of his arguments against it was that the Government would have to pay a high rate of interest.[114] But more important, he regarded reliance on overseas loans as endangering the Government's and the country's independence. Self-reliance would wean the colony 'from a servile dependence on foreign dealers in money'.[115] Foreign capital could not be controlled, nor could it be trusted to act in the colony's interests. It had helped build the large estates instead of contributing to genuine development.[116] So Ballance's 'conservative' approach to government finance aimed at allowing the country to pursue radical policies without external interference.

In a sense Ballance also viewed borrowing as immoral. In the past, he argued, it had 'disorganised our industries and corrupted our people, and driven many from our shores whom it would have been well to have kept here'.[117] Non-borrowing was a political and social creed, not merely economic necessity. It would 'train the people to a policy of industry and self reliance'.[118] It was central to the Government's whole philosophy. 'The only safe policy for the colony is one of self-reliance,' said Ballance,

> one which fosters colonial enterprise and creates a colonising spirit; which recognises that the capitalist equally with the labourer must be identified, by residence and fulfilling all the duties of a colonist, with the progress and destiny of New Zealand. But, above all, it is essential that the Legislature should be free to effect those reforms it may resolve upon without obstruction from outside influences. The Parliament of New Zealand has already shown that it prefers the interests of the people it represents, and I cannot believe it will retire humiliated and beaten before the menaces of a sordid self-interest which resides outside the sphere of its dominion.[119]

A non-borrowing policy and the need, exemplified by the dispute over the Legislative Council appointments, to secure political independence from London, were the key elements of Ballance's self-reliant nationalism.

The arguments against borrowing overseas did not apply to internal loans, and Ballance did not rule out the possibility of raising money within the colony in order to promote development. He was unperturbed by the accusation that securities for this purpose would ultimately find their way to lenders overseas. The Government itself would still not be entering the London loan market.[120] Ballance admitted that internal borrowing would be required for the purchase of Maori land but argued that it would be 'very limited' and that the Government would 'have the land as an equivalent for the money expended'.[121]

The cry of overseas borrowing 'on the sly' also went up when Ballance announced a plan to make foreign investment companies deposit funds with the Public Trust Office 'as a guarantee of good faith'.[122] The companies would receive four percent interest, the money being re-lent at a slightly higher rate to small farmers or to local bodies for public works projects. The exercise would also, Ballance hoped, reduce the general rate of interest.[123] However, following objections from the insurance companies Ballance agreed not to pursue this attempt at controlling investment. 'So long as they show to the satisfaction of the Government that they have a stake in the country,' he said, they could 'lend their money out directly to small farmers . . . provided that the mortgage deeds are deposited in the Public Trust Office'.[124]

In his Financial Statement Ballance gave details of the estimated revenue from the land and income taxes. A major criticism of these taxes had been that they would not bring in as much money as the old. Ballance knew of the difficulties, for example, in assessing improvements (which were exempt from the land tax), but told the House that in most cases valuations had been quickly reached.[125] In fact the taxes were to raise £374,000 in the year to 31 March 1893. In 1889 the old property tax had raised £354,000.[126] There was, however, a longer-term problem with a progressive land tax. Ballance had always argued that the tax aimed to break up the large estates as well as to raise revenue; yet if large holdings were subdivided the revenue from a graduated tax on them would fall. Ballance appreciated this problem[127] but never tackled it, mainly because he died before any disintegrating effects of the tax could be felt. And anyway, with the Government now in a reasonably healthy financial position, concern at the consequences for revenue of taxation changes quickly evaporated.

Indeed the land tax in general soon ceased to be a major political issue. At first sight this might seem surprising, given the outcry against the tax when it was first announced. There were some complaints that assessors were hounding particular landowners,[128] but most people found that they paid only a little more, or actually paid less, under the new system compared to the old. Professionals and farmers were slightly worse off than under the property tax, while tradesmen, shopkeepers, agents and clerks came out better. The new system was certainly more equitable, in that the working classes now contributed a much lower proportion of direct taxation revenue. Widows too were substantially better off.[129]

As far as the tariff was concerned, Ballance told the House that it would remain as it was. He was adamant that it was preferable to maintain employment and wage levels through spending on public works than to reduce the price of 'certain articles of consumption . . . however much we may appreciate the advantage of cheapness'.[130] Ballance said that he would look at measures to increase protection for New Zealand manufactures. But the heavy legislative programme and amount of work involved in drawing up specific proposals meant that action would have to be postponed until the following session.[131] Finally, in his statement Ballance promised a bill to allow the Government to purchase private land. There would be no compulsion (although he did not discount its necessity in the future) and the large estates in Canterbury, where land was scarce, would be the first to receive the Government's attention.[132]

A land purchasing bill was unlikely to find favour in the Legislative Council. Nor could the Land Bill of the previous session, which Ballance said he would now reintroduce, expect an easier time. In July there was more talk of an election being the only way out of the anticipated impasse.[133] Soon, however, a crack appeared in the Governor's defences. The Cabinet asked Glasgow to turn the matter of the council appointments over to the Colonial Office for a ruling, and on 4 August he agreed.[134]

Glasgow sent the correspondence relating to the affair to the Secretary of State for the Colonies, Lord Ripon. In London, Perceval argued the Government's case and passed on to the Colonial Office some papers that Glasgow had withheld.[135] Glasgow defended his position by saying that he did not want to run the risk 'of making the Legislative Council a mere echo of the other House'.[136] Ballance had pointed out that although he personally favoured the preservation of the Upper House, there would undoubtedly be a demand for its abolition if the appointments were rejected. However Glasgow countered that the council's abolition 'would be preferable to its retention in a condition so manipulated as to possess merely a semblance of independence'.[137] When the matter was debated in Parliament, Ballance argued that although the Governor had the power to refuse the appointments, as long as the Government had a majority in the House the constitution required him to take the advice of his ministers.[138] Ballance was genuinely concerned (it was not just a bargaining tactic) at the constitutional consequences of the problem not being resolved in the Government's favour. He made this clear when suggesting to Perceval the arguments to present to the Colonial Office:

> Our party are ready to go straight for the demolition of the Legislative Council, and for an Elected Governor. I have been restraining them a good deal, hoping that by a fair constitution of the Council, we

might have a chance of carrying out measures without there [*sic*] being mutilated in the customary way by a party in the Council, influenced by a minority in the House. If therefore the Colonial Office maintains the Governor in, as I believe, the utterly unconstitutional attitude he has taken up, then I shall be compelled to throw my lot in with those who contend that one Chamber is sufficient, and will have to put before the people the necessity for many changes in other respects: changes, however, which will be quite consistent with the federation of the Empire. I have been one of the principal sticklers for the old Constitution, so long as the party in power had fair play. If, however, the Glasgow Doctrine is to prevail, then I can say that the Liberal Party in this country is doomed, on each occasion it is returned to power, by an Oligarchy in the Council.[139]

Although Ballance hoped to retain 'the old Constitution', he had distinct republican (as can be seen from his attitude to knighthoods, for example) and certainly very strong democratic tendencies. He opposed the idea of an elected council and Governor on the grounds that the political system would as a consequence become less, rather than more, democratic. 'If we are to have a Democracy in this country,' he wrote, 'then the Upper House must either be made weak, or abolished altogether.'[140]

From the New Zealand Government's point of view the move to seek a ruling from the Colonial Office was very sensible. Gladstone's Liberal Ministry had recently been elected and the favourable outcome of the Edwards case appeal was a good indication of the British Government's likely approach to the council appointments. The key was getting Glasgow to agree to the referral. Ballance was optimistic: 'We shall await the verdict of the Home Office with some anxiety, but I am just as confident that the reply will be favourable as I was in the Edwards Case. The whole spirit of Colonial Office relations to the Colonies is in the direction of throwing the entire responsibility upon Local Governments.'[141]

The most important piece of legislation of the session was the Land Bill, which was introduced in the second week of August. Ballance had intended that the new bill be closely modelled on the measure rejected by the council the previous year. He did not want to attach to the perpetual lease the right to acquire the freehold: this was basic to the preservation of the remaining crown lands. The Bill that passed did not allow lessees this right but conceded all of the other major features of the freehold tenure. The lease-in-perpetuity, as it was called, ran for 999 years and unlike the perpetual lease could be mortgaged (and therefore used as security for loans).[142] Further, there would be no revaluations of rents. The state could impose residence and improvement conditions (and the occupier had to pay the land tax on the same basis as freeholders), but would not receive the 'unearned increment' as the land rose in value.

McKenzie proposed the lease-in-perpetuity under pressure from some of the Government's own supporters representing country districts.[143] 'If I were bringing in a Land Bill entirely to suit my own views,' he said, 'it would be a very different Land Bill from what is before the House at present. . . . But we have to be practical: we must study public opinion, and we must study the opinions of members of this House . . . All legislation on this matter must be to a certain extent a compromise.'[144]

Ballance spoke briefly on the second reading but revealed little, saying simply that McKenzie had recognised 'that the time has not come for confining himself entirely to the perpetual lease'.[145] Ballance had earlier drawn the distinction between his own belief in the preservation through leasing of all remaining crown land, and the widespread popularity of the freehold:

> If the people of the colony wish for the freehold tenure, of course they must have it. Who will gainsay the people of the colony? who resist them? I say we believe that the public estate should be saved for the people . . . for all generations to come — through all time. We say that we shall reason this matter out with the people of the colony, and we believe that if the position is fairly put before them they will come to . . . look upon the lands of the colony as a heritage which should be sacred to the people.[146]

Nowhere, either in the House or in his private correspondence, did Ballance admit to the full extent of the compromise involved in the lease-in-perpetuity. His illness may have been a factor in his conceding the issue, though McKenzie had devised the new tenure well before Ballance's major relapse in late August. Ballance did indicate in a letter earlier in the year that if there were no revaluation in the new tenure he would try to bring in periodic assessments of rent through a Fair Rent Court.[147] In 1894 William Earnshaw told the House that he had only supported the Land Bill having been promised in writing by Ballance that a Fair Rent Bill would be introduced.[148] For the time being, however, there was little Ballance could do. If the House had been persuaded to accept a perpetual lease similar to that in the previous year's Land Bill, the Council would almost certainly have thrown it out for a second time. It might well be that had Ballance been able to appoint the new batch of councillors at the start of the new session (which, of course, is what he had urged of Glasgow), he would have been more inclined to persist with the perpetual lease.

Ballance's prime concern was the survival of the Government. As he wrote to Perceval the day after the second reading of the Land Bill:

> The discussion on the Financial Statement is just over: no amendment was tabled, and the result of the debate is that the Government is strengthened. The Opposition, however, are exceedingly active and will table a No Confidence motion on the Land Bill, supposed to be our weakest point as regards the question of the Freehold, but

McKenzie has completely dumbfoundered them by turning the Perpetual Lease with renewals into a Perpetual Lease for ever at the first rent. This seems to have completely captivated a large number of Members who were formerly in favour of the Freehold.[149]

Certainly the lease-in-perpetuity was much more popular than the perpetual lease; but only because it conceded all but the freehold. For the tenant it was cheap land with virtually freehold security and rights. The Government was left with a few powers over residence and improvement conditions.

In allowing lessees to mortgage their holdings, the Government went some way to recognising the demand from farmers for credit to carry out improvements. This demand grew over the following years and resulted in the passage of the Advances to Settlers Act of 1894. Yet Ballance was by no means convinced that substantial funds needed to be provided, arguing in the past that given the low annual rents (much smaller than the repayments under deferred payment schemes) 'there would be no struggle at all' for lessees to make improvements.[150] Many small farmers disagreed.[151] Ballance was also concerned about where the money for loans would come from. He certainly did not wish to borrow it overseas.

Liberals from the cities were, like Ballance, generally unsympathetic to the demands from small farmers for credit. They wanted the break-up of the large estates and the promotion of a leasehold tenure that would secure for the state a continuing share in rural prosperity. Typical of these liberals were McLean, Tanner, Earnshaw, Buick and Joyce. All disapproved

The present state of affairs in the House (NZ Observer, 1892)

of the 1892 Land Bill, which sacrificed this share.[152] If there were any borrowing to be done, they much preferred it to be for the government re-purchase of private land.

As the Land Bill passed through the House Ballance was dying of cancer. All could see that his condition was getting worse, no matter how hard he tried to conceal it. Harry Atkinson had died in late June and as Ballance spoke of his old adversary, many who listened felt he was 'delivering what might serve as his own funeral oration'.[153] A Wellington journalist later described Ballance as he fought against the illness:

> Time after time he would be observed lying back in his place, ashen pale, waiting to reply to some threatened attack from the Opposition benches, forced to get up every little while and retire to his room, there to writhe in agony. Back to the House he would come, and when the expected attack was being delivered, he would take notes in a bold hand upon the foolscap before him, while stimulating his flagging energies with powerful restorative salts. Then, when it came his turn to reply, casting off all signs of weakness, he would, with the fluency of the ready debater, seek to rout his accuser.[154]

In early September Ballance was compelled to withdraw to his bed. A fancy dress ball that Ellen had organised in Kathleen Ballance's honour was postponed as the family held its breath.[155] Soon Ballance was making slow but steady progress and, against the advice of his doctors and colleagues, was back in the House by the middle of the month.[156] 'Mrs Ballance's Butterfly Ball' went ahead, attended by 200 guests. Sons and daughters of politicians and leading Wellington citizens filled the ballroom at the Premier's residence. Kathleen 'received her youthful friends standing beside Mrs Ballance, with her gauzy wings spread, and fluttering with all the pretty graces of a genuine butterfly'. Although butterflies dominated the occasion, there were other assorted costumes. Miss Stafford made a great hit as a pharaoh's daughter and 'Master Churton made a capital Nigger.'[157]

Unfortunately Ballance's recovery did not last long. When he spoke in the House on 23 September it was to be for the last time, for his condition worsened again and he was back in bed days later.[158] The *Herald* played down the seriousness of the latest relapse. There was every hope, it said, that his health would continue to improve and that with rest he would soon be back on his feet.[159] At the same time it blamed Ballance's illness on the 'shameful' obstruction of business by the Opposition, mentioning in particular the activities of Fish, Fisher, George Hutchison and Scobie MacKenzie, and suggesting that these members' constituencies would do well to turn them out at the next election. 'Mr Ballance has had to work from 16 to 18 hours a day ever since the session began, and to put up with an amount of obstruction and worry that would kill many a less courageous man.'[160]

Ballance was still in his bed, at his Tinakori home above Parliament, when he received the Colonial Office's ruling that Glasgow must agree to make all the new appointments to the Legislative Council.[161] It was, perhaps, Ballance's greatest and most significant victory. Regarded as a vindication of his whole policy, it immediately strengthened the Government's position, demoralised the Opposition still further and in the longer term established an important constitutional precedent. It was the beginning of the end of the council's power to stifle a government's key measures. The consequences of the decision were felt well beyond New Zealand's shores. Similar conflicts between governments and governors were occurring in Australian states. The parties to these disputes now knew what the Colonial Office's attitude to a direct clash between duly-elected government and Queen's representative was likely to be.[162] The rest of the Cabinet were jubilant, though the ever-considerate, sensitive Ballance told them to do everything they could to let the Governor down as lightly as possible. Party members were to be informed straight away of the news, so that when the public announcement was made in the House there would be 'no cheering or other demonstration'.[163]

The Colonial Office had also earlier delivered to Ballance a victory over the related issue of pardon for criminals. Until now, governments in the colonies could recommend pardons but governors made the final ruling whether to grant or refuse. Ballance argued, to the other colonies and to London, that governors ought to be obliged to accept the Government's

'Why not call working men to the Upper House?' (NZ Observer, 1892)

recommendation. The Colonial Office agreed, supporting Ballance's view that a governor was bound to accept the constitutional advice of the Government on this as on other matters.[164]

Although the appointments to the council could only now be made, Ballance had long been considering exactly whom to nominate. His aim was not simply to increase the Government's voting strength in the council, but in selecting the 12 new members to fairly represent, reward and as far as possible help secure the loyalty of the various factions within the party. As far back as September 1891, the *Yeoman* had acknowledged that a number of the new councillors would be labour representatives.[165]

During the recess Ballance approached individuals and organisations for suggestions, and these names were subsequently considered by the Cabinet.[166] The final selection included four trade unionists, the first to be appointed to the council: William Bolt, radical freethinker and Secretary of the National Liberal Association in Dunedin; W. T. Jennings, a printing foreman who was a prominent Auckland liberal and member of the Knights of Labour; J. E. Jenkinson, a Christchurch boilermaker; and finally John Rigg, who was president of the Wellington Trades and Labour Council. The other eight were: Henry Feldwick, the Invercargill liberal who had lost his seat at the last election; Thomas Kelly, a farmer and ex-Member for New Plymouth; two journalists, McCullough and Kerr, from Auckland

'*Reinforcing the crew of the HMS* Legislative Council' *(*NZ Observer, *1892)*

'Dawn of a New Era' (NZ Observer, 1892)

and Greymouth respectively; MacGregor, a Dunedin lawyer; William Montgomery, who had held office very briefly in the first Stout-Vogel Government; Edward Richardson, the Christchurch politician who had been Minister for Public Works in a number of administrations (including Atkinson's); and W. C. Walker, a farmer and ex-Member for Ashburton.

It was the presence of the unionists that drew most comment from the press. The *Evening Post* saw Bolt's elevation as a reflection of the influence of Stout and of 'revolutionary Socialistic doctrines' on the Government.[167] Certainly the thought of working-class men sitting in the Upper House was hard for some to swallow. But many people welcomed Ballance's labour nominees as another step in the march towards greater democracy. As for the other selections, most were rightly seen as reward for services rendered to the liberal cause.[168]

The Government still did not have a majority in the Upper House but with these and later appointments, and with the constitutional principle having been established, its measures would now have a much easier passage. Ballance lived only just long enough to see this vital success. Along with the new hope and confidence that sprang from his budget surplus, it firmly established him as the most popular leader the country had ever had.

[CHAPTER 12]

Cut short

W<small>HEN BALLANCE BECAME</small> dangerously ill in September 1892, the Cabinet unanimously appointed Seddon Acting Premier.[1] After Ballance, Seddon was the most prominent member of the party in Parliament. In his end-of-session speech he lamented that Ballance's health had failed just as the Government's policies were beginning to bear fruit. Seddon said that the Premier had been vindicated by the decisions on the Legislative Council appointments and the Edwards case and, more important, by the success of his self-reliant policy. Financial journals in London that had previously been hostile were now praising New Zealand: 'confidence has been restored not only amongst ourselves in this colony, but also in the Old World'.[2]

Ballance's condition improved only gradually through October. By the end of the month he was able to travel to Wanganui,[3] where he told his constituents that he expected to be in 'perfect health' in a matter of weeks.[4] But he soon suffered another relapse and was rushed back to Wellington by special train.[5]

Ballance tried to keep the seriousness of his ailment a secret. He wanted to hold onto the leadership for as long as possible, with the appearance of firmness and confidence. Uncertainty would fuel a prolonged struggle for his replacement and be damaging to the party. Also, if Ballance were to go, he wanted Stout as successor. Stout was out of Parliament and it would take him some time to get back in. Ballance's colleagues acquiesced in the cover-up, in circumstances similar to those surrrounding the illnesses of Savage and Kirk, subsequent New Zealand Prime Ministers who died in office. On 13 December 1892 T. M. Haultain wrote to his old friend Edward Stafford: 'Ballance's party have a very decided majority both in House and in the Country. I hear from Wellington that there is very little hope of their leader's restoration to health and they are keeping this very quiet, for his retirement whether from death or otherwise would be a serious difficulty to them, as there would be a struggle for the Premiership.'[6]

Ballance's doctors could do nothing for him and in desperation he agreed to be seen by a man called Heiden, an old mine manager who had apparently 'effected some remarkable cures by massage and animal magnetism'.[7] A major symptom of Ballance's illness was blockage of the bowel and Heiden's treatment appears to have eased this considerably, though it did not materially affect the progression of the disease.

By the new year Ballance was well enough to do some work. He was able to share in the growing optimism in the future of the Government and the country. 'The Land Tax has turned out very well indeed, and I am looking forward to find [sic] the Income Tax equally successful,' he wrote to Alfred Saunders. 'The Colony as a whole is really more prosperous than it has been for years . . . The Dairy Industry is developing into one of our staples, and there is no reason why, in the course of a few years, the exports in this should not have reached a million: this is the industry for the small farmer . . . We have virtually no unemployed on our hands now, save those that belong to the professional class who are disinclined to move away from the centres of population.'[8] There was also some good personal news for Ballance; the *Herald* company was showing the best profit for years.[9]

Ballance intended to go home soon to Wanganui, hoping that a break away from Wellington would aid his recovery. 'I look forward with pleasure to be able to spend a fortnight or three weeks in my own house,' he wrote to Duigan, editor of the *Herald*.[10] Ballance also planned to meet up with Stout there. 'I have been longing very much to have a chat with you,' he told his old friend and confidant.[11] They had indeed a lot to discuss.

Throughout January, Ballance resolutely struggled to stay out of bed and at work. In part this effort reflected his enormous commitment to his job, his drive and self-motivation, and sheer grit. In part it was an attempt to squash rumours about his uncertain future. On the sixteenth of the month he put out the following statement:

> The Hon. the Premier is much concerned at some statements that have appeared in print to the effect that he was so ill he was unlikely to enter political life again. He has requested the Press Association to state that his present condition is most satisfactory, that he is recovering rapidly, and has every expectation of being in his seat next session.[12]

This was some way from the truth, for Ballance was only just holding his own and Ellen was desperately worried.[13] But the fight continued. On 30 January, Sarah Jane wrote in her diary: 'Mr Ballance very ill. David saw Ellen this morning: another consultation was held . . . result not satisfactory: patient disobeyed orders, dressed, took a chop & attended to business.'

As Ballance worked on in Wellington two political questions in particular were on his mind. The first was the purchase of the Cheviot Estate, the second the women's franchise.

For Ballance and many on the left wing of the Liberal Party land nationalisation meant not only the preservation of existing crown lands through leasing, but the re-purchase of land in private hands. Ballance had earlier promised a purchasing bill[14] and during the session a Land for Settlements Act had been duly passed. It established a Land Purchase Board that was empowered to inspect freehold land being offered for sale. If suitable, the land could be acquired by the Crown and settled under the lease-in-perpetuity. However, largely because the board could not compel a sale and government spending was limited to £50,000 per year, the act did not meet with much initial success.

Meanwhile, under different legislation, the Government bought the 34 400-hectare Cheviot Estate in Canterbury. The estate was acquired under the provisions of the Land and Income Assessment Act, whereby an owner who refused to accept the official valuation of his property could sell it to the Government. The land had been valued for taxation purposes at £359,126, including improvements. However, the trustees of the estate, advised by the lawyer and conservative politician Francis Bell, offered it for sale at £260,220 — hoping to force the Government to lower the valuation and not really intending the sale to go through.[15] Ballance was not particularly keen to purchase the land but the alternative, reducing the valuation, 'would have established a most dangerous precedent'.[16] So the Government called the bluff of the trustees and took Cheviot. Ballance believed that he had 'established for all time the object lesson in the way of cutting up the large estates, which must act as a stimulus to voluntary promptings for the large holders'.[17]

Historians have disputed the extent to which the Land Tax and the Land for Settlement Acts influenced the subsequent reduction in the size of land holdings. It has been argued that rising prices, refrigeration and the spread of dairying were more important factors; that irrespective of the legislation large landowners were quite willing to subdivide.[18] It is certainly true that the legislation worked in the same direction as economic forces of the time.[19] As Ballance realised, small-scale intensive dairy farming had become a viable proposition and was potentially a major export earner. Estate owners who had watched the value of their sheep runs fall over the past decade welcomed the opportunity to subdivide in favour of dairy farmers as land prices rose. Yet the political significance of the legislation was undeniable. The Liberal Government was seen to be beginning to deliver the goods. Ballance's supporters were delighted that large estates were being split into small farms and the cry for 'more Cheviots' was heard far and wide.

Ballance hoped that the Cheviot purchase would enable the Government to 'settle a large number of people on the land, and at the same time avoid a loss to the Treasury'.[20] Although keen to make the exercise self-financing, he did not believe that this required the sale of the land. 'I do not care if we sell not an acre,' he wrote to Stout. 'As the Land Tax department has the disposal of it, I propose to save the unearned increment by leasing it for terms of 30 and 21 years perpetual on a mere rental system.'[21] In the long run the state would receive back in rents what it had paid for the land. In fact, however, the unsold land was eventually settled on the lease-in-perpetuity.[22] This tenure did not allow for revaluation and so the unearned increment was not saved.

The second issue of concern to Ballance at this time was women's suffrage, something he had long advocated. In 1879 he had unsuccessfully attempted to amend an Electoral Bill to enfranchise women. And he had supported an Enfranchising Bill of 1890, saying, 'I believe in the absolute equality of the sexes, and I think they should be in the enjoyment of equal privileges in political matters.'[23] Ballance's views on this were strongly influenced by those of his wife. Ellen was prominent in the growing feminist movement in New Zealand and had recently been elected vice-president of the Women's Progressive Society. Seddon later said that it was she who converted Ballance to women's suffrage.[24] If this was true, it was doubtless an easy conversion. Ballance was a comprehensive democrat.

Ballance knew that there were liberals opposed to female suffrage, some on the grounds that the majority of women would vote against the Government at an election. James Duigan, editor of the *Herald*, advised him that it was 'dead against the interests of the Liberal Party to extend the franchise to women'. Duigan said that Wanganui women would vote for Carson 'because in their opinion he is a good man, and against you because they have been led to believe by your enemies that you are an athiest [sic]'.[25] Yet Ballance argued that the vote should be given irrespective of the political effect it might have.[26] His problem was that his cabinet colleagues were not so enthusiastic:

> It is no secret that Mr Ballance is the only one of the Ministry who is heartily in favour of the concession and confident of its immediate beneficial influence. The warm support such an advanced proposition has received from the Conservative benches has naturally aroused distrust in the breasts of those Liberals who have not thought much on the subject.[27]

One leading conservative in particular, John Hall, favoured women's suffrage. In 1891 he had proposed its introduction through an amendment to the Electoral Bill (which aimed at removing the right of property voters to appear on more than one roll). Ballance had worked hard to gather support for the measure, and his efforts were acknowledged by women's groups[28] and in the press.[29] Ellen too was very active. When, during the debate, one speaker had boldly announced that women did not want the vote, she passed around a petition in the Ladies' Gallery, which drew 68 signatures, assuring the House that in fact they did.[30] The amendment had been carried by a large majority[31] but was subsequently (along with the property vote clause) thrown out by the council.[32]

The following session Ballance had introduced a new bill, this time containing the female franchise from the start.[33] He suggested that Hall wanted women enfranchised only because he (Hall) believed it would be of benefit to the conservative party. Ballance argued that the bill would have the opposite effect and added that although it did not allow women to stand for Parliament, he was personally in favour of this.[34] The Council had again made some changes to the bill, this time allowing women to vote but only by post. Although without a secret ballot women would be open to instruction on how to vote from men,[35] a leading suffragist, Alfred Saunders, had tried to get the House to accept the concession rather than drop the whole bill. At this crucial point Ballance had been taken ill, and with the rest of the Cabinet opposed to the idea[36] the entire measure was lost.

As Ballance lay on his sick bed, public debate on women's suffrage raged throughout the country. In Christchurch a meeting of the Women's Christian Temperance Union was called to censure the Government on its failure to pass the franchise.[37] In Wanganui the *Yeoman* argued that the council's amendment fitted in with Hall's motives, in that it destroyed the secret ballot, thus 'giving the head of a Tory family several votes through the enfranchisement of his wife, daughters, and female domestics'.[38]

Early in the new year Ballance began to consider the prospects of the party at the coming election,[39] and in particular the effect enfranchisement might have on the result. Six months earlier he had told a liberal in Wellington: 'We believe the wives and daughters of working men will vote with their male relations, and that on the whole women's votes will be progressive in the best sense of the term,' adding that democracy would triumph as long as it was organised.[40] But now he was not so sure. He suggested that the vote be given but its operation delayed until January 1894:

> The Women's Franchise Bill will of course be introduced again next session, and it will no doubt pass both Houses. If it be brought into operation before the General Election, there will not be time for the whole of the women of the country to be placed upon the Register. Only the ones who are already organised will be there, and outside the large cities these are all against us. The Party, in my opinion, will be seriously damaged unless there is time to place the whole of the women of the colony on the rolls . . . I do not myself like to . . . disappoint the women workers who are looking forward to the franchise as a means of redressing their grievances: but the present

Liberal Party has done very much for the cause of labor generally. I cannot think they would refuse to wait for one Parliament in order to obtain so great a boon which has been granted in no other country in the world, with the exception of one State in America.[41]

Nevertheless, with this one qualification, Ballance remained firmly in favour of the franchise.[42] He wrote to Saunders:

My own strong opinion is, that we want on the Statute Book as a foundation of our constitution a broad measure taking in all the adults of the colony, male and female, without any experimental legislation such as voting through the Post Office. Then we shall have the freest political system in the world.

I have myself the utmost faith in the good sense of the women of the colony, and have never changed in the slightest for the last fourteen years my views on the subject. I was the first to carry a resolution in favour of the franchise in the House, and believed then, as I believe still, that it would be one of the greatest of social reforms.[43]

So although concerned for the position of the Liberal Party, Ballance was optimistic that women's enfranchisement would not, in the long term, harm it. Despite Seddon's lack of enthusiam, an act was passed in the 1893 session and women voted at the general election at the end of the year.

Ballance travelled to Wanganui in early February, and was accompanied there by Heiden in the hope that the old man might have further success in treating his patient.[44] Ballance worked in spells that lasted as long as his enthusiasm and energy held up, 'and then would lay down State papers and seek solace and relief in Milton or Tennyson or Shakespeare, or upon the chess-board, which was always at hand, throwing his mind into the solution of some intricate problem. Such pursuits he would alternate with dips into works upon gardening and poultry-raising.'[45] But the periods of reprieve were becoming shorter and shorter, and the downward trend was clear. Ballance had lost 25 kilograms in weight in the past few months.[46] Yet, wandering through and enjoying his large garden at 'The Knolls', chatting to Ellen, to his close friends and to Heiden, Ballance was by no means entirely dejected. He looked forward to another expected budget surplus and talked of how the money might be used. He talked of his ideas for extending the role of state farms to provide homes where the elderly could live comfortable but useful and independent lives; and of a communal settlement, where 'dairy factories were to be established, fruit-evaporating plants erected, and fruit-raising encouraged, silk-culture engaged in, and a variety of cognate industries established by the co-operation of the settlers under the fostering care of the State. While this was being done for settlers inland, he hoped to be able to establish settlements on the coast to promote oyster-culture and develop the fishing industry'.[47] It was the idealism of a man sick but still with a lively, intense mind.

Ballance's exercise was not limited to walks around his garden. In mid-February he tramped two miles to see a friend who ran a nearby orchard. There, sampling the fruit, he was found by a government official who had come to Wanganui to discuss some urgent departmental business with him. Together, the two men strolled back to 'The Knolls', where talk continued well into the evening. A few days later Ballance suffered another severe relapse.[48]

The doctors were called in and consultations took place as Ballance lay prostrate on his bed. The local man, Saunders, was joined by Professor Holden, ex-president of the Royal College of Surgeons in England, who was visiting New Zealand at the time. This latter eminent physician pronounced rather obscurely that there was 'no organic derangement, but that as it were, the engine had been too powerful for the ship'.[49] Ellen was advised that an operation was necessary and that Ballance should be persuaded to retire from politics. When told this, Ballance apparently spoke to the effect that he would rather 'die at his post than lay down the reins of office while the people of the country and the men of his Party desired that he should retain them'.[50] Nevertheless, he knew in his heart that he could not hang on much longer. As arranged in January, Stout arrived in the town and discussed the situation with Ballance. Ballance urged Stout to re-enter politics and to contest the leadership with Seddon. 'I must go and Stout must come,' he told Ellen.[51]

Ballance grew weaker but outwardly at least 'retained his old cheerfulness'. He talked to Archie Willis of plans to publish a new 'Liberal Review'. And when Willis suggested that Ballance write a book 'embodying his ideas and schemes for the future', Ballance 'laughed, and said, "that is exactly what I have been thinking about, and if I get over this illness, I shall set about it shortly".'[52] In all his years in politics Ballance had published just one pamphlet, on land nationalisation — and that was simply a series of newspaper articles. Only now, out of active political life, did he consider writing a more comprehensive and substantial work.

In the second half of March Ballance gained another temporary reprieve, and by early April was able to travel to Wellington to consult with his cabinet. He continued to go to extraordinary lengths to conceal his condition. On the train to Wellington he was lying in considerable pain in his private compartment when some journalists came in to speak to him.

> He at once got up, assumed an appearance of ease, and remained standing while he spoke to them; but as they thoughtlessly continued asking him questions, and he felt unable to combat the pain and weakness under which he laboured, he placed his hand upon his side, excused himself, said he felt tired with the journey, and lying down, concluded the interview in that position, his questioners little thinking the agony they were causing him.[53]

Once in Wellington Ballance held a number of cabinet meetings in his own house. Those who had not seen him for a while were shocked by his appearance. 'His intellect was as bright as ever, and his greeting as cordial, but he had fallen away until what had been sturdy limbs could now have been spanned by the hand.'[54] Ellen later wrote to Stout:

> When on our return from Wanganui my husband found he was not getting stronger, he said, 'Stout must come into the House, and the day the House meets I shall resign; I have not the strength for the work, and I shall not attempt to do what I am incapable of doing.' We decided to say nothing about it for a time, but our intention was to return to Wanganui together . . . His relations with his colleagues were most friendly, but none can imagine better than you how many anxieties he had, and how far before his own interests came the interests of New Zealand. He thought if his intention were known it might injure the Party.[55]

In the meantime, Ballance carried on with government business. On 11 April he wrote to William Hall-Jones, the Liberal Member for Timaru, about a range of political matters. Ballance concluded the letter by saying that his health was 'greatly improving' and that he hoped to be well for the coming session.[56] There were also some domestic concerns to be dealt with. Julius Kurth, Ballance's manservant and gardener, gave notice that he was going to leave 'The Knolls' to take up farming. Ballance wished Kurth every success and then asked him to attend to a few matters before his departure:

> I regret you are leaving me, but believe that you are justified in the step you are taking; and my regard for your welfare more than compensates for the loss which I feel. Before you leave, I would like you to prepare a bed at the conservatory for the vines, so that it will be ready to receive them when the time for planting arrives. I suppose the improvements to the house are being pushed on with proper vigor [sic]. I would like very much if the well could be sunk to say a depth of 10ft and bricked on the sides, so that it would be ready for the wind-mill which I intend to acquire.[57]

As he received with great pleasure and satisfaction figures from the various government departments confirming another substantial surplus, Ballance was nearing the end. The press was now speculating on his likely successor, despite having been requested by the Cabinet not to give away the true seriousness of this situation. Ballance saw one comment from a Westland paper about the chances of Seddon, the local man, taking over. The paper also published a telegram from Wellington saying that the Premier's case was hopeless. Ballance was very annoyed and upset, and insisted on issuing a statement contradicting the report.

Shortly after this, Ballance decided to take a trip on a government launch, appropriately the *Ellen Ballance*, around Wellington harbour. John McKenzie accompanied him. Ballance felt the sea air might do him good but rain soon forced him below deck.[58] On his return to shore he suffered a complete intestinal obstruction.[59] A series of consultations involving five doctors was held. Finally, on Thursday 20 April, the medical men decided that an operation was the only hope. Their view was that 'the bowels must be laid bare, opened, cleansed, and the obstruction removed. For more than ten days there had been a cessation of the functions, and the danger was imminent.'[60]

The operation was to be carried out three days later, on the Sunday morning. The waiting was sheer mental agony for Ballance and came on top of his great physical pain. Realising that his chances of survival were slim, he was 'very anxious' to see Stout before the operation began.[61] Stout was due to arrive in Wellington at any moment, and when he did, he found on the wharf a message from Ballance asking him to go immediately to the Premier's residence.[62] Fortunately Stout was in time, and the two men talked while final preparations were made.

When these were completed, Ballance got up from his bed unassisted and walked over to the operating table. He shook hands with the doctors, said goodbye to Ellen and Stout, and then 'bade the operators begin'. Chloroform was administered, 'the right side above the hip was laid open, and the bowel exposed and severed and accumulations removed'.[63] After two and a half hours the operation was still incomplete, but the surgeons stopped, fearing Ballance might survive no longer under the knife. All the members of the Cabinet, alongside Stout and Ballance's relatives, anxiously stood by. By the following morning Ballance had regained consciousness, and spoke to Stout and David Anderson. At a consultation that evening it was decided to resume the operation the next day, Tuesday. This second stage began at 8 am and lasted three hours. At its conclusion the surgeons had cleared the bowel. Given the limited medical knowledge available to them, there was no more they could do. For a brief moment there was hope that the surgery had been successful, but Ballance did not recover full consciousness. On Wednesday the doctors took what would now be considered a somewhat bizarre action in injecting the patient with champagne. It was hoped this would act as a stimulant — a last desperate effort to 'stave off the end'. Ballance's condition deteriorated further and by midday on Thursday it was clear that he would not live much longer. Messengers were sent out in haste to summon ministers, who were at their homes having just finished a cabinet meeting. Ellen was joined at his bedside by her brother and sisters. Stout, McKenzie, Reeves, Buckley, Seddon and Ballance's private secretary, Amelius Smith, were also there.

The people of Wellington speculated quietly as tension in the city grew. At about 4.30 pm some flags (including that over Government House) were lowered to half-mast. Minutes later they were raised to full height again — Ballance had rallied. As dusk fell he gave a brief flicker of consciousness; then suddenly it was all over, and he died at 6.20 pm.[64] He had only just celebrated his fifty-fourth birthday. Many newspapers, including the *Wanganui Herald*, had already announced his death in their 4.00 pm editions.[65]

When the news broke meetings throughout the country were adjourned and flags flown at half-mast. Closing the Resident Magistrate's Court, Judge Martin said that the Premier's death was a national calamity. Public servants were relieved from duty on the Friday and Saturday. The Government Buildings, usually swarming with activity, stood eerily silent. To the quiet, sad house amid the trees beneath the Tinakori hills, messages of condolence for Ellen began pouring in. They came from throughout New Zealand and later from Australia and England.[66] Many wreaths arrived. Over the next days and weeks Ballance's friends and colleagues spoke of their enormous respect and love for the man. Amelius Smith said he had never 'worked for a kinder chief' in his life. 'The thought uppermost in my mind now is the recollection of his invariable kindness and ever cheerful disposition . . . beyond all comparison.'[67] Reeves told a Dunedin meeting that he did not 'expect to follow quite such a leader again — one so generous as a chief, so sympathetic as a colleague, so kind and loyal as a friend . . . Speaking as one of the youngest and least experienced of his lieutenants, I can never express too strongly my feelings of gratitude to him. In the various perplexities and doubts that beset a young Minister one always had a friend as well as adviser in John Ballance. If one committed a mistake he always made the least of it instead of the most; if one scored a success he made the most of it and not the least. He was great enough to be utterly generous. I need not say that he was sincere. Everyone admits that now.'[68]

Meanwhile, a post mortem found that the surgeons had made their incision on the wrong side (it should have been on the left side instead of the right), and 'that the stricture was a swelling and contraction of the interior channel of the descending colon, about three feet from its exterior termination, of a cicatricial appearance. The pressure upon the main channel of the bowel was so great as to deflect it and displace the various organs, and the marvel was how the sufferer had so long suffered without the relief of all-levelling Death.'[69]

Ballance was buried in Wanganui on Sunday 30 April. 'There has been no funeral in New Zealand more largely attended, nor has the death of anyone called forth such public sorrow and regret,' Stout wrote shortly afterwards.[70] For many days the weather had been gloomy, a grey blanket of cloud producing persistent drizzle, but early on the morning of the funeral the sun finally broke through. By 7.00 am, when the kauri coffin was laid on a gun-carriage drawn up outside the Premier's residence in Wellington, crowds already packed the nearby streets. The procession crept down Tinakori Road, then right into Hill Street and past Parliament to the station. The Volunteer Corps came first, followed by 50 sailors from HMS *Katoomba* and then members of the Permanent Artillery, who escorted the gun-carriage and coffin. Ballance's cabinet acted as pall-bearers, and were accompanied by Robert McKnight, men of the Anderson family and Stout. The Governor's representative, judges, heads of government departments, Members of Parliament, mayors, magistrates, foreign diplomats, business leaders, chairmen of the Harbour Board and the Chamber of Commerce, presidents of various local organisations and prison wardens made up the remainder of the official mourners. Some travelled in carriages, of which there were 22. Growing numbers of the general public fell in behind.

> Down Molesworth Street the column moved, and as the railway station was approached it was seen to be surrounded by a sea of people. Arrived at the station, the military opened ranks, the people falling back with them, and through the lane thus formed the coffin was reverently carried to the funeral train drawn up at the platform. Here, in a car specially prepared, and following next to the engines and tender, was the coffin laid, a black velvet pall and the Union Jack covering it, and these in turn were covered with the exquisite wreaths sent by colleague, friend, and sympathiser. Next to the funeral car was a carriage with Mrs Ballance and her relatives, and after it other carriages with the colleagues and brother-legislators of the dead man, with the Judges, the Consuls, the heads of all the departments, the press, the military officers, and representatives of the local officers, and representatives of the local bodies and organisations — some 200 in all. Never has a New Zealand train borne so representative a freight.[71]

As the train stopped for water on its way north crowds greeted it in silence, while bands played slow marches. On arrival in Wanganui the procession continued up Victoria Avenue and by way of Guyton Street to the cemetery. Meanwhile special boats and trains had brought another 2000 mourners to the town from all over the country.[72] The graveside ceremony was brief. A portion of the Masonic service was read and a hymn sung. The coffin, bearing the simple inscription, 'John Ballance, died 27th April, 1893, aged 54 years', was lowered into the grave. The firing party fired three volleys; the muffled drums rolled. Close by Ellen and her relatives stood Robert Stout. He was visibly moved and in tears, a fact which was 'the great topic of conversation after the funeral'.[73]

Two years later Ellen imported a block of Irish black polished granite as headstone for her late husband's grave. It bore the words 'John Ballance, Prime Minister of this Colony. Born in Glenavy, County Antrim, Ireland, 27th March, 1839, died in Wellington, 27th April, 1893. "To live in the hearts of those we love is not to die".'[74]

The Ballance tradition

STOUT RE-ENTERED PARLIAMENT in June 1893 in order to contest the leadership with Seddon. 'Poor Ballance's death I am sure you would deplore, as in fact all must,' Oliver wrote to Sir John Hall in May. 'The existence of the party he led is a fact which there is no ignoring. . . . I suppose Stout will be in parliament next session which will make a difference. I suppose eventually he will join the Government. Seddon altho' he would not stand aside for him is trying all he knows to placate him. The labour party are going to stick to Seddon, at all events for the present.'[1] In his bid for the premiership Stout rightly pointed out that he was Ballance's favoured successor. Yet in spite of this recommendation, which was publicly confirmed by Ellen,[2] he was unable to unseat Seddon. Stout failed because he moved too late and, pinning his hopes on the prohibition issue, divided the left wing of the party and became increasingly isolated from mainstream liberalism.[3]

Stout was conspicuously absent at the unveiling of Ballance's statue by Seddon in 1897. Just over four years after Ballance's death a huge gathering (estimated at the staggering figure of 3000 people) turned out in an extraordinary tribute to the man. The lawn in front of Parliament, at the centre of which stood the statue, was packed with official guests. Outside the grounds thronged the massive public crowd:

> Every point of vantage that presented itself had been eagerly taken advantage of; a swarm had settled on the railings of the Parliament grounds; others were crowded on the verandahs and at the high windows overlooking the scene; expressmen and carriers loitered in the roadway with their carts, from which a fortunate few were able to get a better glimpse of what was going on; numbers had gathered under the pohutukawa tree on the rising ground behind the statue,

and from many windows of the Parliament Buildings knots of people over-looked the scene.[4]

Ellen Ballance, however, made her dislike of Seddon clear by refusing to attend and she simply sent some flowers. Her wreath was placed at the foot of the statue by Robert McKnight. At the ceremony Seddon made a speech in praise of statues as much as in praise of Ballance, saying that he hoped Ballance 'would not be the last man for whose work the people of the colony would show their appreciation'.[5] He also claimed that he had been the closest of friends to his predecessor. The *Evening Post* complained that the Premier's words would not have been approved of by Ballance, who had 'not a particle of vainglorious aspiration' about him.[6]

At the 1893 election Seddon and the Liberal Party were returned to office. Both remained firmly in power until 1912. Gradually, the party came to be dominated by its conservative rural wing. In 1894 Ward, Seddon's Treasurer, obtained Parliament's approval to renew borrowing overseas. The money was to be lent under the Advances to Settlers Act, to the growing number of small farmers. These farmers were predominantly freeholders who over the following years were able to wield increasing political muscle. Of the £3 million made available by 1900, approximately £2.7 million went to freeholders. Leaseholders received a mere £350,000.[7]

Meanwhile the more radical urban wing of the party — followers of Ballance, Stout and Reeves — remained reasonably content as the Liberal Government implemented a range of labour reforms and ushered in the beginnings of the welfare state in New Zealand. As for the land question, the purchasing of estates continued. By 1924, £13 million had been spent on the acquisition of 800 000 hectares under the Land for Settlement Acts.[8] Many large landowners subdivided their estates of their own accord. Urban liberals had no great wish and little reason to push land reform beyond this; closer settlement was being achieved and the land oligarchy success-fully eroded. The rural sector was becoming more prosperous as each year passed. Farmers wanted the freehold and many more could now afford it. Also, with more land being settled and therefore less remaining for settlement, a declining proportion of the growing urban population could be expected to be placed upon it. It was increasingly naive to believe that closer land settlement could hope to solve urban problems. Especially in the cities, and as urbanisation advanced, urban issues inevitably came to dominate urban politics.

Ballance's two years in power had secured the base for Seddon's long reign. As the party changed, Ballance's memory was invoked to a remark-able degree by protagonists from both urban and rural wings, seeking approval for their policies by claiming them to be within the Ballance 'tradition'. That Ballance's influence remained so significant after his death is testimony to his success as a leader and his importance in New Zealand history.

The tradition was so strong because Ballance had formed the Liberal Party, had led it to power for the first time and had played a major role in establishing its ideological roots. Also, in the minds of party members he was associated with party unity. This achievement reflected his leadership qualities. It also sprang from the fact that Ballance died before the stresses and strains within the party came to a head, and before important decisions (for example, on borrowing) had to be made. In the minds of the populace at large, Ballance was associated with the return of prosperity and the democratisation of the political system. He was the people's Premier. Not unnaturally, subsequent politicians were eager to claim some of this kudos.

Throughout the liberal period there were accusations that the party was departing from the principles laid down by Ballance.[9] His style of leadership was contrasted favourably with the brashness and autocracy of Seddon. He was held up by some as representative of the only true liberalism; it was as if, had he not died when he did, things would have been quite different.[10] Most likely, had Ballance lived longer he would only have been able to delay the transformation of the Liberal Party into a body predominantly representing the interests of small farmers. There would perhaps have been some differences, however, as the *Evening Post* suggested:

> Had Mr. Ballance lived a great many things that have happened since he died would never have taken place, and could not have come about, were he Premier. Who, for example, would be more shocked than John Ballance, were he to come amongst us now, on finding that our public debt had been increased millions by the 'non-borrowing' party he left after him? . . . What would he think, too, of the increase of Customs duties to the extent of nearly £30,000 per annum on articles almost exclusively used by the working community? . . . And we should have had a free Parliament and free speech all the time such a man [as Ballance] remained on the Treasury benches.[11]

Not surprisingly, the Ballance tradition was particularly strong in Wanganui, where it was kept alive by A. D. Willis and the *Herald*. Ballance's ghost was abroad in the town and 'those who courted political office and who wished to strike a responsive note among the local electorate paid homage to it'.[12] For Wanganui's politicians the key to success was to be found, as Ballance had shown, in forging an alliance between the working class and small businessmen: rural development bringing trade to the town and work at the railway yards was regarded as much more important than industrial development. 'Lib-labism', epitomised by William Veitch, Wanganui's Member from 1911 to 1935, rather than socialism held sway.

Shortly after Ballance's death Ellen and Kathleen moved from 'The Knolls' to a large house in Wicksteed Street. They later took an overseas trip, visiting relatives in Ireland and travelling throughout continental

Europe. At some stage in their tour, possibly when they were in Germany, Kathleen took ill with meningitis. Sadly this resulted in permanent physical and mental damage and Kit was never well again.

Ellen's widowhood lasted about twice as long as her marriage to Ballance. She spent her time with her brothers and sisters and their children, and in nursing Kathleen. Ellen also remained active in the affairs of Wanganui, and patronised a range of causes including the local Anglican Church, Wanganui Orphanage and the Plunket Society. She died in June 1935, 42 years after her husband.[13] In her will she made provision for Kathleen, who was to be cared for by 'some tactful and capable person or persons'.[14] Kathleen passed away in a home just eight years later. So ended the New Zealand Ballances.

Notes

ABBREVIATIONS

AES   Auckland Evening Star
AJHR   Appendices to the Journals of the House of Representatives
BMSS   Ballance Papers
EH   Evening Herald
EP   Evening Post
LB   Ballance Letter Book, I   1878–79 volume
                              II   1891–92 volume
                              III 1892–93 volume
LT   Lyttelton Times
NZH   New Zealand Herald
NZJH   New Zealand Journal of History
NZT   New Zealand Times
ODT   Otago Daily Times
PD   New Zealand Parliamentary Debates
PRONI   Public Record Office of Northern Ireland
WC   Wanganui Chronicle
WH   Weekly Herald
Y   Yeoman

PREFACE

1. Ballance to Johnston, 19 Oct. 1891, LB III, p. 355.

PROLOGUE

1. Quoted in A. H. McLintock (ed.), *An Encyclopaedia of New Zealand*, vol. 1, Wellington, 1966, p. 146.
2. See W. H. Oliver's poem 'Poor Richard', Wellington, 1982.
3. *Y*, 10 June 1893.
4. T. W. K. Howitt, *A Pioneer Looks Back Again*, Auckland, 1947, p. 268.
5. Sir Robert Stout, 'Character Sketch: The Hon. John Ballance', *Review of Reviews for Australasia*, May 1893, p.115.

6. *Y*, 10 June 1893.
7. G. Scholefield, *Dictionary of New Zealand Biography*, vol. 1, Wellington, 1940, p. 36.
8. *EP*, 7 Apr. 1897.

CHAPTER 1: FROM BELFAST TO BIRMINGHAM

1. Charles Watson, *The Story of the United Parishes of Glenavy, Camlin, and Tullyrusk*, Belfast, 1892, p. 20.
2. Ibid., p. 57.
3. Correspondence of 26 May 1976 in the Ulster Historical Foundation's Ballance file relating to the birthplace of John Ballance.
4. Watson, pp. 11–14.
5. *Belfast Telegraph*, 5 Aug. 1947. The Ballance House is currently being restored by the Ulster-New Zealand Trust. (Readers interested in finding out about the work of the trust should write c/o Lisburn Museum, Market Square, Lisburn BT28 1AG, Northern Ireland.)
6. Glenavy Townland Valuation, 4 Feb. 1835 (PRONI, 1B/171).
7. Tithe Applotment Book, Glenavy, 1834 (PRONI, 5A/147).
8. Family details from births, deaths and marriages registers of Glenavy Parish and Census of Glenavy Parish, 1856.
9. John remarried following Jane's death, and Robert's uneasy relations with his stepmother were largely responsible for his decision to emigrate. Details of the McKnight side of the Ballance family are from a family Bible in the possession of Ms Shirley McKnight of Ohingaiti.
10. Information from Mrs E. Crawford of Lurgan, Co. Armagh.
11. See G. S. Maloney, 'A History of the Ballance Ministry', M.A. thesis, Canterbury, 1931. Maloney says that Ellen Ballance and Robert McKnight (Ballance's second wife and nephew respectively) confirmed this.
12. Stout, 1893, p. 114.
13. See Ordnance Survey Memoirs, Glenavy Parish, 1836 (PRONI, Mic 6/43).
14. Stout, p. 107; Thomas Pakenham, *The Year of Liberty*, London, 1969, pp. 215–31.
15. See H. Senior, *Orangeism in Ireland and Britain, 1795–1836*, London, 1966, ch. 1.
16. On the famine, see the classic work by Cecil Woodham-Smith, *The Great Hunger*, London, 1962. The province of Ulster lost 16% of its population. Donegal was particularly badly hit; the loss for Antrim and Down would be considerably less.
17. J. L. Dighton, 'The Life and Work of John Ballance', M.A. thesis, Victoria University of Wellington, 1929, p. 2.
18. Stout, p. 114; *Y*, 6 May 1893; *Wanganui Herald*, 3 June 1967.
19. Ballance to Johnston, 19 Oct. 1892, LB III, p. 355.
20. I. Budge & C. O'Leary, *Belfast: Approach to Crisis. A Study of Belfast Politics, 1613–1970*, London, 1973, p. 28.
21. Ibid., ch. 3.
22. Ibid., pp. 78–79.
23. *EH*, 30 Oct. 1872.
24. See *EH*, 6 Sept. 1867, 6 Jan. 1868.
25. *Y*, 30 Mar. 1889. See also *Y*, 16 Feb. 1889, 16 Nov. 1889; Ballance to J. A. Tole, 29 Aug. 1892, LB III, p. 306.

26. *EP*, 2 Aug. 1881. See also Ballance's speech at the Home Rule meeting held during Dillon's visit to New Zealand in 1889, *New Zealand Tablet*, 29 Nov. 1889.
27. *EH*, 30 Jan. 1868.
28. *EH*, 4 Apr. 1873; *Y*, 14 July 1877.
29. *EH*, 21 Oct. 1869.
30. *Y*, 6 May 1893.
31. Ballance to Mason, 8 June 1892, LB III, p. 75.
32. *Y*, 23 July 1892.
33. Conrad Gill, *History of Birmingham*, vol. 1, London, 1952, p. 435; see also V. H. T. Skipp, *Victorian Birmingham*, Birmingham, 1983.
34. Trygve Tholfsen, *Working Class Radicalism in Mid-Victorian England*, London, 1976, p. 130. On adult education in England see J. F. C. Harrison, *Learning and Living, 1790-1960 — A Study in the History of the English Adult Education Movement*, London, 1961.
35. Tholfsen, p. 64.
36. A. Charles to Ballance, 1 Dec. 1891, BMSS, 407-08.
37. Stout, p. 107; *Y*, 23 July 1892; Dighton, p. 3.
38. *EH*, 11 Nov. 1867.
39. Tholfsen, p. 132.
40. A. Charles to Ballance, 1 Dec. 1891, BMSS, 407-08; W. M. Charles to Ballance, 10 Aug. 1891, BMSS, 252. See also Scholefield, vol. I, 1940, p. 32.
41. G. Kitson Clark, *The Making of Victorian England*, London, 1962, p. 125.
42. See Asa Briggs, *Victorian Cities*, London, 1963, ch. V.
43. Richard Jay, *Joseph Chamberlain. A Political Study*, Oxford, 1981, p. 5.
44. Quoted by Briggs, 1963, p. 191.
45. Jay, p. 7. See also Gill, pp. 374-80; Briggs, pp. 203-07.
46. Stout, p. 114.
47. Lyndall Greig, 'Wives of the Prime Ministers of New Zealand', Alexander Turnbull Library.
48. *Y*, 6 May 1893.
49. *NZH*, 5 Aug. 1878, 'Biographical Sketch'.
50. *Y*, 23 July 1892.
51. Passenger list of the SS *Ruahine*, Public Record Office, Victoria.

CHAPTER 2: WANGANUI AND WAR: FRONTIER POLITICS AND INSECURITY

1. An account of the voyage appeared in the Melbourne *Argus*, 13 June 1866.
2. *New Zealand Advertiser*, 13 Aug. 1866.
3. *NZT*, 28 Apr. 1893.
4. *WC*, 22 Aug. 1866.
5. Quoted by L. J. B. Chapple & H. C. Veitch, *Wanganui*, Hawera, 1939, p. 113.
6. See M. J. G. Smart & A. P. Bates, *The Wanganui Story*, Wanganui, 1972, ch. 6.
7. *WC*, 19 Sept. 1866.
8. Isaac Earl Featherston, a doctor who emigrated to New Zealand in 1840, was Superintendent of Wellington Province from 1853 until 1871. He was M.H.R. for Wanganui and Rangitikei, and subsequently Wellington City. He died in 1876 when Agent General in London, a post he had held for five years.
9. Buller to the editor of the *Evening Post*, Nov. 1892, pamphlet in the Alexander

Turnbull Library. The sale is also recorded in J. G. Wilson, *Early Rangitikei*, Christchurch, 1914, ch. XX.

10. *EH*, 25 Sept. 1872. The nice allusion is to Sir William Fox, a political opponent of Ballance whose own background was impeccable. Born in Durham, he studied at Oxford and then became a lawyer before emigrating to New Zealand in 1842.

11. *Y*, 6 May 1893; G. H. Scholefield, *Newspapers in New Zealand*, Wellington, 1958, p. 49. Articles and editorials were unsigned and it is speculation as to which were written by Ballance. Issues of the *Times* for the early months of 1867 bear little of his later distinctive, proselytising style though an editorial on 9 April on the 'Irish Difficulty' (advocating home rule) is almost certainly his.

12. There is no record of this brief partnership in newspapers at the time, though shortly afterwards it is mentioned in a court case, *Howe vs Aitken*, involving some wine of dubious quality; *EH*, 4 Nov. 1867. Scholefield, 1940, p. 32, alludes to it.

13. *WC*, 10, 31 Oct. 1866, 21 Nov. 1866 and 6 Feb. 1867. *Wanganui Times*, 19 Apr. 1867.

14. *Wanganui Times*, 3 May 1867.

15. Shortly afterwards he married a Miss Dixon, daughter of a Wellington brewer (and sister to the wives of his old Wellington newspaper employers). See biographical sketches, *Y*, 17 June 1893 and *Cyclopedia of New Zealand*, vol. 1, Wellington, 1897, p. 1361. Willis became an important and influential person in the town in his own right. He later established and built up a very successful printing and publishing, stationery and bookselling business. Amongst other publishing feats he produced the first colour lithograph in New Zealand, which was printed in his *New Zealand Illustrated* in 1889. He followed Ballance as Member for Wanganui in 1893. 'Daddy Willis', as he was known, had a large family that lived on the south side of the river.

16. *Y*, 6 May 1893.

17. Scholefield, 1958, p. 50.

18. *WH*, 16 Nov. 1867.

19. *Wanganui Times*, 7 May 1867.

20. *Wanganui Times*, 13 June 1867.

21. See, for example, *Wanganui Times*, 4 June 1867.

22. *WC*, 28 May 1867. For the manoeuvrings of the *Times* and the *Chronicle* see *EH*, 3 June 1867.

23. *Wanganui Herald*, 3 June 1967. Centennial Issue.

24. Information from Mr Arthur P. Bates, former General Manager of Wanganui Newspapers.

25. *EH*, 2, 6 May 1868.

26. The Wanganui Land, Building and Investment Society, *WC*, 22 Aug. 1866. See also *EH*, 24 Jan. 1868, for an account of the society's annual general meeting.

27. *EH*, 14 June 1867.

28. *EH*, 30 Oct. 1867.

29. *EH*, 12 Nov. 1867, 6 Jan. 1868.

30. For example, *EH*, 21 Nov. 1867.

31. *EH*, 13 Nov. 1868.

32. *EH*, 12 July 1867.

33. *EH*, 12 Aug. 1867.

34. *EH*, 13 Nov. 1867.
35. *EH*, 20 Sept. 1867.
36. *EH*, 22 Oct. 1867.
37. For example in 1860. On the background to Wanganui and the Provincial system, see W. P. Morrell, *The Provincial System in New Zealand 1852–76*, London, 1932, esp. pp. 119, 163–64 & 202.
38. *EH*, 4 June 1867.
39. *EH*, 12 Nov. 1867.
40. *EH*, 31 July 1868.
41. *EH*, 1 Aug. 1868.
42. *EH*, 27 May 1868.
43. *EH*, 19 Feb. 1868.
44. *EH*, 28 Oct. 1867.
45. Ibid.
46. *EH*, 27 Mar. 1868.
47. *Y*, 6 May 1893.
48. *EH*, 22 Oct. 1867, 18 Nov. 1867, 16 May 1868.
49. *EH*, 11, 13 June 1868. See the account of Titokowaru's campaign in James Belich, *The New Zealand Wars and the Victorian Interpretation of Racial Conflict*, Auckland, 1986, chs. 12 & 13.
50. *EH*, 13 July 1868.
51. Wanganui Military Historical Society, 'Wereroa Redoubt', Wanganui, 1948, p. 4. This pamphlet, in the Turnbull Library, gives a brief history of the Wanganui Cavalry Volunteer Corps.
52. Gorton to Haultain, 25 July 1868, AD, 1868/2507; C.L. Lovegrove, *When Wanganui Stood to Arms in the 'Sixties'*, p. 9, a pamphlet reprinted from the *Wanganui Herald*, 1953(?), in the Turnbull Library.
53. E. Gorton, *Some Home Truths about the Maori War 1863–1869 on the West Coast of New Zealand*, London, 1901, ch. X.
54. Gorton to Haultain, 15 July 1868, AD 1868/2385.
55. Gorton, p. 80.
56. For a fuller discussion of this point see T. J. McIvor, 'On Ballance: a political biography of John Ballance, journalist and politician, 1839–1893', Ph.D. thesis, Victoria University of Wellington, p. 63 (footnote 82).
57. Gorton, pp. 82–3.
58. *EH*, 28 July 1868.
59. *EH*, 7 Aug. 1868.
60. See T. McDonnell, *An Explanation of the Principal Causes which led to the Present War on the West Coast of New Zealand*, Wanganui, 1869. This pamphlet was published by Walter Taylor of the *Wanganui Times*. Ballance reviewed it in the *Herald*, 2 June 1869. See also G.S. Whitmore, *The Last Maori War in New Zealand under the Self-Reliant Policy*, London, 1902, ch. III.
61. Gorton to Haultain, 1 Oct. 1868, A.D. 1868/3281.
62. *EH*, 8 Oct. 1868.
63. *EH*, 19 Oct. 1868.
64. *Wanganui Times*, 13 Apr. 1869, gives a survey of the campaign in retrospect.
65. *EH*, 2 Nov. 1868.
66. *EH*, 10 Nov. 1868.
67. *Wanganui Times*, 13 Apr. 1869.
68. *EH*, 10 Nov. 1868.
69. *EH*, 13 Nov. 1868. Only seven men had appeared on militia parade the day

before, *EH*, 12 Nov. 1868.
70. *EH*, 13 Nov. 1868.
71. *EH*, 16 Nov. 1868. Kupapas were Maori who fought on the European side during the war.
72. *EH*, 17 Nov. 1868.
73. *EH*, 20 Nov. 1868.
74. *EH*, 3 Dec. 1868.
75. Both Nukumaru and Wereroa redoubts had been abandoned on 17 November and all forces drawn back to the Kai Iwi stream. See Lovegrove's chronology of the campaign in the *Wanganui Herald*, 29 May 1948.
76. See Gorton, pp. 86–9.
77. *EH*, 2 Dec. 1868.
78. *EH*, 8, 9 Dec. 1868.
79. See *EH*, 14, 15 & 18 Dec. 1868.
80. Rusden's description of Bryce cutting down women and children 'gleefully and with ease' led to a famous action for libel, which Bryce won. See G. W. Rusden, *History of New Zealand*, vol. II, London, 1883, p. 504. It referred to an incident, at Taurangaika Pa, on 1 December. Ballance was not involved. See also J. Bryce, *A Letter from the Hon. John Bryce to the Secretary of State for the Colonies, etc.*, n.p., n.d.; G. W Rusden, *Tragedies in New Zealand in 1868 and 1881*, London, 1888.
81. *EH*, 17 Dec. 1868. See also *WC*, 17 Dec. 1868.
82. *EH*, 19 Dec. 1868. Ballance at the same time denied charges of cruelty that had been made against the cavalry.
83. Ibid.
84. See *AJHR*, 1868, A-8.
85. Haultain to Lyon, 28 Dec. 1868, A.D. 6/19.
86. *EH*, 2 Jan. 1869.
87. *EH*, 4 Jan. 1869.
88. *EH*, 6 Jan. 1869.
89. Belich, pp. 272–73. Belich suggests the main reason was an affair Titokowaru was having with the wife of a lesser chief.
90. See Whitmore, ch. VII.
91. He remained a member until 1872; Lovegrove Papers, vol. 1, p. 661.
92. *EH*, 29 June 1869.
93. See Belich, ch. 15, on the Victorian interpretation of racial conflict.
94. *EH*, 6 Aug. 1870. Maori were first elected to the House in 1868.
95. *Y*, 6 May 1893. Stout, p. 115, also mentions the incident.
96. Lovegrove Papers, vol. 1, p. 660.
97. *Y*, 6 May 1893.
98. The *Wanganui Times*, on its last legs, was similarly critical of Ballance's extreme editorials. See, for example, *Wanganui Times*, 1, 27 Apr. 1869, 4 May 1869.

CHAPTER 3: THE POLITICS OF PROGRESS

1. *EH*, 19 May 1870.
2. Information on David Anderson is from *EP*, 13 Mar. 1889 (his obituary), and from his great-grandson, Mr John Anderson of Wellington.
3. Sarah Jane Spinks married David Anderson junior. Her diaries, kindly lent to the author by Mrs Carol Anderson, give some insights into the personal life

of Ellen and John Ballance.
4. Finnimore was later to desert his wife, going to South Africa where he, bigamously, remarried.
5. See T. M. Barrett, 'The Ballance House', *Historical Record*, Journal of the Wanganui Historical Society, Nov. 1970, p. 2.
6. *EH*, 10 July 1869.
7. *EH*, 7 Aug. 1869.
8. *EH*, 17 Dec. 1870.
9. *EH*, 21 Sept. 1871; see also *EH*, 29 May 1871.
10. *EH*, 10 Aug. 1869; see also *EH*, 14 Apr. 1869.
11. *EH*, 27 Oct. 1870; see also *EH*, 2 June, 16 Aug. 1870.
12. *EH*, 8 Aug. 1870.
13. *EH*, 21 Oct. 1870. On the Waikato see W. M. Robinson, 'The Pacification of the Waikato 1869–76'. M.A. thesis, Auckland, 1949.
14. *EH*, 14 Mar. 1872, 24 Dec. 1874.
15. See S. M. King, 'The Port of Wanganui and its Influence on Wanganui', M.A. thesis, Victoria University of Wellington, 1964, ch. 2.
16. Chapple & Veitch, ch. XVI.
17. The town population increased between 1867 and 1874 from 2157 to 2572, the population of the electoral district, excluding the town, from 1749 to 2335. This represents increases of 19% and 33% respectively. Figures calculated from *New Zealand Census*, 1867 and 1874.
18. *EH*, 24 Aug. 1869.
19. *EH*, 15 June 1869.
20. *EH*, 7 July 1869.
21. *EH*, 24 Apr. 1872.
22. *EH*, 14 Oct. 1869. Also *EH*, 22 July 1870.
23. *EH*, 27 Sept. 1871.
24. For example, *EH*, 20 Sept. 1869.
25. *EH*, 18 Sept. 1873.
26. *PD*, 1870, 7, pp. 102–08.
27. *EH*, 15 Sept. 1870. See also *EH*, 1 July 1870.
28. *EH*, 19 July 1872.
29. *EH*, 4 Aug. 1872.
30. *EH*, 19 Oct. 1871; 17 May 1872.
31. See W. R. Armstrong, 'The Politics of Development: a study of the structure of politics from 1870 to 1890', M.A. thesis, Victoria University of Wellington, 1960; A. M. Evans, 'A Study of Canterbury Politics in the Early 1880s, with special reference to the general election of 1881', M.A. thesis, Canterbury, 1959.
32. *EH*, 27 Oct. 1871.
33. See, for example, 1876, p. 198. On this occasion sections in Wanganui town, at Campbelltown, and 8800 hectares in Manawatu (Foxton, Palmerston, Fitzherbert, etc.) were being sold. By 1877 Wellington Province, an area of some 2.8 million hectares, had disposed of 0.7 million hectares, excluding the confiscated lands; *New Zealand Statistics*, 1877, p. 196.
34. *EH*, 1 Feb. 1872.
35. *EH*, 18 Mar. 1871.
36. *EH*, 18 Apr. 1871.
37. *EH*, 20 Apr. 1871.
38. For example, *EH*, 3, 14 Oct. 1870.

39. See Bryce's entry in Scholefield, 1940.

40. *EH*, 16 Oct. 1867.

41. *EH*, 16 Jan. 1871.

42. See Chapple & Veitch, p. 284. W. H. Watt was elected first mayor, *EH*, 14 Feb. 1872.

43. *EH*, 28 Dec. 1870.

44. *EH*, 5 May 1871.

45. See *EH*, 25 May 1871 for a report of its second meeting.

46. See Tholfsen, ch. 9.

47. *EH*, 19 July 1871.

48. *EH*, 1 July 1874.

49. *EH*, 27 Apr. 1869. The Manchester Unity itself had a much larger membership in New Zealand than the American-based Independent Order of Oddfellows. See *AJHR*, 1877, H-19, Friendly Society Returns. H. Shepherd, 'The Nature and Role of Friendly Societies in Later Nineteenth Century New Zealand', Research Essay, Massey University, 1976, appendix table III, gives I.O.O.F. membership as 396 in 1880, 724 in 1890 and 1941 by 1900. See also H. W. Gourlay, *Odd Fellowship in New Zealand*, Christchurch, n.d. and J. K. Hoar, 'A Descriptive History of the Major Aspects of the Friendly Society Movement in New Zealand, 1840–1900', M.A. thesis, Idaho, 1963.

50. *EH*, 1 Apr. 1869. See also Ballance's admiration for the Owenite co-operatives in England, *EH*, 15 Nov. 1873.

51. *EH*, 1 July 1874.

52. See *Taranaki Herald*, 18 Sept. 1872. The *Taranaki Herald* supported Moorhouse, the *Taranaki News* Atkinson.

53. *EH* 13 Sept. 1872.

54. Quoted by W. K. Howitt, *A Pioneer Looks Back Again*, Auckland, 1947, p. 265.

55. Both meetings were reported in *EH*, 26 Sept. 1872.

56. *EH*, 24 Sept. 1872.

57. *EH*, 23 Sept. 1872. Writing to Stout years later, Ballance said that Stafford had made the suggestion; Ballance to Stout, 17 Nov. 1890, Stout MSS. See also Ballance's account in *Y*, 14 May 1881.

58. *EH*, 19 Sept. 1872.

59. *EH*, 7 Oct. 1872.

60. Atkinson was assisted in this by Bryce, *PD*, 1872, 13, pp. 669–70.

61. See, for example, *EH*, 24 Oct. 1872.

62. *AJHR*, 1872, G-49.

63. After declining between 1867 and 1870, revenue increased continuously over the following few years. The greatest increase was in 1873, the year of the separationist revival, when it rose to £240,433, an increase of 80% on the previous year, *New Zealand Statistics*, 1876, p. 173.

64. *EH*, 22 Apr. 1873.

65. *EH*, 11 June 1873.

66. *EH*, 6 May 1873.

67. *EH*, 23 May 1873.

68. *EH*, 21 June 1873.

69. *PD*, 1873, 14, p. 191; *EH*, 28 July 1873.

70. *PD*, 1873, 14, pp. 662–68.

71. *PD*, 1873, 14, pp. 668–69. See also *EH*, 28 Aug. 1873.

72. *EH*, 25 Sept. 1873.

73. *EH*, 19 Aug. 1874.

74. *EH*, 9 Sept. 1874.
75. *New Zealand Statistics*, 1876, p. 173.
76. *EH*, 4 Dec. 1874.
77. *EH*, 27 May 1875.
78. *EH*, 17 May 1875.
79. *EH*, 24 Feb. 1873.
80. See *AJHR*, 1873, D-13; part III of R. Arnold, *The Farthest Promised Land*, Wellington, 1981.
81. *EH*, 13 June 1870; *EH*, 28 May 1872; *EH*, 15 Sept, 1874.
82. *EH*, 20 June 1870.
83. *EH*, 18 Feb. 1874. See also *EH*, 21 Mar. 1873; *EH*, 27 Dec. 1873.
84. *EH*, 4 May 1874.
85. *EH*, 27 Nov. 1871. See also *EH*, 5 July 1870, 11 Feb. 1871.
86. *EH*, 6 Jan. 1874. See Ballance's memorial to Mill, *EH*, 31 May 1873.
87. *EH*, 7 June 1872.
88. *EH*, 19 Feb. 1875.
89. *EH*, 11 May 1874.
90. *EH*, 11 Dec. 1872.
91. *EH*, 1 Mar. 1875; *EH*, 3 Mar. 1875.
92. See Chapple & Veitch, pp. 39–40, 111.
93. *WC*, 20 Apr. 1875.
94. *WC*, 6 Feb. 1875.
95. *WC*, 30 Mar. 1875. See also *WC*, 4 Mar. 1875; *WC*, 6 Apr. 1875.
96. *EH*, 20 Apr. 1875.
97. *EH*, 14 Apr. 1875. Election notice.
98. *EH*, 13 Mar. 1875.
99. *EH*, 14 Apr. 1875. Report of the Bulls meeting.
100. *EH*, 14 May 1875.
101. *WC*, 14 Apr. 1875.
102. *WC*, 23 Apr. 1875.
103. *WC*, 19 Apr. 1875.
104. *EH*, 24, 26 Apr. 1875.
105. *EH*, 26 Apr. 1874. See also *WC*, 26 Apr. 1875.
106. *WC*, 4 Mar. 1875.
107. *EP*, 27 Apr. 1875.
108. Quoted by *WC*, 16 Jan. 1878.
109. *PD*, 1875, 17, p. 391.
110. Ibid.
111. See Ballance's retrospective comments on his attitude to abolition, *PD*, 1877, 26, p. 538.
112. *PD*, 1875, 17, p. 396.
113. Ibid.
114. *PD*, 1875, 17, p. 465. See also Bryce's comments, ibid., p. 530.
115. *EH*, 18 Aug. 1875; *EH*, 18 Aug, 1875; *EH*, 27 Aug. 1875.
116. *EP*, 18 Aug. 1875.
117. NZH, 19 Aug. 1875; *AES*, 18 Aug. 1875.
118. *LT*, 19 Aug. 1875.
119. See, for example, Wanganui and Rangitikei District Court, *PD*, 1875, 17, p. 123; Wanganui and Manawatu Railway, *PD*, 1875, 17, p. 375.
120. *PD*, 1875, 18, pp. 363–68.
121. *EH*, 27 Sept. 1875.

122. *PD*, 1875, 18, pp. 551, 554, 556.
123. D. A. Hamer, 'The Law and the Prophet: a political biography of Sir Robert Stout (1844–1936)', M.A. thesis, Auckland, 1960, p. 2.
124. Stout, p. 109.
125. See, for example, Spinks Diary, 8 Sept. 1878.
126. Details of Ballance's communications with the Government and of the meeting in Wanganui, from *EH*, 12 Nov. 1875. The result of the Wanganui election was Bryce 379, Vogel 360, Watt 191 (*EH*, 15 Jan. 1876).
127. *EH*, 16, 27 Dec. 1875.
128. See L. J. Wild, *The Life and Times of Sir James Wilson of Bulls*, Christchurch, 1953, pp. 18, 22; M. H. Holcroft, *The Line of the Road: A History of Manawatu County, 1876–1976*, Manawatu County Council, 1977, pp. 83–86.
129. *WC*, 7 Dec. 1875.
130. *WC*, 6 Jan. 1876.
131. *WH*, 8 Jan. 1876.
132. Ibid.
133. J. L. Hunt, 'The Election of 1875–6 and the Abolition of the Provinces', M.A. thesis, Auckland, 1961, p. 244. See also J. Young, 'The Politics of the Auckland Province, 1872–1876', M.A. thesis, Auckland, 1960.
134. *Cyclopedia of New Zealand*, vol. 1, 1897, p. 1369.
135. See *Y*, 6 May, 17 June 1893.
136. *WH*, 25 Mar. 1876.
137. See Municipal Corporations Act, 1876, part X.
138. *PD*, 1876, 20, pp. 403–04.
139. *WH*, 5 Aug. 1876.
140. *PD*, 1876, 20, p. 482.
141. P , 1876, 21, p. 214.
142. Vogel to Ballance, 10 Aug. 1876, BMSS, 2.
143. See his earlier involvement with the Manawatu Small Farm Association, *EH*, 13 June 1870.
144. See *WH*, 10 June, 15 July, 9 Dec. 1876 & 15 Dec. 1877; R. D. Arnold, 'The Opening of the Great Bush, 1869–1881', Ph.D. thesis, Victoria University of Wellington, 1971, p. 358.
145. *EH*, 15 Sept. 1874, *WH*, 3 June 1876.
146. *WH*, 24 June 1876.
147. *WH*, 9 Dec. 1876.
148. *WH*, 3 Feb. 1877.
149. *WH*, 24 Feb. 1877; also *WH*, 10 Feb. 1877.

CHAPTER 4: AN EARLY TASTE OF POWER

1. Jane Maria Atkinson to C. W. Richmond, 19 Sept., 1876, G. H. Scholefield (ed), *The Richmond-Atkinson Papers*, vol 2., Wellington, 1960, p. 426.
2. *WH*, 9 Sept. 1876.
3. *WH*, 9 Sept. 1876.
4. Quoted by *WC*, 25 Nov. 1876.
5. *New Zealand Herald*, 2 Nov. 1877.
6. *WH*, 20 Jan. 1877.
7. *PD*, 1875, 17, pp. 271, 323, 402, 659.
8. *WH*, 19 May 1877.
9. C. G. F. Simkin, *The Instability of a Dependent Economy. Economic fluctuations in*

New Zealand, 1840–1914, Oxford, 1951, p. 160.
10. *WH*, 12 May 1877.
11. *EH*, 1 Feb. 1872.
12. *WH*, 12 May 1877. See T. A. Gibson, *The Purchase and Settlement of the Manchester Block*, Feilding, 1936; *AJHR*, 1877, H-27, 27a (report on the Manchester settlement).
13. *PD*, 1877, 24 227*ff.*
14. Ibid., p. 579.
15. Ibid., pp. 580–81.
16. Ibid., p. 584.
17. Ibid., pp. 585–86.
18. Ballance suggests this in *WH*, 23 June 1877.
19. *PD*, 1877, 24, p. 582.
20. *AES*, 23 Aug. 1877.
21. *WH*, 23 June 1877.
22. *PD*, 1877, 24, p. 261.
23. *WH*, 11 Aug. 1877.
24. *WH*, 18 May 1878.
25. *WH*, 25 Aug. 1877.
26. *PD*, 1877, 26, p. 107. See also his speech of 29 October on the same theme, ibid., p. 542.
27. *LT*, 3 Oct. 1877.
28. Spinks Diary, 2 Oct. 1877.
29. Ballance to Atkinson, 3 Oct. 1877, BMSS, 4. See also Ballance's later account, *WH*, 2 Aug. 1879.
30. Ballance to Vogel, 1 Mar. 1878, Vogel MSS.
31. *EP*, 4 Oct. 1877.
32. *NZH*, 5 Oct. 1877.
33. *AES*, 4 Oct. 1877.
34. *WH*, 2 Aug. 1879; *WH*, 30 Apr. 1881; *EP*, 10 Jan. 1878.
35. *WH*, 2 Aug. 1879.
36. The *Lyttelton Times* (6 Oct. 1877) reported that Ballance had actually joined the middle party.
37. *WH*, 18 May 1878; *LT*, 12 Oct. 1877.
38. *AES*, 12, 13 Oct. 1877; *LT*, 13, 15 Oct. 1877; *WH*, 13 Oct. 1877; *NZH*, 15 Oct. 1877; *New Zealand Gazette*, 15 Oct. 1877.
39. Spinks Diary, 10 Dec. 1877.
40. *PD*, 1877, 26, pp. 539, 542; *EP*, 31 Oct. 1877.
41. *PD*, 1877, 26, p. 537; T. G. Wilson, 'The Rise of the Liberal Party in New Zealand, 1877–1890', M.A. thesis, Auckland, 1951, pp. 47–48.
42. *WH*, 15 July 1879; A. Saunders, *A History of New Zealand*, vol. 2, Christchurch, 1899, p. 387.
43. *EP*, 11 Jan. 1878; *AES*, 15 Jan. 1878.
44. Ballance was dealing with treasury correspondence from at least the end of January, though his appointment was not gazetted until 12 July. See T1 (1878) in the National Archives.
45. *New Zealand Gazette*.
46. These adverse comments were quoted by the *WC*, 12, 16 Jan. 1878.
47. Vogel to Ballance, 12 Apr. 1878, Vogel Letter Book.
48. Stout, p. 109.
49. Quoted by *WH*, 12 Jan. 1878.

50. *WH*, 19 Jan. 1878.
51. 4 Mar. 1878.
52. *EP*, 7 Mar. 1878.
53. 2 Mar. 1878.
54. 9, 12, Apr. 1878.
55. *AJHR*, 1888, B-12; Simkin, p. 147.
56. *PD*, 1877, 27, p. 238.
57. Ballance to Vogel, 1 Mar. 1878, Vogel MSS.
58. R. C. J. Stone, 'The Maori Lands Question and the Fall of the Grey Government', *NZJH*, 1, 1 (1967), p. 59; Alan Ward, *A Show of Justice*, Auckland, 1973, p. 278.
59. *PD*, 1878, 28, p. 80.
60. Vogel to Ballance, 12, 25 Apr. 1878; 20 June 1878, Vogel Letter Book.
61. *PD*, 1878, 28, pp. 88–89.
62. Ibid., p. 89.
63. Ibid., p. 90.
64. Ibid., p. 92.
65. He estimated revenue from the respective tax as the following: land £100,000; beer £30,000; company £10,000; sparkling wines £1000. Total £141,000. Remissions £117,000. Ibid.
66. Ibid., p. 93.
67. Spinks Diary, 6 Aug. 1878.
68. 7, 8 Aug. 1878.
69. 7, 8 Aug. 1878.
70. 7 Aug. 1878.
71. 8 Aug. 1878.
72. *WH*, 18 May 1878; *EP*, 14, 20 May 1878, 8 June 1878.
73. See Wakefield's comments, *PD*, 1878, 28, pp. 628–36.
74. *WH*, 30 June 1877.
75. Spinks Diary, 1878.
76. *PD*, 1878, 28, pp. 613–26, 628–46; 29, pp. 11–51, 58–66, 87–118.
77. E. C. J. Stevens to Stafford, 3 Mar. 1878, Stafford MS, vol. 6.
78. *PD*, 1878, 29, pp. 514–50.
79. *LT*, 13 Sept. 1878.
80. T.G. Wilson, *The Grey Government, 1877-9*, Auckland University College, 1954, p. 27.
81. Land Tax Act 1878; *WH*, 7 Dec. 1878; *EP*, 21 May 1879.
82. *AJHR*, 1888, B-12.
83. *PD*, 1878, 28, pp. 607–08; 29, pp. 114–18.
84. *PD*, 1878, 29, pp. 117–18.
85. *NZH*, 10 Aug. 1878.
86. Wilson, 1954, p. 27.
87. 9 Aug. 1878.
88. *PD*, 1878, 28, p. 609; *EP*, 22 Aug. 1878, a deputation of brewers to Ballance.
89. *PD*, 1878, 29, pp. 556–55; *NZH*, 5 Oct. 1878; *AES*, 4 Oct. 1878.
90. *PD*, 1880, 37, p. 606.
91. *PD*, 1885, 51, p. 263. Stout's retrospective statement.
92. *PD*, 1878, 29, pp. 46, 568ff.
93. *PD*, 1879, 31, p. 193.
94. *WH*, 18 May 1878.
95. *PD*, 1878, 29, p. 279.

96. *PD*, 1878, 28, pp. 355–58.
97. *AES*, 31 Oct. 1878; *NZH*, 29 Oct. 1878.
98. *WH*, 23 Aug. 1879.
99. *PD*, 1878, 29, pp. 586–88.
100. *PD*, 1878, 30, p. 1068.
101. Simkin, pp. 160–61; W. B. Sutch, *Colony or Nation?*, Sydney, 1966, pp. 12, 16.
102. E. C. J. Stevens to Stafford, 3 Dec. 1878, 9 Jan. 1879, Stafford MS, vol. 6.
103. E. C. J. Stevens to Stafford, 3 Dec. 1878, Stafford MS, vol. 6.
104. *AJHR*, 1880, G-2, pp. xxiv*ff*.
105. Fox's later account, *PD*, 1879, 31, pp. 71–72. See also *NZH*, 2 July 1879.
106. *EP*, 26 Apr. 1879.
107. 7 Dec. 1878. See also 14 Dec. 1878.
108. *EP*, 26 Apr. 1879.
109. Ballance to Vogel, 25 Apr. 1879, LB I, p. 118.
110. J. Rutherford, *Sir George Grey, K.C.B., 1812–1898: a study in colonial government*, London, 1961, p. 620; *EP*, 19 May 1879.
111. E. C. J. Stevens to Stafford, 19 June 1879, Stafford MS, vol. 6.
112. *WH*, 14, 28 June 1879.
113. *PD*, 1885, 53, p. 353.
114. *PD*, 1879, 31, p. 6.
115. *PD*, 1879, 32, pp. 232–35; 1880, 36, pp. 185–88; 1881, 38, pp. 337–39; 1891, 72, pp. 116–17; *AES*, 12 July 1879.
116. E. C. J. Stevens to Stafford, 3 Dec. 1878, 9 Jan. 1879, Stafford MS, vol. 6.
117. Scholefield, 1958, p. 35; *NZH*, 5 Aug. 1879; *PD*, 1879, 31, p. 70.
118. Ballance to Sheehan, 28 Nov. 1878, LB I, p. 8.
119. Ballance to Luckie, 10 Jan. 1879, LB I, p. 22.
120. Grey to Ballance, 27 Feb. 1879, BMSS, 8; *Evening Chronicle*, 29 Jan. 1879.
121. Whitmore to Ballance, 24 Jan. 1879, BMSS, 6–7; Ballance to Whitmore, 12 Mar. 1879, BMSS, 9.
122. *Evening Chronicle*, 27 Feb. 1879; *NZH*, 27, 28 Feb. 1879.
123. Grey to Ballance, 8, 16, 18, 23 Apr. 1879, BMSS, 12–30.
124. Whitmore to Ballance, 11 Apr. 1879, BMSS, 1; *WH*, 12 Apr. 1879.
125. *NZH*, 3 Dec. 1879.
126. Hamer, 1962, p. 146.
127. *AJHR*, 1886, H-32.
128. Ballance to Vogel, 25 Apr. 1879, LB I, pp. 117–18; see also Ballance to Larnach, 25 Apr. 1879, LB I, pp. 119–20.
129. *Evening Chronicle*, 28 Jan. 1879.
130. Hamer, 1962, p. 146. See also *PD*, 1879, 31, pp. 30–36.
131. See, for example, *NZH*, 17 Apr. 1879; *EP*, 5 May 1879.
132. Ballance to Vogel, 25 Apr. 1879, LB I, p. 117, see also *EP*, 5 May 1879; and ch. 7 on the Agricultural Company.
133. *WH*, 6 Sept. 1879.
134. Hamer, 1962, p. 147.
135. See *PD*, 1886, 56, pp. 641–44.
136. See Whitmore's explanation, *PD*, 1879, 31, pp. 34*ff* and Ballance's own later account, *PD*, 1885, 51, p. 273.
137. 29 Mar. 1879.
138. 27 Mar. 1879.
139. *WH*, 19 Apr. 1879.
140. J. Murray to Ballance, 2 Apr. 1879, BMSS, 10–11.

141. Bryce to Ballance, 12 May 1879, BMSS, 31.
142. Bryce to Ballance, 25 May 1879, BMSS, 32–33.
143. *PD*, 1879, 31, p. 69; *EP*, 30 June 1879.
144. *EP*, 18 May 1879; *NZH*, 27 May 1879.
145. 16 June 1879.
146. E. C. J. Stevens to Stafford, 19 June 1879, Stafford MS, vol. 6.
147. *NZH*, 1 July 1879.
148. This account is gleaned from *Evening Chronicle*, 30 June 1879; *NZH*, 1 July 1879; *EP*, 1 July 1879; *WH*, 5, 12 July 1879.
149. Grey to Ballance, 30 June 1879, BMSS, 34.
150. 30 June 1879.
151. Quoted by *WH*, 5 July 1879.
152. Ibid.
153. 1, 2, 4 July 1879.
154. *LT*, 5 July 1879; also 1 July 1879.
155. 1 July 1879.
156. Quoted *NZH*, 3 July 1879.
157. *WC*, 7, 14 Aug. 1879. See also *WC*, 11 Aug. 1879.
158. *WH*, 5 July 1879.
159. See, for example, *EP*, 5 July 1879.
160. *NZH*, 24 July 1879.
161. 12 July 1879. He was right, for the session ended on 31 July.
162. 11 Aug. 1879.
163. *AES*, 13 Oct. 1879. See also *NZH*, 26 Sept. 1879, 6 Oct. 1879.
164. *PD*, 1885, 53, pp. 352–53.

CHAPTER 5: DEPRESSION AND DEFEAT

1. See *WH*, 30 Nov. 1878; *WH*, 16 Aug. 1879.
2. For example, see his speech, *WH*, 26 Jan. 1878.
3. Bryce to Ballance, 25 May 1879, BMSS, 33.
4. *WC*, 12, 20 Aug. 1879; *WH*, 23 Aug. 1879.
5. *Evening Chronicle*, 30 July 1879.
6. *EP*, 1, 4, 14, 15, 18 Aug. 1879. Fisher later retired from the contest.
7. *WH*, 23 Aug. 1879; *NZH*, 21 Aug. 1879.
8. On land ownership as a working class ideal, see Miles Fairburn, 'The Rural Myth and the New Urban Frontier', *NZJH*, 9, 1 (1975), pp. 3–21.
9. *NZH*, 1 Aug. 1879.
10. See E. Bohan, 'The General Election of 1879 in Canterbury', M.A. thesis, University of Canterbury, 1958; see also E. Bohan, 'The 1879 General Election in Canterbury', *Political Science*, XII (1960), pp. 45–61.
11. See, for example, 12, 14, 21, 22, 25 Aug. 1879.
12. 15, 30 Aug. 1879.
13. 1 Sept. 1879.
14. Ibid.
15. *WH*, 6 Sept. 1879; *WC*, 3 Sept. 1879.
16. 23 Aug. 1879.
17. *WH*, 6, 13 Sept. 1879.
18. 20 Sept. 1879.
19. R. C. J. Stone discusses the role of the 'native question' in the motivations of the four 'Auckland Rats' in 'The Maori Lands Question and the Fall of the

Grey Government, 1879', *NZJH*, 1, 1 (1967), pp. 51–74.
20. 7 Aug. 1879.
21. *AES*, 1 Oct. 1879.
22. *NZH*, 8, 9, 11 Oct. 1879.
23. See Wilson, 1954, pp. 52–56.
24. *EP*, 8, 9, 10, 23, 28 Sept. 1879.
25. *AES*, 7 Oct. 1879.
26. G. A. Wood, 'The 1878 Electoral Bill and Franchise Reform in Nineteenth Century New Zealand', *Political Science*, 28, 1 (1976), p. 54.
27. *PD*, 1879, 33, pp. 173, 182.
28. 13 Nov. 1879. The *Herald* naturally supported Ballance, *WH*, 15 Nov. 1879.
29. *PD*, 1890, 68, p. 394.
30. *EP*, 5 Dec. 1879; *NZH*, 6 Dec. 1879; *WH*, 6 Dec. 1879; G. F. Thompson, 'The Politics of Retrenchment: the origin and some aspects of the politics of the Hall Ministry, 1879–82', M.A. thesis, Victoria University of Wellington, 1967, p. 79.
31. *PD*, 1879, 34, pp. 704–05.
32. Land Act 1877 Amendment Act, 1879, sections 24 and 25.
33. Ibid., sections 20–23.
34. *Y*, 9 Aug. 1879.
35. See, for example, *Y*, 10 Jan. 1880. The Association claimed a membership of 80; *Y*, 24 Jan. 1880.
36. *PD*, 1880, 35, pp. 287–88.
37. Ibid., p. 290. See also *WH*, 8 May 1880; R. D. Arnold, 'The Opening of the Great Bush 1869–1881', Ph.D. thesis, Victoria University of Wellington, 1971.
38. See A. J. Gray, *An Ulster Plantation*, Wellington, 1950 (2nd ed.); Evelyn Stokes, *A History of Tauranga County*, Palmerston North, 1980.
39. *WH*, 8 May 1880.
40. C. G. F. Simkin, pp. 163–66; W.B. Sutch, 1966, pp. 26–32.
41. *Wanganui Herald*, 3 June 1967.
42. *WH*, 25 Mar. 1876.
43. *WH*, 22 May 1880.
44. I am grateful to Duigan's granddaughter, Rev. S. Koreneff of Patea, for this information.
45. *Y*, 18 Sept. 1880.
46. *Y*, 14 Dec. 1883.
47. See *Y*, 11 Jan. 1884.
48. *PD*, 1880, 35, pp. 371–382.
49. *Y*, 14 May 1881.
50. Ballance to Stout, 23 May 1881, Stout MSS.
51. See, for example, *PD*, 1881, 38, pp. 90–92.
52. *PD*, 1881, 38, pp. 337–39.
53. *PD*, 1881, 39, pp. 548–51.
54. *Y*, 5 Nov. 1881. For Ballance's two other campaign speeches see *Y*, 19 Nov. 1881; *Y*, 17 Dec. 1881.
55. *WC*, 12 Nov. 1881.
56. *WC*, 2 Nov. 1881. See also *WC*, 11, 12 Nov. 1881.
57. *WC*, 14 Nov. 1881.
58. *WC*, 2 Dec. 1881; *Y*, 3 Dec. 1881.
59. *Y*, 5 Nov. 1881.

60. *Y*, 23 Apr. 1881.
61. For example, see the letter in *WC*, 31 Oct. 1881.
62. *WC*, 11 Nov. 1881.
63. *WC*, 8 Dec. 1881.
64. 7 Dec. 1881.
65. *Y*, 5 Nov. 1881.
66. *Y*, 15 Oct. 1881.
67. *Y*, 17 Dec. 1881.
68. *NZH*, 12 Dec. 1881. The *Chronicle* reported however that they did make it in time to vote, 13 Dec. 1881.
69. 14 Dec. 1881.
70. *EP*, 10 Dec. 1881.
71. Quoted by *NZH*, 20 Dec. 1881.
72. Stout to Ballance, 10 Dec. 1881, Stout MSS.
73. *Y*, 17 Dec. 1881.
74. *Wanganui Herald*, 15, 16, 17 Mar. 1882. See also the pamphlet printed by the *Herald*: *Report of the Proceedings in the Election Petition of A.D. Willis and others against W. H. Watt*, Wanganui, 1882.
75. *Wanganui Herald*, 24 Mar. 1882.

CHAPTER 6: PHILOSOPHY FOR IMPROVEMENT:
STATE HELP AND SELF-HELP

1. *Wanganui Herald*, 6 May 1882; *Cyclopedia of New Zealand*, vol. 1, Wellington, 1897, p. 1369.
2. *Wanganui Herald*, 16 Oct. 1882; *Y*, 20 Oct. 1882.
3. *Share Register, Wanganui Herald Newspaper Company Limited*, in Wanganui Museum.
4. *Wanganui Herald: Memorandum of Association*, Companies Office, Wellington, dead file 13694. The directors were Ballance, S. H. Manson, M. V. Hodge, J. W. Jackson, B. N. Manley, W. C. Watkins, S. Austin.
5. Anderson kept an account of loans in the back of his diary. See Anderson Diary, 1881, 1882.
6. Anderson Diary, 22 Sept. 1882.
7. *Y*, 15 Sept. 1882. The *Auckland Weekly News* was the most popular of the colony's weeklies.
8. *New Zealand Statistics*, 1881–86.
9. *Wanganui Herald*, 3 June 1967.
10. Anderson Diary, 25 Oct. 1882, 11 July 1883, 6 Aug. 1883, 16 Aug. 1883, 4 Oct. 1883, 25 Jan. 1884.
11. *Share Register*, share transfers.
12. New Zealand Founders' Society, Wanganui Branch, 'Newsletter', 21 (1963), pp. 15–16.
13. See Roy Douglas, *Land, People & Politics. A History of the Land Question in the United Kingdom, 1878–1952*, London, 1976; A. R. Wallace, *Land Nationalisation*, London, 1882.
14. See J. S. Mill, 'Explanatory Statement of the Programme of the Land Tenure Reform Association', in *Dissertations and Discussions*, vol. IV, London, 1875.
15. *PD*, 1878, 28, p. 606.
16. Henry George, *Progress and Poverty*, London, 1932 edn, pp. 234, 286–89.
17. Ibid., pp. 298–99.

18. Ibid., p. 13.
19. John Ballance, *A National Land Policy Based on the Principle of State Ownership*, Wellington, 1887, p. 3.
20. Ibid., pp. 17, 18.
21. Ibid., p. 8.
22. *Y*, 12 Oct. 1883.
23. Ballance, p.7.
24. Ibid., p. 10.
25. Ibid., p. 8.
26. Ibid., pp. 18–19; *Y*, 1 Feb. 1884.
27. *Y*, 2 Nov. 1883.
28. *Y*, 16 Nov. 1883.
29. See Frank Rogers, 'The Single Tax Movement in New Zealand', M.A. thesis, Auckland, 1949; and Eric Charman, 'Land Tenure Reform in New Zealand, 1875–1896: a study of the opinions of some leading land reformers', M.A. thesis, Auckland, 1953.
30. *Y*, 30 Mar. 1883.
31. *Y*, 26 Oct. 1883.
32. *Wanganui Herald*, 18 Dec. 1883.
33. *Y*, 24 Aug. 1883.
34. Unfortunately the present writer has been unable to trace any copies of this journal. This information is taken from the *Herald*'s comments on it.
35. *Wanganui Herald*, 18 Dec. 1883; *Y*, 6 Dec. 1883.
36. *Y*, 1 Sept. 1882.
37. See W. J. Jourdain, *Land Legislation and Settlement in New Zealand*, Wellington, 1925, pp. 27–28; E. J. Charman, 1953, ch. 6; *Y*, 28 July 1882.
38. Ballance, p. 19.
39. *Wanganui Herald*, 15 Mar. 1884.
40. *Y*, 1 Feb. 1884.
41. *Y*, 27 June 1884. See also *Wanganui Herald*, 26 June 1884.
42. *Y*, 1 Feb. 1884.
43. *EH*, 26 Apr. 1869, 11 Sept. 1869, 22 Sept. 1870.
44. A. R. Vidler, *The Church in the Age of Revolution*, London, 1971, p. 112.
45. See P. J. Lineham, 'Freethinkers in Nineteenth-Century New Zealand', *NZJH*, 19(1), 1985, pp. 61–80.
46. See, for example, *Echo*, 1 Jan. 1881, 13 Aug. 1881, 24 Mar. 1883.
47. *Freethought Review*, 1 Jan. 1883.
48. See, for example, *Freethought Review*, 1 Dec. 1883, 1 Jan. 1884.
49. *Freethought Review*, 1 Oct. 1884.
50. *Freethought Review*, 1 May 1884.
51. *Freethought Review*, 1 June 1884.
52. John Macmillan Brown, *The Memoirs of John Macmillan Brown*, Christchurch, 1974, pp. 122–23.
53. See, for example, *WC*, 23, 26 Sept. 1887.
54. *Y*, 11 July 1884.
55. See, for example, Spinks Diary, 2 Mar. 6 Apr. 1890.
56. Ballance to Stout, 23 May 1881, Stout MSS.
57. See, for example, *EH*, 11 May 1874.
58. See J. Mackey, *The Making of a State Education System — the passing of the New Zealand Education Act, 1877*, London, 1967.
59. See, for example, *PD*, 1878, 28, pp. 104, 137–38, 183; *PD*, 1878, 30, pp. 701,

790–91.
60. *PD*, 1875, 19, p. 431.
61. *Y*, 5 Nov. 1881.
62. *PD*, 1877, 24, pp. 446–49; *WH*, 1, 8 & 15 Sept. 1877.
63. *WH*, 21 July 1877.
64. Ibid.
65. Hamer, 1962, pp. 150–52.
66. Hamer, 1960, p. 101.
67. See T. G. Wilson, 'The Rise of the Liberal Party in New Zealand, 1877–1890', M.A. thesis, Auckland, 1951, ch. 7.
68. *Wanganui Herald*, 6 May 1884, 14 June 1884.
69. *Y*, 25 July 1884.
70. *Y*, 18 July 1884.
71. *Y*, 25 July 1884.
72. *Y*, 18 July 1884.
73. *New Zealand Census* for the respective years.
74. Chapple & Veitch, pp. 131–32.
75. *Y*, 19 Nov. 1881; S. M. King, 1964, ch. 2.
76. *Y*, 18 July 1884.
77. Ibid. There was no mention of borrowing to provide funds for land nationalisation.
78. *WC*, 19 July 1884. See also *WC*, 3 July 1884.
79. *WC*, 12 July 1884; *Wanganui Herald*, 3 July 1884.
80. *WC*, 18 July 1884.
81. *WC*, 19 July 1884.
82. *WC*, 21 July 1884.
83. *Y*, 25 July 1884.
84. Ibid.
85. Ibid.
86. Calculated from 1884 Electoral Rolls.
87. *Y*, 18 July 1884.
88. *NZH*, 12 Aug. 1884; *ODT*, 7 Aug. 1884.
89. *Wanganui Herald*, 4 Sept. 1884.
90. 18 Aug. 1884.
91. *EP*, 12 Aug. 1884.
92. *EP*, 21 Aug. 1884.
93. *EP*, 21 Aug. 1884.
94. Fisher to Ballance, and reply, 29 Aug. 1884, Fisher Family Papers.
95. *NZH*, 26 Aug. 1884.
96. Ballance to Fisher, 31 May 1885, Fisher Family Papers.

CHAPTER 7: A CURIOUS COMBINATION

1. Anderson Diary, 5–15 October 1884.
2. See T. G. Wilson, 1951, ch. 8; Hamer, 1960, ch. 5; *Y*, 28 Nov. 1884.
3. *NZH*, 9 May 1885.
4. *EP*, 25 Sept. 1885.
5. *PD*, 1884, 48, pp. 351–61.
6. C. G. F. Simkin, pp. 147, 165; W. B. Sutch, 1966, p. 24.
7. *PD*, 1885, 51, pp. 68–84.
8. *PD*, 1885, 53, pp. 573, 733–34.

9. In fact this was not enough to save the Agricultural Company, which was wound up in 1890. See Hamer, 1962.
10. *PD*, 1884, 49, p. 433.
11. *PD* 1886, 56, pp. 455–57, 641*ff*.
12. *PD*, 1891, 72, pp. 125–26.
13. *AJHR*, 1885, C-1.
14. Cash land sales were as follows: 1886, 65 267 acres; 1887, 33 336; 1888, 28 626; 1889, 69 626. Figures calculated from *AJHR*, C-1 of the respective years.
15. J. B. Condliffe, *New Zealand in the Making. A survey of economic and social development*, London, 1930, pp. 186, 188. On trends see also G.R. Hawke, *The Making of New Zealand. An Economic History*, Cambridge, 1985.
16. See Ballance's speech at a banquet given in his honour in Wanganui, *Y*, 5 Dec. 1884.
17. *PD*, 1885, 52, p. 45.
18. Ibid. On the passage of the act see *Y*, 3 July 1885; *EP*, 18 July 1885, 24 Aug. 1885; *NZH*, 18 July 1885.
19. Land Act, 1885, sections 135–160.
20. *PD*, 1885, 52, p. 45.
21. Land Act, 1885, section 161.
22. *PD*, 1885, 52, p. 45.
23. Ibid.
24. 3 July 1885.
25. 4 Aug. 1885.
26. Land Act, 1885, sections 166–168.
27. This order-in-council was published by Ballance as an appendix to his *A National Land Policy Based on the Principle of State Ownership*, Wellington, 1887. See also *EP*, 7 May 1886.
28. *AJHR*, 1890, C-1.
29. *AJHR*, 1887, C-1.
30. 'Report on the Village-Homestead Special-Settlement System in New Zealand' by Hon. W. Copley, *AJHR*, 1891 (Sess. II), C-5 p. 16. See also 'Special Settlement Records, 1871–1903', Lands and Survey Department, Series 22, National Archives, Wellington.
31. W. R. Jourdain, *Land Legislation and Settlement in New Zealand*, Wellington, 1925, p. 29.
32. *Y*, 17 Sept. 1886, 5 Nov. 1886; J. Lundon to Ballance, 24 July 1892, BMSS, 626.
33. *AJHR*, 1888, C-11. See also *AJHR*, 1887 (Sess. I), C-1.
34. *EP*, 20 Apr. 1885.
35. *Y*, 15 Jan. 1886.
36. See the *Yeoman*'s defence of the scheme, 17 June 1887, 26 Aug. 1887.
37. J. Lundon to Ballance, 24 July 1892, BMSS, 626.
38. *PD*, 1886, 56, pp. 607–08.
39. *AJHR*, 1891, C-5, p. 12.
40. See McIvor, 1984, table 1, p. 494.
41. *AJHR*, 1891 (Sess. II), C-5, p. 5.
42. *PD*, 1887, 57, pp. 605–06; *PD*, 1891, 70, pp. 38–9.
43. *Y*, 7 Jan. 1887 (Ballance speech at Oamaru); *AJHR*, 1891, C-5, p. 10.
44. *EP*, 18 July 1888.
45. *Y*, 15 Sept. 1888. See also *Y*, 7 Mar. 1891, 6 June 1891, and Lundon's answer

to criticisms of the North Auckland settlements, *Y*, 21 Mar. 1891.

46. Quoted by John Bradshaw, *New Zealand of To-Day (1884–1887)*, London, 1888, p. 194.

47. Ibid., pp. 194–95. On village settlement in Wellington province see S. H. Franklin, 'The Village and the Bush', *Pacific Viewpoint*, 1, 2 (1960), pp. 143–182; A. C. Bagnall, *Wairarapa. An historical Excursion*, Masterton, 1976, ch. XIII.

48. On this theme see Fairburn, 1975.

49. Land Act, 1885, sections 162–165.

50. *PD*, 1885, 52, p. 46. See also *Y*, 12 Dec. 1884.

51. *AJHR*, 1885, C-1.

52. *PD*, 1886, 54, pp. 356, 362.

53. Jourdain, p. 29.

54. See *EP*, 7 Mar. 1885.

55. James Bell, *A Farmers View on Land Nationalisation and the Working of the New Zealand Land Act*, Palmerston North, 1886, pp. 2–3; *EP*, 10 Oct. 1885.

56. *Y*, 16 Sept. 1887. For a typical opposing view see *O.D.T.*, 22 Dec. 1885.

57. Quoted by Bell, p. 19.

58. *AJHR*, 1892, C-1.

59. Jourdain, p. 29. The locations of associations formed by 1887 were as follows: 56 in Auckland land district, 58 in Hawke's Bay and 341 in Wellington, *AJHR*, 1887, C-1.

60. 7 Jan. 1886. Also *EP*, 2 Jan. 1886.

61. *Y*, 7 Jan. 1887.

62. Land Act, 1885, sections 197–219.

63. Jourdain, p. 28.

64. See McIvor, 1984, table 1, p. 494.

65. 4 Oct. 1886.

66. *Y*, 3 Dec. 1886.

67. *Y*, 8 Apr. 1887.

68. Ibid.

69. *Y*, 21 Dec. 1889 and comment *Y*, 28 Dec. 1889.

70. L. J. Wild, p. 256.

71. Bradshaw, pp. 204, 254, 278.

72. Bell, p. 24.

73. *EH*, 13 Jan. 1873.

74. *EH*, 24 Dec. 1874.

75. *PD*, 1881, 39, p. 550.

76. For a useful definition of terms see Joan Metge, *The Maoris of New Zealand*, London, 1976, pp. 302–10.

77. *PD*, 1881, 39, p. 549.

78. *PD*, 1884, 48, pp. 298–300.

79. Alan Ward, 1974, pp. 185–86.

80. 5 Dec. 1884.

81. Ballance, 1887, p. 16; see also *PD*, 1884, 49, pp. 158–59. On the Taranaki war see Keith Sinclair, *The Origins of the Maori Wars*, Auckland, 1961.

82. Ballance, 1887, p. 16.

83. Ibid., p. 15.

84. See *PD*, 1884, 50, pp. 312–26; *NZH*, 29 Oct. 1884, 3 Nov. 1884.

85. *PD*, 1884, 50, p. 317.

86. *Y*, 5 Dec. 1884. Ballance's banquet speech. See also the *Yeoman*'s comment on

'Native Land Reform' in the same issue.

87. 16 Dec. 1884. See also *EP*, 19 Nov. 1884, 28 Nov. 1884.

88. *Y*, 13 Mar. 1885.

89. *EP*, 24 Dec. 1884. See also *PD*, 1885, 52, p. 398.

90. Ibid.

91. 9 May 1885.

92. Ballance, 1887, p. 16.

93. See Ward, p. 290.

94. *AJHR*, 1884 (Sess. II), G-2.

95. Native Land Disposition Bill, 1885, printed with amendments in *AJHR*, 1885, I-2b; *PD*, 1885, 52, pp. 397–98; *Y*, 10 July 1885.

96. For reports of the meetings see *AJHR*, 1885, C-1. See also, on the Wanganui meeting, *Y*, 16 Jan. 1885, *EP*, 12 Jan. 1885; on Ballance's meeting with Te Kooti, *Y*, 13 Feb. 1885; on the Taranaki meeting, *EP*, 17 Feb. 1885; and on Ballance's visit to Parihaka, *Y*, 22 May 1885, 29 May 1885, *EP*, 13 May 1885. See also 'Travelling letter book. Trip to King Country, 3 Feb. 1885–26 Feb. 1885', Maori Affairs Department, Series 30/3, National Archives, Wellington.

97. *PD*, 1886, 54, p. 448.

98. Vogel to Ballance, 8 Feb. 1885, BMSS, 36–7.

99. *PD*, 1886, 54, pp. 1–2.

100. *PD*, 1885, 52, pp. 390–99.

101. 12, 13, 22 June 1885.

102. *PD*, 1885, 52, p. 398.

103. The bill passed its second reading on the basis that full discussion would take place in the Native Affairs Committee. See Ballance's summing-up, *PD*, 1885, 52, pp. 515–20.

104. *AJHR*, 1885, G-1, p. 74.

105. Ibid., pp. 1–2, 30–34.

106. Ibid., p. 7.

107. Ibid., p. 34.

108. Ibid., p. 63.

109. *PD*, 1886, 54, pp. 327–31; Native Land Administration Act, 1886.

110. See Ballance's comments on the changes in a speech delivered at a meeting with Maori at Aramoho, *Y*, 2 Apr. 1886. See also his King Country visit and speech, *Y*, 13 Nov. 1885.

111. *PD*, 1886, 54, p. 330.

112. *PD*, 1886, 54, pp. 460–64.

113. *PD*, 1886, 55, pp. 311–12.

114. Ward, p. 297.

115. *AJHR*, 1887 (Sess. II), G-8.

116. Ward, p. 298.

117. Ballance made vain attempts to influence the result of the Eastern Maori election, see *Y*, 13 May 1887; *EP*, 24 Aug. 1887, 10 Sept. 1887.

118. See Ward, pp. 298–303.

119. *PD*, 1888, 61, p. 673.

120. Ward, p. 297.

121. *PD*, 1884, 50, p. 373.

122. *PD*, 1884, 48, p. 523.

123. See *PD*, 1885, 55, pp. 343–44; *Y*, 15 Jan. 1886; *EP*, 7 May 1886. Ballance also enfranchised the police, see *PD*, 1885, 51, p. 475; *PD*, 1886, 55, p. 344.

124. See Dick Scott, *Ask That Mountain. The Story of Parihaka*, Auckland, 1975, pp. 148–49.
125. *Y*, 29 May 1885.
126. See *PD*, 1885, 53, pp. 716*ff*; *PD*, 1886, 54, pp. 141*ff*; *PD*, 1887, 57, pp. 29*ff*; Ward, pp. 295–96.
127. *AJHR*, 1885, G-4.
128. *AJHR*, 1885, G-8 and G-8a.
129. *PD*, 1885, 51, pp. 275–77.
130. *PD*, 1886, 57, p. 19; telegrams to Ballance re arrest of Te Whiti etc., BMSS, 718–64; Ballance memo to the Governor, 3 Aug. 1886 in *AJHR*, 1887 (Sess. I), A-1, pp. 18–20.
131. *PD*, 1885, 53, p. 355.
132. *Y*, 25 Dec. 1885, 1 Jan. 1886.
133. *PD*, 1887, 57, pp. 399–401; *EP*, 15 Apr. 1887.
134. See, for example, Ballance to Tawhiao, 8 June 1886, concerning the Maori Councils, *AJHR*, 1886, G-14, p. 5.
135. *PD*, 1885, 53, p. 356.
136. See Ward, pp. 30–40.
137. *Y*, 26 Sept. 1884; *PD*, 1885, 52, pp. 122–23, 130–31.
138. Defence Act, 1886; *EP*, 7 May 1886. See also M. H. S. Stevens, 'New Zealand Defence Forces and Defence Administration, 1870–1900', M.A. thesis, Victoria University of Wellington, 1977.
139. Stevens, pp. 99–101; Glynn Barratt, *Russophobia in New Zealand, 1838–1908*, Palmerston North, 1981, pp. 68–72, 86–92; *Y*, 8 May 1885.
140. Barratt, p. 102.
141. *Y*, 15 Jan. 1886. See also *Y*, 8 Apr. 1887. Ballance speech.
142. *PD*, 1885, 53, pp. 540–43.
143. *Y*, 8 Feb. 1890; *PD*, 1890, 69, pp. 590–99.
144. *PD*, 1885, 53, p. 541.
145. *Y*, 6 Mar. 1885.

CHAPTER 8: LEADERSHIP

1. *Y*, 15 Jan. 1886.
2. *LT*, in *Y*, 5 Feb. 1886; see also *Y*, 29 Jan. 1886.
3. Governor to Colonial Secretary, 20 Sept. 1886, 'Confidential despatches and telegrams to the Colonial Office, 31 May 1886–16 May 1889', National Archives, Wellington.
4. Hamer, 1960, p. 143.
5. *PD*, 1886, 56, p. 728; *Y*, 20 Aug. 1886.
6. *Y*, 8 Apr. 1887.
7. Representation Act, 1887. Boundaries had until 1887 been fixed by Parliament. See L. Lipson, *The Politics of Equality: New Zealand's adventures in democracy*, Chicago, 1948, pp. 29–33.
8. M. F. Lloyd Prichard, *An Economic History of New Zealand to 1939*, Auckland, 1970, p. 201.
9. *Y*, 26 Feb. 1886.
10. *Y*, 17 June 1887.
11. See H. Roth, *Trade Unions in New Zealand*, Wellington, 1973, pp. 3–8.
12. *Y*, 17 June 1887.
13. Ibid.

14. *Y*, 24 June 1887. The speech was printed by the *Herald* in pamphlet form: *Mr Ballance's Speech to the Electors of Wanganui*, Wanganui, 1887.
15. *Y*, 15 July 1887.
16. See, for example, *WC*, 14 July 1887.
17. *Y*, 30 Sept. 1887.
18. *WC*, 23 Sept, 1887. See also 26 Sept. 1887.
19. *WC*, 16, 21, 22 July 1887, 13 Sept. 1887.
20. *WC*, 19 Sept. 1887, also 20 Sept. 1887.
21. *Y*, 22 July 1887.
22. *EP*, 6 Aug. 1887, 12 Aug. 1887; see also *WC*, 9, 12 Aug. 1887.
23. Ballance's letter to the *EP*, 25 Aug. 1887; *Y*, 10 Sept. 1887.
24. *EP*, 10, 20, 21 Sept. 1887.
25. See the meeting of ratepayers reported in *WC*, 8 Sept. 1884.
26. *PD*, 1884, 49, pp. 11*ff*; *Y*, 7 Nov. 1884.
27. *Y*, 14 Nov. 1884.
28. See King, p. 15.
29. *PD*, 1885, 52, pp. 174*ff*; *PD*, 1886, 55, pp. 401*ff*.
30. *PD*, 1887, 57, pp. 94*ff*; *Y*, 13, 27 May 1887.
31. *Y*, 24 June 1887, 30 Sept. 1887.
32. *Y*, 30 Sept. 1887.
33. *Y*, 7 Oct. 1887; *WC*, 1 Oct. 1887.
34. Bassett, pp. 137–38.
35. *Y*, 14 Oct. 1887.
36. *Y*, 21 Oct. 1887.
37. On the first report of Ballance's illness see *EP*, 6 Sept. 1887.
38. Ballance played for the parliamentary team against the City of Wellington, see L. E. Ward, *Early Wellington*, Wellington, 1928, p. 180; see also the match between Ballance and Bryce discovered by the *NZT*, 13 Feb. 1983.
39. *WH*, 19 May 1877.
40. *Y*, 24 Mar. 1877; J. P. Belcher, *Wanganui from 1856 to 1929*, Wanganui, 1930, p. 12.
41. *Y*, 23 Dec. 1887; Anderson Diary, 17, 22, 25 Dec. 1887.
42. Anderson Diary, 31 Dec. 1887, 4 Jan. 1888, 17 May 1888.
43. Ballance to Stout, 3 Jan. 1888, Stout MSS.
44. Ballance to John Notman, 27 May 1888, letter in the possession of the author (copy in the Turnbull Library).
45. *EP*, 20 Apr. 1888.
46. Ballance to Stout, 3 Jan. 1888, Stout MSS.
47. Ballance to Notman, 27 May 1888.
48. *EP*, 12 May 1888.
49. See Lance's retrospective statement, *NZH*, 27 Feb. 1890.
50. *NZH*, 8 Aug. 1888.
51. McKenzie to Stout, 8 July 1888, Stout MSS.
52. Ballance to Stout, 7 July 1888, Stout MSS.
53. *PD*, 1888, 62, pp. 407–33, especially Ballance's speech, pp. 416–17.
54. *PD*, 1888, 63, p. 497.
55. Ibid., p. 498.
56. See Ballance's speeches on the bill, *PD*, 1888, 61, pp. 671–76; 62, pp. 266–68; 63, pp. 75–78.
57. *PD*, 1888, 63, p. 507.
58. *EP*, 1 Feb. 1889.

59. *EP*, 11 July 1888.
60. *EP*, 12 Apr. 1889.
61. Anderson Diary, 15 Aug. 1888, 17 Feb. 1889.
62. Anderson Diary, 1 Feb. 1889.
63. Spinks Diary, 17 Mar. 1889; *EP*, 18 Mar. 1889; Will of David Anderson, High Court, Wellington.
64. *Y*, 12 Nov. 1892.
65. *Y*, 8 June 1889.
66. *Y*, 6 July 1889; Wilson, p. 227.
67. *Y*, 6 July 1889.
68. *NZH*, 6 June 1889.
69. *EP*, 29 June 1889.
70. See Hamer, 1960, ch. 17.
71. *EP*, 29 June 1888.
72. Hamer, 1960, p. 346; Andre Siegfried, *Democracy in New Zealand*, Wellington, 1982 edition, p. 78.
73. *Lyttelton Times* on how opponents viewed Ballance, quoted by *Y*, 6 July 1889.
74. *PD*, 1889, 64, p. 128.
75. Ibid., pp 643–47; see also *PD*, 1889, 65, pp. 19–20.
76. *PD*, 1889, 65, pp. 114–16.
77. *Y*, 27 July 1889, 10 Aug. 1889.
78. *EP*, 24 July 1889.
79. *EP*, 25 July 1889.
80. *EP*, 8 July 1889.
81. See Barron's motion to this effect, *PD*, 1889, 64, p. 321.
82. *PD*, 1889, 65, p. 215.
83. Ibid., p. 216.
84. *PD*, 1889, 65. p. 228. See also *PD*, 1889, 66, pp. 549–50.
85. *EP*, 14 Aug. 1889.
86. *PD*, 1889, 65, p. 268.
87. *PD*, 1889, 65, p. 434; *Y*, 17 Aug. 1889.
88. *PD*, 1889, 66, p. 556; *Y*, 14 Sept. 1889.
89. *EP*, 16 Sept. 1889.
90. See Ballance to Fisher, 16 Apr. 1889, 21 May 1889, Fisher Family Papers.
91. *Y*, 9 Nov. 1889.
92. Judith Bassett, 'Sir Harry Atkinson and the Conservative Faction in New Zealand Politics, 1879–1890', *NZJH*, 2, 2 (1968), p. 141.
93. *PD*, 1889, 66, pp. 604–05.
94. Ibid., p. 604.
95. *Y*, 9 Nov. 1889.
96. W.C. Walker to Ballance, 24 Oct. 1889, BMSS, 44.
97. *Y*, 9 Nov. 1889.
98. *EP*, 2 Nov. 1889.
99. Quoted by *Y*, 9 Nov. 1889.
100. All the foregoing press reaction to Ballance's speech was reprinted in the *Y*, 30 Nov. 1889.

CHAPTER 9: THE TIDE OF EVENTS

1. Spinks Diary, 11, 13, 26 Jan. 1890.
2. Anderson Diary, 3 Mar., 3 July 1886.

3. Ernest D. Hoben, *John Ballance*, Wellington, 1893, p. 6.
4. Anderson Diary, 3 Mar. 1886.
5. Anderson Diary, 25 Dec. 1886.
6. Neither property has survived. 'The Knolls' was located near the present-day St. Chad's Church.
7. Spinks Diary, 28 Feb. 1890.
8. On the meeting see also *Y*, 15, 22 Feb. 1890, 1 Mar. 1890.
9. Spinks Diary, 12 Feb. 1890.
10. Spinks Diary, 3 Feb. 1890.
11. For example, Spinks Diary, 16 Feb. 1890, 2 Mar. 1890, 6 Apr. 1890.
12. Spinks Diary, 22 Mar. 1890.
13. *EP*, 27 Oct. 1885. See also her obituary, *Wanganui Herald*, 15 June 1935.
14. Spinks Diary, 20 Apr. 1890.
15. *EP*, 8 May 1890.
16. *Y*, 17 May 1890.
17. Ibid.
18. Ibid.; *PD*, 1890, 67, pp. 14, 190–200 & 307–08; *PD*, 1890, 69, pp. 909–10; *EP*, 14 Mar. 1890.
19. *Y*, 17 May 1890.
20. Bassett, 1975, p. 157.
21. H. Roth, *Trade Unions in New Zealand*, Wellington, 1973, pp. 13–14; Sweating Commission report, *AJHR*, 1890, H-5.
22. *PD*, 1890, 67, p. 10. See also *Y*, 28 June 1890 on the same theme.
23. Condliffe, 1930, p.188; *Y*, 7 June 1890.
24. *Y*, 21 June 1890.
25. Rogers, appendix, p. 1.
26. H. W. Farnall, *The Industrial Depression in New Zealand*, Auckland, 1890.
27. Rogers, ch. 3.
28. *EP*, 13 June 1890.
29. *NZH*, 2 July 1890.
30. *PD*, 1890, 67, p. 197.
31. 7 July 1890.
32. 29 Mar. 1890.
33. *EP*, 9, 15 July 1890; *Y*, 12 July 1890; *WC*, 15, 16 July 1890.
34. *Y*, 9 Aug. 1890.
35. For example, *Y*, 26 July 1890, 2 Aug. 1890.
36. *PD*, 1890, 69, pp. 197–200. Ballance was one of four opposition members on the committee. *Y*, 9 Aug. 1890 gives a full account of the affair.
37. See Roth, pp. 14–15; and for some press comment, *EP*, 5 Sept. 1890.
38. *PD*, 1890, 69, pp. 749–50 & 810–12; *Y*, 27 Sept. 1890.
39. *PD*, 1890, 69, p. 813.
40. *Y*, 27 Sept. 1890.
41. *PD*, 1890, 69, p. 263. See also *PD*, 1890, 69, pp. 394–95; *Y*, 30 Aug. 1890.
42. *PD*, 1890, 68, pp. 124–25.
43. *PD*, 1890, 69, p. 813.
44. Ibid., p. 961.
45. Ibid., p. 962.
46. *ODT*, 25 Sept. 1890.
47. *Y*, 27 Sept. 1890.
48. *Y*, 13 Sept. 1890; *WC*, 6 Sept. 1890.
49. *Wanganui Herald*, 28 May 1959.

50. *Y*, 27 Sept. 1890. See also the article entitled 'A Land and Income Tax', 20 Sept. 1890.
51. 24 Sept. 1890.
52. *ODT*, 25 Sept. 1890; *LT*, 24, 26 Sept. 1890; *AES*, 24 Sept. 1890; *WC*, 25 Sept. 1890.
53. Ballance spoke at the following venues: Turakina, *Y*, 4 Oct. 1890, 15 Nov. 1890; Mosstown and Fordell, *Y*, 11 Oct. 1890; Brunswick and Okoia, *Y*, 18 Oct. 1890; Aramoho, *Y*, 25 Oct. 1890; Taylorville, *Y*, 29 Nov. 1890; and St. John's, *Y*, 6 Dec. 1890.
54. *PD*, 1890, 68, pp. 176–77.
55. *Y*, 4, 11 Oct. 1890.
56. Bassett, p. 160.
57. For example, *ODT*, 7 Nov. 1890.
58. Keith Sinclair, *William Pember Reeves*, London, 1965, p. 119.
59. *Y*, 19 July 1890; see also *WC*, 16, 21 July 1890.
60. *WC*, 12 Aug. 1890.
61. *Y*, 19 July 1890.
62. *Y*, 1 Nov. 1890; *WC*, 23, 28 Oct. 1890.
63. *Y*, 8 Nov. 1890.
64. *EP*, 1 Oct. 1890.
65. *WC*, 8 Aug. 1890; Ballance to Barnicoat, 27 Mar. 1893, LB III, p. 488. Ballance appointed C. E. Allsworth as editor, see Ballance to Allsworth, 21 July 1892, LB III, p. 224; Ballance to Allsworth, 10 Jan. 1893, LB III, p. 409 and Ballance to Allsworth, 29 Mar. 1893, LB III, p. 489.
66. See, for example, 'The Graduated Land Tax', *Y*, 4 Oct. 1890; 'The Land Tax', *Y*, 25 Oct. 1890.
67. From *Y*, 4 Oct. 1890.
68. In 1887 the Wanganui constituency had a population of 6360 and there were 1631 electors on the roll. In 1890 the figures were 8377 and 2113 respectively. *AJHR*, 1887 (sess. II), H–13, 1890 (sess. I), H–2.
69. *Y*, 29 Nov. 1890.
70. *WC*, 15 Oct. 1890.
71. Young, 1964, p. 172. At Carson's opening meeting 15 of his 38 supporters on the platform were farmers; at Ballance's only 4 out of 31.
72. For example, *WC*, 27 Nov. 1890.
73. For example, see Rees's retrospective statement on receiving instructions from Ballance concerning the conduct of the Auckland campaign, *PD*, 1892, 76, p. 289.
74. For example, see Ballance's letter to Joyce in Akaroa, *LT*, 2 Oct. 1890; also *WC*, 18 Nov. 1890.
75. Ballance to Stout, 17 Nov. 1890, Stout MSS.
76. *NZH*, 7 Nov. 1890.
77. For the election results see *AJHR*, 1891 (sess. I), H–2.
78. C. Campbell, 'Parties and Special Interests in New Zealand, 1890–93', M.A. thesis, Victoria University of Wellington, 1978, p. 34.
79. Ballance to Stout, 17 Nov. 1890, Stout MSS.
80. Ibid.
81. Campbell, pp. 12, 33–34; Sinclair, 1965, p. 116.
82. *ODT*, 8 Nov. 1890.
83. *Y*, 29 Nov. 1890.
84. W. K. Howitt, 1947, p. 264.

85. *Y*, 13 Dec. 1890.
86. Analysis of Wanganui Electoral Roll of 1890. The proportion of electors describing themselves as farmers or settlers was approximately as follows: Okoia 52%, Turakina 40%, Brunswick 65%, Fordell 28%, Mosstown 30%, Aramoho 23%.
87. T. J. Young, p. 178, calculates that 19% of electors in 1890 were farmers, compared to 11% in 1887.
88. In the 1890 Electoral Roll, 51 out of 81 Aramoho electors identified were labourers or artisans.
89. *AJHR*, 1891 (sess. I), H-2.
90. T.G. Wilson, 1951, p. 250; Sinclair, 1965; Erik Olssen, 'The 'Working Class' in New Zealand', *NZJH*, 8, 1 (1974), pp. 44–60; W. H. Oliver, 'Reeves, Sinclair and the Social Pattern' in P. Munz (ed.), *The Feel of Truth*, Wellington, 1969, pp. 163–78.
91. Ballance to Joyce, 27 Sept. 1890, published in *LT*, 2 Oct. 1890. The letter was later quoted by Fisher in the House, *PD*, 1892, 76, p. 617.
92. *Y*, 13 Dec. 1890.
93. H. Crook, 'The Significance of the 1890 Election', M.A. thesis, Auckland, 1953, pp. 128–29.
94. *WC*, 6 Dec. 1890.
95. *EP*, 6 Dec. 1890.
96. *WC*, 9 Dec. 1890; *ODT*, 8 Dec. 1890; *NZT*, 9 Dec. 1890.
97. Bassett, p. 163.
98. *WC*, 8 Dec. 1890.
99. *NZT*, 11 Dec. 1890, interview with Ballance. On the agreement see *Y*, 27 Sept. 1890, 13 Dec. 1890; *EP*, 9 Dec. 1890.
100. *EP*, 11 Dec. 1890; *ODT*, 12 Dec. 1890; Fisher's statement, *PD*, 1892, 76, pp. 178–79.
101. *PD*, 1893, 79, p. 107.
102. *ODT*, 12 Dec. 1890; also *NZT*, 13 Dec. 1890.
103. *EP*, 23 Dec. 1890; *NZT*, 19 Jan. 1891.
104. Hall to Ormond, 15 Dec. 1890, Hall Letter Book, p. 236.
105. Bassett, p. 164.
106. See *AJHR*, 1891 (sess. I), A-1a.
107. *Y*, 27 Dec. 1890; *EP*, 23 Dec. 1890.
108. For example, *EP*, 16 Dec. 1890, 17 Jan. 1891; *NZT*, 19 Dec. 1890.
109. W. Rolleston to J. Hall, 9 Jan. 1891, Hall MSS, folder 173.
110. *Y*, 24 Jan. 1891.
111. *NZT*, 23 Jan. 1891.
112. *PD*, 1891, 70, p. 6.
113. *NZT*, 24 Jan. 1891.
114. *Y*, 31 Jan. 1891, telegraph, Wellington 24 Jan.
115. *Y*, 31 Jan. 1891, 'The New Ministry'.
116. Scholefield, vol II, 1940, p. 281.
117. *Y*, 31 Jan. 1891.
118. For example, *EP*, 6 Dec. 1890; *NZH*, 9 Dec. 1890.
119. *EP*, 26 Jan. 1891; *ODT*, 26 Jan. 1891, 7 Feb. 1891 (supplement); *Y*, 31 Jan. 1891.
120. *EP*, 26 Jan. 1891.
121. Ibid.
122. *EP*, 23 Jan. 1891.

123. *PD*, 1891, 70, p. 39.
124. *Y*, 17 Jan. 1891.

CHAPTER 10: NEW ZEALAND FOR NEW ZEALANDERS

1. *EP*, 3 Jan. 1891.
2. *EP*, 26 Jan. 1891.
3. *Y*, 21 Feb. 1891; *EP*, 13 Feb. 1891.
4. *Y*, 7 Feb. 1891; *EP*, 18 Feb. 1891. Bruce had been defeated by Hutchison for Waitotara at the general election.
5. Ballance to W. C. Smith, 2 Apr. 1891, LB II, p. 127.
6. Ballance to W. Tanner, 14 Mar. 1891, LB II, p. 87.
7. *Y*, 28 Mar. 1891.
8. *Y*, 7 Mar. 1891.
9. *Y*, 11 Apr. 1891, 16 May 1891.
10. *PD*, 1891, 71, pp. 57–69; *Y*, 20, 27 June 1891.
11. *PD*, 1891, 71, pp. 177–83.
12. Ibid., pp. 239–45.
13. Vogel to Ballance, 30 Jan. 1891, BMSS, 57.
14. *EP*, 11 July 1891; *Y*, 18 July 1891.
15. J. Evison, 'The Hon. John Ballance', in *Political Portraits*, Wellington, 1892, p. 1.
16. *PD*, 1891, 72, p. 127.
17. Ibid.
18. Ibid., pp. 126, 128–29.
19. Spinks Diary, 30 July 1891, 1, 7 Aug. 1891.
20. *EP*, 6, 10 Aug. 1891, 14 Sept. 1891.
21. *Y*, 22, 28 Aug. 1891, 19 Sept. 1891; *EP*, 13 Aug. 1891.
22. *EP*, 21 Aug. 1891.
23. Ibid.
24. Raewyn Dalziel, *The Origins of New Zealand Diplomacy: the Agent-General in London 1870–1905*, Wellington, 1975, pp. 149–50.
25. *EP*, 15 Sept. 1891. On criticism of the Government's treatment of Bell see *EP*, 20 Nov. 1891.
26. *PD*, 1891, 73, p. 99.
27. *Y*, 22 Aug. 1891. 'A Lady's Letter from Wellington.'
28. *PD*, 1891, 73, pp. 372–73.
29. Ibid., pp. 373–74.
30. Land and Income Assessment Act, 1891; Property Tax Act, 1891.
31. *NZH*, 24 Oct. 1891; see also *PD*, 1891, 74, p. 881.
32. *EP*, 23 Sept. 1891.
33. *PD*, 1891, 74, p. 875.
34. *Y*, 26 Sept. 1891; W. K. Jackson, *The New Zealand Legislative Council: a study of the establishment, failure and abolition of an Upper House*, Dunedin, 1972, ch. 10.
35. Ballance to Hildreth, 24 Aug. 1891, LB II, p. 361; Ballance to Parr, 24 Aug. 1891, LB II, p. 363.
36. *PD*, 1891, 74, p. 515; see also *PD*, 1891, 73, pp. 463–65.
37. *PD*, 1891, 72, p. 426. See also Ballance to Onslow, 13 Aug. 1891, LB II, 349–50.
38. Knutsford to Onslow, 11 Apr. 1891, in *AJHR*, 1891 (sess. II), A-2.
39. *PD*, 1891, 74, pp. 176–78, 187–89. See also *Y*, 27 June 1891; Onslow to

Ballance, 10 July 1891, BMSS, 212.
40. For example, People of Wellington to Ballance, 4 Sept. 1891, BMSS, 281.
41. *Times*, 9 Nov. 1891.
42. See M. R. Stenson, 'The Origins of the Government Advances to Settlers Act, 1894', Auckland, 1962, ch. 10.
43. *PD*, 1891, 73, pp. 402–03, 408–09.
44. See the league's resolution contained in W. Hutchison to Ballance, 9 July 1891, BMSS, 210–11.
45. *EP*, 16 July 1891.
46. Knights of Labour to Ballance, 23 May 1891, BMSS, 172; Anti-Poverty Society to Ballance, 15 June 1891, BMSS, 185.
47. *PD*, 1891, 72, pp. 119–20.
48. *PD*, 1891, 73, p. 100.
49. W. C. Walker to Ballance, 18 June 1891, BMSS, 187. See also *EP*, 11 Apr. 1891.
50. See Ballance to Mills, 1 Dec. 1891, LB II, p. 509; Auckland Liberal Association to Ballance, 13 Oct. 1891, BMSS, 323.
51. W. Berry to Ballance, 18 June 1891, BMSS, 186.
52. *Y*, 25 Apr. 1891.
53. See J. R. Moody to Ballance, 5, 7 Mar. 1891, BMSS, 95–103; J. Watkin to Ballance, 7 Mar. 1891, BMSS, 104–07; R. M. Houston to Ballance, 9 Mar. 1891, BMSS, 108–09.
54. *EP*, 21 Mar. 1891.
55. Ballance to Bond, 20 Apr. 1891, LB II, p. 160.
56. W. T. Bond to Ballance, 27 Apr. 1891, BMSS, 141.
57. C. H. Mills to Ballance, 30 Apr. 1891, BMSS, 143–44; Ballance to Mills, 20 May 1891, LB II, p. 222.
58. *PD*, 1891, 74, pp. 723*ff.*; *EP*, 21 Sept. 1891.
59. *PD*, 1891, 74, p. 1026; *Y* 10 Oct. 1891.
60. *PD*, 1891, 70, p. 58.
61. *PD*, 1892, 75, pp. 213–16, 230–32; I. S. Ewing, 'Public Service Reform in New Zealand 1866–1912', M.A. thesis, Auckland, 1979, p. 137.
62. Evison, pp. 1–2.
63. See Ballance to Stout, 7 July 1888, Stout MSS; *EP*, 11 Apr. 1891.
64. See W. Earnshaw to Ballance, 23 Nov. 1891, BMSS, 388; H. S. Fish to Ballance, 23 Jan. 1891, BMSS, 50.
65. For a typical clash in the House, see *PD*, 1891, 73, p. 551.
66. Ballance to Fish, 28 Sept. 1891, LB II, pp. 390–91.
67. *EP*, 24 Nov. 1891.
68. W. Earnshaw to Ballance, 16 Nov. 1891, BMSS, 360–61; Ballance to Earnshaw, 26 Nov. 1891, LB II, pp. 485–91; D. Pinkerton to Ballance, 16 Nov. 1891, Ballance BMSS, 362–63; Ballance to Pinkerton, 24 Nov. 1891, LB II, pp. 479–83; Stout to Ballance, 16 Nov. 1891, telegram, Stout MSS, folder 75.
69. *NZT*, 13 Dec. 1890.
70. *PD*, 1891, 73, pp. 173–79, 210, 361.
71. *PD*, 1891, 74, p. 698.
72. *Y*, 25 July 1891.
73. *Y*, 30 Apr. 1892.
74. *Y*, 22 Aug. 1891, 'A Lady's Letter'.
75. Ballance to Stout, 20 Nov. 1891, LB II, pp. 457–58.

76. On a libel action Hutchison later brought against Ballance, see McIvor, pp. 404–05.
77. *PD*, 1891, 74, pp. 94–98; *EP*, 29 Aug. 1891.
78. *PD*, 1891, 74, pp. 122*ff.*
79. J. Wilson to W. A. Buller, 10 Sept. 1891, BMSS, 289; also W. A. Buller to Ballance, 16 Sept. 1891, BMSS, 290; *EP*, 1 Sept. 1891.
80. *Y*, 5 Sept. 1891.
81. *Y*, 10 Oct. 1891. See also *PD*, 1891, 74, p. 1025.
82. *PD*, 1891, 74, p. 1039.
83. *EP*, 26 Sept. 1891.
84. *EP*, 13 Nov. 1891.
85. *EP*, 18 Nov. 1891.
86. *EP*, 9 Nov. 1891.
87. 4 Dec. 1891.
88. Ballance to Mills, 1 Dec. 1891, LB II, p. 509.
89. Auckland Liberal Association to Ballance, 13 Oct. 1891, BMSS, 323.
90. H. S. Rees to Ballance, 14 Nov. 1891, BMSS, 359; Ballance to J. Adams, 3 Nov. 1891, LB II, p. 406.
91. J. J. Smith to Ballance, 5 Oct. 1891, BMSS, 320–21; Ballance to J. J. Smith, 13 Oct. 1891, LB II, p. 401; *Y*, 19 Sept. 1891.
92. J. T. M. Hornsby to Ballance, 22 Sept. 1891, BMSS, 295.
93. W. E. Akroyd to Ballance, 16 Oct. 1891, BMSS, 324. See also, on the plight of Woodville's *Examiner*, E. A. Haggan to Ballance, 23 Mar. 1892, BMSS, 557.
94. See, for example, D. Pinkerton to Ballance, 7 Nov. 1891, BMSS, 346; Ballance to Pinkerton, 10 Nov. 1891, LB II, p. 424.
95. Ballance to A. L. Smith, 18 Nov. 1891, LB II, pp. 447–49.
96. J. T. M. Hornsby to Ballance, 25 Nov. 1891, BMSS, 396.
97. Ballance to Hornsby, 20 Nov. 1891, LB II, p. 460; Ballance to Rees, 20 Nov. 1891, LB II, p. 461.
98. Ballance to Jackson, Palmer, Mills, Pinkerton, 13 Nov. 1891, LB II, pp. 432–35; Ballance to Fraser, 14 Nov. 1891, LB II, pp. 437–38.
99. D. A. Hamer, *Liberal Politics in the Age of Gladstone and Rosebery*, Oxford, 1972, pp. 46, 173–74.
100. For example, Ballance to Mills, 26 Nov. 1891, LB II, p. 498.
101. Scholefield, vol. I, 1940, pp. 84–87.
102. T. Bracken to Ballance, 7 May 1891, BMSS, 156.
103. Ballance to Bracken, 25 Nov. 1891, LB II, p. 495.
104. Ballance to Buick, 13 Nov. 1891, LB II, p. 436.
105. Scholefield, p. 117.
106. Ballance to Hornsby, 20 Nov. 1891, LB II, p. 460; Ballance to Rees, 20 Nov. 1891, LB II, p. 461.
107. Ballance to Stout, 20 Nov. 1891, LB II, pp. 457–58.
108. See Ballance's letter to prospective council members, 13 Nov. 1891, LB II, pp. 432–38; also C. H. Mills to Ballance, 23 Nov. 1891, BMSS, 389, Ballance to C. H. Mills, 26 Nov. 1891, LB II, p. 498.
109. Ballance to Firth, 3 Dec. 1891, LB II, p. 511.
110. *EP*, 25 Nov. 1891; see also *EP*, 16 Nov. 1891, 1 Dec. 1891, *Y*, 28 Nov. 1891.
111. See the account of an Auckland Liberal Association public meeting, 14 Aug. 1891, BMSS, 256; also Ballance to Jennings, 24 Aug. 1891, LB II, p. 362.
112. *EP*, 5 May 1891, 28 Apr. 1891.

113. *EP*, 25 Nov. 1891.
114. See Ballance to Rees, 20 Nov. 1891, LB II, p. 461.
115. *Y*, 10 Oct. 1891; also *EP*, 8, 9 Oct. 1891.
116. Spinks Diary, 14 Oct. 1891.
117. *Y*, 24 Oct. 1891; *EP*, 6 Nov. 1891.
118. *EP*, 2 Oct. 1891.
119. *Y*, 24 Oct. 1891.
120. Spinks Diary, 1 Nov. 1891.
121. *EP*, 10 Nov. 1891.
122. *EP*, 14 Nov. 1891.
123. *EP*, 11, 13 Nov. 1891.
124. For example, *EP*, 30 Nov. 1891.
125. *EP*, 4 Dec. 1891.
126. *Y*, 12, 19, 26 Dec. 1891, 30 Jan. 1892, 27 Feb. 1892, 30 Apr. 1892.
127. *Y*, 12 Dec. 1891.
128. Ballance to McLean, 26 Nov. 1891, LB II, p. 499.

CHAPTER 11: THE RAINMAKER

1. Ballance to Perceval, 4 Feb. 1892, LB II, p. 578.
2. *Y*, 16 Jan. 1892.
3. Ibid.
4. Quoted by *Y*, 23 Jan. 1892.
5. Ballance to Perceval, 4 Feb. 1892, LB II, p. 578.
6. Ballance to Hildreth, 20 Feb. 1892, LB II, p. 617a; Ballance to F. H. Fraser (the Federation's Treasurer), 20 Feb. 1892, LB II, p. 617b; A. Smith (Ballance's Private Secretary) to Hildreth, 25 Feb. 1892, LB II, p. 627.
7. A. Smith to Sandford, 4 Feb. 1892, LB II, p. 566; A. Smith to Fraser, 4 Feb. 1892, LB II, p. 569.
8. See, for example, Ballance to Perceval, 7 Nov. 1891, LB II, pp. 422–23.
9. C. W. Reardon to Ballance, 20 Apr. 1891, BMSS, 139; Ballance to C. W. Reardon, 24 Apr. 1891, LB II, p. 170.
10. Knights of Labour to Ballance, 14 July 1891, BMSS, 220; Ballance to Parr, 24 Aug. 1891, LB II, p. 363.
11. Reform Special Settlement Association to Ballance, 20 Nov. 1891, BMSS, 378–79; Ballance to the Association, 23 Nov. 1891, LB II, p. 473. The Association had been formed by the Masterton Knights of Labour.
12. Palmerston North Knights of Labour to Ballance, 30 Aug. 1892, BMSS, 592.
13. *Y*, 14 Nov. 1891.
14. J. Stallworthy to Ballance, 9 Feb. 1892, BMSS, 513; see also Ballance to Knights of Labour, 19 May 1891, LB II, p. 211.
15. T. L. Buick to Ballance, 8 Jan. 1892, BMSS, 457.
16. *Y*, 6 Feb. 1892.
17. *Y*, 21 May 1892.
18. W. F. Gayne to Ballance, 15 Apr. 1892, BMSS, 569.
19. See Ballance to Carley, 12 Feb. 1892, LB II, p. 599.
20. *EP*, 12 Apr. 1892.
21. Ballance to Sievwright, 28 Apr. 1891, LB II, p. 166. See also R. W. Jones to Ballance, 12 Aug. 1892, BMSS, 643, on the Cook County Association.
22. Auckland Liberal Association to Ballance, 13 Oct. 1891, BMSS, 323.
23. J. Palmer to Ballance, 23 Nov. 1891, BMSS, 385–86; *EP*, 25 Nov. 1891.

24. See W. J. Napier to Ballance, 17 Feb. 1892, BMSS, 534–35.
25. W. O'Donoghue to Ballance, 19 Jan. 1892, BMSS, 461–62; *EP*, 28 June 1892.
26. Evison, p. 2.
27. Pinkerton to Ballance, 29 Dec. 1891, BMSS, 434; Ballance to Adams, 1 Feb. 1892, LB II, p. 559; J. A. Tole to Ballance, 13 Feb. 1892, BMSS, 524–25.
28. W. O'Donoghue to Ballance, 18 Jan. 1892, BMSS, 456.
29. Ballance to Shera, 25 Feb. 1892, LB II, p. 625.
30. 2 May 1892.
31. *EP*, 21 Mar. 1892. See also *Y*, 9 Apr. 1892, 'The Bogey Man Again'.
32. Ballance to Beeham, 20 May 1892, LB II, p. 744.
33. W. J. Napier to Ballance, 17 Feb. 1892, BMSS, 534–35.
34. W. J. Napier to Ballance, 25 July 1892, BMSS, 627–28.
35. Ballance to J. Adams, 4 June 1892, LB III, p. 62; J. Adams to Ballance, 9 Aug. 1892, BMSS, 641.
36. Ballance to Beeham, 20 May 1892, LB II, p. 744.
37. See J. A. Tole to Ballance, 13 Feb. 1892, BMSS, 524–25.
38. W. A. Buller to Ballance, 19 Jan. 1892, BMSS, 460.
39. Ballance to Stout, 2, 4 Feb. 1892, telegrams, Stout MSS, folder 38; J. G. Ward to Ballance, 29 Feb. 1892, BMSS, 549.
40. W. A. Buller to Ballance, 12 Dec. 1891, BMSS, 418.
41. Ballance to Stout, 2 Feb. 1892, telegram, Stout MSS, folder 38.
42. Ballance to Stout, 12 Feb. 1892, telegram, Stout MSS, folder 38. Stout gave £1000 to the project; see also Ballance to Perceval, 25 Feb. 1892, LB II, p. 631; *Y*, 5 Mar. 1892.
43. Ballance to Stout, 5 Feb. 1892, telegram, Stout MSS, folder 38.
44. See the Company Prospectus, printed in *Y*, 12 Mar. 1892.
45. Ballance wanted a Wanganui man, J. M. Bullock, for the job. See J.M. Bullock to Ballance, 3 Dec. 1891, BMSS, 409. As with the choice of name for the paper, Ballance seems to have given in to Reeves's preference.
46. Scholefield, 1958, p. 35.
47. See, for example, W. P. Reeves to Ballance, 28 Feb. 1893, BMSS, 695.
48. See Ballance to Reed, 23 Mar. 1892, LB II, p. 661.
49. Ballance to Smith, 29 Mar. 1892, LB II, 645.
50. *AJHR*, 1893, A-7a, p. 13.
51. Ballance to Perceval, 25 Feb. 1892, LB II, p. 631.
52. *Y*, 12 Mar. 1892.
53. *PD*, 1892, 77, p. 434.
54. Onslow to Ballance, 12 Dec. 1891, BMSS, 416–17.
55. *Y*, 6 Feb. 1892.
56. Perceval to Ballance, 11 Dec. 1891, BMSS, 410–15.
57. Ballance to Perceval, 4 Feb. 1892, LB II, p. 578; see also Ballance to Vogel, 19 May 1892, LB II, p. 732.
58. Perceval to Ballance, 8 Jan. 1892, BMSS, 49.
59. Ballance to Perceval, 4 Feb. 1892, LB II, p. 578.
60. Perceval to Ballance, 22 Jan. 1892, BMSS, 469–72.
61. *Y*, 12 Mar. 1892, 'Interview with the Premier'; Onslow to Ballance, 23 Jan. 1892, BMSS, 474. See also R. M. Dalziel, 1975, pp. 139–40.
62. Ballance to Perceval, 25 Feb. 1892, LB II, p. 631; also Ballance to Perceval, 4 Jan.(?) 1892, telegram, BMSS, 444.
63. Onslow to Glasgow, 16 Feb. 1892, *AJHR*, 1893, A-7a, pp. 13–14. For Onslow's views see also his speech on leaving the colony, *EP*, 13 Feb. 1892.

64. Glasgow to Knutsford, 8 Aug. 1892, *AJHR*, 1893, A-1, pp. 7–8.
65. Glasgow to Knutsford, 22 June 1892, *AJHR*, 1893, A-7 pp. 1–3.
66. See W. K. Jackson, 1972, p. 147.
67. Ripon to Glasgow, 26 Sept. 1892, *AJHR*, 1893, A-7, p. 5.
68. Ballance to Vogel, 19 May 1892, LB II, p. 732.
69. For example, *Y*, 12 Mar. 1892.
70. *Y*, 4 June 1892.
71. C. G. F. Simkin, pp. 166–67.
72. *Official Year Book*, 1894, statistical summary.
73. *Y*, 7, 28 Nov. 1891, 20 Feb. 1892.
74. W. Kennaway to Ballance, 12 Nov. 1891, BMSS, 353–55; Perceval to Ballance, 24 Dec. 1891, BMSS, 423–29.
75. *PD*, 1892, 75, p. 133.
76. Hall to Oliver, 1 Feb. 1891, Hall MSS.
77. Vogel to Ballance, 19 Feb. 1892, bound as a pamphlet in the Turnbull Library.
78. *PD*, 1891, 73, pp. 370–71.
79. Perceval to Ballance, 12 May 1892, BMSS, 583–88.
80. Ballance to Vogel, 19 May 1892, LB II, p. 731.
81. Ballance to Willis, 30 May 1892, LB III, p. 28.
82. Ballance to Pirani, 25 May 1892, LB III, p. 10.
83. Ballance to J. Boyle, 24 June 1892, LB III, p. 122.
84. Ballance to Perceval, 4 Feb. 1892, LB II, p. 578.
85. Ballance to Shrimski, 9 Feb. 1892, LB II, p. 591.
86. Ballance to Perceval, 16 June 1892, LB III, p. 87.
87. See the correspondence between Ballance and Edwards published in *Y*, 23 May 1891.
88. *Y*, 30 May 1891.
89. Ballance to Kelly, 17 June 1892, LB III, p. 98.
90. See the correspondence in *AJHR*, 1892, H-28; *Y*, 4 June 1892; also Edwards's petition to Parliament, *AJHR*, 1892, J-2.
91. In fact Ballance argued that an extra judge was not needed: Ballance to Hall-Jones, 30 May 1892, LB III, p. 34; Ballance to Kelly, 17 June 1892, LB III, p. 98.
92. Ballance to Willis, 30 May 1892, LB III, p. 28; *EP*, 30 May 1892; *Y*, 20 May 1893, 'The Dead Tribune'; A. D. MacLaren to Ballance, 1 June 1892, BMSS, 593; C. Hall to Ballance, 25 June, 1892, BMSS, 613.
93. 15 June 1875.
94. Ballance to Steward, 15 Jan. 1892, BMSS, 448.
95. *NZT*, 29 Apr. 1893.
96. Glasgow to Knutsford, 22 June 1892, *AJHR*, 1893, A-7, p. 2.
97. *Y*, 4 June 1892.
98. A. J. Cadman interviewed by the *Auckland Star*, reported in *Y*, 5 Mar. 1892; also *Y*, 27 Feb. 1892.
99. Ward, 1974, p. 302.
100. *Y*, 27 Feb. 1892.
101. Reeves to Ballance, 1 May 1892, BMSS, 578.
102. *PD*, 1892, 75, p. 129; *Y*, 20 Aug. 1892.
103. Ibid., p. 130.
104. *Y*, 29 Aug. 1892.
105. Hoben, p. 8.

106. See the Department of Labour reports on the State Farms in *AJHR*, 1893, H-10, p. 5; 1895, H-6, pp. 3, 17; 1896, H-6, pp. vii–viii; 1897, H-6, p. viii.
107. Reeves to Ballance, 1 May 1892, BMSS, 578.
108. *PD*, 1892, 75, p. 131.
109. Evison, p. 2.
110. Simkin, p. 147.
111. *Y*, 9 July 1892.
112. Quoted by *Y*, 15 Oct. 1892.
113. Ballance to Saunders, 11 July 1892, LB III, p. 109.
114. See, for example, Ballance to C. C. McMillan, 20 July 1892, LB III, p. 217.
115. *PD*, 1892, 75, p. 131.
116. *PD*, 1892, 76, p. 473.
117. Ibid., p. 472.
118. Ballance to Meath, 20 Oct. 1892, LB III, p. 358.
119. *PD*, 1892, 75, p. 133.
120. Ibid., p. 131.
121. Ballance to Saunders, 11 July 1892 LB III, p. 190.
122. *PD*, 1892, 75, p. 132.
123. Ballance to Saunders, 11 July 1892, LB III, p. 190; *Y*, 16 July 1892.
124. *PD*, 1892, 76, p. 486.
125. *PD*, 1892, 75, p. 128.
126. *Official Year Book*, 1894, p. 250.
127. See G. L. Peacocke to Ballance, 27 Oct. 1892, BMSS, 327–29.
128. See *PD*, 1892, 76, pp. 466–67.
129. *Official Year Book*, 1894, p. 250.
130. *PD*, 1892, 75, pp. 131–32.
131. Ibid., p. 131.
132. Ibid., p. 127.
133. Ballance to Kerr, 21 July 1892, LB III, p. 221.
134. Glasgow to Ballance, 4 Aug. 1892, *AJHR*, 1892, A-7, pp. 4–5.
135. Ballance to Perceval, 10 Aug. 1892, LB III, pp. 276–77; Dalziel, 1975, p. 136.
136. Glasgow to Knutsford, 22 June, 1892, *AJHR*, 1893, A-7, pp. 1–3.
137. Ibid.
138. *PD*, 1892, 77, p. 249.
139. Ballance to Perceval, 10 Aug. 1892, LB III, p. 276.
140. Ballance to Hall-Jones, 30 May 1892, LB III, p. 34.
141. Ballance to J. A. Tole, 29 Aug. 1892, LB III, p. 306.
142. Holders of the lease-in-perpetuity had the 'power of sale, sub-lease, disposition by will, or mortgage', *Official Year Book*, 1894, p. 201.
143. *PD*, 1892, 76, p. 574; 77, p. 497.
144. *PD*, 1892, 77, pp. 529–30.
145. *PD*, 1892, 76, p. 549.
146. Ibid., p. 471.
147. Ballance to J. Taylor, 27 Apr. 1892, LB II, p. 707.
148. *PD*, 1894, 84, pp. 171–72.
149. Ballance to Perceval, 10 Aug. 1892, LB III, p. 274.
150. Ballance, 1887, p. 12.
151. See M. R. Stenson, 'The Origins of the Government Advances to Settlers Act', 1894; M.A. thesis, Auckland, 1962.
152. *PD*, 1892, 77, p. 531.
153. Hoben, p. 8.

154. Ibid., p. 7.
155. *Y*, 10, 24 Sept. 1892; EP 5, 8 Sept. 1892.
156. *EP*, 13 Sept. 1892; *Y*, 24 Sept. 1892; Ballance to Wellington Liberal Association, 10 Sept. 1892, BMSS, 657.
157. *Y*, 24 Sept. 1892.
158. *PD*, 1892, 78, p. 361; *Y*, 1 Oct. 1892.
159. *Y*, 17 Sept. 1892, 'Our Parliamentary Letter'.
160. *Y*, 10 Sept. 1892.
161. *Y*, 1 Oct. 1892; Spinks Diary, 26 Sept. 1892; see also *AJHR*, 1893, A-2, pp. 26–27.
162. See Jackson, pp. 121, 149–50.
163. Stout, 1893, p. 114.
164. Ibid., p. 112. See also *AJHR*, 1893, A-2, pp. 2, 4.
165. *Y*, 19 Sept. 1891, 'A Lady's Letter From Wellington'.
166. Ballance to J. T. Fisher, 9 Feb. 1892, LB II, p. 590; S. P. Andrews to Ballance, 9 Sept. 1891, BMSS, 285 and Ballance's note in reply.
167. *EP*, 28 June 1892.
168. *Y*, 22 Oct. 1892.

CHAPTER 12: CUT SHORT

1. *NZT*, 7 Sept. 1892.
2. *PD*, 1892, 78, p. 901.
3. Spinks Diary, 26 Oct. 1892.
4. *Y*, 5 Nov. 1892.
5. Spinks Diary, 10 Dec. 1892; *Y*, 3 Dec. 1892.
6. T. M. Haultain to Stafford, 13 Dec. 1892, Stafford Papers, vol 6.
7. Hoben, p. 8.
8. Ballance to Saunders, 30 Dec. 1892, LB III, pp. 395–96.
9. *Y*, 12 Nov. 1892: Ballance to J. Boyle, 10 Jan. 1893, LB III, p. 412.
10. Ballance to Duigan, 16 Jan. 1893, LB III, p. 434.
11. Ballance to Stout, 10 Jan. 1893, B III, p. 415.
12. *Y*, 21 Jan. 1892.
13. Spinks Diary, 26 Jan. 1893.
14. *PD*, 1892, 75, p. 127.
15. *Official Year Book*, 1895, pp. 264–65.
16. Ballance to Saunders, 16 Jan. 1893, LB III, p. 396; also Ballance to Perceval, 9 Jan. 1893, LB III, p. 404.
17. Ballance to Walker, 10 Jan. 1893, LB III, pp. 410–11.
18. W. H. Oliver, *The Story of New Zealand*, London, 1960, p. 144; see also J.D. Gould, 'The Twilight of the Estates, 1891 to 1910', *Australian Economic History Review*, X, 1 (1970).
19. Condliffe, p. 184; G. R. Hawke, pp. 95–96.
20. Ballance to Tanner, 16 Jan. 1893, LB III, p. 432.
21. Ballance to Stout, 10 Jan. 1893, LB III, p. 414.
22. *Official Year Book*, 1895, p. 266.
23. *PD*, 1890, 68, p. 394.
24. *NZT*, 2 Nov. 1893; see also Patricia Grimshaw, 'Politicians and Suffragettes. Women's suffrage in New Zealand, 1891–1893', in *NZJH*, 4, 2 (1970), p. 164n.; Patricia Grimshaw, *Women's Suffrage in New Zealand*, Auckland, 1972, p. 48.

25. Duigan to Ballance, 27 Aug. 1891, BMSS, 267. See also E. Hackett to Ballance, 28 Aug. 1891, BMSS, 268–69.
26. *PD*, 1890, 68, p. 394.
27. *Y*, 19 Sept. 1891, 'A Lady's Letter From Wellington'.
28. Women's Franchise Committee to Ballance, 13 July 1891, BMSS, 217; Miss L. W. Dalrymple to Ballance, 7 Sept. 1891, BMSS, 284.
29. *EP*, 19 June 1891.
30. Grimshaw, 1972, p. 68.
31. See *Y*, 29 Aug. 1891.
32. See *PD*, 1891, 74, pp. 719–22, 898–99; *EP*, 10 Sept. 1891.
33. See Ballance to Mrs A. Daldy, 12 July 1892, LB III, p. 196.
34. *PD*, 1892, 75, pp. 151–52, 189–93; *Y*, 16 July 1892.
35. See *Y*, 15 Oct. 1892.
36. Grimshaw, 1972, p. 72.
37. *Y*, 29 Oct. 1892.
38. Ibid.
39. See, for example, Ballance to Duigan, 16 Jan. 1893, LB III, pp. 434–45.
40. Ballance to Rae, 19 July 1892, LB III, p. 214.
41. Ballance to Pinkerton, 11 Jan. 1893, LB III, p. 420. See the very similar sentiments in Ballance to W. C. Smith, 11 Jan. 1893, LB III, p. 422 and Ballance to Stout, 10 Jan. 1893, LB III, pp. 416–17. See also Raewyn Dalziel, 'The Colonial Helpmeet. Women's Role and the Vote in Nineteenth-Century New Zealand', *NZJH*, 11, 2 (1977).
42. Ballance to Saunders, 30 Dec. 1892, LB III, p. 396.
43. Ballance to Saunders, 11 Apr. 1893, L III, p. 766.
44. Hoben, p. 8.
45. Ibid., p. 9.
46. R. M. Burdon, *King Dick*, Christchurch, 1955, p. 104.
47. Hoben, p. 9.
48. Ibid.
49. Hoben, p. 10.
50. Ibid.
51. Ellen Ballance's letters to Stout printed in *EP*, 11 Aug. 1894.
52. Willis's 'Personal Reminiscences of the Late John Ballance', in *Y*, 6 May 1893.
53. Hoben, pp. 11–12.
54. Ibid., p. 10.
55. *EP*, 11 Aug. 1894.
56. LB III, p. 509.
57. LB III, p. 503.
58. Hoben, p. 11.
59. Having read the limited medical evidence available, Dr John Chrisp of Wellington suggested that an annular (constricting) carcinoma (cancer) of the upper sigmoid colon was the most likely cause of Ballance's illness and death. The tumour would have led to the bowel obstruction and dehydration. 'The illness was organic. It would have weakened him and debilitated him but could not I think be said to have been worsened by the stresses of his political life at that time.'
60. Hoben, p. 11.
61. *EP*, 11 Aug. 1894.
62. Hoben, pp. 10–12; Spinks Diary, 20, 21, 22 Apr. 1893.
63. Hoben, p. 13.

64. *Y*, 29 Apr. 1893; Spinks Diary, 23, 24, 25, 26, 27 Apr. 1893; Hoben, pp. 13–14.
65. Hoben, p. 15.
66. 'Letters and Telegrams of Condolence Received by Mrs Ballance', Wanganui, n.d. (1893?), pamphlet in possession of the author.
67. *NZT*, 29 Apr. 1893.
68. *Y*, 10 June 1893.
69. Hoben, p. 17.
70. Stout, 1893, p. 115.
71. Hoben, p. 19.
72. *NZT*, 1 May 1893.
73. Ibid.
74. *New Zealand Mail*, 8 Mar. 1895.

EPILOGUE

1. Oliver to Hall, 16 May 1893, Hall MSS, folder 196.
2. *EP*, 11, 13, 16 Aug. 1894.
3. R. T. Shannon, 'The Liberal Succession Crisis in New Zealand, 1893', *Historical Studies*, 8, 30 (1958); Hamer, 1960, ch. 18.
4. *New Zealand Mail*, 15 Apr. 1897.
5. Ibid.
6. Apr. 1897.
7. *AJHR*, 1900, B-13.
8. Jourdain, p. 36.
9. For example, *PD*, 1896, 93, p. 574; *PD*, 1896, 95, p. 131; *PD*, 1900, 115, p. 236.
10. *PD*, 1907, 139, p. 128; *PD*, 1909, 148, p. 160.
11. 8 Apr. 1897.
12. K. L. Stewart, 'The Ballance Tradition and its Permeation in Wanganui', M.A. thesis, Massey University, 1970, p. 22.
13. *Wanganui Herald*, 15 June 1935.
14. Will of Ellen Ballance, 26 Feb. 1934.

Bibliography

PRIMARY

OFFICIAL PAPERS

(i) *New Zealand Government Records, National Archives, Wellington*
Army Department
AD 1:   Inwards letters, Colonial Defence Office, 1863–72.
AD 6:   Outward letter books.

Lands and Survey
LS 22:   Special Settlement records, 1871–1903.
LS 36(13):   Crown Lands Guide No. VIII, published by authority of Minister
                of Lands, Wellington, 1887.

Maori Affairs
MA 4 (40–47):   Letter books 1884–87.
MA 5 (17–23):   Telegrams 1884–87.
MA 30 (3):   Travelling letter book. Trip to King Country, 3 Feb. 1885–26
                Feb. 1885.

(ii) *Public Record Office of Northern Ireland, Belfast*
1A/1/63:   Valuation map, Glenavy
1B/171:   Glenavy Townland valuation, 4 Feb. 1835.
5A/147:   Tithe applotment book, Glenavy 1834.

MANUSCRIPTS

(i) *Alexander Turnbull Library, Wellington*
Ballance Papers.
Fisher Family Papers.
Hall Papers.
Thomas McDonnell Papers.
Stafford Papers.
Stout Papers.
Vogel Papers.

(ii) *Wanganui Public Library*
Lovegrove Papers.

CHURCH RECORDS

Glenavy Parish Church, registers of births, marriages and deaths.

DIARIES

David Anderson (Turnbull).
Sarah Jane Spinks (in the possession of Mrs Carol Anderson, Wellington).

OFFICIAL PUBLICATIONS

Appendices to the Journals of the House of Representatives.
Electoral Roll, Wanganui, 1884 & 1890.
Journal of the Proceedings of Wellington Provincial Council.
New Zealand Census.
New Zealand Gazette.
New Zealand Parliamentary Debates.
New Zealand Statistics.
New Zealand Statutes.
Official Year Book.
Wellington Provincial Council, Land Regulations, 1872.

NEWSPAPERS

Auckland Evening Star.
Belfast Telegraph.
Echo (Dunedin).
Evening Chronicle (Wellington).
Evening Herald (Wanganui).
Evening Post (Wellington).
Freethought Review (Wanganui).
Lyttelton Times (Christchurch).
New Zealand Herald (Auckland).
New Zealand Times (Wellington).
Otago Daily Times (Dunedin).
Wanganui Chronicle.
Wanganui Herald.
Wanganui Times.
Weekly Herald (Wanganui).
Yeoman (Wanganui).

PAMPHLETS

Ballance, John, *A National Land Policy Based on the Principle of State Ownership; with the regulations of the village homestead system*, Wellington, 1887.
Ballance, John, *Mr Ballance's Speech to the Electors of Wanganui*, Wanganui, 1887.
Bell, James, *A Farmer's View on Land Nationalisation and the Working of the New Zealand Land Act*, Palmerston North, 1886.
Farnall, H. W., *The Industrial Depression in New Zealand*, Auckland, 1890.
Hoben, E. D., *John Ballance. Premier of New Zealand. The Story of his Illness, Death, and Burial*, Wellington, 1893.
Interesting Chapters from the Early History of Wanganui, Wanganui, 1887.

Lovegrove, C. L., *When Wanganui Stood to Arms in the 'Sixties'*, pamphlet reprinted from the *Wanganui Herald*, 1953(?), in the Turnbull Library.

McDonnell, Thomas, *An Explanation of the Principal Causes which led to the Present War on the West Coast of New Zealand*, Wanganui, 1869.

Wanganui Herald, *Handbook of the Law Relating to Crown Land in New Zealand*, Wanganui, 1880, with an introduction by John Ballance.

Wanganui Herald, *Report of the Proceedings in the Election Petition of A. D. Willis and others against W. H. Watt*, Wanganui, 1882.

Wanganui Military Historical Society, *Wereroa Redoubt*, Wanganui, 1948.

SECONDARY

UNPUBLISHED THESES

Armstrong, W. R., 'The Politics of Development: a study of the structure of politics from 1870 to 1890', M.A., Victoria University of Wellington, 1960.

Arnold, R. D., 'The Opening of the Great Bush, 1869–1881. A social history of the bush settlements of Taranaki, Hawke's Bay and Wellington', Ph.D., Victoria University of Wellington, 1971.

Bohan, E., 'The General Election of 1879 in Canterbury', M.A., University of Canterbury, 1958.

Campbell, Christopher, 'Parties and Special Interests in New Zealand, 1890–93', M.A., Victoria University of Wellington, 1978.

Charman, E. J., 'Land Tenure Reform in New Zealand, 1875–1896. A study of the opinions of some leading land reformers', M.A., University of Auckland, 1953.

Crook, Harry, 'The Significance of the 1890 Election, M.A., University of Auckland, 1953.

Dempsey, P. E., 'The Land Policy of the Stout-Vogel Ministry, 1884–1887', M.A., University of Auckland, 1945.

Dighton, J. L., 'The Life and Work of John Ballance', M.A., Victoria University of Wellington, 1929.

Evans, A. M., 'A Study of Canterbury Politics in the Early 1880s with Special Reference to the General Election of 1881', M.A., University of Canterbury, 1959.

Ewing, I. S., 'Public Service Reform in New Zealand, 1866–1912', M.A., University of Auckland, 1979.

Hamer, D. A., 'The Law and the Prophet: a political biography of Sir Robert Stout (1844–1936)', M.A., University of Auckland, 1960.

Hoar, J. K., 'A Descriptive History of the Major Aspects of the Friendly Society Movement in New Zealand, 1840–1900', M.A., University of Idaho, 1963.

Hunt, J. L., 'The Election of 1875–6 and the Abolition of the Provinces', M.A., University of Auckland, 1961.

King, S. M., 'The Port of Wanganui and its Influence on Wanganui, M.A., Victoria University of Wellington, 1964.

Maloney, G. S., 'A History of the Ballance Ministry', M.A., University of Canterbury, 1931.

McIvor, T. J., 'On Ballance: a biography of John Ballance, journalist and politician, 1839–1893', Ph.D., Victoria University of Wellington, 1984.

Robinson, W. M., 'The Pacification of the Waikato 1869–76', M.A., University of Auckland, 1949.

Rogers, Frank, 'The Single Tax Movement in New Zealand', M.A., University of Auckland, 1949.

Shepherd, H., 'The Nature and Role of Friendly Societies in Later Nineteenth Century New Zealand', Research Essay, Massey University, 1976.

Stenson, M. R., 'The Origins of the Government Advances to Settlers Act, 1894', M.A., University of Auckland, 1962.

Stevens, M. H. S., 'New Zealand Defence Forces and Defence Administration, 1870–1900', M.A., Victoria University of Wellington, 1977.

Stewart, K. L., 'The Ballance Tradition and its Permeation in Wanganui', M.A., Massey University, 1970.

Thompson, G. F., 'The Politics of Retrenchment: the origin and some aspects of the politics of the Hall Ministry, 1879–82', M.A., Victoria University of Wellington, 1967.

Whitehead, C., 'The 1887 General Election in Canterbury', M.A., University of Canterbury, 1961.

Wilson, T. G., 'The Rise of the Liberal Party in New Zealand, 1877–1890', M.A., University of Auckland, 1951.

Young, John, 'The Politics of the Auckland Province, 1872–1876', M.A., University of Auckland, 1960.

Young, T. J., 'The Political Career of John Ballance, 1875–1890', M.A., Victoria University of Wellington, 1964.

ARTICLES

Bohan, E., 'The 1879 General Election in Canterbury', *Political Science*, XII, 1 (1960).

Campbell, C., 'The 'Working Class' and the Liberal Party in 1890', *NZJH*, 9, 1 (1975).

Fairburn, Miles, 'The Rural Myth and the New Urban Frontier. An Approach to New Zealand Social History, 1870–1940', *NZJH*, 9, 1 (1975).

Franklin, S.H., 'The Village and the Bush. The Evolution of the Village Community, Wellington Province, New Zealand', *Pacific Viewpoint*, 1, 2 (1960).

Gould, J. D., 'The Twilight of the Estates, 1891 to 1910', *Australian Economic History Review*, X, 1 (1970).

Grimshaw, Patricia, 'Politicians and Suffragettes. Women's suffrage in New Zealand, 1891–1893', *NZJH*, 4, 2 (1970).

Hamer, D. A., 'The Agricultural Company and New Zealand Politics, 1877–1886', *Historical Studies of Australia and New Zealand*, X, 38 (1962).

———— 'Towns in Nineteenth-Century New Zealand', *NZJH*, 13, 1 (1979).

Oliver, W. H., 'Social Policy in the Liberal Period', *NZJH*, 13, 1 (1979).

Olssen, Eric, 'The "Working Class" in New Zealand', *NZJH*, 8, 1 (1974).

Shannon, R. T., 'The Liberal Succession Crisis in New Zealand, 1893', Historical Studies of Australia and New Zealand, VIII, 30 (1958).

Stone, R. C. J., 'The Maori Lands Question and the Fall of the Grey Government, 1879', *NZJH*, 1, 1 (1967).

Stout, Sir Robert, 'Character Sketch: The Hon. John Ballance', *Review of Reviews for Australasia*, May 1893.

Toynbee, Claire, 'Class and Social Structure in Nineteenth Century New Zealand, *NZJH*, 13, 1 (1979).

Wood, G. A., 'The 1878 Electoral Bill and Franchise Reform in Nineteenth Century New Zealand', *Political Science*, XXVIII, 1, (1976).

Young, John, 'The Political Conflict of 1875', *Political Science*, XIII, 2 (1961).

BOOKS

Arnold, R. D., *The Farthest Promised Land. English Villagers, New Zealand Immigrants of the 1870s*, Wellington, 1981.

Bagnall, A. G., *Wairarapa. An Historical Excursion*, Masterton, 1976.

Barratt, Glynn, *Russophobia in New Zealand, 1838–1908*, Palmerston North, 1981.

Bassett, Judith, *Sir Harry Atkinson, 1831–1892*, Auckland, 1975.

Belcher, J. P., *Wanganui from 1856 to 1929*, Wanganui, 1930.

Belich, James, *The New Zealand Wars and the Victorian Interpretation of Racial Conflict*, Auckland, 1986.

Bradshaw, John, *New Zealand of To-Day (1884–1887)*, London, 1888.

Briggs, Asa, *History of Birmingham. Volume II, Borough and City, 1865–1938*, London, 1952.

———— *Victorian Cities*, London, 1963.

Budge, Ian & O'Leary, Cornelius, *Belfast: Approach to Crisis. A Study of Belfast Politics, 1613–1970*, London, 1973.

Burdon, R. M., *New Zealand Notables*, 2 vols., Christchurch, 1941, 1945.

Chapman, R. & Sinclair, K., *Studies of a Small Democracy: essays in honour of Willis Airey*, Hamilton, 1963.

Chapple, L. J. B. & Veitch, H.C., *Wanganui*, Hawera, 1939.

Condliffe, J. B., *New Zealand in the Making. A survey of economic and social development*, London, 1959.

Cyclopedia of New Zealand, vol. 1, Wellington, 1897.

Dalziel, Raewyn, *The Origins of New Zealand Diplomacy: the Agent-General in London 1870–1905*, Wellington, 1975.

———— *Julius Vogel. Business Politician*, Auckland, 1986.

Davis, R. P., *Irish Issues in New Zealand Politics 1868–1922*, Dunedin, 1974.

Downes, T. W., *Old Whanganui*, Hawera, 1915.

George, Henry, *Progress and Poverty*, London, 1932 edn.

Gill, Conrad, *History of Birmingham. Volume I, Manor and Borough to 1865*, London, 1952.

Gisborne, William, *New Zealand Rulers and Statesmen: from 1840 to 1897*, London, 1897.

Gorton, E., *Some Home Truths about the Maori War 1863–1869 on the West Coast of New Zealand*, London, 1901.

Gourlay, H. W., *Odd Fellowship in New Zealand*, Christchurch, n.d.

Grimshaw, Patricia, *Women's Suffrage in New Zealand*, Auckland, 1972.

Gudgeon, T. W., *The Defenders of New Zealand*, Auckland, 1887.

Hamer, D. A., *Liberal Politics in the Age of Gladstone and Rosebery. A Study in Leadership and Policy*, Oxford, 1972.

———— *The New Zealand Liberals: The Years of Power, 1891–1912*, Auckland, 1988.

Harrison, J. F. C., *Learning and Living, 1790–1960. A Study in the History of the English Adult Education Movement*, London, 1961.

Hawke, G. R., *The Making of New Zealand. An Economic History*, Cambridge, 1985.

Howitt, W. K., *A Pioneer Looks Back Again*, Auckland, 1947.

Jackson, W. K., *The New Zealand Legislative Council: a study of the establishment, failure and abolition of an Upper House*, Dunedin, 1972.

Jay, Richard, *Joseph Chamberlain. A Political Study*, Oxford, 1981.

Jourdian, W. R., *Land Legislation and Settlement in New Zealand*, Wellington, 1925.

Lipson, L., *The Politics of Equality: New Zealand's adventures in democracy*, Chicago, 1948.

Macmillan Brown, John, *The Memoirs of John Macmillan Brown*, Christchurch, 1974.

Morrell, W. P., *The Provincial System in New Zealand, 1852–76*, London, 1932.

Pakenham, Thomas, *The Year of Liberty*, London, 1969.

Reeves, W. P., *The Long White Cloud*, London, 1899 edn.

_____ *State Experiments in Australia and New Zealand*, 2 vols., London, 1902.

Roth, H., *Trade Unions in New Zealand. Past and Present*, Wellington, 1973.

Ross, Angus, *New Zealand Aspirations in the Pacific in the Nineteenth Century*, Oxford, 1964.

Rusden, G. W., *History of New Zealand*, 3 vols., London, 1883.

Rutherford, James, *Sir George Grey, K.C.B., 1812–1898: a study in colonial government*, London, 1961.

Scholefield, G. H., *A Dictionary of New Zealand Biography*, 2 vols., Wellington, 1940.

_____ *Newspapers in New Zealand*, Wellington, 1958.

_____ *Notable New Zealand Statesmen: Twelve Prime Ministers*, Christchurch, 1946.

Scott, Dick, *Ask That Mountain. The Story of Parihaka*, Auckland, 1975.

Senior, H., *Orangeism in Ireland and Britain, 1795–1836*, London, 1966.

Simkin, C. G. F., *The Instability of a Dependent Economy. Economic Fluctuations in New Zealand, 1840–1914*, Oxford, 1951.

Sinclair, Keith, *William Pember Reeves*, London, 1965.

Smart, M. J. G. & Bates, A. P., *The Wanganui Story*, Wanganui, 1972.

Stewart, W. D., *Sir Francis H.D. Bell. His life and times*, Wellington, 1937.

_____ *William Rolleston. A New Zealand Statesman*, Christchurch, 1940.

Sutch, W. B., *Poverty and Progress in New Zealand*, Wellington, 1941.

_____ *Colony or Nation? Economic Crises in New Zealand from the 1860s to the 1960s*, Sydney, 1966.

Tholfsen, Trygve R., *Working Class Radicalism in Mid-Victorian England*, London, 1976.

Wakefield, E. J., *Adventure in New Zealand, from 1839 to 1844*, London, 1845.

Wallace, A. R., *Land Nationalisation*, London, 1882.

Ward, Alan, *A Show of Justice. Racial 'amalgamation' in nineteenth century New Zealand*, Auckland, 1974.

Watson, Charles, *The Story of the United Parishes of Glenavy, Camlin, and Tullyrusk*, Belfast, 1892.

Whitmore, Sir George Stoddart, *The Last Maori War in New Zealand under the Self-Reliant Policy*, London, 1902.

Wild, L. J., *The Life and Times of Sir James Wilson of Bulls*, Christchurch, 1953.

Wilson, J. G., *Early Rangitikei*, Christchurch, 1914.

Wilson, T. G., *The Grey Government, 1877–9*, Auckland University College, 1954.

Index